The Psychology of Tactical Communication

MONOGRAPHS IN SOCIAL PSYCHOLOGY OF LANGUAGE SERIES

Series Editor
Howard Giles, *Department of Communication, University of California, Santa Barbara, CA 93106, USA*

Editorial Advisory Board
John Wiemann, *Department of Communication, University of California, Santa Barbara, CA 93106, USA*

Miles Patterson, *Department of Psychology, University of Missouri, St Louis, MO 63121-4499, USA*

Bella DePaulo, *Department of Psychology, University of Virginia, Charlottesville, VA 22903-2477, USA*

Other Books in the Series
Perspectives on Marital Interaction
    P. NOLLER and M.A. FITZPATRICK (eds)

Other Books of Interest
Talk and Social Organisation
    G. BUTTON and J.R.E. LEE (eds)

Communication and Crosscultural Adaptation
    Y.Y. KIM

Conversation
D. ROGER and P. BULL (eds)

Communication and Simulation
    D. CROOKALL and D. SAUNDERS (eds)

Afrikaner Dissidents: A Social Psychological Study of Identity and Dissent
    J. LOUW-POTGIETER

Language and Ethnicity in Minority Sociolinguistic Perspective
J.A. FISHMAN

Please contact us for the latest information on all our book and journal publications:

Multilingual Matters Ltd.
Bank House, 8a Hill Road,
Clevedon, Avon BS21 7HH,
England

MONOGRAPHS IN SOCIAL PSYCHOLOGY OF LANGUAGE 2
Series Editor: Howard Giles

The Psychology of Tactical Communication

Edited by

Michael J. Cody and Margaret L. McLaughlin

MULTILINGUAL MATTERS LTD
Clevedon · Philadelphia

Library of Congress Cataloging-in-Publication Data

The psychology of tactical communication/edited by Michael J. Cody and
Margaret L. McLaughlin.
   p. cm. — (Monographs in social psychology of language: 2)
   Bibliography: p.
   Includes index.
   1. Interpersonal relations. 2. Communication—Social aspects.
   3. Influence (Psychology) 4. Self-presentation. 5. Persuasion (Psychology)
   I. Cody, Michael J. II. McLaughlin, Margaret L.
   III. Series
   HM132.P79 1989 89-2878
   302.2—dc19   CIP

British Library Cataloguing in Publication Data

The psychology of tactical communication —
   (Monographs in social psychology of language; 2)
   1. Interpersonal relationships. Communication.
   Psychological aspects
   I. Cody, Michael J. II. McLaughlin,
   Margaret L. *1943*– III. Series
   158'.2

   ISBN 1-85359-040-1
   ISBN 1-85359-039-8 Pbk

HM
132
P79
1990

Multilingual Matters Ltd
Bank House, 8a Hill Road   &   1900 Frost Road,
Clevedon, Avon BS21 7HH   Suite 101,
England   Bristol, PA 19007, USA

Typeset by Photo·graphics, Honiton, Devon
Printed and bound in Great Britain by WBC Print, Bristol

Contents

Preface and Acknowledgements

Early in 1985, we were invited by Howard Giles and Peter Robinson, both of the University of Bristol, to serve as Convenors for the section on 'accounts' for the Third International Conference on Social Psychology and Language, to be held in Bristol on 20–24 July 1987. We were pleased to accept their invitation and set to work organising a panel. By the summer of 1987, our efforts had been rewarded with the scheduling of not one but two panels, the first dealing with accounts and the second with social influence. Panellists from the USA, England, Canada, Wales and the Federal Republic of Germany, representing communication, psychology and other disciplines, produced a group of thoughtful essays and cutting-edge research reports which are the foundation of this volume.

Chapters in the book reflect the considerable current interest in everyday tactics for influencing others and managing self-presentation. The contributors draw upon diverse perspectives, reflecting the fact that tactical communication as a topic occupies the attention of researchers in a broad range of disciplines. One can find without difficulty studies of influence tactics in the family, in the small work group, and in the organisation; scholars have examined how relational partners disengage, how children learn to use argument, how strangers manage self-presentation through the construction of accounts, how traffic offenders attempt to avoid penalty, how subordinates attempt to influence their managers, and so on.

Chapters in this volume are grouped into two broad categories, *social influence* and *presenting and defending the self*. The reader unfamiliar with the general topic of tactical communication will soon discover that although the two lines of enquiry represent two relatively distinct research traditions, they none the less are not entirely unrelated with respect to their conceptual underpinnings. A number of the authors draw heavily from the assumptions of interactionist and/or cognitive social psychology schools of thought.

A number of persons have contributed to our efforts to produce *The Psychology of Tactical Communication*. We are grateful to Howard Giles and the Editorial Board of Multilingual Matters Ltd for their advice and helpful comments. Our attendance at the Bristol Conference, partially funded by the Conference itself and the University of Bristol, was also generously underwritten by the University of Southern California. We are grateful to Dr Kenneth K. Sereno, Chair, Communication Arts and Sciences; Paul Bohannon, immediate past Dean, Social Science and Communication; and Sylvester Witaker, Dean, Social Sciences and Communication, for their support. We also acknowledge, with gratitude, the assistance of Gwen and Michael Brown with preparation of manuscripts and Larry Kersten for completing the index.

Introduction

MICHAEL J. CODY and MARGARET L. MCLAUGHLIN
Department of Communication Arts and Sciences, University of Southern California, Los Angeles, USA

Contributions to this volume on tactical communication each focus on one of two general areas: social influence, and presenting and defending the self. All contributions are concerned with how and why actors attempt to achieve goals (to manage a desired impression, to change a target's attitude, opinion, or behaviour, and so on), and are concerned with the consequences of messages used to achieve goals. All contributions focus on social relations, and deal with influence that is primarily interpersonal in nature. All contributions (as Tedeschi notes in Part III) share an interactionist perspective, in that behaviour is produced from the interplay of a number of contemporaneous factors.

Despite these, and other, commonalities, substantial differences exist between our chapters—for good reason. Our goal is not to produce a volume that presents a single theory or approach to the study of influence tactics or strategies, nor is it to present a homogeneous set of papers. Rather, our goal is to produce a volume that reflects the current, and healthy, diversity of approaches focusing on social behaviour and influence. Contributions differ widely in theoretical premises, and we have selected contributions that have extremely divergent research histories. Our intention is to provide a volume that serves as a 'sourcebook', that thoroughly prepares the scholar new to the area, and that facilitates the comparison of, and contrasts between, different lines of theory and research.

Part I presents six chapters in the area of interpersonal influence, and Part II contains seven chapters on self-presentation and accounts. Any student of tactical communication should be familiar with research in each area. James Tedeschi, in Part III, develops an overarching framework of communication, influence and impression management, and integrates chapters into the framework.

Given the diversity and density of the volume, we believe that the best way of 'prefacing' the book would be to discuss historical developments in each area, and discuss how present contributions represent important extensions of theory and research.

Social Influence

'Influence', by whatever label (power, manipulation, ingratiation, compliance-gaining, and so forth) is one of the most popular and robust areas in psychology, sociology, communication, management and marketing. Years of research on power, for example, have produced an impressive amount of data on (to mention only a few topics): (a) managerial influence and the effectiveness of different types of power (e.g. Bachman, Bowers & Marcus, 1968; French & Raven, 1959; Raven & Kruglanski, 1970; Student, 1968; see also Seibold, Cantrill & Meyers, 1985); (b) exchange theory (Marwell & Schmitt, 1967b; Michener & Suchner, 1972); (c) the corrupting effects of power (Kipnis, 1976; Kipnis et al., 1976); (d) the relative effectiveness of expertise and referent influence in sales (for instance, Busch & Wilson, 1976; Weitz, 1981); and (e) laboratory studies, research in bargaining, and game-theoretic research on the credibility, and effectiveness, of threats and promises (see Tedeschi's chapter; and Chapter 11 in Bettinghaus & Cody, 1987). A second line of research spanning three decades is manipulation (Godfrey, Jones & Lord, 1986; Jones, 1964; Jones & Wortman, 1973).

While both lines of enquiry (influence and manipulation) are still quite popular, for obvious reasons (also see Smith and her colleagues, this volume, Chapter 4; Arkin and Shepperd, this volume, Chapter 7), we have witnessed several fundamental changes in theory and research since the early 1970s. First, there has been emphasis on developing a theory of the production of tactics, cast in terms of cognitive processes (Chapters 1 and 2). Second, increased interest in 'implicit theories' (e.g. Wish, Deutsch & Kaplan, 1976) and lay explanations (Furnham, 1988) during the 1970s and 1980s prompted more researchers to view the research participant as an active, planning, protagonist, as opposed to a 'subject' who was merely reacting to the immediate stimulus materials provided by the experimenter. Ten years ago, for example, it was common to provide participants with a description of a hypothetical situation (which they could not reject), and provide strategic choices for them to evaluate on 'likelihood-of-use' scales. Today, it is common both to rate events in terms of relevance, importance, realism, or frequency of occurrence, and to elicit open-ended responses concerning tactics empoyed (see Chapter 4, by Smith and her colleagues; and Roloff *et al.*, 1988). The two developments involving basic issues of ecological validity dealt with (a) studying tactical choices actors claim they actually use, and (b) understanding the nature of influence processes by examining the basic types of influence goals actors claim they pursue (see Dillard, this volume, Chapter 3; also Smith *et al.*, this volume, Chapter 4).

Following research on describing the nature of influence goals which actors claim they pursue, research currently focuses on the basic reasons why actors and targets believe compliance should be granted to a wide number of interpersonal requests: relational obligations and implicit reciprocity obligations among friends. Another trend assesses the fundamental question of how person-variables (e.g. gender of actor or target) or personality constructs (locus of control, self-esteem, self-monitoring) impact both on social participation (actors differ in how frequently they pursue particular goals and in their amount of contact with others) and tactical choices. Another, growing, concern focuses on influence in particular contexts: e.g. groups, organisations, marriages.

A final trend is still not fully apparent in the social influence literature: the study of influence as an interactional process. Any specific attempt at influencing others can be met with a resistance tactic, but only a few studies have explicitly studied attempts at compliance–resistance (McLaughlin, Cody & Robey, 1980; McQuillen, 1986; McQuillen, Higgenbotham & Cummings, 1984). However, a number of studies have assessed what actors would say or do as a 'second-attempt' tactic, and literature on accounts assess sequential steps routinely (see below, and Chapter 10).

Cognition and tactical communication

First, research in the last several years or so has focused on fundamental questions of cognition and production of messages. Schank & Abelson (1977) argued that the knowledge that can be used to understand stories or events stems from one of two sources: scripts (for understanding routine events), and plans (for understanding novel events). As Rule and Bisanz note (this volume, Chapter 2), a plan-based theory of understanding assumes that we are aware of the particular goal an individual pursues, as well as the method used to achieve the goal. Hence, Rule, Bisanz & Kohn (1985) assessed the goals actors reported (see below), as well as the influence methods reportedly used. In their contribution to this volume, Gay Bisanz and Brendan Rule present their findings concerning the operation of a persuasion schema, represented in memory as a general canonical form of a culturally shared, single-ordered list of tactics, ordered from Ask, to (in descending order of preference and probable use) Self-oriented, Dyad-oriented, Social Principles, and Negative Tactics. Their chapter focuses on the organisation of knowledge about persuasion, how such knowledge is developed, and, ultimately, the production of behaviour. As such, it represents one of the chapters richest in implications for future research and theoretical elaboration.

The first chapter, by John Greene, is a perfect companion to Bisanz and Rule's chapter. Greene presents a theoretical discussion in which he argues that strategic message production cannot be explained adequately, or at least fully, without recourse to a model of the representation, selection and utilisation of procedural information (rules, scripts, relations among goals, situations, and actions). Bisanz and Rule have already tackled the first two concerns, and further work has progressed on the issue of representation (Greene, Smith & Lindsey, 1988). According to Greene, theories of tactical selection that rely on social exchange or costs/ risks analyses will not fully account for the processes and mechanisms of selection and utilisation (i.e. how the individual moves from an abstract representation of a plan to the actual implementation of specific behavioural components necessary in order to effect or carry out any plan). Research on representation is fundamental.

Message tactics and influence goals

As noted above concerning issues of ecological validity, the current emphasis on influence goals and how actors attempt to achieve them stems (for those in the communication discipline) from concerns over both the relevance and exhaustiveness of tactics studied, and the relevance (and generalisability) of situational effects on strategic choices. French and Raven had earlier developed and outlined five original bases of power (referent, expert, reward, coercive, and legitimate), and later added a sixth (information; see Raven & Kruglanski, 1970). While these bases of power are (and have proven to be) very useful in studying managerial influence, sales, etc., questions can be raised as to how powerless actors influence others; if an actor isn't particularly attractive (referent influence is sometimes referred to as attraction power: see Tedeschi & Bonoma, 1972), does not control the target's rewards and punishments, and is not an expert, what does the actor do?

In 1975 Raven and his colleagues (Goodchilds, Quadrado & Raven, 1975) presented a paper at the Western Psychological meetings entitled 'Getting One's Way', that fuelled considerable interest in identifying actors' attempts to influence (Cody, McLaughlin & Jordan, 1980; Falbo, 1977; Falbo & Peplau, 1980; Kipnis, Schmidt & Wilkinson, 1980; Wiseman & Schenck-Hamlin, 1981; see review in Cody, Canary & Smith, in press; and see Kearney *et al.*, 1984, concerning tactics used in classrooms). Other projects explored tactics used in seeking particular goals, such as relational initiations (Berger, in press (a)), relational de-escalation (Cody, 1982; Wilmot, Carbaugh & Baxter, 1985; and see Chapter 4 by Smith and her colleagues), what actors say to traffic officers (Cody & McLaughlin, 1985b) and what actors say to traffic court judges (Cody & McLaughlin, 1988; and see Chapter 11, by McLaughlin and her colleagues).

Briefly, the results of several multidimensional scaling projects indicated that there exists a finite set of tactics which actors employ, and that these tactics are differentiated from each other on the basis of a few salient dimensions. Falbo (1977) identified 16 tactics that were arrayed along two dimensions, defined as 'indirect vs. direct' and 'rational vs. non-rational', and Falbo & Peplau (1980) obtained two dimensions of the kinds of compliance-gaining tactics people used in intimate relationships ('direct vs. indirect' and 'bilateral vs. unilateral'). Wiseman & Schenck-Hamlin (1981) identified 14 tactics, and four dimensions: directness of tactics, manipulation of sanctions (punishing vs. rewarding), locus of control, and explicitness of rationale. Cody and his colleagues (1980) obtained solutions for essays written for three separate compliance-gaining events, and obtained tactics and dimensions similar to ones in Falbo, Falbo & Peplau, and Wiseman & Schenck-Hamlin. In these studies direct methods of influence include simple statement ('Ask' in Bisanz and Rule's work), and persistence, while indirect methods include deceit, hinting, and some emotionally oriented tactics (flattery, other forms of ingratiation, and nonverbal methods, such as looking disappointed, etc.). Rational approaches include reason, compromise, bargain, persuasion and expertise, while less rational ones include evasion, *fait accompli*, and threat.

Independently of the work by Cody *et al.* and Wiseman & Schenck-Hamlin, Kipnis and his colleagues (1980) analysed essays written by managers on 'How I Get My Way' and identified 14 categories of tactics (clandestine, personal negative actions, administrative sanctions, exchange, persistence, training, reward, self-presentation, direct request, weak ask, demand, explanation, gathering supporting data, and coalitions); a subsequent factor analytic project produced eight factors, and Kipnis and his colleagues later created the POIS (Profiles of Organisational

Influence Strategies) measure of the tactics reason, friendliness, assertiveness, coalition, higher authority, and bargaining, etc. (see this volume, Chapter 6).

Rule & Bisanz (1987) analysed open-ended responses in order to investigate, and extend, Schank and Abelson's theory. They identified 15 tactics, and grouped them on the basis of the five general types previously mentioned: Ask, personal benefits and personal expertise (Self-oriented Tactics), invoke role relationships and bargain (favour) (Dyad-oriented Tactics), appeal to norms, moral principles, and altruism (Social Principles), and butter-up, bargain (object), emotional appeals, personal criticism, deceive, threaten, and force (Negative Tactics). They ordered the tactics, as noted above, in terms of preference, social desirability, and costs, from the simple, unelaborated Ask, to Negative Tactics.

Rule and Bisanz are not the only ones who propose that tactics form a single dimension. Marwell & Schmitt (1967a) wrote 16 items to measure compliance-gaining activities and obtained five factors which reflected, in their interpretation, the first five, original bases of power (French & Raven, 1959). They also obtained two second-order factors (pro-social and anti-social). However, Hunter & Boster (1987) re-analysed their data and found that the items in fact fail to measure distinct factors of reward power, coercive power, etc. Instead, the 16 items collapse to form a single continuum, a Guttman scale, of pro-social to anti-social tactics.

Besides the similarity in reporting a single dimension, there is little other commonality between the approaches of Rule and Bisanz and of Hunter and Boster. Rule and Bisanz argue that tactics are ordered from direct and rational (in which the actor first attempts compliance using a simple request, before using a tactic that requires greater force) to the more negative tactics. Also, it is critically important, according to their work, to treat each specific tactic as a qualitatively different tactical move (see Rule & Bisanz, 1987; Chapter 2 of this volume). The Hunter–Boster set of items do not include asking or bargaining (Kipnis *et al.*'s exchange tactic), or any rationality tactics (information power was added late in the French & Raven work). Hunter and Boster argue that tactics span a 'pro-social to anti-social' continuum, and that likelihood-of-use ratings of items should be summed to form a single number ('message selection'), that reflects the actors' use of verbal assertiveness.

To the student new to the area of 'compliance-gaining', the different results of the multidimensional scaling projects, factor analytic projects and studies coding open-ended essays produce an array of apparently different terms and dimensions that are at first difficult to reconcile, especially if one includes typologies of tactics used in particular goals or contexts such as relational disengagement and traffic courts. Clearly, there cannot be a typology of message tactics for every different setting or goal! In fact, if there is a single persuasion schema that is culturally shared (i.e. invariant to gender differences, etc.: see Rule & Bisanz, 1987), then the various typologies ought to be reconcilable in terms of the schema. The reader should keep in mind that the theory makes several important assumptions; for example, (a) goals associated with the use of a persuasion schema constitute a small finite set; (b) there exists a standard set of methods that can be used to pursue goals; (c) if any of the standard methods fail, the actor may use additional ('auxiliary') methods; and (d) the use of methods is ordered so that once an initial method is selected and fails, the individual will select a tactic further down in the sequence. Further, it is possible for the actor to 'skip over' a number of methods. We also have to assume that statements reflecting general categories are phrased differently in various goals and relationships; that is, how an actor phrases a dyad-oriented tactic may differ in work relationships, romantic relationships, family relationships, etc., but that despite different operationalisations, each attempt represents a relevant form of a dyad-oriented tactic.

Given these assumptions, we can easily reconcile goal-specific typologies with the five categories included in the persuasion schema. Romantic and emotional involvements are unlikely to be terminated (at least effectively) with a mere direct request statement (e.g. 'Is it okay with you if we never see each other again?')(unless attempted by a partner who is completely uninvolved in the relationship and lacks emotional commitment to the other partner). Rather, the tactics obtained in disengagement literature (see Cody, 1982; Wilmot, Carbaugh & Baxter, 1985; Chapter 4, by Smith and her colleagues, in this volume) can be grouped on the bases of self-oriented, dyad-oriented, and negative tactics. For instance, integrative tactics clearly reflect dyad-oriented attempts, de-escalation tactics largely reflect self-oriented attempts, and assertive/ultimata or 'negative identity management tactics' (Cody, 1982) are clearly negative tactics. In traffic court, actors 'skip over' ask and dyad-oriented tactics (since no relationship exists), and rely on social principles (appeals to fairness, equity, logical proofs, norms), self-oriented (justifications) and negative tactics (challenge the authority of the ticketing officer; see Chapter 11 in this volume by McLaughlin and her colleagues; and Cody & McLaughlin, 1988).

Actors possess knowledge of relationships and situations that govern how and when they 'skip over' the ordered list to produce influence methods. Both person variables (gender, Machiavellian orientations, self-monitoring, verbal assertiveness; see Chapters 10 and 13 in Bettinghaus & Cody, 1987; Chapter 4 by Smith *et al.* in this volume) and situational variables have been studied over the years. Two chapters in our volume focus attention on how goals (and goals and personality constructs jointly) influence strategic choices. James Dillard, in Chapter 3, reviews recent literature on the popularity of the goal construct, and the goal–planning–action (GPA) sequence, and explicates the assumptions, claims and relevance of the goal construct to the area of tactical communication. Dillard proposes that primary goals are the types of changes actors desire to implement in their social and physical environments; a primary goal specifies why the interaction is taking place (i.e. to get a date, to convince the neighbour that something is in fact wrong with the dog, etc.). Secondary goals specify a change one intends to induce in the target. Dillard provides evidence that interpersonal goals include Give Advice (Lifestyle), Gain Assistance, Share Activity, Change Political Stance, Give Advice (Health), and Change Relationship. Secondary goals include interaction, identity, personal resource, relational resource and arousal management goals. As one would expect, influence goals are strongly related to the amount of cognitive and behavioural effort respondents claim they would commit to the achievement of the goal, and 'logic' was more likely to be used in the pursuit of influence goals than of other types of goals.

Like Dillard, Sandi Smith, Michael Cody, Shannon LoVette and Daniel Canary also focus attention on goals (Chapter 4). Dillard differentiated influence goals from one another on the basis of a number of situation variables: source benefit, target benefit, group benefit, publicness, normative pressure, improvement, voluntary vs. nonvoluntary relationships, relational growth/maintenance, and specificity (see Chapter 3). Smith and her colleagues had earlier proposed and developed a typology of influence goals from a somewhat different set of situation features (see Cody & McLaughlin, 1985a; Wish, Deutsch & Kaplan, 1976): dominance, intimacy, perceived benefits, perceived right to persuade (i.e. the actor's beliefs that the request is a legitimate one), perceived or anticipated resistance to influence, situation apprehension, homophily, and relational consequences (short-term vs. long-term change in the definition of the relationship: see Cody, Canary & Smith, in press). However, the proposed typology of goals is largely the same: Obtain Permission, Gain Assistance, Give Advice, Change Opinion, Share Activity, Third Party/Elicit Support (i.e. an actor requests help in influencing a third person; influencing brothers and sisters to help parents during a health crisis), Change Ownership (selling and buying), Violate Law/Harm, Enforce Obligation, Protect a Right, and Change Relationship (i.e. initiate, maintain, escalate or de-escalate one: see Chapter 4). Rule, Bisanz & Kohn (1985) identified many of the same categories in their open-ended categorisation project: Activity, Opinion, Permission, Object (to acquire an object), Information, Agency (to get a target to do something for the actor), Ownership, Relationship, Habit (to give advice on health), Assistance, Third-party, and Harm.

It is important that these studies obtained similar types of goals. The studies agree on which goals are most frequently pursued, and the differences that exist between the studies are due to two simple factors (other than some differences in labels). First, it is clear that actors pursue qualitatively different goals in different relationships. For example, Cody *et al.* found that almost all requests made of parents involved obtaining permission, gaining assistance and giving advice, while almost all requests made of room-mates involved gaining assistance, sharing activities and enforcing obligations. Since Dillard focused attention on interpersonal goals, Rule *et al.* focused on friends, fathers, enemies and others, and Cody *et al.* encouraged participants to list all influence attempts involving parents, brothers/sisters, room-mates, neighbours, strangers and bureaucrats, some differences in goals were evidenced.

There is a second factor accounting for differences in goal taxonomies. Cody *et al.* clustered 42 events sampled from 10 years of research in compliance-gaining literature, and obtained two clusters not identified in the other studies. Protect a Right includes events in which the actor believes that the target has infringed his or her rights, as when neighbours' dogs bark at night, neighbours play their stereos loudly at night, room-mates borrow clothing or eat food without permission, and so forth. Similarly, Enforce Obligation goals were obtained in Cody *et al.* which included those relatively infrequent events in which the actor has to take action to ensure that others will fulfil some implicit or explicit obligation (pay the rent on time, pay the phone bill on time, share class notes as previously promised, etc.). These two types of events are not representative of the major goals actors pursue; both types of goals represent fewer than 3% to 5% of all influence attempts (see Cody, Canary & Smith, in press). In fact, most episodes occurred in relationships with room-mates, although sometimes with brothers/sisters, and friends/acquaintances. Note, however, that a social actor who effectively exerted control over his or her social relationships and social environment would not have to pursue such goals often.

We wish to draw attention to two critically important aspects of a goal-based study of influence and communication. The first of these deals with basic research issues. After uncovering criteria laypersons use to differentiate situations from one another and assign meanings to events, the research issue became one of assessing how actors used such information in making strategic choices. Early studies naturally used analysis of variance (ANOVA) or MANOVA designs to study two or three situational features at a time (for instance, Miller et al., 1977, who studied intimate vs. non-intimate relationships, and short-term vs. long-term relational change), and results were often interpreted in terms of two criteria (the desire to be effective, and the desire to conform to particular situational constraints; see this volume, chapter 3, by Dillard; and Cody, Canary & Smith, in press). However, situation perceptions per se do not explain behaviour; rather, as Dillard notes in Chapter 3, goals are culturally viable explanations for behaviour, and are used to 'partition the stream of behaviours into meaningful units' (Dillard, Chapter 3; see also von Cranach et al., 1982). However, goal-types, as repetitively re-occurring objectives which actors pursue (e.g. seeking permission from parents) are intimately linked to situation perceptions (see Canary, Cody & Marston, 1986; Canary, Cunningham & Cody, 1988; Cody, Canary & Smith, in press; Dillard, this volume, Chapter 3; Smith et al., this volume, Chapter 4). While conceding that we still need to know more about the content and organisation of influence goals (as in the seminal work by Cantor, Mischel & Schwartz, 1982a, b), situational features of rights, benefits, apprehension, aspects of the relationship and its history, anticipated resistance, etc., are a significant part of the meaning actors assign to events.

In practical research terms, research using goals offers several extremely important advantages over using 'situations'. First, there is the issue of parsimony. If seven (or more) situation features are needed to 'cover' perceptions of events, then studying situational effects becomes a complex task relative to studying the effects of a finite set of goals. This is especially evident if one is interested in studying the sequence of activity required to achieve success (i.e. the process of interpersonal influence). It is by far more straightforward to study how influence attempts (and resistance) unfold in ten or so goals, rather than a matrix of 7 × 7 cells defined by situation perceptions. Second, simplistic studies relying on ANOVA or MANOVA designs often produced interaction effects that failed to replicate (see review by Cody, Canary & Smith, in press), either because some of the sampled situations may have differed on additional and unmeasured situational criteria, or through some other sampling problem or methodological issue. For example, a situation involving high intimacy and long-term relational consequences may reflect either a relational initiation goal, a relational de-escalation goal, an advice giving (health) goal or the making of a 'selfish request' that results in a re-definition of the relationship (see examples in Cody, Canary & Smith, in press). Since different tactics are used in giving advice than in de-escalating relationships, for example, a significant Intimacy × Relational Change interaction effect obtained in one study may not replicate in another study. We need to examine how actors attempt to achieve goals over time, when they are effective (or fail), and the interpersonal as well as psychological consequences of failure and success.

Relational obligation and tactical communication

Studies on influence goals conducted to date indicate two unsurprising findings. First, nearly all requests are made of friends and family members: and, secondly, most of these requests are ones which involve obligations among friends and family members, or requests that at least imply reciprocity (see Cialdini, 1984). Cody et al., for example, found that only 20% of requests made by college students were directed towards neighbours, strangers, and bureaucrats; 21% to 29% of all requests were directed towards parents, brothers and sisters, and 50% to 60% of all requests involved friends and room-mates. Rule & Bisanz (1987) similarly found that 64% of all requests involved close friends and family members. Further, the most common requests involved sharing activities, changing opinions, securing objects or gaining assistance (according to Rule & Bisanz, 1987), or gaining assistance, giving advice, and sharing activities (according to Cody, Canary & Smith, in press). The single most popular compliance request among college students is to ask a favour of a friend (i.e. to borrow notes, get a lift to campus, etc.).

Only recently, however, has attention focused directly on demonstrating the impact of implicit obligations in relationships on tactical choices. Roloff et al. (1988) investigated the common request of borrowing class notes and found, as expected, that actors believed the obligation to lend notes was greater with intimates than with strangers. Roloff and his colleagues had college students role-play what they would say when asking either a friend, an acquaintance, or a stranger to loan them class notes days before a mid-term examination, and to suppose they wanted to ask for the notes for half an hour or for three days (small vs. large request, thus manipulating resistance). Role players were also asked what they would say to the target if the target rejected the request for a loan.

Roloff et al. studied the degree to which requests involved 'elaborations' (a frequency count of the number of clauses employed in the written essays), apologies, explanations, inducements and contingencies.

They found that when making requests of friends, actors merely used an unelaborated simple request, relative to the requests made of acquaintances and strangers, and that the requests of intimates contained fewer elaborations, fewer apologies (for the small request of borrowing notes for 30 minutes), fewer explanations and fewer inducements. Intimacy substitutes for persuasion, according to Roloff and his students, and since we expect intimates to help us in times of need, we produce messages minimally sufficient to induce compliance. To influence strangers, however, actors have to justify their requests. However, when intimates refused to loan notes, actors responded with less polite responses than their first-attempt messages, and used more counterpersuasion than if strangers refused to lend them notes. Clearly, when friends fail to fulfil implicit obligations actors increase their effort to persuade, as Rule and Bisanz argue.

In one of the studies in Cody, Canary & Smith (in press), we found that 77% of the actors merely used the simple direct request when seeking assistance from a friend; and if the friend refused, 25% justified the request, 18% relied on some type of exchange, and another 29% withdrew (they claimed they would ask another friend). When seeking assistance from strangers, most actors used rationality (57%), and if the stranger refused, actors claimed to use exchange (23%), a justification tactic labelled 'other benefit' (21%—actors would point out some positive consequence that the target would derive from giving assistance), and direct request (19%: i.e. wait and ask again). Another approach was to become hostile if a stranger failed to help (15%). Cody *et al.* used different operationalisations of assistance than Roloff, and so the results are not precisely the same for the second-attempt requests. However, it is clear that actors do not feel obligated to justify initial requests of a routine nature with friends (compared to strangers).

The importance of obligations, implicit or explicit, was even more strongly demonstrated in Canary, Cunningham & Cody (1988). Canary and his colleagues had respondents write an essay on a recent conflict, and studied preferences for conflict-coping tactics. The essays were coded in such a way as to address the question: Which compliance-gaining goals escalate to conflict episodes? Influence goals involving giving advice, seeking assistance (from professors), eliciting support, escalating relationships and initiating relationships rarely, if ever, escalated to conflict. However, one set of conflict episodes (accounting for 35% of all conflicts) involved rights and obligations dealing with specific actions: protect a right (barking dogs, room-mates eating one's food), enforce obligations (room-mates not cleaning their part of the house as previously agreed), and defend self (i.e. the actor had to defend against another person's claim that he or she failed to uphold an obligation). In addition, approximately 30% of the conflict episodes involved disputes in maintaining obligations and reciprocity in relationships; for instance, sharing activities (one friend refused to engage in an activity preferred by the actor even though the actor had participated in the friend's activity), disputes about maintaining a current level of intimacy in a relationship, and de-escalating relationships. Clearly, issues of relational obligations and expected reciprocity are fundamental to both compliance-gaining and to conflict.

Person variables and tactical communication

One of the important features of the current interest in goals deals with integrating person variables or measures into a framework of social participation. Some years ago psychologists debated earnestly over the extent to which personality variables could predict relevant behaviours; why weren't correlations routinely higher than 0.30? Today, we routinely assess two important effects of person variables: entering or avoiding situations, and behavioural choices once actors enter the situation. It is obvious that some personality variables exert a very strong influence on social participation. For instance, an anxious or apprehensive person may cope for years with a neighbour's barking dog because he or she dreads the confrontation. The apprehensive person may also avoid relational initiation goals for fear of being rejected or negatively evaluated.

The research on gender differences and social influence clearly demonstrates how our knowledge of person–motive–behaviour is enhanced by assessing social participation and goals. Years ago, the claim was made that females (compared to males) use more indirect tactics and rely on fewer power-oriented strategies, and research in fact confirms that females are expected to behave differently (Johnson, 1976). However, there is increasing evidence that females differ little from males in power or politeness in organisational or task settings (especially after controlling, statistically, for ratings of self-confidence: see Instone, Major & Bunker, 1983; Kipnis, Schmidt & Wilkinson, 1980; Steffen & Eagly, 1985). If females want to be effective in influencing others, then they will adapt to organisational rules as they are socialised into organisations (Putnam & Wilson, 1982), or increase their use of rationality when influencing bureaucrats or strangers, in order to overcome lower initial levels of credibility assigned to females in our society, or to ward off biases. For instance, Cody *et al.* found some evidence that parents are biased in favour of sons' permission requests (to extend curfew, etc.); if females want the same privileges, they have to justify their requests.

However, if females are socialised and encouraged to be more communal or relationally oriented, then this motivation should be reflected in some of the types of activities and goals pursued. In fact, Cody *et al.* found that females more frequently pursued goals of sharing activities with brothers, sisters, friends and room-mates, gave advice to parents and to brothers and sisters, spent more time involved in volunteer work, and spent considerably more time involved in relational changes with friends (prompting friends to confide more in them, planning and proposing relational escalations, tests of trust, etc.). While there was some evidence of the female-as-weak-and-dependent (i.e. males still apparently control relational initiations, females made more requests for assistance from others, females claimed less success in obtaining permission from parents, and when influencing employers), a stronger case can be made for the view of females as communally oriented (for at least some portion of college-aged females). In fact, females rated persistence at achieving goals higher than males in events involving eliciting support (for a third party), de-escalating relationships, protecting rights, enforcing obligations, and giving advice, and females can be just as assertive when relationally disengaging as males (see Chapter 4 in this volume). Other research in social participation indicates that females are status neutralising (see Reis *et al.*, 1982: 994), whereas males are more likely to be status assertive.

Another person variable which has figured in studies in person–motive–behaviour is self-monitoring. Mark Snyder (1987) argued that the low self-monitoring individual is a 'principled and honest' individual who behaves in accordance with his or her own attitudes, feelings and inner states. Snyder also presents evidence of how self-monitoring is related to preferences for entering or avoiding events. Smith, Cody, LoVette and Canary, in Chapter 4 of this volume, present a series of studies that assess how the low self-monitor (male) (a) employs different standards when considering entering or avoiding events; (b) rejects (relative to the high self-monitoring male) emotionally oriented as well as relationally oriented tactics (e.g. compromise, referent power); and (c) manages relational de-escalation. Their findings are complex and presented in considerable detail.

After reviewing literature on females as 'communal and friendly' and self-monitors as 'principled and honest', Smith and her colleagues argue that the low self-monitoring male should be the least expressive type of social actor. The central thesis is simple: if self-monitoring does in fact measure whether a person is principled and honest, then the measure should correspond with a rejection of a number of specific tactics (e.g. pout, sulk, deception, etc.), and an adherence to a set of behaviours concerning relational obligations and reciprocity. Smith and her colleagues found support in the first two studies for the hypothesis that low self-monitors reject 'manipulation' (positive feelings, negative feelings, referent influence, compromises). In their second study they also found that while high and low self-monitors were likely to pursue practical goals with equal frequency (e.g. seeking permission from parents), low self-monitors were reluctant to pursue a small number of 'interpersonal goals' (sharing activities with friends, gaining assistance from friends, initiating relationships, and gaining assistance from strangers). Low self-monitors also rejected attempts at talking a traffic patrolman out of ticketing them. In the third study—focusing on relational disengagement—Smith *et al.* found that low self-monitoring males were least likely to demand changes in their dating partners, and, whereas high self-monitors withdrew commitment when accepting (and desiring) to change relational partners, low self-monitors withdrew emotional feelings and commitments when the partner caused problems. In sum, low self-monitors (or low self-monitoring males) decline to employ tactics that might be labelled as 'manipulative', place value on being independent and allow friends to do as they please; apparently, if guilty of speeding they would accept the ticket with little counter-arguing (relative to high self-monitors). While provocative, research of this nature would certainly benefit from assessing directly relational rules and obligations believed to be operating by high and low self-monitors (see, for instance, Roloff *et al.*, 1988).

Tactical communication in the organisation and small group

David Kipnis and Stuart Schmidt have played a prominent role in the study of influence methods and goals in the 1970s and 1980s. They have played an active, and quite visible, role in uncovering laypersons' tactics, as well as in the study of organisational goals pursued by actors (Kipnis, 1984; Kipnis, Schmidt & Wilkinson, 1980). In their contribution to this volume (Chapter 6), Kipnis, Schmidt and Braxton-Brown briefly overview their earlier projects, and propose that the 'Shotgun' style of influencing others is related to lower performance evaluations (compared to Tacticians, Ingratiators and Bystanders). They propose that the Shotgun style is also related to increased stress (while Tacticians, who rely on rational argument, experience the least amount of stress). To us, far too much emphasis has centred, in recent years, only on the issue of predicting tactical selections. It is refreshing to secure more evidence on the effectiveness of tactics and their consequences—a trend we hope accelerates.

Kipnis and his colleagues remind us, first, that having power does not necessarily mean that influencers will use power. Powerful people have a wider range of tactics available to them, but being selective, strategic and rational is more likely to correspond to effectiveness, reduced stress, promotions, and salary increases. Second, Kipnis *et al.* also remind us to look either at the structure of the organisation or the relationships between target and actor when considering tactic selection and outcomes. More than 20 years ago Cartwright (1965) suggested that the truly powerful person need use very few influence attempts, since he or she may have others who anticipate needs and desires, or he or she may only need to use simple requests. Roloff *et al.* argued that relational obligations can substitute for persuasion; power positions, as well as a well-groomed image as a competent, invaluable worker who controls resources, or an intimidator, etc., may also substitute for persuasion in the sense that others do favours for such people automatically, or are willing to comply with simple requests.

Sources of influence in the small group context have been a subject of interest to social scientists for several decades. One of the most enduring lines of research in social psychology has concerned itself with the choice shift or group polarisation phenomenon, in which group decisions (or, alternatively, the post-decision choices of group members) become either more risky or more cautious than the mean of the individual members' pre-discussion choices (Dion, Baron & Miller, 1978; Laughlin & Earley, 1982; Murningham & Castore, 1975; Pruitt, 1971a, b; Stoner, 1961; Vinokur, Trope, & Burnstein, 1975). There is also an interest in group polarisation among communication researchers (Alderton, 1981, 1982; Boster & Mayer, 1984; Kellerman & Jarboe, 1987; Meyers, in press).

One of the leading accounts of group polarisation is Persuasive Arguments Theory (Burnstein, 1982; Burnstein, Vinokur & Trope, 1973; Vinokur & Burnstein, 1974). Persuasive Arguments Theory holds that with respect to any given decision choice there is a set of arguments which is consensually shared within a given social community; that individual group members possess some of these arguments; and that communication during group discussion serves as a vehicle for displaying the argument resources collectively shared by the group. Key factors in the translation of pre-discussion arguments into sources of group influence are argument novelty and persuasiveness.

Persuasive Arguments Theory is a non-interactional model in the sense that factors which we might expect to emerge and be ratified through talk, such as the unequal distribution of member power and influence, or the accumulating weight of favourable statements towards a particular decision alternative, are not regarded as important determinants of group choice. In their chapter (Chapter 5), Meyers and Seibold offer a critical analysis of Persuasive Arguments Theory, arguing for increased attention to the role of interaction processes in group decision-making. The authors review research on interaction patterns and decision quality, consensus and group shift; interpersonal argument, including reason-giving; and the 'structuration' (Poole, Seibold & McPhee, 1986; Seibold & Meyers, 1986) of group argument. Four argument strategies are proposed which appear to be capable of influencing group decision-making.

Presenting and Defending the Self

Although John Greene, in Chapter 1, reminds us of the basic distinction between tactics (a specific move executed in a sequence) and strategies (a sequence of tactics), all of the work presented in Part I assesses tactical deployments. The goal of self-presentation research is to assess how social actors engage in verbal or nonverbal displays in order to create and maintain particular, and desired, impressions. As Jones & Pittman (1982) define it, the key to self-presentation involves ' . . . those features of behavior affected by power augmentation motives designed to elicit or shape others' attributions of the actor's dispositions' (p. 233). Further, Jones and Pittman are quite explicit in grounding a proposed theory of self-presentation in terms of identifiable social motives. Five assumptions form the basis of their theory (p. 235):

1. Actor A wants to make secure or to augment his power to derive favourable outcomes from target B;
2. The desired growth of consolidation of power may or may not be directed towards these outcomes in the immediate future. Actor A may invest strategic outcomes in a 'power bank', whose resources may be tapped in unspecified future encounters with target B;
3. Actor A's getting the kind of power he wants will be facilitated

TABLE 1 *A taxonomy of self-presentational strategies classified primarily by attribution sought*

	Attributions sought	*Negative attributions risked*	*Emotion to be aroused*	*Prototypical actions*
1. Ingratiation	likeable	sycophant, conformist, obsequious	affection	self-characterisation, opinion conformity, other enhancement, favours
2. Intimidation	dangerous (ruthless, volatile)	blusterer, wishy washy, ineffectual	fear	threats, anger (incipient), breakdown (incipient)
3. Self-promotion	competent (effective, 'a winner')	fraudulent, conceited, defensive	respect (awe, deference)	performance claims, performance accounts, performances
4. Exemplification	worthy (suffers, dedicated)	hypocrite, sanctimonious, exploitative	guilt (shame, emulation)	self-denial, helping, militancy for a cause
5. Supplication	helpless (handicapped, unfortunate)	stigmatised, lazy, demanding	nurturance (obligation)	self-deprecation, entreaties for help

Source: Jones & Pittman (1982)

if target B has a certain impression of actor A; that A is expert, competent, etc.;

4. Creating an impression will be easy or difficult depending on A's resources, which in turn are defined by A's cognitive and behavioural capacities within the settings available for interaction with B;

5. The linkage of a particular power motive with the self-presentational features of behaviour is mediated by cognitive processes in the self-presenting actor. The behaviour is further shaped by evaluative or moral constraints. The complex interaction of motive, cognition and morality determines the choice of self-presentational strategies.

Table 1 presents succinctly five basic self-presentational strategies, and the desired attributions, emotions to be aroused, and actions that must be displayed. The *ingratiator* desires others to find him or her *likeable* and desires to elicit *affection* from others. There are standard tactics used to seek approval, praise others, etc., that can be used to effect liking, and apparently nonverbal, subtle and indirect methods are considered more effective (see Godfrey, Jones & Lord, 1986). An *intimidator* desires others to view him or her as dangerous, and desires to evoke fear. In extreme cases, violence-prone men (Toch, 1969) may even go out of their way to violate the rights or space of others and engage in fights in order to promote an image of a 'tough guy', with whom others should not tangle. Once an intimidator is successful at creating the desired image at bars, football stadiums, etc., he (or she) need rarely worry about 'persuading' others or overcoming counter-arguments.

A *self-promoter* may run the risk of being perceived as conceited, or a braggart, but there are undoubtedly many benefits which follow from successful self-promotion that would compensate for the risk. Of course, less risk is involved if the self-promoter arranges for others to make claims on his or her behalf (Jones & Pittman, 1982; McLaughlin *et al.*, 1985). An *exemplifier* desires others to view her or him as dedicated, and seeks to elicit emulation, guilt, or shame. Such a style involves the actor in righteous denial, sacrifice, helping others, etc. Finally, *supplication* requires the actor to appear helpless (unfortunate, handicapped) in order to elicit nurturance from others. Actors highly dependent on others are perceived as more likely to use supplication (Howard, Blumstein & Schwartz, 1986).

Oddly, little work by compliance-gaining researchers has integrated the self-presentation framework (except in the attention given by some to the classic works in ingratiation). Such integrative emphasis would certainly be welcome, especially in light of the atheoretical orientation of a large number of compliance-gaining projects. One obvious link is between research on powerless actors (a factor of locus of control) and tactical preferences (Canary, Cody & Marston, 1986; Doherty & Ryder, 1979; Lefcourt, 1982; Lefcourt et al., 1985; Levenson, 1976). Canary et al., for example, concluded that powerless actors (those actors who were more likely to believe that the world is controlled by powerful others) preferred compliance-gaining contexts in which they are dependent on the target. They then exploit that dependence by manipulating positive or negative feelings, or by using referent influence (appeals to similarity). They also avoided events involving strangers, and giving advice—when success depends on one's own personal efforts. Thus, people who believe that the world is run by powerful others will establish some dependent relationship with people who have power (or ability), then manipulate feelings and relational obligations in order to exploit them. However, a few of the compliance-gaining projects have assessed how actors create and maintain a desired public (targeted) image over time, or engaged in the actual exploitation over time.

Strategic self-presentation

The first two chapters in Part II deal directly with self-presentation theory. The remaining chapters focus on how actors defend themselves from accusations, and the psychological consequences of providing accounts. Robert Arkin and James Shepperd (Chapter 7) first present a brief history of self-presentation theory, provide an overview of self-presentational styles, and introduce the distinction between assertive and defensive strategies. After introducing these issues, Arkin and Shepperd emphasise research and theory on the topic of self-protection. Besides using excuses and disclaimers to protect the self from negative evaluations, actors will undoubtedly find ways to regulate anxiety that is likely to be experienced in events in which they feel obliged to protect an image. A highly anxious person, for example, may feel obligated to speak during jury deliberations, but fears evaluation and fears that he or she will stutter, make speech errors, etc. A protective self-presentational style is one in which an actor takes a conservative social orientation towards interaction; one wants to be safe. Thus, the juror may appear to be attentive and thoughtful (to fulfil the role of 'concerned juror'), and speak rarely, control message length and speech errors, and agree with statements made by others (thus avoiding risk). 'Getting along' becomes more important than 'getting ahead'. Self-serving biases, self-handicapping and other tactics can be used to avoid risks, and to protect, preserve, maintain or enhance one's image.

Arkin and Shepperd focus attention on *direct* methods of presenting and protecting the self. Robert Cialdini, John Finch and Maralou DeNicholas review the fascinating processes of *indirectly* enhancing one's image (Chapter 8). First, Cialdini *et al.* note that actors implicitly know (and behave) in ways to associate themselves with good news and successful teams, universities, and institutions (compared to bad news and failures). They review evidence that, when an actor's positive self-image is threatened, the actor is likely to engage in two indirect tactics to enhance personal prestige. Actors can *bask* in the victories and successes of others, and they can *blast* by devaluing or derogating their rivals. Another tactic, distancing one's self from failures (e.g. an unsuccessful football team that the actor could be linked to) is also presented ('cutting off reflected failure'; see Snyder, Lassengard & Ford, 1986).

Indirect methods (the MUM—keeping mum about unpleasant messages—effect, basking, blasting, cutting off reflected failure) obviously benefit the actor's *public* image and prestige, but do indirect tactics also benefit the *private* self? That is, regardless of the presence of an audience to impress, do actors (especially an actor whose image is threatened) engage in indirect methods in order to bolster their own, inner view of self? Apparently they do. People who were led to believe that they had the same birthday as Rasputin privately rated the infamous character as less negative than people who did not share the same birthday, even though all participants read the same description of the man. Further, Cialdini and his colleagues present some evidence that actors who possess impoverished views of the self (external locus of control, low self-esteem) are particularly likely to engage in ego-protection. The latter findings are quite compatible with the literature discussed earlier—that which shows that powerless individuals attempt to benefit from associations with those who are more powerful (and successful).

Defensive self-presentation

C.R. Snyder and his colleagues have devoted considerable research effort over the last decade to the study of how accounts, especially excuses, are used to 'negotiate reality'. They begin their chapter, the first of five devoted to defensive self-presentation, by presenting dimensions of appraisal: an actor who is party to a 'failure event' (Schönbach, 1980) can perceive, on one dimension, the extent to which he or she is linked to the act (or the outcome). On the second dimension, the actor perceives the act as located on a continuum ranging from 'very negative' to 'very positive'. Because actors are motivated to protect (if not enhance) a positive self-image and avoid a negative self-image, they will perceive links to positive acts (even if there are no legitimate grounds for doing so, as Cialdini *et al.* point out), and distort or otherwise reduce links to negative acts. Protective reality negotiation (avoiding the repulsive and vivid negative view of self) may play a greater role in the normal person's coping with feedback from the world at large than do the enhancing processes (linking self to positive acts).

Of course, feedback from external reality (friends, police, family, etc.) limits or constrains the perceived linkage to acts. External feedback can also shape a better, revised theory of self. In the Snyder and Higgins framework, justifications reflect strategies that operate on the valence-of-act dimension of appraisal, and excuses operate on the linkage-to-act dimension. Since excuses are fundamentally related to linking the actor to good acts, or lessening the linkage of the actor to bad ones, excuse-making represents the 'overarching protective process that employs both the linkage-to-act and the valence-of-act dimensions'. Excuses can be offered to both the internal audience (the self) or the external audience (the jury, judge, friends, etc.); in the latter case there is less room (obviously) for self-deception. As acts increase in negativity and links to self become less deniable, audience members (who, if friends, might be biased towards the accounter's excuse) will show less bias or tolerance for the accounter.

Excuses have beneficial effects in maintaining or bolstering esteem, and in influencing other affects, such as depression, especially if the accounter attributes the cause of behaviour to external, variable and specific (rather than internal, stable and global) factors. Snyder and Higgins focus some attention in their contribution on interpreting the ten specific excuse episodes from President Reagan's speech on the Iran arms scandal, noting how each excuse was linked to either (or both) the dimensions of appraisal. Clearly, their theory of excuse-making and its consequences is applicable to a wide variety of contexts.

The fact that verbal messages, accounts, can be used to neutralise questionable actions surfaced a long time ago (Scott & Lyman, 1968; Sykes & Matza, 1957; and see Semin & Manstead, 1983). However, little systematic empirical research focused on the antecedents and consequences of accounts until the 1980s, immediately following on the heels of a number of taxonomic projects (for instance, Schönbach, 1980; Tedeschi & Reiss, 1981). Accounts are, briefly, verbal messages used to manage failure events (Schönbach, 1980). By failure event we refer to some action committed by one party (alone or in concert with others) to which a second party or parties take exception. A failure event may also refer to action which was expected but which failed to materialise or at least to come off in the conventional way (Cody & McLaughlin, 1985b). Accounts include four general forms (see Cody & McLaughlin, in press):

1. When using an *excuse*, the 'offender' admits that the act in question occurred, and that it was in fact harmful, but denies that he or she was fully responsible for it (e.g. 'my alarm failed to go off, so I was late'). Excuses, according to the classic typology provided by Scott & Lyman (1968), may include *appeal to accident, appeal to biological drives, scapegoating,* and *appeal to defeasibility* ('I had no idea it would turn out that way').

2. When offering a *justification* the offender accepts responsibility for the questionable action, but denies that it was harmful, or claims that there were positive consequences to the act ('I was late for work today because I had to stop and rescue injured passengers in an accident'). Justifiers can use *denial of injuries* ('nothing happened'), *denial of victim* ('he got what he deserved'), and *appeal to loyalties* ('I couldn't betray a friend').

3. When offering a *concession*, the 'offender' neither denies responsibility nor attempts to justify untoward conduct, but simply confesses or admits to the failure in question. Concessions are often accompanied by apologies, expressions of remorse, offers to make restitution, and so on.

4. A *refusal*, however, might be offered if the 'offender' believes that the 'reproacher', the one asking for the account, does not have the right to make the request, believes that the questionable act did not take place, or disagrees with labelling the act as a questionable or offensive one.

In a recent elaboration of his earlier taxonomic work, Schönbach (1985, 1986) introduced the notion of a *theme*, a sort of topical device which can be used to construct a variety of different accounts. For example, the theme 'provocation by the accuser' can be used to fashion either an excuse ('I was so upset by what you said that I just wasn't myself'), or a justification ('you deserved it after what you said to me'). Schönbach (1985) has also redefined excuse to focus on the offender's request for mitigation of judgement, using 'various arguments including, but not limited to, claims of impairment and hence reduced causal responsibility' (p. 10).

As we turn to the chapters by Schönbach and Kleibaumhüter, McLaughlin, Cody and French, Antaki, and Jellison, it is appropriate to return to two of the issues we considered in our earlier discussion of current developments in the study of social influence tactics: the role of social cognition processes, particularly causal attribution, in the production of accounts and explanations, and the role of person variables, especially gender. It is particularly striking to note that most of the current research on accounting for untoward conduct has been conducted without even a passing nod to attribution theory. (Similarly, with the exception of a recent paper by Weiner *et al.* (1987) on the differences between withheld and communicated excuses, attribution theorists have shown little direct interest in how people explain their own questionable conduct to others and how those explanations are shaped in talk.) We would note here that Leddo & Abelson (1988) argue that specialised knowledge structures are not necessary to account for the ways events are explained: '. . . the same knowledge structures used in understanding ought to be implicated in explanation' (p. 103). To extend the argument further, we would suggest that the processes by which we create explanations for others must be guided in part by conventional and consensually shared schemata for understanding events—what Abelson & Lalljee (in press) call explanation prototypes. These explanations are available to parties to failure events as resources for remedial action.

Often a person who is called upon to account for his conduct is required to provide a *contrastive explanation*: '. . .the individual must account for departure of an event from what might normally be expected' (Leddo & Abelson, 1988: 106). An account can be constructed from the sequence of actions associated with correct performance, and could be addressed to goal failure, planning failure, execution failure, interference, and so forth (see Read, 1987a, for a full account of causal scenarios and the knowledge structure approach to attribution).

Although the notion of causal schemata discussed above has not yet been incorporated into research on communicated explanations, there is another traditional bailiwick of attribution theorists that is beginning to be incorporated: moral judgement and the attribution of responsibility (Darley & Zanna, 1982; Finchem, 1985; Hamilton, 1978; Hamilton, Blumenfeld & Kushler, 1988; Schultz & Wright, 1985). McLaughlin, Cody and French, in Chapter 11 of this volume, argue that among the contents of the knowledge structures available for the fashioning of accounts are abstract moral principles and propositions about the situated evaluation of conduct. Following Backman (1985), they stress the interplay between moral 'knowledge' and moral decision-making, arguing that the availability of plausible accounts plays a crucial role in the decision to undertake a morally dispreferred action. Recent work by Hale (1987) and Weiner *et al.* (1987) lend credence to the notion that certain kinds of explanations can in fact redefine a failure event and relieve the account-giver of attributed responsibility and/or blame. Hale found that the use of justifications tended to result in judgements that the failure event was only slightly wrong and not a cause for severe penalties. Weiner *et al.* found that excuses which laid the blame for untoward conduct on external, uncontrollable and unintentional causative factors positively influenced perceptions of the accounter's dependability, responsibility and consideration.

McLaughlin, Cody and French, in their chapter, report a study in which they examined the influence of conventional accounting schemata on attributions about the moral character of the account-giver. Using a sample of accounts given by defendants in traffic court for such offences as 'speeding' and 'running through a red light' (along with a description of the offence), they had respondents read the accounts and evaluate the defendants on a series of scales measuring moral responsibility; *the extent to which the defendant was to blame, the influence of the defendant's personality, the defendant's intent to violate the law*, and so forth. Severity of the offence was also rated for each account. McLaughlin *et al.* report that significant multivariate main effects were obtained for account type for both 'speeding' and 'red light' accounts; offence severity, entered as a covariate, interestingly did not account for variation in the ratings of moral character beyond what could be explained by type of account. Among their findings are: that the use of justification produced the strongest attribution of the offence to the defendant's personality across both types of offences, and the strongest attribution of intent to violate the law in the cases of speeding offences.

According to classic attribution theory (Kelley, 1967, 1971), individuals use information about consistency, consensus and distinctiveness to determine whether a particular action can be attributed to dispositions of the actor, or characteristics of the situation. In his chapter, Charles Antaki argues that in the classical account of attribution processes, an explanation is entirely divorced from the context in which it is offered; that is, characteristics of the explanation and the audience for the explanation are not taken into consideration. Antaki established through examples from a large corpus of naturally occurring conversations that an adequate account of explanation must include the interpersonal function which explanation is intended to fulfil; that is, it must recognise that the communicated account cannot be interpreted without a context. Antaki demonstrates that in ordinary discourse many 'because' statements are not explanations for *events* but *justifications for speech acts* (Grice, 1975) or *warrants for assertions* (Searle, 1969). Further, he shows that many apparently 'non-causal' conjunctions ('if', 'when', 'else') are used in ordinary talk to mark an upcoming explanation. Antaki makes a compelling case that the traditional way of thinking about explanations as 'non-negotiable representations of internal information processing' is flawed by its failure to take into account their social construction in talk.

Role of person variables

Work in the early 1980s established that accounts seemed to conform to a *canonical form* (McLaughlin, Cody & O'Hair, 1983; McLaughlin, Cody & Rosenstein, 1983; Cody & McLaughlin, 1985b) or a sequence of 'slots' first suggested by Schönbach (1980); the *failure event*, the *reproach*, the *account*, and the *evaluation*. The *contingent* nature of the steps in the accounting sequence, that is, the dependence of each step on the immediate step, has been demonstrated, as has the tendency for actions in the sequence to mirror the affective tone of the preceding action (Cody & McLaughlin, 1985b). Thus, 'aggravating' reproaches tend to elicit 'aggravating' account forms (justifications and refusals), which can lead to failure to honour the account, and to continued conflict.

In Schönbach's (1986) theory of conflict escalation in account episodes, a harsh reproach for a failure event, or a refusal to account for the failure, can lead parties to the account episode to experience a felt loss of control and a subsequent loss of self-esteem. In their chapter in this volume, Schönbach and Kleibaumhüter test the hypotheses: (1) that a severe reproach results in a defensive account; (2) that actors with strong needs for control offer more defensive accounts given a severe reproach than those with a lower need for control; and (3) that the accounts of male actors are more defensive than those of female actors, given a higher male need for control.

Recent research on sex differences in the use of aggressive verbal behaviour has been inconsistent. Johnson (1976, and other researchers; see Bettinghaus & Cody, 1987) found that coercive tactics were stereotypically associated with masculinity. Studies of self-reported verbal behaviour favouring few or no differences in the use of 'strong' tactics include Kipnis, Schmidt & Wilkinson (1980), Instone, Major & Bunker (1983), and Steffen & Eagly (1985). Infante & Wigley (1986), analysing scores on the Verbal Aggressiveness Scale, report significantly higher means for male respondents. DeTurck (1985) reported that males, responding to hypothetical compliance-gaining situations (for instance, a neighbour's loud stereo, disagreements concerning sharing activities with friends, etc.), were more likely than females to use coercion initially, whereas females were more likely to *escalate* to the use of threats. Burggraf & Sillars (1987) found that women cannot be expected to be any less assertive or more complacent or indirect when communicating with their spouses. They found that conflict styles were so strongly reciprocal (assertiveness by speaker A was matched by speaker B) that gender effects dissipated. The chapter by Schönbach and Kleibaumhüter embeds the issues of sex and aggressive verbal behaviour in the context of a well-developed theory of conflict escalation in account episodes, incorporating not only the traits and dispositions of *both* parties to the episode but interactional constraints as well. Most previous research on sex and verbal aggression has tended to locate the actor and his or her verbal output in a virtual vacuum. Among their several findings Schönbach and Kleibaumhüter report that reproaching an actor's self-esteem or sense of control produced more defensive accounts (justifications and refusals), and that males offered fewer excuses but slightly more justifications and significantly more refusals when their sense of control was threatened in a reproach.

The last two chapters in this volume represent more general discussions on the nature of accounts (Chapter 13) and a framework for the study, and interpretation, of tactical communication (Chapter 14). Jerald Jellison establishes a point that the reader should keep in mind concerning the role played by accounts, or explanations in general, in society as a whole. The Norm of Internality, largely adopted by all members of society, dictates a close adherence to attending to (and emphasising) the individual's claim that he or she caused his/her own behaviour. Many publicly portrayed behaviours have been shaped externally, and may have sociological or historical developments that pre-date the individual. This norm of internality helps legitimate society's use of rewards and punishments to affect the future behaviour of its members.

As previously mentioned, James Tedeschi, in Part III, summarises a model of compliance developed from many years of research, and integrates the various contributions to this volume into a viable framework, emphasising both the role of source characteristics (truthfulness, authority, control of resources, expertise, and (mediation of) rewards) and self-presentational theory. Clearly, the self-presentational theory outlined in this introduction (see Jones & Pittman, 1982), and in many of the chapters in this volume, provide the most general framework for studying influence processes, emphasising, as they do, both a proactive and reactive (or assertive vs. defensive) and strategic vs. tactical nature of interpersonal influence, and emphasising features of the relationship between source and target, and the target's perceptions of the source. Tedeschi outlines a number of future hypotheses to be tested, and draws our attention to the role of self-esteem as a mechanism associated with social power.

We hope the reader will find the review pieces and studies presented in this volume useful in her or his research. Considerable work, we believe, needs to focus on cognition and the production and interpretation of tactical behaviours, and on mechanisms for integrating person variables (gender or personality) with goals and behaviour choices (as Tedeschi noted). We believe that additional work should deal with the consequences (i.e. salaries, promotions, evaluations, loss of friendships, etc.) of tactical communication. It is hoped that the publication of this volume will accelerate work in each of these areas, and advance our understanding of everyday influence.

Part I:
Social Influence

1 Tactical social action: Towards some strategies for theory

JOHN O. GREENE
Department of Communication, Purdue University, West Lafayette, Indiana, USA

Conceptions of tactics and strategic behaviour have come to pervade descriptive and theoretical approaches to human social interaction. As evidence in support of this assertion, consider the myriad of reports focusing on compliance-gaining message strategies (e.g. Marwell & Schmitt, 1967a; Miller *et al.*, 1977; Wiseman & Schenck-Hamlin, 1981), the work on strategies for resisting compliance-gaining attempts (e.g. McLaughlin, Cody & Robey, 1980; McQuillen, 1986), that on strategies for initiating relationships (e.g. Berger, in press (a); Berger & Bell, 1987), and that for terminating those relationships (e.g. Baxter, 1979; Cody, 1982), as well as research on strategies relevant to a host of other communication phenomena (e.g. Baxter & Wilmot, 1984; Burleson, 1984; Shea & Pearson, 1986; Richmond *et al.*, 1984). This current focus on strategy is due in part to a fundamental shift in assumptions concerning the intrinsic character of human beings. Rather than automatons buffeted by environmental reward contingencies, people have come to be viewed as purposeful, planning, social actors (Dowling & Roberts, 1974; Mischel, 1975; Gardner, 1987). From this philosophical perspective, conceptions of strategies, plans and allied entities are readily accorded the status of legitimate theoretical constructs and admitted as desirable foci of study.

Particularly noteworthy amidst the profusion of scholarly work in this domain have been the various attempts at building theories of strategic communication by explicating the processes by which this strategic behaviour is produced. Although these models invoke a range of distinct assumptions and constructs, they typically rely upon two essential premises:

first, that people possess a repertoire of communicative strategies or tactics that specify the behavioural information used to produce action; and, second, that the essential process involved in behavioural production is one of selecting a strategy appropriate to one's goal(s) and personal and/or situational constraints.[1] The aim of this essay is to evaluate these points in the interests of prompting more refined and rigorous accounts of the processes of strategic communication.

The argument to be advanced here is that both of these fundamental premises are flawed in that they represent overly simplistic conceptions of behaviour and the processes of behavioural production. In effect, such models assume an isomorphism between abstract memory repesentations and overt behaviour which is untenable in light of current knowledge of the structures and processes of the output system. To demonstrate this point, we begin with a consideration of the nature of behaviour and strategic action. This conception of action is then employed as a basis for evaluating the principle of isomorphic manifestation, and, by extension, models of strategic communication which reflect this principle. In the final section of the paper, this view of action is used to identify a set of formal requirements for a minimally adequate cognitive model of strategic social behaviour.

The Nature of Behaviour and Strategic Action

While it may appear patently true and beyond gainsaying, there is, nevertheless, value in reminding ourselves that strategic communicative actions are the products of an output system responsible for the formulation and execution of behaviour. A central assumption of this essay is that because this output system governs the production of strategic action and ultimately defines its content, form and dynamics, our understanding of strategic behaviour will be enhanced by focusing on the properties of this system. Indeed, a failure to consider the nature of the output system may lead to assumptions concerning processes of strategic communication that are inconsistent with fundamental principles of behavioural production and efferent control.

Behaviour as a dynamic collocation of features

Our commonsense conception of behaviour is that it consists of a series of abstractly defined units, or acts, such as 'throws', 'gestures', 'promises' and 'threats'. From such a perspective, it seems quite reasonable to view behavioural production as a process of stringing together an appropriate series of acts to accomplish our various goals. Such an 'act-sequence' conception of behaviour has intuitive appeal in that it is consistent with our phenomenal experience of behavioural control in most, or all, of our daily activities (see Vallacher & Wegner, 1987). Thus, when I go to a restaurant, I perceive that I am 'ordering', 'eating', 'paying the bill', and so on. Despite its phenomenal appeal, however, this view is limited in that it captures only a single facet of a complex output system and obscures essential properties of human action relevant to strategic communication.

In order to unpack this claim it is useful to begin with two observations concerning fundamental properties of human behaviour. The first of these is that any abstract act or co-ordinated activity involves the control of a large number of degrees of freedom in the efferent system (see: Reed, 1982; Saltzman & Kelso, 1983, 1987; Stelmach & Diggles, 1982; Turvey, 1977). In other words the motor output system permits an extremely wide range of effector unit configurations and trajectories that must be constrained and co-ordinated in order to behave effectively. However, while execution of action requires this low-level control, our phenomenal experience of our own behaviour is considerably more abstract than this (see Vallacher & Wegner, 1987). Indeed, there are simply too many degrees of freedom in the output system to effect control at the level of motor commands (Greene, 1982; Turvey, 1977).

The second fundamental property of behaviour is that all acts or action sequences are creative in the sense that they reflect novel output characteristics. Certainly this is true of abstractly defined acts such as 'ordering a meal' where I am virtually certain to produce a novel configuration of verbal and nonverbal behaviours in executing that act. More compelling, however, is the fact that even the most concretely defined acts exhibit this same creative character. Consider the simplest possible case, that of reaching from one precisely defined position to another, as in moving from a 'home' button to a 'target' button in a reaction-time experiment. At the level of our phenomenal experience, repeated reaches from one point to the other will seem devoid of any creative or novel character. Despite this, such reaches do exhibit considerable variation in movement parameters from trial to trial (Marteniuk & Romanow, 1983; Reed, 1982; Stelmach & Diggles, 1982). Thus, even the simplest and most repetitive acts are characterised by creativity and change.

Recognition of the complex and creative character of action has given rise to a view of behaviour radically different from that implicit in the act-sequence perspective. Rather than a sequence of abstract acts, behaviour is more properly seen as a dynamic organisation of constituent features, or properties, in which each feature represents some limited component of the matrix of properties defining the behaviour (see: Greene, 1984a; MacKay, 1982; Pew, 1984; Reed, 1982; Saltzman & Kelso, 1987; Stelmach & Diggles, 1982). These features defining the parameters of action reflect a range of levels of abstraction in that some features are represented in terms of abstract propositional and linguistic codes, while others are represented in terms of low-level sensorimotor symbolic primitives (see: Greene, 1984a; Rosenbaum, Kenny & Derr, 1983; Saltzman, 1979; Turvey, 1977).

It is the organisation of these features which effectively defines the semantic and physical properties of any action. This collocation of features can be likened to a matrix of parameter values which reflects two dimensions. Most obviously, there must be a temporal dimension representing the order in which features are manifested. The second dimension is suggested by the fact that the output system is fundamentally hierarchical in that it is characterised by a downward, constraint-setting process through which more abstract representations of action functionally constrain the specifications for behaviour represented in less abstract codes (see: Greene, 1984a; MacKay, 1982, 1983; Marteniuk & MacKenzie, 1980; Pew, 1984). The second dimension is thus an abstraction dimension bounded by abstract behavioural specifications at the top and specific motor programmes at the bottom.

The key point of this discussion is that all behaviours are represented at a variety of levels of abstraction. This conception of a hierarchical organisation of elemental behavioural features provides a basis for addressing the problems of creativity and complexity noted above. The large number of degrees of freedom involved in behavioural production are controlled through specification of more abstract representations of action. In other words the hierarchical nature of the output system makes it unnecessary to act through conscious specification of individual motor commands. Instead, the output system functions to allow the control of lower-level activities through specification of more abstract representations of action which, in turn, constrain the operation of effector units. Within the constraints imposed by more abstract behavioural specifications, however, lower levels of the output system remain relatively autonomous in their concretisation of more abstract representations (see: Fowler & Turvey, 1978; Gallistel, 1980; P. Greene, 1982; Greene, 1984a; Marteniuk

& MacKenzie, 1980; Pew, 1984; Reed, 1982; Rosenbaum, 1984). Thus, an abstract specification for action such as 'threaten' may be manifested in behaviour in a variety of ways due to the operation of lower levels of the output system which serve to concretise this act in less abstract features. The creativity in manifestation of a specific act is the inevitable result of lower-level behavioural specifications marshalled to concretise the abstract act within the context of environmental and intrasystemic states relevant to the operation of those lower levels.

In summary, recognition of the creative and complex character of human action has led to a view of behaviour that is radically different from that of the act-sequence view. Behaviour is not a series of unitary abstract acts, but instead is a hierarchical collocation of elemental features reflecting a range of levels of abstraction. From this perspective, the 'acts' of our phenomenal experience, those captured in the act-sequence view, are simply particular abstract features of action comprising a portion of the action specifications employed in production of behaviour.

Strategies, tactics and mental representations of action

Before tracing the implications of this view of behaviour and behavioural production, it is useful to establish the terminological conventions to be used here. Scholars have used single terms such as 'plan', 'strategy' and 'tactic' to refer to distinct conceptual and phenomenal entities, and in other cases, terms such as these have been used interchangeably (Seibold, Cantrill & Meyers, 1985; Wheeless, Barraclough & Stewart, 1983). For this reason it is important to specify the use of essential terms in this chapter. My purpose, then, is not to suggest that the terminology proposed here is in some sense more 'correct' than other proposals; instead, the primary purpose is one of expository clarity. Further, it is important to emphasise that whether one employs this terminology is irrelevant to the arguments concerning theories of production processes developed below.

The focus of this chapter is upon the relationship of cognitive structures to observable strategic behaviour. For this reason it is important that we adopt terminology which preserves and emphasises the distinction between cognitive representations and externally available behavioural phenomena. With respect to observable phenomena, we shall use the term 'strategy' to refer to a behavioural sequence enacted in pursuit of some goal or goals. The term 'tactic', on the other hand, refers to a single abstract act, so that a single strategy may comprise several tactics.

It should be clear from the preceding section that what constitutes a tactic will depend upon the level of analysis employed in describing a behavioural sequence, but those acts commonly given in taxonomies of compliance-gaining techniques (e.g. 'threat', 'direct request', 'moral appeal') should typically fall in the domain of tactics. This approach to the relationship of tactics and strategies is generally in keeping with other recent treatments (e.g. Hazelton, Holdridge & Liska, 1982; Seibold, Cantrill & Meyers, 1985; Wheeless, Barraclough & Stewart, 1983), but it does emphasise that both strategies and tactics refer to *observable phenomena*. This focus on externally available cues is consistent with the treatment of strategies and tactics as methods of *interpersonal* influence, but it also restricts the range of application of the term so that, as used here, 'strategy' is not considered to include: (1) mental representations such as 'anticipated discourse patterns' (Seibold, Cantrill & Meyers, 1985), (2) inferred reasons or principles underlying a behavioural sequence (e.g. Wheeless, Barraclough & Stewart, 1983), or (3) groups of *potential* acts (defined either by the social actor or the theorist) that share some element or feature in common (e.g. Hazelton, Holdridge & Liska, 1982; Wheeless, Barraclough & Stewart, 1983).

In addition to such observable phenomena we need to consider the internal representation of behavioural information. We have previously noted that procedural information is typically held to be represented in modular elements which reflect a range of levels of abstraction in their specification of features of behaviour. Although a variety of terms and specific conceptions have been introduced in an attempt to capture this basic notion (e.g. Allport, 1979; Greene, 1984a; Kerr, 1983; MacKay, 1982; Norman & Shallice, 1980; Pew, 1984; Schmidt, 1975, 1976), here we shall employ the general term 'procedural element' to denote the basic structural/representational elements of the output system. A second major structural element emphasised in current understanding of the output system is a hierarchical structure composed of the activated subset of procedural elements. The term 'output representation' is used here to refer to this organisation of behavioural features.

In addition to these two representational structures, there are two additional terms that are useful in clarifying the conceptual stance articulated here. 'Plan' is used here to refer generally to the abstract levels of the output representation. As such, plans are mental representations of states and transitions leading to accomplishment of goals (de Beaugrande, 1980; Hayes-Roth & Hayes-Roth, 1979; Newell, 1980). Thus, 'plan' is reserved for use in speaking of a mental representation while 'strategy' refers to sequences of observed acts, a convention which is consistent with previous usage of these terms (e.g. de Beaugrande, 1980; Hayes-Roth & Hayes-Roth, 1979; Hobbs & Evans, 1980; Young, 1978). Finally, it is useful to introduce some concept corresponding to the general principle(s) which underlie plans and, more indirectly, strategies. Such general procedural knowledge, or 'heuristics', relevant to interpersonal compliance-gaining might include such principles as 'begin with the least effortful tactics' or 'when all else fails, threaten or coerce the other'.

Some Theories about Strategies: The Principle of Isomorphism

As was noted at the outset, a central focus of this chapter is on previous efforts to develop cognitive and quasi-cognitive theories of strategic social action. In this section the focus is upon a particular class of models of strategic action defined by a commitment to a principle of structural isomorphism between long-term memory representations of tactical information and behaviour. Following an evaluation of this principle based on the properties of the output system outlined above, the final section focuses on elements necessary for more refined models of strategic behaviour.

From a cognitive perspective, explanations for social phenomena consist of descriptions of the cognitive structures, processes and content that have given rise to those phenomena (Greene, 1984b; Greene & Cody, 1985). This process of theory building is essentially an inferential task in which the theorist seeks to posit a description of the 'black box' based upon observed input–output regularities. In essence, then, cognitive models comprise unobservable conceptual entities 'invented' by the theorist. Although this orientation towards the process of explanation gives the theorist considerable latitude in proposing specific components of the cognitive system, such theoretical entities remain subject to evaluation in terms of their conceptual and empirical adequacy (Greene, 1984b).

The principle of isomorphism examined here concerns the relationship between behaviour and the content of procedural elements in long-term memory. More specifically, isomorphism refers to a one-to-one correspondence between elements in the representational domain and the domain of abstract acts. In essence, models of strategic message production that reflect a commitment to isomorphism identify abstract tactical acts with the content of long-term memory structures. Thus, an act such as 'direct request' is held to be represented as the symbolic content of a procedural element (schema, rule, production, etc.).

There are two facets of this principle of isomorphism with far-reaching implications for the development of theories of strategic message behaviour. First, because there is an assumed correspondence between tactical acts and cognitive structures, a description of those acts effectively defines the memory structures relevant to production of strategic messages. For example, an individual who uses the tactic 'threat' must possess a memory structure corresponding to threat. Second, because it is these structures which are held to give rise to the message phenomena of interest, these descriptions are assigned explanatory status. To continue the example, an individual employs a threat because this tactic was selectively retrieved from her repertoire of strategic information. Thus, abstract descriptions of behaviour come to constitute essential components in explanations of that same behaviour (see Saltzman & Kelso, 1983; Summerfield et al., 1980). With this assumption of isomorphism intact, the search for a complete explanatory account of strategic action can be reduced to identifying the set of goals, situational features, and/or personal constraints that will cause certain elements to be selected from the tactical repertoire.

Although these two components of isomorphism make the task of constructing theories of strategic communication appear much more tractable, neither facet fares well under closer scrutiny. Instead of a one-to-one correspondence between act descriptions and cognitive structures, the link between the behavioural and representational domains is characterised by structural and behavioural indeterminacy that undermine the principle of isomorphism.

Structural indeterminacy

That abstract act descriptions correspond to long-term memory structures is assumed to permit identification of the cognitive structures underlying strategic action. In contrast to this position, however, there is, in fact, a structural indeterminacy that characterises the link from act to cognitive structure. By this I mean that an act description does not uniquely determine or identify the structure which produced that act.[2] A single act may be the result of any of a number of distinct structural representations such that identification of a particular structure on the basis of an act description is unwarranted (see Vallacher & Wegner, 1987).

To illustrate this point, assume that a person is observed to use the statement 'I'm going to bust your head if you do that again', as a compliance-gaining message. Now, the approach informed by the principle of isomorphism would be to attach some abstract tactical description such as 'threat' to this behaviour, assume that the individual possessed a long-term memory structure representing threat, and claim that this statement was the result of that behavioural specification being called into play. The problem with this approach is that rather than a procedural element corresponding to 'threaten', the person in question might have possessed any of a vast number of other abstract procedural elements that would have led to the same statement. For example, our hypothetical rhetor might have procedural elements such as: 'say: "I'm going to bust your head if you do that again"', or 'repeat the most recent compliance-gaining statement you heard your brother use', or 'make clear that you aren't going to be intimidated', any of which might have resulted in the statement in question. In such cases the ascription of causality to the procedural content 'threaten' would be erroneous. More importantly, the fact that social actors may possess multiple abstract procedural elements relevant to any influence tactic suggests that rather than a one-to-one correspondence between behaviour and procedural representations, there exists a one-to-many relationship, and as a consequence, inferences about the role of any particular structure on the basis of simple observation are unwarranted.

This structural indeterminacy suggests at least three significant implications. First, observing precisely the same tactic or abstract act on the part of different people does not necessarily indicate that this behaviour was produced by the same procedural representations. To observe similar actions and lump people together on the basis of some assumed common procedural content is unwarranted and violates a fundamental injunction of cognitive science (see: Kail & Bisanz, 1982; Newell, 1973; Young, 1978). Second, the fact that a person may possess multiple representations that could give rise to a single behavioural act (Vallacher & Wegner, 1987) indicates that simply because a person engages in the same behaviour at two different times does not necessarily mean that the same abstract procedural elements are responsible for each instance of that action. Finally, even if we know that a person possesses some procedural content, and we observe a strategic act consonant with that content, we cannot know that it was that structure which gave rise to his/her behaviour. That is, I may possess procedural content such as 'threaten' but that content may not play a role in the production of a specific threatening act.

Behavioural indeterminacy

Paralleling the structural indeterminacy of moving from act description to cognitive structure is the problem of behavioural indeterminacy in moving from cognitive representation to behaviour. In contrast to the principle of isomorphism, there is a lack of correspondence between the cognitive representation of an act, or tactic, and behaviour. As was noted above, our current understanding of behavioural production emphasises the conception of a hierarchical system in which abstract action specifications are concretised through the successive application of lower-level procedural information. Thus, if I decide to 'ask' in order to secure the assistance of another, then I must identify appropriate propositional content to implement this tactic, choose lexical items to deliver this propositional content, develop suitable articulatory and nonverbal programmes, and so on. At each successive level of behavioural specification there is considerable opportunity for variation. Because no behaviour is fully specified by an abstract act, there exists a one-to-many relationship between that act representation and behaviour.

In and of itself, this fact is not particularly damaging to the principle of isomorphism. As long as the abstract act is manifested as a feature of behaviour it is possible to maintain a one-to-one mapping between the features of abstract structures and those of the resultant behaviour. The problem with respect to isomorphism arises from the fact that a high level feature may, in some cases, not be manifested in action. An individual simply may not possess (or retrieve) lower-level procedural and/or declarative information necessary for implementation of the abstract act. To illustrate, my abstract plan may specify that a threat is in order, but a lack of skill or knowledge appropriate to delivering a threat in this social and communicative context may result in a behaviour which has no vestiges of threat. The point, then, is that even when a tactic is specified at upper levels of the output representation, the hierarchical nature of the output system may prevent that feature from being manifested in action.

Summary

Vestiges of the principle of isomorphism can be found in a variety of theoretical approaches to strategic communication. Unfortunately, this assumption involves an overly simplistic view of the relationship between procedural knowledge and behaviour. It is important to recognise that use of some abstract tactic does not necessarily mean that that tactic is represented as a long-term memory structure. Similarly, a long-term memory representation of a tactic, should it exist, need not correspond in any direct manner to the features of strategic action. Given this, it is useful to consider the theoretical elements necessary for more complete characterisations of the processes of strategic communication.

Towards some Strategies about Theories: Beyond Isomorphism

To date there has been considerable progress in understanding strategic message production—progress signalled by theoretical developments in conceptions of planning (e.g. Berger, in press (a); Cohen & Perrault, 1979; Hobbs & Evans, 1980; Infante, 1980), representation of strategic information (e.g. Rule & Bisanz, 1987; Rule, Bisanz & Kohn, 1985; Smith, 1982, 1984; Schmidt & Sherman, 1984), and so on. Further, in light of the widespread concern with interpersonal influence and strategic social action, there is every reason to believe that such theoretical advances will continue. A key question, then, concerns those issues that will need to be addressed by the next generation of models of strategic production. From the standpoint of cognitive science the pressing issues can be seen to fall into three broad categories; representation of strategic information, selection of appropriate elements from this strategic store, and utilisation of selected information in behavioural production.

Representation

Representation concerns the structure and symbolic coding of information in long-term memory. The preceding discussion of the first-order isomorphism fallacy should make clear that questions of representation are not easily resolved by recourse to observations of regularities in social behaviour. Despite this, the conceptual significance of the structure and coding of skill-relevant information suggests that questions of representation are among the most compelling issues for the next generation of strategic message production models.

Although the problems of structure and coding are far from resolution, it is possible at this point to advance some rudimentary conclusions about the nature of eventual solutions. With respect to the symbolic coding of procedural information, it seems virtually certain that there are multiple symbolic codes reflecting a number of levels of abstraction that play a role in strategic social action (see discussion above). For this reason, it is inappropriate to think of the information underlying the production of strategic messages in terms of a single abstract symbolic code. However, while we may recognise the existence of multiple procedural codes, their specific nature, role in message production, and availability to introspection and verbal report must await further theoretical and empirical developments.

Distinct from questions concerning the symbolic primitives of strategic information is the issue of the nature of the larger structural entities built up from these simpler units. One key issue here is that of the size of these structures. We can point to a number of treatments that emphasise highly macro-level structures such as scripts (Schank & Abelson, 1977) and MOPs (Schank, 1982), but again it is difficult to make unequivocal claims about the existence of such structures on the basis of behavioural observation. To illustrate this point, suppose that a person is observed to repeat a series of acts in pursuit of some recurrent goal. On the basis of this observation it would be tempting to conclude that there is some underlying memory structure that preserves this sequence of steps. It is equally plausible, however, that this sequence is a result of functional (rather than structural) factors, and that the elements of memory are much smaller than the complex sequence. This issue of the extent of structural elements is further complicated by the fact that even if we demonstrate that one person possesses a particular macro-structure (see J. Anderson, 1981), another person may exhibit the same sequence of acts without possessing that structure. The chief implication of this point is that claims concerning the characteristics of such macro-structures must be embedded in specific conceptions of process in order to allow empirical substantiation of those characteristics (J. Anderson, 1976; Greene, 1984b).

One final representational issue that demands attention in future models of message production concerns what might be termed the representational fidelity of procedural information. Various conceptions of procedural knowledge (e.g. productions, certain conceptions of regulative rules) involve representations of clear-cut relations among specifications for action and the eliciting conditions for that action (e.g. 'Given goal X, in context Y, then engage in behaviour Z'). In contrast to such conceptions, however, it appears that information in memory is actually represented in 'noisy' structures which contain many relations among a variety of primitive nodes corresponding to features of situations and action (McClelland & Rumelhart, 1985; McNicol & Stewart, 1980). Conceptions of clear-cut representations thus are probably too simple. The advantage of invoking 'noisy' conceptions of procedural structures is to allow more rigorous accounts of structural development, retrieval, and utilisation.

Selection

Regardless of the specific structural formalisms invoked in a model of strategic message production, there must be some mechanism that allows selection of appropriate elements from the procedural repertoire. The most straightforward conception of the selection process involves a representational scheme in which certain eliciting conditions are stored with the behavioural specifications appropriate for those conditions, as in a production (e.g. 'If situation X, then behaviour Y'). In principle, there is nothing wrong with a selection mechanism that works along these lines, but there are several complications that need to be addressed when such conceptions are extended to the realm of strategic message production. The first of these complications stems from the all-or-none matching process implicit in such conceptions of retrieval. To illustrate this point, suppose that situation X is defined by the conjunction of several features relevant to interpersonal compliance-gaining (f_1, f_2, f_3 ... f_x). It should be immediately obvious that the occurrence of some subset of these features (e.g. f_2, f_3 ... f_x) will not correspond to situation X, and as a result an all-or-none matching process will not result in retrieval of the procedural content associated with situation X. Because all social situations are almost certain to reflect novel configurations of relevant features, the social actor may be in the unfortunate position of not being able to select any appropriate procedural knowledge. The most obvious analogue of this point is the case in which the name of an existing computer file is misspelled, so that while most eliciting features match, the appropriate file is not retrieved. There are two general approaches that one might take to solve this problem. First, rather than think of situations as complex configurations of features, we might focus on individual features (e.g. f_1) or subsets of features (e.g. f_1, f_2 or f_2, f_3). This approach leads to the second complicating factor, which, in one sense, is the opposite of the first. In the first case, we saw that an all-or-none conception of situational matching and a conception of situations as the conjunction of relevant features leads to the problem of no appropriate procedural information being retrieved when the configuration of situational features is novel. If we alter the conception of eliciting conditions to include single features (or subsets of features), then the possibility of multiple procedures being activated at one time is raised. This suggests that models of message production need to move beyond conceptions of simple matching processes to incorporate two types of mechanisms. First, models probably need to incorporate matching mechanisms that function according to degrees of correspondence rather than an all-or-none match, so that those procedural elements that most closely correspond to the current situation are selected (e.g. Greene, 1984a, 1987). Second, if there need not be a perfect match for selection to occur, or if situations can be defined in terms of subsets of features, then models need to incorporate some type of contention scheduling device to handle situations in which multiple procedures are simultaneously selected (see: J. Anderson, 1982; Kerr, 1983; Norman & Shallice, 1980).

One final problem relevant to selection, that of feature equivalence, involves a more difficult set of issues. To illustrate this problem, if situation X is defined by the conjunction of features 'needing a favour from a higher-status other' then needing a favour from my boss represents only a partial symbolic match with the representation of situation X. However, my boss clearly qualifies as a higher-status other. The issue then is one of feature equivalence—does a particular symbolic feature (e.g. my boss) 'count' as an instance of a more general class (e.g. higher-status other), under what conditions will this be true, and, when it is true, how is this operation resulting in feature equivalence executed? Taken together, then, issues of partial matches, contention scheduling and feature equivalence suggest that the process of selection is considerably more complex than it appears at first blush, and that our commonsense conception of situations serving to elicit appropriate strategic information may actually embody a number of complex theoretical problems.

Utilisation

Once particular elements of procedural information have been selected, they may be used in subsequent processing. The end result of these processes is the production of the sequence of verbal and nonverbal behaviours comprising the strategic message. Utilisation, then, encompasses those processes that allow us to move from selected elements of procedural memory to the production of behaviour. As such, utilisation must include at least two functions that need to be addressed in models of strategic message production. First, there must be a concretisation mechanism that functions to translate abstract act representations and plans into specific behaviours. It is important to emphasise that while behaviour may reveal tactics, or be guided by tactics, the tactics are *not* themselves the behaviour, and they do not fully specify that behaviour. One implication of this fact is that models of tactical selection and/or formulation cannot stand as adequate accounts of strategic message production. Instead, a minimally adequate model of message production would have to specify the nature of the system linking abstract tactical representations and behaviour. Without such a component the social actor is left in a behavioural netherworld, capable of formulating elaborate plans for accomplishing his/her goals, but never able to say or do anything to bring those plans to fruition; with such a mechanism, on the other hand, he/she is capable of creative behavioural manifestations of abstract acts.[3]

The second function involved in utilisation is that of specifying the serial order of the various action specifications comprising a strategic message. Recall from the discussion above that behaviour may be characterised as an organisation of individual features or action specifications. This organisation reflects two basic dimensions, one hierarchical and one temporal. The concretisation function is responsible for the organisation of the hierarchical dimension. The serial-order function, then, is concerned with the sequencing of individual action specifications within a given hierarchical level. At the level of tactical acts, a serial order mechanism will probably take into account enablement conditions, obstacles, distractions (Schank & Abelson, 1977), and so on, relevant to planning. Similarly, at the level of utterance production, syntactical constraints will need to be considered in establishing serial order. In the interests of parsimony we should note that while the serial ordering mechanism appropriate to each level of the output representation may be subject to different constraints, that does not necessarily mean that the mechanism by which the serial order function is executed is itself different at each level (e.g. Greene, 1984a).

Summary

Our current understanding of behavioural production emphasises the conception of behaviour as an organisation of features or properties reflecting a range of levels of abstraction. This suggests that a minimally adequate model of strategic message production would need to address issues of representation of procedural information, selection of procedural elements from memory, and utilisation of information once it has been selected. The aim of this section has been to outline some of the fundamental conceptual problems attendant to representation, selection, and utilisation. A number of the issues touched on here have received considerable attention from scholars working in areas other than the production of strategic messages, and, for some problems, relatively straightforward solutions have been proposed. In these cases, theorists need to incorporate such approaches explicitly in models of strategic social action. Other problems will doubtless require considerable additional effort before tentative solutions can be advanced. For these issues, theorists concerned with strategic messages may be able to take the fore in the development of new theoretical approaches.

Conclusion

The focus of this chapter has been upon the development of theories of strategic message production, but theory building constitutes only one facet of systematic enquiry, so I wish to conclude with a comment about methods of investigation in this domain. The discussion above should make clear that models of the structures and processes underlying strategic message behaviour cannot be tested simply by observing regularities in social acts. Although examination of such behavioural regularities is essential, such data must be augmented by investigations incorporating techniques capable of revealing in greater detail the properties of the output system. In other words, progress towards more adequate models of strategic communication will require examination of temporal characteristics of tactical production, processing capacity requirements, production errors, and so on (see: Greene, in press; Taylor & Fiske, 1981). This information is no less important to understanding the production of strategic action than describing the content of the tactical acts themselves.

Notes to Chapter 1

1. Although these claims are not often made explicit in models of strategy *selection*, such models may be subject to the same points developed in this essay. Models of selection processes may be seen to reflect one of three possible stances with respect to the explanation of psychological processes underlying strategic behaviour: (1) models of selection are irrelevant to processes of strategic behaviour, (2) models of selection are relevant to processes of production in some unspecified way (i.e. such models do not specify the processes underlying the production of strategic behaviour and the

link between these processes and those of strategy selection), or (3) models of strategy selection implicitly or explicitly assume that people possess strategies and that the essential process is one of selection. To the extent that either of the first two characterisations is true, the model is necessarily incomplete as an account of strategic behaviour in interpersonal interaction; to the extent that the third case applies, the comments developed in this essay apply.

2. The point here is not simply that the cognitive representation and description may employ a different term to specify the act. The theorist's act description 'butter up' (Rule, Bisanz & Kohn, 1985) might well involve an isomorphic mapping with the actor's representation 'brown nose' despite the terminological difference. The essential question with respect to isomorphism is whether there is a one-to-one correspondence between action features in the representational and behavioural domains.

3. There is an additional reason for incorporating conceptions of lower-level processes in models of tactical communication. It may well be that in addition to top-down, constraint-setting processes, the output system includes bottom-up influences, of either a structural or functional nature, so that an understanding of abstract tactical formulation is impossible without considering the influences of the lower levels of the output system.

2 Children's and adults' comprehension of narratives about persuasion[1]

GAY L. BISANZ and BRENDAN G. RULE
Department of Psychology, University of Alberta, Edmonton, Alberta, Canada

Introduction

The issue of how prior knowledge affects performance is central to work in cognitive science. As Schank and Abelson have so elegantly described it, 'The psychologist who studies "knowledge systems" [in this tradition] wants to know how concepts are structured in the human mind, how such concepts develop, and how they are used in understanding and behavior' (1977: 1). Our work follows in this tradition. Specifically, it is related to research on natural language understanding in which the focus is on the development of models about how human observers interpret human events, especially purposeful action sequences (e.g. Abbott, Black & Smith, 1985; Black & Bower, 1980; Bower, 1978; Bower, Black & Turner, 1979; Bruce & Newman, 1978; Lichtenstein & Brewer, 1980; Omanson, 1982; Schank, 1975; Schank & Abelson, 1977; Trabasso, Secco & van den Broek, 1984; Warren, Nicholas & Trabasso, 1979). Our interest has been in how people understand narratives when knowledge about goals and methods of persuasion is a prerequisite to understanding characters' actions. Thus, although we share an interest in tactical communication with the other investigators whose work is described in this book, both our orienting framework for research and our particular focus on the problem are radically different.

Given the large number of schemata one might choose to examine in relation to story understanding, those working in other traditions might well ask how knowledge about persuasion comes to be a focus for study. Initially, our attention was directed to this schema because of its purported importance to understanding the behaviour of characters in a wide range of stories. In their influential book, *Scripts, Plans, Goals, and Understanding*, Schank & Abelson (1977) suggested that there are two modes by which individuals (or computers) can apply knowledge to understand stories: script-based and plan-based understanding. Script-based understanding is a theory about how we use knowledge to interpret routine events; plan-based understanding is a theory about how we use knowledge to understand novel situations. Within the theory of plan-based understanding, understanding actions is assumed to be a two-part process of ascertaining (a) an individual's goal and (b) the particular method being used to achieve that goal. Knowledge of persuasion, or in Schank and Abelson's terminology, the 'Persuade Package', was a central component of this theory.

Because Schank and Abelson's monograph is a 'thought piece' in the artificial intelligence tradition, our work on persuasion can be viewed as an attempt to examine their assumptions, extend their ideas and provide empirical support for this work. In this sense it is akin to two other lines of research in cognitive psychology that have explored the implications of concepts, discussed in this book, central for a theory of human understanding, namely, the very productive lines of work on scripts, originally initiated by Bower, Black & Turner (1979), and the work of Trabasso and his colleagues on causal chains (e.g. Trabasso, Secco & van den Broek, 1984; Trabasso & Sperry, 1985; Trabasso & van den Broek, 1985). Although these theories and lines of research are focused on story understanding, we should make clear that the theoretical constructs and data are relevant to the development of a general theory for understanding human actions whether they are described in stories, seen in visual media presentations, or occur in everyday events.

Although our attention was directed to this knowledge structure because of its hypothesised importance for story understanding, our interest has been sustained by the realisation that this schema is a cornerstone knowledge structure important for an integrated understanding of cognitive and social phenomena. There are several reasons for holding this view. First, and of importance to understanding the relationship between our work and that of other investigators in this book, theories that explain how individuals *understand* compliance-gaining interactions should be relevant to recent studies in social psychology and communication research focused on how individuals *generate* persuasive appeals and how those appeals influence others; related knowledge, if not the same knowledge systems, must be involved (see Bisanz & Rule, 1989). Second, as we will illustrate in this chapter, detailed study of this knowledge structure and its effect on information processing has the potential to integrate literatures in social psychology such as those on sex differences and compliance-gaining interactions.

Third, it is our intuition that a process approach to understanding the operation and acquisition of this schema can provide a means for achieving an integrated picture of the child's developing abilities in both cognitive and social domains. Specifically, we believe that this approach can clarify links between the ability to understand narratives and, for example, the development of communication skills, moral reasoning, and compliance-gaining strategies. We intend to develop this argument more fully in future work. Finally, of significance in applied settings, more precise models of knowledge, like knowledge about methods of persuasion, required for successful social interactions can provide the clinician with the basis for developing more principled and theory-driven tools to assess an individual's competence for purposes of clinical intervention (cf. Spivack & Shure, 1974).

To date our research programme has reflected the tripartite interest in the structure of knowledge, its effects on processing and/or behaviour, and concept development described by Schank and Abelson. The first three sections of this paper will describe these phases of our research, respectively. In the first section, we will briefly summarise findings from our earliest work designed to determine the nature and organisation of knowledge about persuasion in adults. We will also describe in more detail a newer study that both extends this early work and illustrates how such work can integrate literatures in social psychology. In the second section, we will describe two studies intended to demonstrate the psychological validity of the persuasion schema by demonstrating that, like scripts and story schemata, it affects measures of information processing or memory for texts. In the third section, we will describe preliminary work intended to trace the development of this knowledge structure in children and, ultimately, explore how it affects their ability to understand and remember compliance-gaining interactions. In the fourth and final section, we will comment on future directions for research and our view of the potential significance of this work.

Anatomy of a Persuasion Schema: A Search for Cognitive Invariants

In developing their theory of plan-based understanding, Schank & Abelson (1977) formulated a number of hypotheses about the nature and organisation of the goals and methods that constitute knowledge about persuasion. First, they suggested that goals associated with the use of a persuasion schema constitute a small finite set. Second, they assumed that these goals are linked to use of a standard set of methods. Third, if these methods fail, they assumed that additional methods (referred to as auxiliary methods) may be tried. Finally, Schank and Abelson hypothesised that use of the methods is ordered so that once an initial method is selected and fails, the individual will select a strategy further down in the sequence. In proceeding through the sequence, however, the persuader might skip some strategies.

In our early work (see Rule, Bisanz & Kohn, 1985), we used open-ended questions and rating of schematic elements to examine Schank and Abelson's hypotheses about the invariant properties of this schema. Although these studies confirmed the basic structure of the cognitive representation proposed by Schank and Abelson, certain details were discrepant with their ideas. Specifically, based on the data, we concluded that, although goals associated with the persuasion schema constitute a small infinite set, that set is larger than suggested by Schank and Abelson and is better conceptualised as finite with respect to various role relationships. In addition, goals do seem to be linked to a standard set of methods that are ordered. However, again the set is larger than Schank and Abelson proposed and its order differs from the one they suggested. Instead, as we had hypothesised, the set of strategies can be grouped into five major types. These types and the order of use we predicted are: (a) asking; (b) self-oriented methods; (c) dyad-oriented methods; (d) appeals to social principles, and (e) negative tactics (see Table 2.1). Significantly, this order is identical for both men and women ranking the strategies in the order that 'people in general' would use each method. We had hypothesised that this order might be obtained both because it reflects the order in which these strategies might be learned developmentally and because it saves the potentially most effective, yet socially more desirable, appeals until later. Only when these tactics fail would negative strategies be employed. According to Rule & Bisanz (1987), collectively these studies support the view that there is a culturally shared schema that will be employed by people to understand the events that occur in compliance-gaining interactions.

TABLE 2.1 *Methods of persuasion as labelled and described for participants*

Name	Description
Ask	Simply ask the friend to try to get co-operation. No particular reason is given.
Self-Oriented	
Present Information (Invoke personal expertise)	The individual presents facts or evidence to try to get co-operation.
Mention Personal Benefits (Inform personal reason)	In asking, the individual mentions how he or she personally would benefit to try to get co-operation; or the individual mentions how the friend personally would benefit from co-operating.
Dyad-Oriented	
Mention Relationship (Invoke role relationship)[a]	In asking, the individual mentions an existing relationship to try to get co-operation. For example: 'A good friend would do this.'
Bargain (favour)	The individual offers to do a favour in exchange for co-operation.
Social Principles	
Mention Similar Behaviour of Others (Invoke norm)	In asking, the individual tells the friend about others who would do the same thing to try to get co-operation.
Mention Benefit to Others (Invoke altruism)	In asking, the individual mentions how the friend's co-operation will benefit others.

Make Moral Appeal (Invoke moral principle)	In asking, the individual makes an appeal to a moral value (e.g. it's the right thing to do) to try to get co-operation.
Negative Tactics	
Butter-up	The individual attempts to make the friend feel wonderful or important to try to get co-operation.
Bargain (object)	The individual offers a highly desired physical object (could be money) in exchange for co-operation.
Emotional Appeal	The individual cries, begs, throws a tantrum, sulks or uses some other emotional display to try to get co-operation.
Criticise	The individual attacks the friend on a personal level, trying to make him or her feel personally inadequate for not co-operating.
Deceive	The individual misleads the friend to try to get co-operation.
Threaten	The individual informs the friend of negative things that will result from not co-operating.
Force	The individual physically assaults the friend or uses some other means of force to try to get co-operation.

[a] The names in parentheses after the labels provided for participants are the more technical labels used in the taxonomy developed by Rule, Bisanz & Kohn, 1985.

Asking men and women to rank-order methods as they would be used by 'people in general', however, provides only tentative evidence for a culturally general schema. As mentioned previously, a critical step beyond characterising the structural properties of this schema is to demonstrate that it functions as other schemata do in guiding information processing as reflected in, for example, encoding time, recognition or recall (cf. Bower, Black & Turner, 1979; Mandler & Johnson, 1977; Mandler & Goodman, 1982). However, gender is an inescapable attribute of individuals and fictional characters. Thus determining whether there are culturally general or sex-specific expectations associated with the order of use of strategies is crucial to the design of stimulus materials for studies intended to assess the psychological validity of this knowledge structure. In a recent study (Bisanz & Rule, 1989), we addressed this issue more directly by asking men and women to think of 'men in general' and 'women in general' as they put methods in the order that they would be used for two different targets (friend, father) over nine different goal situations.

Our previous work led us to hypothesise that the rank order of the 15 strategies would be invariant for men and women. From our theoretical perspective, support for this hypothesis would provide evidence that knowledge utilised by men and women to understand persuasive attempts can be represented in memory as a single ordered list of strategies. Yet, like Schank and Abelson, we acknowledge that a complete model of how knowledge of persuasion affects information processing must include other types of knowledge.

Specifically, knowledge in the form of rules or heuristics is needed to explain our understanding of how individuals select an initial strategy and how they proceed down that list. Within our framework, determining that the order of strategy use is a cognitive invariant implies that these rules encompass the knowledge utilised to understand individual differences and situational effects. Thus support for this hypothesis is preliminary evidence that these heuristics are the source of differences in expectations about behaviour related to sex in this domain.

In an effort to examine one further cognitive invariant, namely, the role of social approval in explaining the order of strategy use, respondents in this study were also asked to use a rating scale to indicate 'how much you would approve of each method if you saw it being used by a man [woman] in a situation like the one described'. Specifically, we wanted to determine whether, as hypothesised by Rule & Bisanz (1987), strategies that invoke social principles were more approved than some of the self-oriented and dyad-oriented methods used earlier in the sequence, and all of the negative strategies applied later.

The results from the ranking data were clear-cut. A comparison was made by calculating a Kendall's W (rank coefficient of concordance for multiple samples) for the eight sets of ranks created by summing across goals and examining the two types of participants (men, women), two types of persuaders (male, female) and two types of targets (friend, father). It was highly significant: W (8,14) = 95, $p < 0.001$.

Also highly significant were the coefficients making pairwise comparisons of men's and women's rankings given each target (e.g. friend) and type of persuader (e.g. man): $Ws(2,14) > 0.95$, $ps < 0.02$. Thus, it can be said that irrespective of whether men or women are doing the ranking, the basis for the rankings is the same. In our view that common basis is the culturally shared schema that men and women have about the order in which persuasive strategies are applied.

When W is significant, Kendall (see Siegel, 1956) suggested that the best estimate of the 'true' ranking is provided by the order of the summed ranks. The order of the summed ranks obtained in this study was so similar to those obtained by Rule, Bisanz & Kohn (1985) that we present the summed ranks pooled across the two studies in Table 2.2. We take this pooled ranking to be the best estimate of the 'true' order. Comparing the order of methods listed in Tables 2.1 and 2.2, it should be clear that, with the exception of 'butter-up', the strategies fall into the categories and order of use we predicted. Listing 'butter-up' under self-oriented strategies in Table 2.2 is to acknowledge the empirical data. Using hindsight, butter-up does not seem to involve reciprocity (the defining feature of dyad-oriented strategies) but rather seems to be a tactic designed to appeal to the ego of the persuadee much like the strategy 'personal benefit'.

The approval data are relevant to the second issue addressed in this study, namely, what factors might account for the particular order embodied in the list of strategies. Recall that Rule & Bisanz (1987) hypothesised that the order was a joint function of two factors: the order of acquisition in development and degree of social approval. Specifically, it was hypothesised that strategies invoking social principles (hypothesised to be acquired later developmentally) would be more approved than some of the self-oriented and dyad-oriented methods used earlier in the sequence and all of the negative strategies applied later. As indices of the operation of social norms, the approval ratings obtained in this study provide an opportunity to assess the importance of the latter factor.

TABLE 2.2 *Summed ranks, approval ratings and rank orders of methods*

Methods	Pooled over two studies		Approval by individual method		Approval pooled over category	
	Sum of Mean Ranks	Rank	Mean Rating	Rank	Mean rating	Rank
Ask	12.0	1.0	8.3	1.0	8.3	1.0
Self-Oriented						
Personal expertise	28.0	2.0	8.1	2.0	6.7	2.0
Personal benefit	37.5	3.0	7.1	3.0		
Butter-up	47.5	4.0	4.8	8.5		
Dyad-Oriented						
Role-relationship	69.5	5.0	4.7	10.0	5.3	4.0
Bargain (favour)	75.0	6.0	5.9	5.0		
Social Principles						
Moral principle	90.0	7.0	5.6	6.0	5.8	3.0
Norm	91.0	8.0	5.3	7.0		
Altruism	93.0	9.0	6.5	4.0		
Negative Tactics						
Bargain (object)	117.5	10.0	4.8	8.5	2.8	5.0
Emotional appeal	131.5	11.0	3.3	11.0		
Personal criticism	145.5	12.0	2.9	12.0		
Deceive	153.0	13.0	2.3	13.0		
Threaten	165.5	14.0	2.0	14.0		
Force	180.0	15.0	1.4	15.0		

The mean approval ratings for each method pooled over goals, sex of participant, sex of the persuader, and target along with its rank are shown in Table 2.2. Deviations of these ranks from numerical order reflect inabilities of social approval as a factor to account for order of use. The correlation between rank order of use and approval was high ($r = -0.95$, $p < 0.001$), providing evidence that social approval as a factor does play a role in order of use.

The ratings shown in Table 2.2 pooled over category provide some evidence that strategies invoking social principles are more approved than some self-oriented and dyad-oriented strategies (primarily due to low social approval for 'butter up' and 'invoking a role relationship') and such strategies are clearly more approved than are negative tactics.

Although the analyses on the approval data just described were summed over gender, identical analyses conducted separately on the data derived from men's and women's ratings produced similar results. Thus in terms of accounting for the order of strategy use, degree of social approval is another cognitive invariant with respect to the sex of the individual. We submit that this study illustrates how detailed examination of this knowledge structure and its effect on processing has the potential to help integrate such literatures in social psychology as those on compliance-gaining strategies and sexual stereotypes.

Psychological Validity: Evidence from Memory for Texts on Persuasion

The goals of our research programme are similar to those of other work in cognitive psychology in which well-articulated theories of specific schemata have been developed and their effects on information processing and memory examined (e.g. Bower, Black & Turner, 1979; Graesser, 1981; Mandler & Goodman, 1982). As we have indicated, in this research, methodologies like those employed in our research — open-ended questions and rating of schematic elements — are commonly used in determining the nature and organisation of a schema. However, such work must be followed by research designed to assess the psychological validity of the knowledge structure (cf. Mandler & Goodman, 1982; Wiseman & Schenck-Hamlin, 1981).

Ordering of strategies is an important property of the persuasion schema as we have characterised it. It is also an important characteristic of some of the other schemata that have been studied, specifically, the story schema and scripts with strongly ordered actions (e.g. the Restaurant script). The predominant means of assessing the psychological validity of these knowledge structures has been to give individuals versions of texts in which the constituents of the schema appear in either canonical or atypical order, and to look for effects on memory (either in the amount remembered or memory for serial order), reorganisations of text material, or reading time (e.g. Bower, Black & Turner, 1979; Mandler, 1978; Mandler & Goodman, 1982; Stein & Nezworski, 1978). Evidence for pausing at the boundaries of constituents while reading well-formed sequences has also been used as a dependent measure (cf. Haberlandt, Berian & Sandson, 1980; Mandler & Goodman, 1982).

As evidence for the psychological validity of the story schema, research focused on the effects on free recall of stories presenting atypical sequences (e.g. Mandler, 1978; Mandler & DeForest, 1979; Stein & Nezworski, 1978) has generally shown that the amount of information recalled is greater for stories presented in canonical than in atypical order. In fact, the recall of atypical stories shows a tendency for the order of recall protocols to be more highly related to the canonical rather than the presented sequence and for more distortions and repetitions to occur in the recall of 'ill-formed' stories. Indeed, even when presented with an atypical story initially, individuals have no difficulty reproducing the canonical sequence when instructed to do so.

In the only study to use a reconstruction measure to assess memory for order in adults, Stein & Nezworski (1978) found that individuals hearing well-formed stories were significantly better than those receiving slightly disordered stories in reconstructing the order of presentation. Individuals in both of these conditions performed significantly better than those who heard randomly ordered stories or unrelated sentences. Performance in the latter conditions did not differ. With this measure, however, there was no tendency for individuals to reconstruct ill-formed stories to conform to canonical order. Stein & Nezworski (1978) attributed this finding to individuals' recognising that the stories were disorganised, and using this knowledge to reconstruct distorted sequences.

Research using reading time as an index of psychological validity (e.g. Haberlandt, 1980; Mandler & Goodman, 1982) has shown that movement of story constituents increases reading time for those constituents. This effect occurs even when the unit is displaced only one position, when the movement is marked in the surface structure of the text, and when it is a permissible movement as captured by the rules of story grammar theory (Mandler & Goodman, 1982).

Research on the psychological validity of scripts shows similar effects. For example, using a reconstruction measure, Bower, Black & Turner (1979) demonstrated that memory for serial position was better for texts describing ordered scripts as compared to texts describing unordered scripts. In turn, memory for serial order of the latter was better than for texts describing ordered scripts in which some of the actions were misordered. These investigators also found evidence that misordered actions 'drifted back' towards their canonical positions during reconstruction. Like Stein & Nezworski (1978), however, they found that if respondents were presented with actions from ordered scripts in random order, 'backward drift' disappeared. Under these conditions, participants remembered that the script actions were 'all mixed up' and preserved this property in their reconstructions.

In two studies, we undertook to demonstrate the psychological validity of the persuasion schema by presenting individuals with texts in which characters were described as using methods of persuasion in either standard or atypical order, and examining the effect on various dependent measures. In the first study (Bisanz & Rule, 1987), participants were tested in small groups and told that we were interested in people's reactions to the same material presented orally (as in radio or a lecture) or visually (as in reading) after a time delay. They were told that they were in the visual condition. They were then shown four short stories projected on a screen. In each story, a protagonist attempted unsuccessfully to get another person to comply. Four different goals identified by Rule, Bisanz & Kohn (1985) were employed, including 'ownership', 'activity', 'agency' and 'permission'.

To minimise story effects irrelevant to our purposes, we controlled a number of variables across stories. Characters were always women described as being friends. Stories were constructed so as to have uniform structure as determined in relation to Mandler & Johnson's (1977) story grammar theory. In the context of that theory, each story could be characterised as having 11 components: two Setting statements, a statement representing the Beginning Event category, a statement representing the Goal category, a dialogue that began with two statements that can be characterised as a 'preliminary attempt' and a 'neutral' outcome, statements representing five Attempt–Outcome pairs in which the outcome was always negative, and an Ending statement. The five attempts were instantiations of five different persuasion strategies: ask, give personal reason, bargain for a favour, give altruistic reasons and threaten. Each strategy was representative of one of the five major strategy types we had identified previously. Strategies were presented in one of three orders: Standard or Canonical, Mildly Disordered (r of -0.50 with Canonical), or Greatly Disordered (r of -0.70 with Canonical). In constructing the stories, care was taken to equate the importance of the goal to the persuader, the cost of the goal to the target, the degree of resistance of the target in terms of the nature of their responses to each attempt, and the extremity of the persuader's final reaction. An example of one of these stories is shown in the Appendix to this chapter.

Given the structure of these stories, we assume that the persons who read them used one of two modes of processing associated with understanding stories. These modes are processing in terms of their general knowledge about human social interactions (e.g. scripts, plans) or processing in terms of their knowledge of story structure (see Bisanz, 1982). Whichever general strategy was utilised, we assume that specific knowledge, in the form of the persuasion schema, was cued by aspects of the text and utilised to understand the series of five attempt–outcome pairs. Related to this, the 'preliminary attempt' was included in the stories on the grounds that it made the dialogue seem more natural. It seemed to us as we created these stories that such an opening exchange may be optional; however, its function in a conversation may be to allow the persuader to 'test the waters' of target receptivity before 'diving in' or it may be a conventional signal to the target that some demand is about to be made so that the persuader will not appear to have 'sprung' the demand on the target. Note, however, that to the reader trying to comprehend these stories these sentences almost certainly had the potential to serve as a text cue that could activate the persuasion schema.

After two days, participants were given the first part of each story as a cue and four decks of cards, randomly ordered, containing the five attempt–outcome pairs. Half were instructed to put them in the order of presentation and the other half were told to put them in the order that people would normally use them.

To determine the degree of relationship between *presented order* and *reconstructed order* for participants receiving the two types of instructions and three types of stories, we calculated a Spearman's rank order correlation between these orders for each participant and converted these correlations to z-scores. Of greatest importance are the mean correlations between presented order and reconstructed order for the participants asked to put the events in the order of presentation. The mean z-scores for the Canonical, Mildly Disordered and Greatly Disordered conditions for participants receiving these instructions were 1.35, 0.50 and 0.65, respectively. The difference between the canonical and atypical story conditions was significant. This finding provides evidence that memory for presented order was greater for stories in which methods of persuasion were described in canonical order than it was for the other two types of stories. It constitutes evidence for the psychological validity of the persuasion schema as a mental structure that affects memory for the order of events.

To determine the degree of relationship between *canonical order* and *reconstructed order*, we also calculated Spearman's rank order correlations between these orders for each participant. Like the data from work on the story schema and ordered scripts, the mean z-scores for the Mildly and Greatly Disordered conditions in which participants were instructed to put events in the order of presentation showed no evidence for 'drift backward' (0.17 and -0.13, respectively). When participants were asked to put the attempts to persuade in normal order, there was a high degree of relationship between their view of 'normal order' and canonical order. Unlike the data from work on the story schema, however, there was a difference in the degree to which participants' 'normal order' corresponded with canonical order, depending on the type of story they saw 48 hours earlier. Recall that in story schema research under similar conditions, regardless of the type of story participants heard, the order of their recall was canonical. The mean z-scores for the correlations between canonical order and reconstructed order for participants given instructions to put events in normal order were 1.43, 0.86 and 0.91 for the Canonical, Mildly Disordered and Greatly Disordered conditions, respectively. Statistically, there was a greater correspondence with canonical order when participants read canonical stories, rather than either type of atypically ordered story, 48 hours earlier. In fact, the degree of relationship in the former condition was similar to that of participants who had seen canonical stories and were instructed to reconstruct the order of presentation (1.43 and 1.35, respectively). Taken together, these results provide strong support for the schematic representation of persuasion strategies in memory.

In an effort to replicate and extend these findings, we conducted a second study in collaboration with John Pullyblank. In this study, we added an additional story to the original set focused on the goal of 'gaining assistance' and developed a parallel set of stories in which the five attempts were again representative of the five major categories, but differed in the specific strategies utilised by the characters. In this second set, the strategies were ask, mention personal expertise, invoke role relationship, invoke norm, and personal criticism. We also collected two additional measures per participant, reading time and character attributions. Participants were given one of the three types of stories (Canonical, Mildly Disordered, Greatly Disordered) with either the original (first set) or second set of methods. As before, half of the participants were instructed to put the methods in the order of presentation and the other half to put them in the order that people would normally use them.

Participants were tested individually with equal numbers of males and females assigned to each condition. Participants were told that we were interested in the effects of different types of media on people's evaluations of materials. They were told that they would see the material on a computer screen and would be asked to return and evaluate it in two days' time. Stories were presented one component at a time on a monitor run by a microprocessor. As subjects pressed the space-bar on the microprocessor to read the title and each component of a story, their reading time for each component was stored. Upon return, participants were given the first part of each story as a cue and were asked to order the five attempt–outcome pairs in accord with their condition. They then answered a series of 26 questions designed to determine their impressions of each story in general and the behaviour of the persuader and target in particular.

We had made some minor modifications to our four original stories in the interest of reducing minor variations in the content and grammar of story sentences over the total pool of ten stories; also, the method of presentation was quite different from the first study. Despite these changes, we expected to replicate the findings obtained in our first study for memory of order of events for both sets of stories. Based on previous work on the story schema, we also expected that, relative to canonical stories, atypical stories would slow reading times. Finally, we hypothesised that such stories would alter character attributions: characters who utilised strategies in atypical orders, thus violating social expectancies, would be perceived as 'odd' or different. We will focus here on the memory data.

All analyses on memory were originally conducted with sex as a factor. There was no main effect for sex nor were there any significant interactions, so all the analyses we will discuss are pooled over sex. As before, we examined correlations to determine the degree of relationship between the *presented order* and the *reconstructed order* for participants receiving the two different sets of methods under the two types of instruction for each type of story. Analyses on the z-scores showed that there was a significant effect of condition ($p < 0.001$) as well as a significant interaction between condition and the set of methods described in the stories ($p < 0.01$).

Of greatest importance are the mean correlations between presented order and reconstructed order for participants instructed to put the events in the order of presentation. Again, for both sets of methods, the data provide evidence that memory for presented order was greater for stories in which methods of persuasion were described in canonical order than it was for the other two types of stories. The pattern of means obtained for the second set of methods nicely replicates the pattern of means obtained in the first study. The interaction between condition and the set of methods described in the stories can be explained in terms of deviations from this pattern by participants reading the first set of stories. *Post hoc* comparisons revealed that the major differences between this pattern and the pattern obtained for the first set of methods in this new experiment were in (a) the very high degree of relationship obtained between presented and reconstructed order for participants reading the first set in canonical order (a z-score of 1.80 as compared to 1.14 for the second set), and (b) the relatively low correlations between presented and reconstructed order for participants receiving both types of instructions and reading stories containing the first set of methods in the Mildly Disordered Condition (z-scores of 0.02 and -0.01, respectively). These differences, however, are minor. As in the first study, the data again provide evidence for the psychological validity of the persuasion schema as a mental structure that affects memory of the order of events.

Again, to determine the degree of relationship between *canonical* and *reconstructed order*, we examined the correlations between these orders for each participant. These same correlations for participants instructed to put events in 'normal order' did not provide evidence that the degree to which participants' 'normal order' corresponded with canonical order depended upon the type of story that they saw 48 hours earlier. Rather, the relationship between canonical and normal order was high and similar whether participants read Canonical, Mildly Disordered or Greatly Disordered stories (1.38, 0.97, and 1.28 for the first set of methods and 1.12, 0.79 and 1.09 for the second set, respectively). In sum, while the new set of methods and the procedure of reading stories on a sentence-by-sentence basis resulted in some variation in the magnitude and nature of the effects obtained, the data from both studies provide strong support for the schematic representation of persuasion strategies in memory.

Characterising Cognitive Growth

We plan to extend our work on the psychological validity of the persuasion schema by continuing to map its effects on other measures of adults' information processing and memory as well as exploring the boundary conditions of those effects. In some sense, however, this work has been a prelude to our primary interest: characterising the development of this knowledge structure in children. Because there had been no previous work on whether schemata for complex social events operate in a manner similar to those for routine events, this first stage was crucial. With the completion of the series of studies we conducted on how the schema is organised and affects memory in adults, however, we have sufficient data to begin to address our interest in development.

There are two lines of related research in the developmental literature. The first is research focused on characterising the development of schematic structures, like the story schema and scripts, and their effects on children's information processing and memory. There are several assumptions common to this work. Like the work with adults, it is assumed that schemata facilitate the encoding, storage and retrieval of events. For example, with respect to narrative understanding, because of schematic knowledge, a reader or listener generates expectations about the kind of information that should occur in a text. If incoming information conflicts with expectations, the reader or listener uses prior knowledge to construct a representation of the mismatched information. Thus misordered sequences of events are likely to be remembered more in accord with the reader's schematic expectations. If there are gaps in important parts of the story, schematic knowledge will be used to draw inferences.

Although some research has demonstrated that children's memory is affected by the order, structure and content of stories (for reviews see Mandler, 1983; Trabasso, Stein & Johnson, 1981), there remain several gaps in the literature. First, to date, there has been no attention given to identifying schemata relevant to understanding complex social events like knowledge of persuasion. Second, once identified, the development of such schemata must be charted much as Nelson (1978) has studied the development of scripts for routine events like eating at McDonald's.

Third, the memorial consequences of these knowledge structures need to be documented, and we need to ascertain whether those consequences are similar for children and adults. For example, Mandler (1983) has argued that, if anything, children may be *more* dependent than adults on the story schema and scripts to understand and remember events. Fourth, most of the research has relied on recall measures of memory, which provide a limited view of the role of knowledge-related expectations in the comprehension process. Trabasso, Stein & Johnson (1981) argued for the use of generation methods, whereas we think that these must be supplemented by other measures such as reconstruction or recognition. Finally, this body of work has focused entirely on the role of knowledge in story comprehension. While that is our current focus as well, we are interested in extending our work to encompass real events as well as events portrayed in visual media presentations.

The second line of related research is a small set of studies focused on the development of persuasion strategies (e.g. Clark & Delia, 1976). Each of these studies has a slightly different agenda and the set as a whole encompasses a broad spectrum of theoretical perspectives. Perhaps because of this diversity, the only conclusion one can draw from reading these studies is that the number of persuasive strategies children use, or report they use, increases with age. The primary advantage our approach offers over these studies is that it is research in which an inductive strategy is applied to identify the number and types of strategies available to children of different ages, yet this strategy is applied within the context of a theoretical framework that has testable psychological implications (see Rule & Bisanz, 1987). We hope that such an approach can lead to a consensus about both the cognitive invariants and developmental differences important to understanding the development of persuasive skill.

In an attempt to begin to characterise the development of the persuasion schema in children and to examine its effects on processing, we have completed our first developmental study. The children in this study were in school grades 3, 5 and 9. A pilot study had helped us to identify four goals of the set discussed by Rule, Bisanz & Kohn (1985) that were familiar to children in each of these grades; these goals were 'to get someone to do something for you' (agency), 'to get someone to go somewhere with you' (activity), 'to get someone to give you something' (object), and 'to get someone to help you with something' (assistance). In the first phase of this study, children were asked to tell how someone would get a friend to accomplish each of these goals. In the second phase, they were each given four stories and asked to put the methods in the order that they thought they would be used by the character in the story. For half of the participants the attempts to persuade were instantiations of the strategies of ask, personal reason, bargain for a favour, give altruistic reasons, and threaten. For the other participants, the attempts were instantiations of the strategies ask, mention personal expertise, invoke role relationship, invoke norm, and personal criticism. As before, we refer to these as the first and second set of methods, respectively. This procedure gave us the opportunity to assess both what children of different ages would generate as well as a preliminary way to assess when children's expectations can be characterised as an ordered list of strategies.

Consistent with other studies, the data obtained in the first phase of this study provided evidence that the number of methods generated increased from 10, to 11, to 13 for the three grades, respectively. The major types of methods generated are shown in Table 2.3. We did not collect data from adults in this study; however, for purposes of comparison the data collected by Rule, Bisanz & Kohn (1985) for a broader sample of goals and targets are shown in the right-most column of the table. Examination of the totals for the five major types of strategies reveals that 'asking' actually decreased in frequency over the age range studied. The frequency of 'self-oriented' and 'dyad-oriented' methods generated increased until Grade 9, when the frequency either levelled off or declined. Only the frequency of generating methods in the category of 'appeals to social principles' increased over the entire age range studied. There is no trend with respect to 'negative tactics'.

Recall that nine methods (ask, plus one method representing each of the major strategy types) were used to examine the development of the ordering principle in the second phase of the study. Interestingly,

TABLE 2.3 *Percentage of total responses generated by children*

Major types of methods	Groups			
	Grade 3	Grade 5	Grade 9	Adults[a]
Ask	41.5	26.3	31.4	18.5
Self-Oriented	12.3	14.9	23.8	25.9
Dyad-Oriented	5.8	7.8	12.4	8.7
Social Principles	0.0	0.7	1.9	6.9
Negative Tactics	26.9	41.8	23.4	40.2

[a] Adult data are obtained from Rule, Bisanz & Kohn, 1985.

three of those comprising the second set of methods (mention personal expertise, invoke role relationship, invoke norm) were generated infrequently or not at all by the children. The situation was similar for 'give altruistic reasons' in the first set. This raises the question of whether children who do not generate these strategies were able to order them in the second phase of the study.

The data from the second phase are presented in Table 2.4. Shown in this table is the degree of relationship between the order which children constructed and canonical order for the two sets of methods. An analysis of variance conducted separately for stories incorporating the two sets of methods showed a significant effect of grade for the second set ($p < 0.01$) and a marginally significant effect for the first set ($p < 0.10$). There was no story effect or significant interaction in either analysis. It should be noted, however, that the magnitude of the correlations in Grades 5 and 9 (z-scores of 1.17 to 1.73) was similar to that obtained for adults seeing Greatly Disordered stories and instructed to put the methods in 'normal order' (1.28 and 1.09 for the two story sets, respectively). We take these findings to be preliminary evidence that children's expectations can be characterised as an ordered list of strategies at least in late elementary school. We should be able to obtain converging evidence for this finding by examining memory for texts on persuasion with children as we have done for adults.

Interestingly, the greatest degree of relationship between children's reconstructed order and canonical order occurred with the set of stories in which three of the five methods described were not, or infrequently, generated by the children. Use of the reconstruction measure followed directly from our attempt to examine Schank and Abelson's assumptions developmentally. Many previous studies have used generation as the primary measure of children's knowledge about methods of persuasion.

TABLE 2.4 *Mean Z-scores of correlations between children's order and canonical order*

Grade	First set	Second set
3	0.77[a] (.65)	0.79[b] (.66)
5	1.17[a] (.82)	1.51[a] (.91)
9	1.34[a] (.87)	1.73[a] (.94)

Note: Shown in parentheses are the values of Spearman's rank order correlations. Within each column cells sharing common superscripts do not differ.

Clearly, this latter measure does not reflect adequately all that children know about these methods. We think this finding is a good example of the potential our approach has to provide new insights into the development of children's knowledge about methods of persuasion.

Implications and Future Directions

In this chapter we have described a programme of research addressed to the tripartite concerns of documenting how knowledge of persuasion is organised in the mind, how it develops, and how it is utilised in understanding and affects behaviour. Given our data, one can envision several additional phases of research. As mentioned previously, we need to examine how the development of this schema affects narrative comprehension in children of different ages. We must address the question of how the medium of encoding, whether real-life events, film, or stories, affects schema utilisation. We must assess how the comprehension of compliance-gaining interactions relates to the individual's ability to produce effective sequences of persuasive appeals. This latter issue is what links our work to a number of other programmes of research described in this book. Indeed, we have begun preliminary work on this problem (Bisanz & Rule, 1989). Finally, there is the issue of how one might model formally the phenomena identified in these studies, perhaps using computer simulation as a vehicle.

In our view, the lasting contribution of the programme of research we have described will probably not be that it provides the final word on the nature and organisation of the persuasion schema in adults, its development in children, and how it affects performance. Indeed, we anticipate that we will continue to refine our ideas as we, and perhaps others, study these phenomena. Rather, one hope we have is that, through our work, we can convince others of the centrality of this particular knowledge structure to an integrated perspective on human cognition. Our second hope is that our work will serve to illustrate one fruitful approach to the study of this knowledge structure.

Note to Chapter 2

1. Preparation of this chapter and the authors' research was facilitated by grants from the Natural Sciences and Engineering Research Council of Canada. Early drafts of this chapter were written while the first author was on study leave at the Department of Psychological Sciences, Purdue University. The

first author is grateful to members of that department for resources and services made available during that interval.

Appendix: Sample Story (Canonical or Standard Order)

Setting (2)

Sue and Ann were close friends. They lived in the same apartment.

Beginning Event (1)

One evening Ann felt a need to relax and unwind before a big exam.

Goal (1)

She decided to ask Sue to go with her to see a play their friend Doug was directing.

Preliminary Attempt and Outcome (1)

She found Sue and asked: 'Do you have any plans for tonight?'
Sue looked up and said: 'I thought I might study'

Attempt–Outcome Sequences (5)

Ask
Ann: 'Would you like to come to a play with me ?'
Sue: 'Not really.'

Personal Reason
Ann: 'Please come to a play with me. I have an important exam tomorrow and I need to unwind.'
Sue: 'No thanks.'

Bargain Favour
Ann: 'I'll do you a favour some time if you come to a play with me.'
Sue: 'Not this evening.'

Invoke Altruism
Ann: 'Please come to a play. Doug is directing and he'll be so disappointed if we don't come.'
Sue: 'Maybe next time.'

Threaten
Ann: 'Come to a play with me or I'll simply move out of this apartment.'
Sue: 'So move.'

Ending (1)

Ann fretted about what else to do.

3 The nature and substance of goals in tactical communication

JAMES PRICE DILLARD

Department of Communication Arts, University of Wisconsin, Madison, USA

One account that can be given of human behaviour is found in the goal–planning–action (GPA) sequence (Frese & Sabini, 1985; Miller, Galanter & Pribram, 1960). Goals are desired future states which an individual is committed to achieving or maintaining (see e.g. Hobbs & Evans, 1980; Klinger, 1985). Goals cause planning to occur, which in turn guides action. When necessary, goals are modified by feedback, and corresponding adjustments in planning and action are the result (J. Anderson, 1985; Bandura, 1986).

The generality of the GPA sequence is made evident by the diversity of its application. The formulation has been utilised as explanation by scholars in areas as diverse as discourse analysis (Levy, 1979), cognitive science (Schank & Abelson, 1977), organisational behaviour (Locke *et al.*, 1981), social cognition (Higgins, McCann & Fondacaro, 1982), story comprehension (Wilensky, 1978), social psychology (Carver & Scheier, 1983), and communication (Tracy, 1984). It would seem that the GPA sequence might be fruitfully applied to the study of tactical communication.

However, the risk run by such generality is that the 'explanatory account' may be so adaptable as to be content-free. Retrospectively, the GPA sequence can account for virtually any behaviour. For example, when studying human action within the GPA framework, it is tempting to infer people's goals on the basis of their behaviour, to conclude on the basis of what they said, what was intended. From a logical standpoint, this commits the *post hoc fallacy*. One cannot conclude that it is raining simply because people are carrying umbrellas. If the GPA sequence is to have any predictive power, and thus true explanatory power, then it is necessary to specify *a priori* the nature and substance of the components in the sequence. It is necessary to put some theoretical meat upon the skeletal, conceptual framework of GPA. To meet this requirement completely would mean the development of a full-fledged theory — one which drew its general structure from GPA but whose content was specific to the substantive area under study. My aim in this chapter is less ambitious.

To begin with, I emphasise the goals portion of the GPA sequence. Considerably less attention is allocated to the planning and action components. In the initial sections of the chapter, I outline the assumptions inherent in any goal-driven account of human behaviour, and further specify the nature of goals by making three additional claims. This 'top-down' theoretical analysis is followed in the second half of the chapter by a description of two empirical studies. Those investigations contribute to our understanding of goals in tactical communication in a phenomenologically grounded, or 'bottom-up' fashion. The purpose of this two-pronged attack is to move us closer to the development of a middle-range, goal-driven theory of tactical communication.

Conceptual Explication: The Nature of Goals

Assumptions

It is usually presumed that people act for a variety of reasons. From this premise, we may infer that (Assumption 1) individuals possess multiple goals. For example, Clark & Delia (1979) contend that people are motivated to meet instrumental, relational and identity goals. Further, it will be taken as axiomatic that (Assumption 2) goals can be arranged on at least three dimensions: in terms of hierarchy, importance and temporality (cf. Greene, this volume; Smith, Cody, Lovette and Canary, this volume).

The hierarchical claim asserts that higher-level goals subsume other, lower-level, goals. That is to say, some goals exist in the service of other goals. Although logically the hierarchy could have any number of levels (cf. Carver & Scheier, 1983; Parks, 1985), for our purposes a simple three-tiered system composed of motives, goals and subgoals is sufficient. Motives exist at the top of the hierarchy. They are conceived here in much the same way that motivation theorists discussed needs (see e.g.

Alderfer, 1969; Murray, 1938; Maslow, 1943). Thus, motives are broad and deep-seated determinants of behaviour. Goals themselves occupy the next tier in the hierarchy, with subgoals at the base. Subgoals, which exist at the lowest level, are governed by goals.

The importance dimension offers another means of arraying goals. From this perspective some goals are viewed as more attractive than others. Presumably, it is the most important goal at any given time which guides behaviour (Kuhl, 1985). Goals also vary in importance or attractiveness *over time*. Goals which are reached often diminish in importance and are replaced by other desires. At other times, goals are seen as unobtainable and, consequently, may be forsaken entirely or may enter into 'top-spin' (Heckhausen & Kuhl, 1985). Top-spin is a state in which the individual recognises that the goal is not attainable at present, but he or she remains vigilant to the possibility that changes in the situation will make it attainable. In this way the goal affects perception, but not action.

Finally (Assumption 3), although only one goal is dominant at any one time, people usually try to achieve more than one goal simultaneously. In accordance with this assumption, Tracy & Moran (1983) provide qualitative evidence that interactants are capable of dealing with attentiveness and topic change goals concurrently. In more recent work, O'Keefe and her associates (O'Keefe & McCornack, 1987; O'Keefe & Shepard, 1987) argue that the ability to act upon multiple goals simultaneously is largely a matter of individual/developmental differences.

Additional claims

With the preceding theoretical backdrop established, I turn next to a discussion of the special features of goals. These features provide goals with their unique conceptual status, and set them off from related ideas such as motives and subgoals.

First, goals are *culturally viable explanations for behaviour*. As social actors, we look to goals to provide a plausible understanding of why people choose certain courses of action and persist in those directions. When we provide ourselves or others with a verbal account of our past or future actions it is often couched in terms of what our primary goal was or is. The reasons we depend upon goals as explanation are contained in the two remaining claims.

It has been said that 'the sine qua non of goal categories...is their ability to conjoin otherwise isolated actions into coherent, connected, rule-guided (and in some cases, sequential) patterns' (Hoffman, Mischel & Mazze, 1981: 212). Thus, goals are *used to partition the stream of behaviour into meaningful units* (von Cranach *et al.*, 1982: 111–47). To clarify this point it may be helpful to consider the notion of an 'action unit' (Beach, 1985). At one boundary of the action unit is the goal itself — the state of affairs that the individual is striving to achieve or maintain. At the other end is the decision to act. When one considers action units retrospectively, the 'distance' between decision and goal is filled with behaviours. In contrast, a prospective view is less concrete. From this vantage point the action unit is composed of potential tactics, contingency plans, and probably large gaps. These gaps may result from lack of knowledge about the way in which one's social partner will respond, or from an unwillingness to consider all of the many different potential courses of action (Reither, 1981). But in either case the claim applies: goals are used to segment the flow of actions over time.

The third claim is that *goals represent the level in the hierarchy at which planning occurs*. Rosch's (1973, 1978) work on categorisation is instructive on this point (see Cody & McLaughlin, 1985a, for a review). Rosch argues that natural, fuzzy categories exist at three levels of abstraction: *superordinate* categories (e.g. animal) encompass *basic* categories (e.g. bird) which in turn encompass *subordinate* categories (e.g. robin). The middle-level or basic categories exhibit several intriguing properties. They are accessed most quickly when a relevant stimulus is encountered, they are learned first during language acquisition, and they normally have brief, single-word names (Rosch *et al.*, 1976). Rosch contends that basic-level concepts possess these special features because they provide the best trade-off between informativeness and cognitive economy. Concepts at the basic level offer reasonably fine discrimination between stimuli, but are still broad enough to be useful as a means of reducing cognitive load. Basic concepts constitute the happy medium, that is, the level of abstraction at which people normally operate.

While Rosch's efforts have concentrated on establishing that hierarchical relationships exist among objects, colours and other physical stimuli, a second group of researchers have extended this line of work into the realm of social perception. Cantor, Mischel & Schwartz (1982b) have demonstrated that persons possess and utilise basic situational categories which may be grouped under such superordinate headings as 'ideological situations', 'social situations' and 'stressful situations'. Yet, while Rosch's work and the Cantor *et al.* investigation are compelling, neither bears directly on the issue at hand. Are nonstatic entities, such as goals and action units, organised similarly and for similar reasons? The third claim asserts that they are similar (see also Cody, Canary & Smith, in press; von Cranach *et al.*, 1982).

Application to tactical communication

Thus far I have concentrated on examining conceptual aspects of goals without regard for any specific context or type of interaction. The purpose of this section is to consider the implications of the foregoing assumptions and claims for tactical communication.

As noted earlier, many theorists have claimed that persons possess multiple goals. Students of interpersonal influence have often operated from the same assumption. For instance, Marwell & Schmitt (1967b) suggest the existence of two general types of goals in compliance-gaining attempts. They contend that would-be influencers strive to produce behavioural change, while at the same time avoid the costs that might be incurred from different means of influence. Brown & Levinson (1978) theorise that persons making requests must juggle their desire to be efficacious with the need to preserve the face of the other interactant. Sillars (1980c) and deTurck (1985) both argue that sources seeking compliance weigh the likelihood of the message's being effective against the likelihood of relational damage. This same general theme is evident in Cody *et al.*'s (1986) claim that persuasive strategy use is based on twin criteria: (1) the desire to be effective and (2) the desire to conform to the particular situational constraints in which the influence attempt takes place. In short, all of these writers specify the existence of two classes of goals: one which drives the influence attempt, and another set of goals which shape it. I will refer to the two goal types as primary and secondary goals, respectively.

Primary and secondary goals differ in a number of ways which flow directly from the conceptual distinctions drawn earlier. In any given instance, the influence (primary) goal is considered the more important of the two kinds of goals because it defines the interaction. The influence goal explains *why* the interaction took (or will take) place.

The primary goal also distinguishes the influence attempt from other communication activities. Hence, it segments the flow of behaviour into meaningful units. In the case of tactical communication, the primary goal separates interpersonal influence attempts from other kinds of interaction. This segmentation can be done retrospectively, as in the case of a naive account ('I was trying to convince her to . . .'), or prospectively ('I intend to persuade him to . . .'). The former constitutes a culturally viable explanation, while the latter is indicative of planning. Further, it is assumed that awareness of an influence goal stimulates a consideration of the secondary goals. That is, the influence (primary) goal provides the initial push which activates the cognitive calculus that, in turn, incorporates the relevant secondary goals. Secondary goals then function to shape the behaviours whose overriding purpose is to alter the behaviour of the target.

This embryonic theorising about primary and secondary goals pushes us towards certain questions. First, are influence goals undifferentiated? Or might it not be useful to consider whether there are distinct types of influence goals? Surely the answer to these questions would move us closer to being able to address the claim that goals (and action units) are similar to basic categories. Second, what kind of concerns are these secondary goals? And how do they shape influence behaviour? Both questions are essentially concerned with the substance of goals. The remainder of this chapter reports two studies designed to address questions about substance.

Empirical Explication: The Substance of Goals

Types of influence (primary) goals

One of the earliest treatments of influence goals comes from Schank & Abelson's (1977) work on story comprehension. They suggest the existence of a set of persuasive techniques, called a *persuade package*, which is called on to serve change goals. Four goal types are relevant to interpersonal influence: (1) to acquire information, (2) to gain control of an object, (3) to gain social control, e.g. power or authority, and (4) to get a target person to act on behalf of the source.

Rule, Bisanz & Kohn (1985) gathered data from 64 men and women by asking, 'What kind of things do people persuade other people/their friends/their fathers/their enemies to do?' Their content analysis of those data indicated that only 23% were classifiable using the Schank and Abelson (1977) categories. Thus, they proposed the existence of eight additional goals. Such findings suggest the need to expand the Schank and Abelson scheme. Another data-based effort, which leads to the same conclusion, is by Cody, Canary & Smith (in press). Their cluster-analytic work suggests the existence of 12 distinct goal types, some of which exhibited substantial similarity to the categories settled on by Rule, Bisanz & Kohn (1985).

My intention in the first of the investigations reported here was to build upon the foundation laid by Rule *et al.* and Cody *et al.* Its purpose was to determine the types of influence goals that might exist. As in the Rule *et al.* study, it was deemed important to work with first-hand reports of what individuals' goals were, and like the Cody *et al.* investigation, systematic, quantitative methods for developing groups of goals were preferred. But in contrast to both previous efforts, this study was limited to influence goals in close relationships. The justification for this last decision was that (1) close, personal relationships are vitally important to individuals and comparatively under-researched (Berscheid & Peplau, 1983; Duck, 1985), and (2) close, personal relationships may be one of the most active arenas in which social influence attempts take place.

Phase 1

In the first segment of the investigation, a sample of influence goals was generated by asking students ($N = 152$) and business persons ($N = 49$) to recall a self-initiated influence attempt and to describe their goal in that situation. Thus, the goals the participants provided should have been plausible explanations for behaviour (at least as seen by the participants). Three judges examined the pool of statements for the purpose of drawing a representative sample. After several examinations of the data, ten content categories were established: social relations, companionship, entertainment, political activity, health, values and morality, financial matters, career, tasks/labour, and changes in locale. Six goals were chosen to represent each category except political activity, for which only five were retained. This gave a total of 59 goals which were used as stimuli in the next phase.

Phase 2

In this part of the study a group of students ($N = 100$) were asked to assign the goals to groups based on their similarity to one another. Data from individual respondents were compiled to form a summary matrix of similarities which was then submitted to a series of non-hierarchical cluster analyses. Five through 11 group solutions were computed. To assist in choosing among the solutions, the next phase of the investigation was carried out.

Phase 3

This validation segment of the project had another set of participants ($N = 240$) rate each of the goals on several Likert-type rating scales which represented nine conceptually separate dimensions (see Table 3.1). The purpose of these ratings was to ascertain which dimension(s) subjects might be using to discriminate among the goal categories produced by the cluster analysis. The scales were used as predictors in a series of discriminant analyses: goal categories were the dependent variables. The results of the discriminant analysis indicated that 68% of the cases were correctly classified for the five-group solution, 73% for the six-group, 73% for the seven-group, 70% for the eight-group, 71% for the nine-group, 73% for the ten-group, and 68% for the eleven-group solution. Inspection of the cluster analyses revealed that the seven-group and above solutions had at least one cluster which contained only one member. Thus, attention was focused on the five- and six-group solutions. Although both were interpretable, classification efficiency was maximised in the six-group solution. Hence, it was retained (see Dillard, 1987, for details of the analysis).

Types of Influence Goals

The goals in the first cluster were perceived as low in source benefit, above average in target benefit, and were directed primarily at family members. Because of the emphasis on lifestyle issues, the cluster was named *Give Advice (Lifestyle)*. Some examples of the types of goals which appeared in this group are given in Table 3.2.

The second cluster was characterised by high source benefit and a low degree of target benefit. It appeared to be conceptually similar to the Cody, Canary & Smith (in press) *Gain Assistance* category. Consequently, it was given that label (see also Smith *et al.*, this volume, Chapter 4). Again, Table 3.2 provides examples. The goals in the third cluster were also high in source benefit. However, in contrast to the previous cluster, this group focused exclusively on targets in a voluntary relationship with the source, i.e. non-kin, and on topics concerned with how to manage the shared activities in that relationship. In line with the earlier work, this cluster was labelled *Share Activity* (cf. Cody, Canary & Smith, in press; Smith *et al.*, this volume, Chapter 4).

Two characteristics of the fourth cluster set it off from the other goal clusters. First, the goals were aimed at benefiting a group rather than either one of the two interactants. In addition, these influence attempts tended to take place amidst a number of other people: they were high in 'publicness'. An examination of the content of the cluster showed that every one of the goals was concerned with convincing the target to engage in some politically related behaviour. This group of goals was given the label *Change Political Stance*.

TABLE 3.1 *Scales used to aid in interpreting the cluster solutions*

Source Benefit (alpha = 0.73)
1. . . . would be very beneficial to the source.
2. . . . is purely in the interest of the source.

Target Benefit (alpha = 0.94)
3. . . . would be very beneficial to the target.
4. . . . is for the good of the *individual* target person.

Group Benefit (alpha = 0.68)
5. . . . is an activity that should be done for the good of some larger group, e.g. community, society, etc.
6. . . . benefits some third person or group, i.e. not the source or target.

Publicness (alpha = 0.90)
7. . . . pertains to a very public activity.
8. . . . represents an activity that involves many other people.

Normative Pressure (alpha = 0.82)
9. . . . emphasises an obligation.
10. . . . refers to something that 'should' be done because of social norms.

Improvement (alpha = 0.80)
11. . . . tries to remedy an important problem.
12. . . . is concerned with making things better.
13. . . . focuses on trying to prevent something bad from happening.(R)[a]

Voluntary–Nonvoluntary Relationship (alpha = 0.93)
14. . . . focuses on friends or lovers (as opposed to family).
15. . . . involves a person with whom the source chose to have a relationship.

Relational Growth/Maintenance (alpha = 0.95)
16. . . . concerns how often the source and target can or will interact with one another.
17. . . . has to do with the potential for two persons in a relationship to become closer to one another.
18. . . . reflects a concern for building/maintaining a relationship.

Specificity (alpha = 0.72)
19. . . . is concerned with specific issues in how a relationship will work rather than global matters (like will the relationship continue).
20. . . . refers to a concrete, material problem (e.g. money).

---

[a] Items followed by (R) were reflected.

The goals grouped into the fifth cluster were unique in their focus on convincing the target to eliminate some self-destructive behaviour. In light of these features, it is not surprising that target benefit was perceived as high. In addition, the raters saw goals in this set as being high in normative pressure or the extent to which the goal represented something that society said the target should do. This cluster was labelled *Give Advice (Health)* (cf. Cody, Canary & Smith, in press; Smith *et al.*, this volume).

TABLE 3.2 *Six clusters of influence goals*

Cluster label	Goal statement ('I wanted . . .')
Give Advice (Lifestyle)	. . . the person to buy a computer for the family.
	. . . my mother to start buying light salt instead of ordinary salt.
Gain Assistance	. . . my girlfriend to type my paper.
	. . . the person to leave a party and take me to another city so I could see my boyfriend.
Share Activity	. . . her to go to the restaurant of my choice.
	. . . this person to walk to the store with me.
Change Political Stance	. . . the person not to participate in a political demonstration on campus.
	. . . the person to vote in the Wisconsin Student Association election, specifically for the High Tide Party.
Give Advice (Health)	. . . my friend not to see someone because it was bad for my friend's mental health.
	. . . the person to use some form of birth control because she is sexually active.
Change Relationship	. . . the person to attend church with me on a regular basis.
	. . . two good friends to live with me next year in the apartment we are living in now.

The final cluster was similar to the Share Activity category in that it was high on source benefit, voluntary relationship and relational growth. The difference between the two clusters appears to lie in the type of change that is sought. Whereas goals in the Share Activity category focus on joint, short-term endeavours, goals in this last group represent long-term matters that require continuous effort or at least a major one-time effort. Consequently, the last cluster was named *Change Relationship* (cf. Cody, Canary & Smith, in press; Smith *et al.*, this volume).

After inspecting these findings, at least three conclusions suggest themselves. One is that there is considerable convergence between the results of this study and the previous efforts. Four of the six goal clusters are conceptually quite similar to groupings reported in Cody, Canary & Smith (in press) and in Rule, Bisanz & Kohn (1985). In an attempt to prevent the proliferation of names/categories in the literature, I have adopted (or slightly modified) Cody *et al.*'s labels for those four clusters: Gain Assistance, Change Relationship, Give Advice (Health), and Share Activity. In contrast to these near-perfect matches is the Give Advice (Lifestyle) category. It is somewhat similar to Cody *et al.*'s Obtain Permission in its focus on family members, but has no apparent mate in the Rule *et al.* scheme. Finally, Change Political Stance is unique to the present study.

A second point that can be made is that persons are capable of differentiating between types of influence goals and that they do so on a variety of different dimensions. This is clearly compatible with Rosch *et al.*'s (1976) claim that 'in the real world information-rich bundles of perceptual and functional attributes occur that form natural discontinuities' (p.358).

A third conclusion pertains to the ways in which people distinguish between the goal types. At once it seems clear that the goals imply more than the simple statements which the study participants judged. It would appear that persons made use of relational and situational information in distinguishing between the statements as well as the actional information contained in the goal description itself. This suggests that influence goals are probably not context-free (cf. Schank & Abelson's (1977) goals which are context-free), but that they either exist within situations or that they are defining features of situations.

Summary

My purpose in this study was to generate descriptive knowledge about the substance of influence goals. The study was successful in isolating six distinct types of goals, four of which had clear correlates in previous research. To the question 'Are there different types of goals?', the answer seems to be yes.

Secondary goals

A number of researchers (Carver & Scheier, 1983; Clark & Delia, 1979; Greene, 1984a; Higgins, McCann & Fondacaro, 1982; Schank & Abelson, 1977; M.J. Smith, 1982) have developed lists of goals. Each of these lists contains a number of goals which might reasonably be construed as 'recurring goals' (Wilensky, 1978), and therefore relevant to many situations including interpersonal influence attempts. A recent study by Dillard, Segrin & Harden (1987) took those existing lists as a starting point and attempted to synthesise them into a compact, but reasonably exhaustive, set of secondary goals. Our conceptual analysis of the lists suggested that they could be reduced to four general categories. We conducted an investigation to provide an empirical test of our thinking.

Phase 1

One hundred students were presented with 10 different compliance-gaining scenarios (two per student). Accompanying each scenario was a label, a brief description, and an example of each of the Schenck-Hamlin, Wiseman & Georgacarakos (1982) compliance-gaining strategies. The students were asked to indicate which strategies they would and would not use in each situation; for the strategies they would not use they were asked to say why.

The purpose of this procedure was twofold. The first aim of this phase was to gather data which were reflective of the concerns which individual sources face in interpersonal influence attempts. By obtaining open-ended self-reports of the constraints which individuals perceive to shape their own influence behaviour, we hoped to gain some sense of the extent to which our theorising about the substance of secondary goals was grounded in the phenomenology of the actor. The other purpose of this phase was to generate a pool of statements closely tied to the decisions which shape tactical behaviour. Our intention was to use those statements as a basis for constructing a series of closed-ended scales for use in phase 2.

First, the open-ended justifications for not using particular compliance-gaining strategies were content-analysed (*N* of justifications = 1,959). Our coding scheme consisted of the four hypothesised secondary goals as well as an Ineffectiveness category (which corresponds to a concern for the primary goal).

Phase 2

In the second phase, the open-ended responses were translated into item format. The eventual result was a questionnaire which was composed of closed-ended items based on the open-ended data. A group of students ($N = 604$) responded to the questionnaire after being asked to recall an instance in which they had attempted to influence someone whom they knew well. They were instructed to imagine themselves back in that situation and then to respond to the goals items. The sample was split in half and a series of confirmatory and exploratory factor analyses were conducted on the first half. The results indicated the existence of five secondary-goal factors, rather than the originally hypothesised four. These results were then validated on the second half of the sample (see Dillard, Segrin & Harden, 1987, for the details of these analyses). The five secondary goals are described below, and the scales used to measure people's perceptions of their secondary goals are given in Table 3.3. Also included is the scale used to assess perceptions of the importance of the primary or *Influence* goal.

Interaction goals are concerned with social appropriateness (Price & Bouffard, 1974). They represent the source's desire to manage his or her impression successfully (Schlenker, 1980), to ensure a smooth flow to the communication event (Goffman, 1967), and to maintain politeness (Brown & Levinson, 1978). Interaction goals revolve around a person's public persona and the way in which that persona meshes with others in joint social activities.

Identity goals are objectives related to the self-concept. As such, they are *internal* standards of behaviour which may or may not overlap with expectations about how others would or should behave (Schwartz, 1977; M.J. Smith, 1982). They derive from one's moral standards, principles for living, and personal preferences concerning one's own conduct.

There are two types of *Resource* goals, both of which attempt to increase or maintain valued assets. The domain of *Personal Resource* goals is the material, physical, and probably temporal assets a person possesses. Persons attempt to conserve or increase their time, energy and material possessions, as well as their mental and physical health (cf. Berger, 1985: 488). *Relational Resource* goals focus on the maintenance or enhancement of all those personal rewards and gratifications which arise from participation in a relationship with the target. The substance of these goals would be likely to include such things as attention from the target, positive stimulation, emotional support and social comparison information (C. Hill, 1987).

Finally, there are *Arousal Management* goals. Similar to theories which seek to explain aspects of interpersonal interaction (Burgoon, 1978; Cappella & Greene, 1982; Patterson, 1976), it is assumed that persons have a desire to maintain a state of arousal which falls within certain individually specified boundaries. Most often this will mean that people attempt to dampen the apprehension (McCroskey, 1982) induced by engaging, or anticipation of engaging, in communication. For others, however, such as highly extroverted individuals or persons high in sensation-seeking, the influence process itself may be enjoyable and they may be attracted to it for that reason.

Given the limited empirical base (only one study), this set of secondary goals must be regarded as tentative. In retrospect, the concept of arousal management may be too limited. It takes into account one type of affect (anxiety) which persons may experience in the course of influencing another, but ignores a wide range of other emotions. Whether these other emotions play a role in interpersonal influence processes remains to be seen.

Summary

The aim of this study was to provide an answer to the question 'What is the substance of secondary goals?' We found evidence for five separate concerns that qualify as secondary goals.

Goals and tactical communication

Up to this point the bulk of the discussion has centred around explicating the substance of goals. The long range purpose of that enterprise, however, was to aid us in understanding the determinants of

TABLE 3.3 *Goals items/scales and scale reliabilities*

Goals/Scales

Influence Scale (alpha = 0.85, 0.87)
1. It was very important to me to convince this person to do what I wanted him or her to do.
2. I was very concerned about getting what I wanted in this persuasive attempt.
3. I really didn't care that much whether he or she did what I asked or not. (R)[a]
4. The outcome of this persuasion attempt had important personal consequences for me.
5. Although I wanted the person to do as I asked, it really wasn't that important an issue. (R)

Identity Scale (alpha = 0.78, 0.76)
6. In this situation, I was concerned with not violating my own ethical standards.
7. In this situation, I was concerned about maintaining my own ethical standards.
8. I was concerned about being true to myself and my values.
9. I wanted to behave in a mature, responsible manner.
10. I was not concerned with sticking to my own standards. (R)

Interaction Scale (alpha = 0.71, 0.72)
11. I was concerned with making (or maintaining) a good impression in this persuasion attempt.
12. In this situation, I was careful to avoid saying things which were socially inappropriate.
13. I was very conscious of what was appropriate and inappropriate in this situation.
14. I was concerned with putting myself in a 'bad light' in this situation.
15. I didn't want to look stupid while trying to persuade this person.

Relational Resource Scale (alpha = 0.76, 0.71)
16. I was not willing to risk possible damage to the relationship in order to get what I wanted.
17. Getting what I wanted was more important to me than preserving our relationship. (R)
18. I didn't really care if I made the other person mad or not. (R)

Personal Resource Scale (alpha = 0.80, 0.71)
19. This person could have made things very bad for me if I kept on bugging him/her.
20. This person might have taken advantage of me if I tried too hard to persuade him/her.
21. I was worried about the threat to my safety if I pushed the issue.

Table 3.3 *Continued*

Goals/Scales

Arousal Management Scale (alpha = 0.75, 0.76)
22.   In this persuasive attempt, I avoided saying things which might have made me apprehensive or nervous.
23.   This situation did *not* seem to be the type to make me nervous. (R)
24.   This situation's potential for making me nervous and uncomfortable worried me.
25.   I was afraid of being uncomfortable or nervous.

[a] 'R' indicates that the item was reverse scored. The two alpha reliabilities are for the first and second subsamples, respectively.

interpersonal influence behaviour from a GPA perspective. If goals, as elaborated here, do not show any correspondence to planning or behaviour, then this exercise in explication is trivial. The final segment of Dillard, Segrin & Harden's (1987) paper addressed this issue by using persons' reports of their goals as predictors of selected aspects of the interpersonal influence process. It is to those particular features of the influence process that we now turn.

Several investigations directed at isolating the perceptual dimensions of influence messages were useful in guiding our decisions about which aspects of the influence process to study (Cody, McLaughlin & Jordan, 1980; Falbo, 1977; Falbo & Peplau, 1980; Wiseman & Schenck-Hamlin, 1981). Although the findings are not perfectly consistent across these studies, there are some strong similarities which indicate the existence of at least three perceptual dimensions of influence messages. *Directness* refers to the extent to which a message makes clear the change that the source is seeking in the target. *Positivity* is the degree to which the positive outcomes associated with compliance, or negative outcomes associated with non-compliance, are specified. The third dimension, *logic*, refers to the degree to which the source makes use of evidence and reason. Each of these three dimensions of tactical communication was examined in the study. Our expectation was that the set of goals would share substantial variance with the set of message dimensions.

Method

The data ($N = 304$) for the analyses came from the holdout sample on which the factor structure of the goals was validated (see previous section). Besides making judgements on the closed-ended goal scales, and on measures of cognitive and behavioural effort, persons in that sample also provided open-ended descriptions of (1) their influence goal and (2) the content of the interaction. The questionnaire instructed respondents to unitise their report of the dialogue by presenting them with an alternating series of prompts such as, 'First, you said:', 'Then, s/he said:', 'Next, you said:', and so on. Each prompt was followed by several blank lines. Respondents were encouraged to be as descriptive as possible.

These interaction descriptions were rated by three trained judges for logic, directness and positivity. Each rater read the entire interaction description on three separate occasions, and after each reading, rendered a global judgement concerning the source's behaviour for one of the dimensions. All judgements were made on five-point scales.

Judgements regarding the use of logic considered the degree to which the source employed plausible and compelling reasons in his or her influence attempt. Hints and direct requests exemplify a minimal use of logic, while offering several realistic and compelling reasons demonstrates a high degree of logic. Cronbach's alpha for this set of ratings was 0.81. The directness rating reflects the extent to which the source was explicit in his or her request for behavioural change. If a source made a direct request immediately in the interaction it was rated as very direct. Interactions in which the source never made an explicit request, but only hinted at it, were judged low in directness. Cronbach's alpha for this dimension was 0.86. Finally, the interaction descriptions were rated for the degree to which the source alluded to the positive or negative consequences which would result from the target's compliance (or lack thereof). References to desirable material or relational consequences were rated as positive, while references to aversive, unpleasant outcomes were rated as negative (i.e. low in positivity). Instances in which there were few or no references to any outcomes were judged as neutral. Cronbach's alpha for this dimension was 0.81.

The measures of cognitive and behavioural effort were both self-report. Planning (cognitive effort) was assessed with a single item: 'I put a lot of thought (or would have if s/he had resisted) into figuring out what was the best way to persuade this person.' Two items were combined to assess the source's perception of his or her own behavioural effort: 'I tried (or would have tried) everything I could think of to persuade this person' and 'I put a great deal of effort (or would have done) into persuading this person' (Cronbach's alpha =0.77). The response scales for each of the three items were 1 = 'not at all true', 2 = 'somewhat true', and 3 = 'completely true'. A hierarchical regression analysis was conducted for cognitive and behavioural effort and for each of the three dimensions of influence messages. The predictors in each analysis were the scales designed to assess the importance of the primary and secondary goals.

Results

Overall, the results are quite compatible with the claim that goals shape influence behaviour. The analyses revealed that, with one exception, each goal was uniquely associated with one or more aspects of the influence message (see Table 3.4).

The influence goal emerged as a major predictor of both cognitive and behavioural effort. Further, the positive relationship between the importance of the influence goal and the use of logic reveals another point at which the primary goal enters the influence process. The data indicate that important goals (1) stimulate planning in anticipation of the influence event, that they (2) result in the creation of messages characterised by reliance on reason and evidence, and that they (3) cause the source to persist in his or her efforts to obtain compliance from the target.

The identity and interaction goals both reflect the desire to conform to certain standards of behaviour, internal standards in the case of identity goals and external standards in the case of interaction goals. This conceptual demarcation is, to a degree, empirically fuzzy because external standards may become internalised, usually by socialisation processes (see e.g. Berkowitz & Daniels, 1964). However, as Table 3.4 indicates, the two goal types have unique impacts on the influence process. Identity goals were positively associated with cognitive effort and the use of logic, but negatively associated with directness. Interaction goals were positively associated with expenditure of cognitive effort and the use of more positive messages.

Concern for the relationship, i.e. relational resource goals, showed a direct association with the use of positive messages. This finding is similar to earlier work which has generally found a tendency for persons to report that they would be more likely to use messages which emphasise

TABLE 3.4 *Goals as predictors of aspects of the interpersonal influence process*

Goals	Standardised Regression Coefficients				
	Cognitive Effort	Behavioural Effort	Directness	Positivity	Logic
Influence	0.29***	0.55***	0.04	−0.04	0.28***
Identity	0.13*	0.09	−0.17**	−0.06	0.15*
Interaction	0.19**	0.07	0.06	0.31***	0.07
Relational	−0.04	0.01	0.06	0.22***	−0.05
Personal	−0.08	−0.01	0.02	−0.02	−0.00
Arousal	0.05	−0.06	−0.14*	−0.24***	−0.19*
R	0.46***	0.57***	0.23*	0.39***	0.32***
Corrected R^a	0.51	0.68	0.24	0.48	0.37

[a] These coefficients are corrected for both measurement error and shrinkage.
$N = 294$.
  *$p < 0.05$
 **$p < 0.01$
***$p < 0.001$

desirable consequences with highly intimate targets than with non-intimate targets (e.g. Dillard & Burgoon, 1985; Miller *et al.*, 1977; Raven, Centers & Rodrigues, 1975; Roloff & Barnicott, 1978). However, it extends our knowledge base by demonstrating a unique effect for relational concerns in the influence process and by linking those concerns to a specific dimension of influence messages.

Although arousal management goals were apparently unrelated to either cognitive or behavioural effort, the source's concern for his/her own level of arousal exhibited significant associations with all three message dimensions. Highly aroused sources were less direct, less positive, and relied less on the use of logic than did less aroused sources (cf. Smith & Cody, 1986). Taken together, these findings suggest that the influence episodes of apprehensive persons are more like emotional outbursts than considered attempts at producing behavioural change. The implications of such messages for the health of the source–target relationship are obviously negative.

The personal resources goal did not show a reliable statistical association with any of the aspects of the influence process that we chose to study. Although this suggests that this goal may be unimportant to compliance-gaining activities, it is probably too soon to make such a determination. One possibility is that concern for personal resources exerts an influence on the actor's decision regarding whether to enter a compliance-gaining situation at all (Emmons, Diener & Larsen, 1986).

Summary

Overall, the results are supportive of the assumption that the goals of the actor are important determinants of behaviour. In a more specific vein, the results also support the distinction between primary and secondary goals. As Table 3.4 indicates, the influence, or primary, goal has its strongest associations with the energic aspects of the influence process, i.e. cognitive and behavioural effort. In contrast, secondary goals have their most consistent relationships with the communication variables. While the pattern is not a perfect dichotomy, it is consistent with the claim that there are two types of goals. The primary goal serves to initiate and maintain the influence attempt, while the secondary goals act as a set of boundaries which delimit the verbal (and, no doubt, nonverbal) choices available to the source.

Summary and Conclusion

The guiding purpose of this chapter was to elaborate a structurally promising, but substantively vacuous, account of interpersonal influence: the GPA sequence. In the service of that end I presented two different, yet complementary, approaches to theory development. The top-down approach involved the conceptual elaboration of the notion of goals. Three assumptions thought to be inherent in any goal-based account of human behaviour were specified. Three additional claims regarding the nature of goals were also advanced. From this groundwork, primary and secondary goals were distinguished.

Efforts at using a bottom-up approach to theory development were necessarily data-driven. Two investigations were reported, one which sought to describe types of primary goals, and one which aimed to give substance to the secondary goals. The first study indicated the existence of different kinds of primary goals. The second study suggested a small and intuitively reasonable set of secondary goals. The last section of the second study showed that variations in the importance of the primary goal and the secondary goals were correlated with alterations in effort and content of the influence messages used by the source.

Although the attempts at explicating a theoretical perspective moved from the top down and from the bottom up simultaneously, these attempts did not simply meet in the middle. Rather, much remains to be done before a goal-driven model of tactical communication is complete. My hope is that the foundational concepts examined in this chapter will prove durable enough for a stronger and more complete theory to be constructed upon them.

Acknowledgement

I am grateful to Mike Cody, Quana Jew and Peggy McLaughlin for their comments on an earlier version of this manuscript.

4 Self-monitoring, gender and compliance-gaining goals

SANDI W. SMITH
Department of Communication, Purdue University, West Lafayette, Indiana, USA

MICHAEL J. CODY and SHANNON LOVETTE
Department of Communication Arts and Sciences, University of Southern California, Los Angeles, USA

DANIEL J. CANARY
Speech Communication Department, California State University, Fullerton, USA

Compliance-gaining communication offers an excellent example of goal-driven behaviour. A social actor perceives a deviation from an ideal state and acts in order to reduce the perceived discrepancy between the present and ideal states (Carver & Scheier, 1982; Hobbs & Evans, 1980). For example, a couple have been dating for several months, but one of them perceives that the relationship is becoming too serious. He (she) is uncomfortable and therefore wants to de-escalate the relationship in order to achieve a more comfortable state. The communicative behaviour that such a person uses to de-escalate the relationship serves to reduce the perceived discrepancy between the present and ideal states. Of course, there are many methods and potential messages that could be used to de-escalate a dating relationship, as there are many interacting goals that could constrain choices of behaviour in this situation. Our purpose in this chapter is to explore the ways in which self-monitoring and gender influence goal-driven compliance-gaining behaviour. Our expectations and findings are that *low self-monitoring actors (particularly males) will be less expressive and rely on fewer emotionally based and relationally oriented tactics when influencing others*, and that *low self-monitoring actors will pursue influence goals differently from their high self-monitoring counterparts.* First, however, we need to consider compliance-gaining goals and the nature of goal-driven behaviour.

Compliance-Gaining Goals

'Compliance-gaining goal' refers to an actor's intention to induce some change in his/her social or physical environment by influencing others through communication (either verbally or nonverbally—via affiliative cues, or, conversely, by pouting, sulking, etc.). A growing body of literature has focused on typologies of compliance-gaining goals, and how actors pursue specific goals (Berger, in press(a,b), 1985; Canary, Cody & Marston, 1986; Dillard, 1987, and this volume; Dillard, Segrin & Harden, 1987; Kipnis, 1984; Kipnis, Schmidt & Wilkinson, 1980; McCann & Higgins, 1987; Rule & Bisanz, 1987, and this volume; Rule, Bisanz & Kohn, 1985; Schank & Abelson, 1977; Schmidt & Kipnis, 1984). We have reviewed these studies elsewhere (Cody, Canary & Smith, in press), and have proposed a typology of goals that might drive most of the compliance-gaining events described in the studies noted above.

Table 4.1 presents the typology. *Obtain Permission* goals involve influencing people in authority to approve or grant permission to engage in an activity, or to approve a change in a norm (e.g. increased autonomy from parents, etc.). *Gain Assistance* is one of the most commonly pursued goals, reflecting an element of dependence on parents and friends to help the actor fulfil a desired outcome (e.g. buy a new computer printer, help to pay a credit card bill on time). Such goals range from soliciting advice or information from others, to borrowing money or objects, to running errands (or related favours from others), to making selfish requests (the actor hopes to achieve his/her goal at the expense of the target's ability to fulfil his/her goal) (see Cody, Canary & Smith, in press). *Give Advice* goals are reflected in the actor's attempt to influence, for example, whom the target should (or should not) date, or the target's habits, appearances, and future plans—motives that provide a benefit to the target.

Change Opinion goals motivate an actor's efforts to influence the target's evaluation of (or attitudes towards) objects or events, while *Share Activity* goals primarily involve influencing the target to engage in an activity, usually with the actor, such as shopping or going out together. Our category of *Elicit Support* includes what Rule and Bisanz refer to as 'Third party' goals—for example, the actor forms a coalition with a target in order to influence a third person (see examples in Table 4.1, and in

Cody *et al.*). To *Change Ownership*, the actor engages in selling or buying objects or services, although charity selling may also be included. *Enforce Obligation* goals involve the actor's motivation to ensure that the target fulfils his/her contract or other obligation, such as paying the phone bill or rent on time. A *Protect Right* goal is typified by the actor's defence against an infringement of his/her rights to privacy, property, or health (e.g. stopping a neighbour's dogs from barking at night). Finally, *Change Relationship* goals may lead the actor either to initiate, escalate, or de-escalate a relationship. Rule *et al.* also included a goal labelled 'Harm', and Cody *et al.* included a goal labelled *Violate Law* (buying or selling drugs, tests, term papers, etc.). We do not include such a goal in research reported here.

Sufficient work has been done in the area of influence goals to suggest four general conclusions. First, there exists (at least among college-aged actors) a standard set of goals actors pursue, and the frequency by which goals are pursued varies as a function of role relationships (Cody, Canary & Smith, in press; Rule & Bisanz, 1987; Rule, Bisanz & Kohn, 1985). For example, actors are frequently involved in seeking permission, gaining assistance and advice-giving in interactions with parents, while a wider range of goals is pursued with friends. More conflicts (e.g. Protect Right and Enforce Obligation) occur with room-mates and siblings, and a very restricted range of goals occurs when influencing bureaucrats and strangers. Also, it is likely that certain goals differ in frequency over time, since it is probable, for example, that youths make more requests for permission from parents prior to entering college and more requests for assistance from parents after matriculating. Most of the requests made by college students involve family members and friends as targets (Cody *et al.*, in press; Rule *et al.*, 1985).

Second, the extent to which actors claim success in gaining compliance varies as a function of both the goal and the role relationship. Actors claim more success in pursuing the goal types Gain Assistance, Share Activity, Change Relationship, Change Ownership and Elicit Support than when pursuing other goals. Actors also claim more success when influencing friends, room-mates and strangers (most requests made of strangers involve Assistance goals), than bureaucrats and parents (parents did not frequently grant permission requests; see Cody, Canary & Smith, in press).

Third, several studies indicate that goals differ significantly from one another on the basis of perceptions dealing with cognitive, affective and behavioural features (Canary, Cody & Marston, 1986; Cody, Canary

TABLE 4.1 *A typology of compliance-gaining goals*

Goal		Subcategories and examples
Obtain Permission	single activity:	to go to an all-night graduation party
	ongoing activity:	to have curfew extended
	personal activity:	to have ears pierced
	increased autonomy:	freedom from going to church
Gain Assistance	information:	gain information about an object to purchase
	fund activity:	pay for airfare home
	purchase goods:	pay for a new printer for home computer
	financial assistance:	borrow money for new expenses
	favour/borrow object:	lend a car, borrow clothing
	favour/consideration:	run an errand for the actor
	selfish request:	keep job so actor can receive discount
Give Advice	relational:	give advice on who should date whom
	health/habit:	give advice on breaking habits
	social skills/appearance:	give advice on public behaviour
	financial plan:	give advice on making plans, money
	career plan:	give advice on the target's career
Change Opinion	opinion change:	change opinion of film, Greek system
Share Activity	mutual activity:	shop together, walk together
	target's activity:	target should engage in a behaviour

Elicit Support (third party)	family coalition:	seek aid in persuasion of another
	resolve conflict:	seek aid from a target to speak to a third person
	acquire information:	seek aid from a target to investigate a third person's attitudes
	relational initiation:	seek aid from a target to introduce actor to a potential dater
Change Ownership (buying and selling)	selling:	to sell something to others
	charity:	to sell raffle tickets, etc.
	buying:	to purchase materials from others
Enforce Obligation	obligation:	target should fulfil contract or other obligation
Protect Right	annoyance:	a target's behaviour infringes on the actor's rights, property, health
Change Relationship	initiation:	actor plans to begin or to initiate a relationship
	escalation/test of relationship:	actor plans to engage in an activity or persuade a dating partner to advance to a more intimate or personal level
	de-escalation:	actor plans to reduce the level of intimacy in an existing relationship

Source: Cody, Canary & Smith (in press).

& Smith, in press; Dillard, Segrin & Harden, 1987; Pervin, 1986). A common set of situation perceptions discriminates among goal types: actor–target *Intimacy*, *Homophily*, target *Dominance*, perceptions of *Rights to Persuade*, anticipated target *Resistance to Persuasion*, levels of *Personal Benefits* (self vs. other benefit), length of *Relational Consequences* (short-term consequences or long-term relational changes or changes in the relational definitions), and *Situation Apprehension* (see Cody & McLaughlin, 1985a, for a discussion of situation perceptions). For instance, a goal to Escalate a Relationship is characterised by high levels of intimacy, homophily and rights to persuade, and by low levels of target resistance, situation apprehension and personal benefits. However, a goal to Obtain Permission (from a parent) is characterised by high intimacy, high target dominance, short-term relational consequences and low levels of situation apprehension (see Cody, Canary & Smith, in press). Although we still need to know more about the content of various compliance-gaining goals (in terms of a more exhaustive range of beliefs, expectations, behavioural requirements and emotions), it is clear that social actors develop, from past experiences in various relationships, social knowledge about goals that affect how frequently goals are pursued (or avoided) and whether actors plan a course of action to influence others. In the studies described here we asked respondents to rate various goals in terms of *familiarity, confidence of success, willingness to enter* (or avoid), anticipated *persistence*, and how *easy it is to imagine* the particular situation. We did so in order to compare different goals in terms of general reactions, and to assess the role of personality differences in general reactions (see below).

Fourth, actors use different message tactics when pursuing most goals (see also Canary, Cody & Marston, 1986). *Rationality* (justification or 'logical proofs') (see Falbo, 1977; Falbo & Peplau, 1980; Kipnis, 1984; Cody & McLaughlin, 1988) is more likely to be used in goals involving requests for permission from parents, when influencing bureaucrats, when giving advice, and when proposing relational changes, but is used *infrequently* in Share Activity goals (for which actors use simple direct requests) or relational initiations (for which indirect tactics are preferred; see Cody, Canary & Smith, in press). *Coercive Influence* tactics (as first attempts) were reserved for Protect Right and Enforce Obligation goals, and *Compromises* were offered when proposing changes in relationships, when asking for assistance, and when pursuing Enforce Obligation and Protect Right goals. Three emotionally oriented tactics have been studied—ones requiring greater expressivity. *Manipulation of Positive Feelings* (putting on a 'happy face': Falbo, 1977; or ingratiation tactics:

see Bettinghaus & Cody, 1987) are most often used when actors attempt to gain permission from parents, when gaining assistance from others, when escalating relationships and when attempting to influence bureaucrats. *Manipulation of Negative Feelings* (pouting, sulking, looking disappointed, etc.) appears to be used rarely as a first-attempt tactic, but is used as a second-attempt tactic when others fail to follow advice, share an activity together, or grant permission (i.e. actors would make sure they showed disappointment if parents did not grant permission requests), when friends or dating partners decline to escalate relationships, and when others at first refuse to give assistance to the actor. Pouting, sulking or looking disappointed also reflects a general tactic used when bureaucrats at first refuse to comply with requests (see Cody, Canary & Smith, in press). Finally, *Referent Influence* or appealing to the quality of the relationship (i.e. 'oneness') is used in Relational Change goals, when giving advice and when involved in Elicit Support goals—and is almost never used on strangers or bureaucrats.

Goal-driven behaviour, gender and self-monitoring

Social actors develop beliefs and expectations about goals. We believe that the cognitive representations or prototypical conceptions of goals are similar to those described by Cantor and her colleagues for various types of situations (Cantor & Kihlstrom, 1987; Cantor & Mischel, 1977, 1979a, 1979b; Cantor, Mischel & Schwartz, 1982a, 1982b; Neidenthal, Cantor & Kihlstrom, 1985); that is, that actors possess person-in-situation images, that particular events are exemplars of a domain of category members, and that a basic level of organisation is more predictive of tactical choices than either a superordinate or subordinate level (Cody, Canary & Smith, in press; Dillard, this volume; Pavitt & Haight, 1985; Rosch, 1978; Tversky, 1977). The fact that actors possess knowledge of situations or goal types does not tell us precisely *why* actors behave the way they do. Certainly, the pursuit of some tasks, such as making an oral argument in traffic court (Cody & McLaughlin, 1988), or asking directions from strangers, involves a limited range of influence options. Other goals are *reactive* (i.e. in Enforce Obligation and Protect Right goals the actor is forced to engage in behaviours to correct, or to defend against, the behaviour of others), and reactive goals may induce certain behavioural choices more so than proactive goals. For example, in one study we found that persons were more likely to use aggressive tactics when protecting a right or defending the self against a verbal attack than when seeking proactive relational change goals (Canary, Cunningham & Cody, 1988).

Pursuit of many other goals, however, not only allows for considerable freedom of choice, but also reflects on the actors' public image and self-concept. That is, actors develop some idealised self-image about the kind of persons they are, the kind of relationships they have (or find ideal), and the kind of behaviours in which they can or cannot engage (Cantor & Kihlstrom, 1987; M. Snyder, 1987). Decisions to enter into (or avoid) some events, to be persistent and active in pursuing goals, and the selection of behavioural choices when pursuing goals are strongly constrained or influenced by the actor's reference to concepts of desired self-images. One social actor adopts the view of self as 'friendly and communal', for instance, while another adopts the view of self as 'principled and honest'. Both might desire reducing the level of intimacy in a dating relationship, but a friendly-communal actor may do so quite differently (e.g. 'positive tone', see below) from a principled-honest one (e.g. 'justifying' his/her intentions). Understanding why and how actors pursue goals requires that we understand how particular types of communicators possess superordinate goals (e.g. to be friendly) and use such superordinate goals in interacting with the external environment. One important group of actors are females (as opposed to males), who traditionally are socialised to be friendly and communal.

If females, in fact, possess a superordinate goal to be 'friendly and communal' (and much literature on college-aged females indicates that this is true), then females ought more frequently to pursue communal types of goals and goals that affect the quality of relationships (e.g. Share Activities, Give Advice, perform acts of charity or engage in volunteer work, Escalate or De-escalate Relationship), and females ought to adjust a good deal (but not all) of their tactical choices to reflect such a superordinate motive. Indeed, several studies over the years found that females frequently are 'found in' different situations than males (Booth, 1972; Cody, Canary & Smith, in press; Wheeler & Nezlek, 1977); that is, females (as opposed to males) seek more frequent contact with, confide more in, and engage in more spontaneous activities with friends (especially the same sex best friend) and develop deeper, more affectively rich friendships.

Specific details of how gender is related to the pursuit of more communal and relationally oriented goals were obtained in the 'nominating study' reported in Cody, Canary & Smith (in press). Some 135 females and 75 males recalled all compliance-gaining events in different categories (first listed by role relationship and then listed by motive: Gain Assistance, Give Advice, etc.). Respondents rated their own levels of success in achieving the goals (successful, partially successful and unsuccessful). Episodes were coded into a typology of goals (see above) and several gender differences were obtained. Females more frequently pursued the following goals than males:

1. *Share Activity* with brothers/sisters, room-mates and friends;
2. *Gain Assistance* from parents, brothers/sisters, and room-mates;
3. *Give Advice* to parents and to brothers/sisters;
4. *Sell for Charity* (i.e. females were more likely to sell raffle tickets, etc.);
5. *Change Relationship*—females were more likely to prompt friends to confide more in their partners, to plan a relational escalation, to devise a test of trust, and to initiate a relationship using indirect tactics;
6. *Protect Right* and *Enforce Obligation* goals with room-mates; and,
7. *Change Ownership* using qualitatively different objects and services. That is, males sold expensive objects such as cars, stereos and cameras, while females sold services and handmade products (babysitting, typing, etc.).

In terms of claimed success, females (as opposed to males):

1. Sold charity more effectively, and with parents were somewhat more successful in *Share Activity* and *Change Opinion* goals, but were less effective than males in gaining permission;
2. Were more effective in gaining compliance from brothers and sisters to *Share Activity* but were less effective in gaining assistance from brothers/sisters, and in giving advice to brothers/sisters;
3. Were more effective in pursuing *Elicit Support* goals (seeking assistance for a third party: see definitions below), but were less effective in *Share Activity* goals with friends; and,
4. Were more effective in securing special favours (*Gain Assistance* goals) from bureaucrats, especially guards and police, but were less successful in *Give Advice* to superiors (i.e. bosses at work).

Some of the major differences between males and females, then, involve the fact that females want to share activities with others (and succeeded in doing so), that females spend more time thinking about and planning relational escalations and de-escalations (see also Baxter & Wilmot, 1984), and that females engage in (and are more effective in) charity work. Note that the relative ineffectiveness of females in giving advice to others, obtaining permission from parents, and influencing superiors may prompt some females to increase reliance on *Rationality* as a preferred influence method in order to overcome lower initial levels of credibility. We did find that females rated Rationality higher in preference across many goal types (see Cody, Canary & Smith, in press). Also, if females do adopt the superordinate goal of being 'friendly and communal' then females should rely less on Direct Request, Coercive Influence, and Manipulation of Negative Feelings (e.g. pouting, sulking, making the target feel guilty), and rely more on Compromise (with friends) and Manipulation of Positive Feelings (e.g. putting on a 'happy face': see Falbo, 1977). However, there could be some goals that are important enough to prompt females to discard the immediate interactional goal of 'friendliness' in order to achieve a more important goal pertaining to self-image. That is, it appears that being treated fairly in interpersonal relations is another salient feature, producing more direct and assertive behaviours—females can be quite persistent and assertive when de-escalating relationships, re-asserting equity in dating relationships, and when involved with the goal types of Protect Rights and Enforce Obligation (see below and see Cody *et al.*).

A second variable relevant to the purpose of understanding goal-driven behaviour is self-monitoring. The self-monitoring construct (M. Snyder, 1974, 1979, 1983, 1987; Snyder & Cantor, 1980) is a class variable (Snyder, 1987: 157–69) that segregates persons into one of two types. The high self-monitor is pragmatic and behaves strategically and appropriately to obtain outcomes, regulating his or her expressive self-presentations for the sake of desired public appearances. The low self-monitor is principled and behaves in accordance with his or her own attitudes, feelings, and other inner states. These persons are self-presentational to their own inner audiences.

The social worlds and behaviours of high and low self-monitors have been shown to differ along many dimensions that reflect differences in their self-images. High and low self-monitors differ in several aspects of their social functioning. For example, high self-monitors choose specific friends for specific activities, especially if they are experts in the activity, but low self-monitors are likely to choose the same friends for most of their activities (Snyder, 1987; Snyder, Gangestad & Simpson, 1983). High self-monitors prefer relatively non-exclusive and uncommitted relationships initiated on the basis of physical appearances, but low self-monitors prefer close and exclusive relationships initiated on the basis of interior qualities (Snyder, 1987; Snyder, Berscheid & Glick, 1985; Snyder & Simpson,

1984). Further, high self-monitors respond to image-oriented advertisements, while low self-monitors respond to quality-oriented advertisements (Snyder, 1987; Snyder & De Bono, 1985). Also, high self-monitors become depressed over failures to be seen as capable, but low self-monitors become depressed when they act in ways not consistent with their beliefs and values (Snyder, 1987). In terms of behavioural differences, high self-monitors are more expressive, better able to control and modify self-presentations and expressive behaviours, better able to communicate a wide variety of emotions, and better able to deceive others under certain conditions than are low self-monitors (Elliott, 1979; Lippa, 1976; Miller, deTurck & Kalbfleisch, 1983; Snyder, 1987).

While the social worlds and behaviours of high and low self-monitors have been shown to be strikingly different, conflicting findings have emerged as to whether the social knowledge held by high and low self-monitors is significantly different as well. One body of research indicates that high self-monitors are more attentive to social information and have category systems of social knowledge that contain more breadth and depth than is the case with low self-monitors. Snyder (1974, 1987) reports that high self-monitors are particularly attentive to social information that might guide their expressive self-presentations. They consult information about their peers more often and for longer periods of time (Snyder, 1974), turn to others for guidance more often (Rarick, Soldow & Geizer, 1976), and generate more strategies to induce others to like them, as well as rate these strategies higher in likelihood of use (Bell & Daly, 1984). Snyder (1987: 23) also notes that high self-monitors are particularly skilled at 'reading' others nonverbally.

Lindsey & Greene (1987) tested for differences between high and low self-monitors in six categories of declarative social knowledge including situational attributes, social roles and relationships, physical appearance and artifacts, general mental and behavioural dispositions, thoughts, feelings and mental states, and specific behaviours. They found that although low self-monitors possess more self-oriented than other-oriented representations of social knowledge, the same is also true of high self-monitors. Similarly, Douglas (1983) found that the social knowledge of high and low self-monitoring persons did not differ significantly. However, he also found that high self-monitors generated responses judged more likely to promote friendly interaction even though both high and low self-monitors possessed the same amount of information about the situation.

Another important issue concerns potential differences in how high and low self-monitors use social knowledge to guide them in goal-directed action. Snyder (1979) and Snyder & Cantor (1980) suggested that social knowledge is held in 'person-in-situation' units and that high self-monitors tend to possess more information about prototypical actors in situations while low self-monitors tend to possess more information about themselves in situations. Although the recent research by Lindsey & Greene (1987) casts doubt on this proposal, a study by Neidenthal, Cantor & Kihlstrom (1985) may offer an explanation as to how high and low self-monitors use social information in different ways in order to produce goal-directed behaviour. Neidenthal *et al.* found that high and low self-monitors operating within the constraints of practical goals did not show differences in matching self-prototypes to others. However, persons operating within the constraints of interpersonal goals did show differences. Both high and low self-monitors relied primarily on interpersonal evaluations when they assessed their knowledge of prototypical persons in living situations, but used this information in different ways. The high self-monitor was willing to enter a wide variety of living situations because he or she believed that it was possible to adapt to what was prototypical in the situation. The low self-monitors chose living situations that more closely matched their self-prototype. Apparently, the low self-monitor uses his or her information about a prototypical person in a situation and compares it to his or her own self-prototype. If the match is sufficient, he or she is willing to enter the situation; if not, he or she is more likely to avoid it.

On the basis of this evidence, we investigated which compliance-gaining tactics high and low self-monitors rate as generally characteristic of self, as well as which tactics they would use in pursuit of a variety of different goals, and on which goals high and low self-monitors differ. We anticipated that self-monitoring is not related to practical or task-oriented goals such as Enforce Obligation, Protect Rights, Obtain Permission, or to those involving bureaucrats. We anticipated that high self-monitors would be more likely to possess, and to react more favourably towards, interpersonal goals such as Share Activity (being communal and affiliative), Elicit Support (reflecting a desire to shape another's behaviour by overcoming resistance), Gain Assistance (displaying a dependence on others), Give Advice, and Change Relationship (particularly when initiating a relationship). If the low self-monitoring actor is a principled person, he/she would be unlikely to hold such goals (or to be persistent in pursuing them), because doing so would be perceived as dishonest and manipulative. High self-monitors, however, ought to use information as a model to know how to behave. To explore these issues we asked actors how they would respond to 14 common goal types (Study Two below).

We had several hypotheses and expectations:

1. High self-monitoring actors will rate a wide variety of compliance-gaining tactics as more characteristic of self, particularly the emotionally oriented tactics of Manipulation of Positive Feelings and Manipulation of Negative Feelings, and the relationally based tactics of Referent Influence and Compromise. Given that females are more expressive and communal we expect that as a general rule low self-monitoring males rely least on emotionally oriented and relationally based tactics. We further expect low self-monitors, particularly males, to rate all tactics with the exception of avoidance as significantly less characteristic of the self than high self-monitors.

2. We expect high self-monitors to rate their reactions to Ease of Image, anticipated Persistence, Willingness to Enter, Familiarity and Confidence of Success significantly higher than low self-monitors, but only in goals of an interpersonal nature.

3. If self-monitoring is related to preferences for expressive tactics, then it follows that self-monitoring would be related to how actors de-escalate relationships (reviewed in Baxter, 1982; Banks *et al.*, 1987; Cody, 1982). We anticipate that low self-monitoring actors will rely less on some of the basic, emotional approaches to de-escalation ('positive tone' and 'integrative solutions', see examples below), and would prefer 'emotional detachment' approaches. These expectations were tested in Study Three.

We also had two research questions. First, do high and low self-monitors perceive situations in similar ways and thus have similar bodies of social knowledge? That is, do social actors differ in declarative knowledge of situation perceptions dealing with Intimacy, Resistance, etc.? Given the studies cited above, we anticipate that high and low self-monitoring actors may not differ from one another in terms of content of goal perceptions—rather, high and low self-monitors might differ in terms of tactical preferences or in terms of 'procedural' knowledge.

We further investigate the issue 'What does the self-monitoring scale measure?' Researchers have questioned the unidimensional nature of the original scale (Briggs, Cheek & Buss, 1980; Cappella, 1986; Dillard & Hunter, 1987; Furnham & Capon, 1983; Tobey & Tunnell, 1981; Tunnell, 1980) and Snyder & Gangestad (1986) recently proposed an 18-item scale. For each of the studies presented here we obtained nearly identical factor solutions for Acting Ability, Extroversion and Other-Directedness, and we re-analysed our results using the 18-item inventory. Some studies have found that the use of some sub-scales (i.e. Acting Ability) provide results more strongly related to a criterion variable or outcome than the original 25-item scale, or, at least, equal to the effects of the 25-item scale (Cappella, 1986; Snyder & Gangestad, 1986). If there are different factors and different types of outcomes, how does the self-monitoring scale work both in reflecting levels of expressiveness and in influencing outcomes? Since we study situation perceptions, reactions to goals, frequency of pursuing goals, and preferences for using tactics, we hope to shed some light on why the self-monitoring scale works the way it does.[1]

Overview of studies

Study One examines the links between role relationships, self-monitoring, gender and compliance-gaining. We asked 282 respondents to rate seven general types of social influence methods on the degree to which they were typical or characteristic of self. We also asked them to rate one of eight compliance-gaining situations involving professors, friends or strangers in terms of anticipated persistence, willingness to enter the situation, anticipated success and familiarity. Study Two examines the relationships among 14 goal types, self-monitoring, gender and compliance-gaining. We asked 351 respondents to rate each of 14 compliance-gaining episodes on a variety of scales, and also to report their preferences among eight social influence methods (including avoidance). Rated reactions included ease of image, confidence of success, willingness to enter the situation, anticipated persistence, and familiarity. Study Three examines self-monitoring, gender and social influence as they relate to relational de-escalation. We presented 297 respondents with scenarios in which a romantic partner was either dependent or independent. Six problems were presented: three indicated that the partner was responsible for the change in relational definition, and three indicated the actor was responsible. Respondents rated each scenario in terms of the importance of image, relational and instrumental goals, as well as confidence of success, anticipated persistence and familiarity. Respondents then wrote essays about what they would do in each situation.

Study One: Role Relationships, Self-Monitoring and Gender

Methods and procedures

One hundred and thirty-four males and 148 females completed a questionnaire in which they (a) rated social influence tactics on the degree to which the tactics reflected their characteristic or typical way of influencing others, and (b) rated a compliance-gaining situation in terms of reactions, perceptions, and likelihood of using a set of representative tactics. Reactions involved four variables: Anticipated Persistence, Willingness to Enter the situation (as opposed to avoiding the situation), Anticipated Success, and Familiarity of the situation (alphas ranged from 0.731 to 0.906). Perceptions included Resistance to Persuasion, Rights to Persuade, Target Dominance, Relational Consequences, Intimacy, Personal Benefits, and Situation Apprehension (items are listed in Cody, Woelfel & Jordan, 1983). We also indicated items to measure Homophily; for example, 'The person in this situation and I are NOT very similar to each other'. Influence methods assessed in this study included Direct Requests, Coercive Influence, Referent Influence, Rationality, Compromise, Manipulation of Positive Feelings, and Manipulation of Negative Feelings. (Median alphas were 0.749 for self-characteristic ratings and 0.780 for likelihood of use ratings.)

The specific social influence events we sampled are listed in Table 4.2, reflecting three types of relationships: those with professors, with friends and with strangers. Respondents were randomly assigned to one of the eight events. We looked at the impact of type of relationship, gender and self-monitoring on reactions, perceptions and tactical preferences.

Self-monitoring, gender and characteristic methods of influencing others

Table 4.3 presents the correlations between self-monitoring (and its sub-scales) with ratings of how typical the tactics are to the subjects (a) for females, and (b) for males. For females, self-monitoring total scores only correlated significantly with ratings of Manipulation of Positive Feelings and Negative Feelings. On the other hand, the correspondence between self-monitoring and tactics was more substantial for males: self-monitoring total scores correlated with Referent Influence ($r = 0.360$, $p < 0.001$), Compromise ($r = 0.300$, $p < 0.01$), Manipulation of Positive

TABLE 4.2 *Description of the eight compliance-gaining events (Study One)*

I *Professors*

1. *Letter Situation*

Professor Jenkins is a professor with whom you have taken several classes, and whom you know fairly well. You are going to have some job interviews soon and you want to persuade Professor Jenkins to write a letter of recommendation for your file in the placement centre. What would you say or do?

2. *Grade Scale Situation*

You are enrolled in an important senior-level class in your major subject. Professor Jenkins, a senior faculty member, is a great lecturer, but is very tough when it comes to grading. You know of no one in the class who is expecting a B+ or better. You want to convince Professor Jenkins that his grading scale is too hard and should be changed. What would you say or do?

II *Friends*

3. *Black-Tie Party Situation*

Your fraternity/sorority is having a formal black-tie dinner in two weeks. You want your boy/girlfriend, whom you have dated for over a year, to go with you to this important event. However, his/her parents are arriving in town that particular weekend on their way to Hawaii. He/she wants to spend as much time as possible with his/her parents. You, however, want to convince him/her to go to the formal dinner. What would you say or do?

4. *Date Others Situation*

You have been dating a particular boy/girlfriend for several months. Recently you have begun to feel that things may be a little too serious between the two of you. You want to persuade the boy/girlfriend that there is nothing wrong in occasionally dating another person. What would you say or do?

Feelings ($r = 0.279$, $p < 0.01$), Manipulation of Negative Feelings ($r = 0.232$, $p < 0.01$) and Coercive Influence ($r = 0.155$, $p < 0.05$). For males, then, self-monitoring is significantly associated with emotionally oriented and relationally based tactics (tactics generally related to greater expressiveness), with low self-monitoring males rating the tactics as less characteristic of typical influence methods.

Self-monitoring and reactions

A Relationship (professors, friends and strangers) × Gender × Self-monitoring ($3 × 2 × 2$) MANOVA for reactions (familiarity, persistence, willingness to enter and success) revealed a significant Gender × Self-monitoring interaction effect (approximate $F (4,267) = 3.12$, $p < 0.05$),

TABLE 4.2 *Continued*

---

5. *Confide More Situation*
   You have been dating a particular boy/girlfriend for several months. Recently, you've given the relationship a good deal of thought and you are convinced that you love your boy/girlfriend. However, you also feel that he/she is uncertain about his/her love for you and is reluctant to trust you completely. You want to convince him/her to confide in you more. What would you say or do?

III *Strangers*

6. *Used Car Situation*
   The car you presently own is beginning to require large maintenance costs, and you would like to trade it on a new car. You are interested in getting the best deal possible on your new car. You want Mr Buckley, the car dealer with whom you are only slightly acquainted, to give you a $2,500 trade-in for your new car. What would you say or do?

7. *Use Phone Situation*
   You have just moved into an apartment complex and you do not yet have any of the utilities turned on. You have been waiting all day for the representative of the gas company to arrive, and he/she is late. Thus you will be late for a meeting of your fraternity/sorority. You need to call the house to tell them that you will be late, but your telephone is not yet connected. You go to the neighbours, whom you do not yet know, to ask them to let you use their phone. What would you say or do?

8. *Noisy Neighbour Situation*
   You've just moved into an apartment complex and you've discovered that your neighbour, whom you do not know, has friends over for get-togethers frequently. Usually about 10:30 or 11:00 someone will turn on the stereo and it will get progressively louder as the guests get louder. You want to persuade the neighbour to keep the noise down when it gets late. What would you say or do?

---

defined solely in terms of anticipated success (univariate F (1,270) = 6.92, $p<0.01$). The significant interaction effect was due to the fact that low self-monitoring males expected to be less successful ($M = 5.85$) than high self-monitoring males ($M = 7.08$). There was no difference between females who scored high ($M = 6.33$) or low ($M = 6.42$). (Nine-point scales were used, with 9 indicating high expected success.)

Self-monitoring and perceptions of events

A Relationship × Gender × Self-monitoring (3 × 2 × 2) MANOVA did not reveal any significant effects for actors' perception of events in terms of Dominance, Resistance, etc. However, there were significant

TABLE 4.3 *Correlations of self-monitoring and self-monitoring sub-scales of acting, other-directedness, and extroversion with self-rating of characteristic use of compliance-gaining tactics for females and males (Study One)*

	Self-monitoring (total scale)			Other-Directed-ness	Extrover-sion
	25-item	18-item	Acting		
a. Females					
Referent Influence	0.081	0.053	0.009	0.058	0.04
Negative Manipulation of Feelings	0.140	0.077	0.056	0.245**	0.039
Rationality	0.053	0.087	0.148*	−0.152*	0.125
Compromise	0.082	0.105	0.054	0.032	0.081
Positive Manipulation of Feelings	0.363***	0.313***	0.155*	0.293***	0.229**
Coercive Influence	−0.121	−0.129	−0.147*	−0.028	−0.044
Direct Request	−0.092	−0.124	−0.189*	0.101	−0.011
b. Males					
Referent Influence	0.360***	0.381***	0.241**	0.186*	0.277**
Negative Manipulation of Feelings	0.232**	0.244**	0.120	0.176*	0.158*
Rationality	0.110	0.106	0.053	−0.024	0.116
Compromise	0.300***	0.311***	0.177*	0.139	0.244**
Positive Manipulation of Feelings	0.279**	0.288***	0.213**	0.233**	0.022
Coercive Influence	0.155*	0.169*	0.030	0.144*	0.169*
Direct Request	0.049	0.050	0.020	0.077	−0.077

*$p<0.05$
**$p<0.01$
***$p<0.001$

main effects for acting and extroversion sub-scales (see summary and Table 4.11).

Self-monitoring and tactical preferences

A significant Relationship × Gender interaction effect was obtained (approximate $F(14,528) = 2.375, p <0.01$), defined by Coercive Influence (univariate $F(2,270) = 4.902, p <0.01$) and Manipulation of Positive Feelings ($F(2,270) = 7.654, p <0.001$). Males and females did not differ in likelihood of use of Coercive Influence with professors (males, $M =$

1.78; females, $M = 1.69$) and with friends (males, $M = 2.07$; females, $M = 2.09$). However, males rated coercive influence higher in likelihood of use ($M = 3.31$) when influencing strangers than did females ($M = 2.11$). A breakdown of the ratings for Positive Feelings revealed that males and females have different rules about when one should manipulate the positive feelings of others—females rated the approach higher in preference with strangers ($M = 6.13$) relative to professors or friends ($M = 5.78, 5.07$), but males rated the approach higher in preference with friends ($M = 6.12$) relative to professors and strangers ($M = 5.53, 5.33$).

There was a significant main effect for self-monitoring (approximate $F (7,264) = 4.674$, $p < 0.001$), defined by Referent Influence (univariate $F (1,270) = 16.544$, $p < 0.001$), Negative Feelings ($F (2.270) = 13.221$, $p < 0.001$) and Compromise tactics ($F (2,270) = 5.870$, $p = 0.016$). Low self-monitoring persons rated Referent Influence ($M = 3.57$), Positive Feelings ($M = 5.17$), Compromise ($M = 4.51$) and Negative Feelings ($M = 2.49$) lower in preference than did high self-monitors ($Ms = 4.29, 6.00, 5.03$ and 3.28, respectively). As expected, low self-monitors relied less on emotionally oriented and relationally based approaches to social influence.

Study Two: Goal Types, Self-Monitoring and Gender

Methods and procedures

Three hundred and fifty-one respondents completed a questionnaire that provided 14 compliance-gaining episodes involving different motives and relationships (see Table 4.4). The respondents were required to indicate their reactions to each goal type and to indicate their preferences for using a representative set of social influence methods. We did not include the less frequently pursued goals of Change Opinion and Change Ownership.

The five reactions were Ease of Image ('This situation is easy to imagine'), Confidence of Success ('I would be very confident of my success in persuading the other(s) in this situation'), Willingness to Enter ('I would probably actively enter this situation'), Anticipated Persistence ('If the person in this situation first said no to my request, I would probably be very persistent; that is, I'd continue to persuade him/her') and Familiarity ('I have often experienced a situation like this one'). Seven general modes of influence were assessed (and respondents were also asked to indicate the extent to which they would prefer to avoid using any attempts—i.e. to let the issue simply resolve itself, etc.): Direct Request ('Without going into details, I'd simply ask, "Can you do it?" I wouldn't feel obliged to give any reasons or supporting arguments for my request'); Positive Feelings ('I'd put on my happy face and act particularly nice when trying to persuade him/her. I'd get him/her in the "right frame of mind" before asking'); Compromise ('I would suggest that we talk over some compromise, and work something out'); Negative Feelings ('I would show how disappointed I was in him/her. I'd act sad, hurt and/or dejected when trying to influence him/her to make him/her feel guilty'); Rationality ('I would explain the reasons why I wanted the person(s) to agree with my request'); Coercive Influence ('I would threaten to punish the person(s) if they did not go along with my request'); Referent Influence ('I would appeal to the person(s) by referring to the nature of our relationship, and our sense of togetherness and mutual liking'); and Avoidance ('I probably wouldn't do anything about persuading the person(s) in this situation. I'd drop the matter and just hope that the person(s) would come around'). Additional details concerning methods and reliabilities can be found in Canary, Cody & Marston (1986). We are only interested here in reporting results dealing with self-monitoring.

Self-monitoring, gender and characteristic methods of influence

The impact of self-monitoring on general tactical preferences was assessed by summing ratings across goal types and correlating the personality measures with the summed ratings. Table 4.5 presents the correlations (a) for females, and (b) for males. For females, self-monitoring total scores were positively correlated with Referent Influence ($r = 0.361$, $p < 0.001$), Compromise ($r = 0.185$, $p < 0.01$), Direct Request ($r = 0.200$, $p < 0.01$), Coercive Influence ($r = 0.252$, $p < 0.001$), Manipulation of Negative Feelings ($r = 0.256$, $p < 0.001$), and Manipulation of Positive Feelings ($r = 0.230$, $p < 0.001$), but total self-monitoring is negatively correlated with Avoidance ($r = -0.112$, $p < 0.05$). High self-monitoring total scores for men correlated with the same types of tactics: Referent Influence ($r = 0.363$, $p < 0.001$); Compromise ($r = 0.261$, $p < 0.01$); Direct Request ($r = 0.191$, $p < 0.05$); Coercive Influence ($r = 0.182$, $p < 0.05$); Manipulation of Negative Feelings ($r = 0.361$, $p < 0.001$); and Manipulation of Positive Feelings ($r = 0.454$, $p < 0.001$). Thus, both male and female high self-monitors indicated that the use of a wide variety of tactics is characteristic or typical across goal types; however, self-monitoring was not as strongly associated with 'avoidance' as we had

TABLE 4.4 *Fourteen goal types and exemplars (Study Two)*

Routine Activities—Friends

Please imagine the following situation: *You want to have a routine night out with your friends.*

Example: You and your friends haven't gone out for a night on the town in some time and you want to persuade them into going with you this Friday evening.

Bureaucracy

Please imagine the following situation: *You want to persuade a person in authority or in a bureaucracy to do something.*

Example: On a recent trip back to school from a vacation, you were going 'about' 60mph when you were stopped by a police officer for speeding. You want to persuade the officer not to give you a ticket.

Advice-Giving—Friend

Please imagine the following situation: *You are giving advice to someone about whom you care.*

Example: A close friend of yours at college has been spending a good deal of time on his/her non-academic activities and has neglected his/her grades. You want to persuade him/her to study more and, generally speaking, to set some career goals.

Relational De-escalation

Please imagine the following situation: *You want to break off a dating relationship with a person you have dated for a few months.*

Example: While you first liked dating a particular person, you now realise that the two of you really do not have a lot in common. You want to persuade him/her that you only want to be friends, nothing more.

Assistance—Acquaintance

Please imagine the following situation: *You want to persuade an acquaintance to help you do something.*

Example: You find that the math homework you need to have finished for class each period absorbs a good deal of your time—time that you really do not have since you started working three days a week. You want to persuade someone you know in class to help you with the homework.

Enforce Obligation

Please imagine the following situation: *You want to persuade a person to fulfil his/her obligation to you.*

Example: You have lived in your apartment complex for some months. One Saturday morning you woke up late and found the kitchen plumbing dripping very badly. You want to persuade the landlord to fix the plumbing promptly.

Relational Initiation

Please imagine the following situation: *You want to initiate a relationship with a person of the opposite sex or to increase the intimacy in a relationship.*

Example: There is a person of the opposite sex in your Mass Communication class whom you would like to know better. You run into him/her after class and

Cont'd

TABLE 4.4 *Continued*

start a conversation. You want to persuade him/her to get together again and get to know each other.

Gain Assistance—Professor
Please imagine the following situation: *You want a professor to do you a special favour.*
Example: You find that one of the classes you desperately need to enrol in has been closed out. You want to persuade the professor into letting you enrol in this class.

Third Party (Elicit Support)
Please imagine the following situation: *You want to persuade an acquaintance to help a third party.*
Example: You believe that a friend of yours is drinking (alcoholic beverages) too much, and you also believe that the drinking problem has become quite apparent to many people over the last several weeks. You want to persuade this person's closest friend to talk about the problem with him/her so that he/she might stop drinking.

Advice-Giving—Parents
Please imagine the following situation: *You want to give advice to your parents about some long-term goal of theirs.*
Example: On a visit home recently you see that your father looks tired and overworked. You want to persuade him to take time off from work and find something relaxing to do.

Relational Escalation
Please imagine the following situation: *You want to include someone special to you into your social world by including him/her in activities with your friends and family.*
Example: You have dated your boyfriend/girlfriend for some time and the two of you really get along well. You want to persuade him/her into coming home for the weekend to meet your relatives.

Annoyances (Protect Right)
Please imagine the following situation: *You want to persuade someone from engaging in an annoying habit.*
Example: Your neighbour frequently has friends over for small parties. Usually, about 10:30 or 11:00 at night someone will turn on the stereo, and it will get louder as the guests get louder. You want to persuade your neighbour to keep the noise down when it gets late.

Assistance—Stranger
Please imagine the following situation: *You want a stranger to do a special favour for you.*
Example: For a social science class that you are taking, you (and your group members) need to have a group of students participate in your experiment. The project counts as a large percentage of your grade. You want to persuade a group of people in the cafeteria to participate in your project.

Cont'd

TABLE 4.4 *Continued*

Assistance—Parents
   Please imagine the following situation: *You want to gain permission from your parents to do something.*
   Example: You want to persuade your parents to send (or loan) you more money for college.

Source: Canary, Cody & Marston (1986).

expected (although self-monitoring was related to other reactions; see below).

Self-monitoring, gender, goals, tactical preferences and reactions

The linear effects reflected in the correlations in Table 4.5 average over potential interactions between self-monitoring and goals. Two repeated measures ANOVAs, one for reactions and one for tactical preferences, were computed to assess the multivariate tests of significance. There were significant Goal Types × Self-Monitoring interactions or Goal Types × Self-Monitoring × Gender interactions:

1. Self-monitoring was not significantly associated with ratings of Avoidance. There were significant main effects only in the analyses of Easy to Imagine, Anticipated Persistence, Direct Requests, Compromise, Manipulation of Negative Feelings, Coercive Influence and Referent Influence. Correlations were 0.169, 0.292, 0.225, 0.185, 0.297, 0.268 and 0.357, respectively.
2. There were significant Goal Types × Self-Monitoring interactions for Confidence of Success (F (13,4485) = 2.27, $p < 0.01$), Familiarity (F (13,4485) = 1.96, $p < 0.05$), and Willingness to Enter (F (13,4485) = 1.73, $p < 0.05$). Means for these three reactions are listed in Table 4.6. (We set alpha at 0.01 when testing differences between pairs of means.) As a general rule, high self-monitors rated Confidence of Success, Willingness to Enter and Familiarity significantly higher than low self-monitors in five of the goal types: Activity (friend), Assistance (friend, stranger), Initiate Relationship, and Bureaucracy.
3. There was a significant Gender × Self-Monitoring interaction effect for Manipulation of Positive Feelings (F (1,345) = 4.59, $p < 0.05$). Females rated Positive Feelings as a popular tactic at both high and low levels of self-monitoring (Ms = 2.45, 2.85),

TABLE 4.5 *Correlations of self-monitoring and self-monitoring sub-scales of acting, other-directedness, and extroversion with tactical preference across goal types for females and males (Study Two)*

	Self-monitoring (total scale)		Acting	Other-Directed-ness	Extro-version
	25-item	18-item			
a. Females					
Referent Influence	0.361***	0.366***	0.339***	0.201***	0.194***
Negative Manipulation of Feelings	0.256***	0.196***	0.217**	0.184**	0.038
Rationality	0.086	0.159*	0.100	−0.070	0.215**
Compromise	0.185**	0.194**	0.145*	0.100	0.125*
Positive Manipulation of Feelings	0.230***	0.242***	0.160**	0.066	0.214**
Coercive Influence	0.252***	0.178*	0.290***	0.279***	−0.054
Direct Request	0.200**	0.145*	0.277***	0.065	0.052
Avoidance	−0.112*	−0.165*	−0.084	0.012	−0.177*
b. Males					
Referent Influence	0.363***	0.250***	0.357***	0.276**	0.046
Negative Manipulation of Feelings	0.371***	0.244***	0.463***	0.378***	0.074
Rationality	0.062	0.071	−0.024	−0.058	0.171*
Compromise	0.261**	0.218**	0.275**	0.205*	0.030
Positive Manipulation of Feelings	0.454***	0.390**	0.340***	0.449***	0.112
Coercive Influence	0.182*	0.032	0.343***	0.269**	−0.229**
Direct Request	0.191*	0.044	0.303***	0.291**	−0.207*
Avoidance	−0.042	−0.164*	0.161*	0.200*	−0.419***

*$p<0.05$
**$p<0.01$
***$p<0.001$

while low self-monitoring males rated Positive Feelings lower in preference ($M = 3.76$) than high self-monitoring males ($M = 2.83$).

4. There was a significant Goal Types × Self-Monitoring × Gender interaction for Rationality ($F (13,4485) = 2.10$, $p<0.05$). In one event, Give Advice (friend), females rated Rationality levels high in preference at both high ($M = 1.50$) and low ($M = 1.66$) levels of self-monitoring, while low self-monitoring males rated Rationality lower in preference ($M = 2.51$) than high self-monitoring males ($M = 1.74$).

TABLE 4.6 *Mean differences between high and low self-monitors by types of events (Study Two)*

Events	Confidence of success		Willingness to enter		Familiarity	
	High S–M	Low S–M	High S–M	Low S–M	High S–M	Low S–M
Activity—friend	1.684	2.178	1.633	2.109	2.469	2.914
Assistance—friend	2.277	2.931	2.339	2.885	3.588	4.207
Assistance—stranger	2.554	3.167	2.633	3.161	4.305	4.776*
Initiate Relationship	2.582	3.109	2.373	3.328	3.209	4.149
Bureaucracy	3.333	4.132	2.780	3.425	3.876	4.667
Give Advice—parent	3.130	3.379*	2.390	2.592*	3.853	4.052*
Permission—parent	2.164	2.184*	2.169	2.328*	2.893	2.966*
Give Advice—friend	2.554	2.879*	2.266	2.546*	3.073	3.552*
De-escalation	2.554	2.701*	2.503	2.730*	2.814	3.276*
Escalation	1.842	2.000*	1.757	1.919*	3.051	3.379*
Obligation	1.898	2.144*	1.780	1.948*	3.701	3.828*
Assistance—professor	2.322	2.632*	1.949	2.155*	2.588	3.506
Elicit Support (third party)	2.633	2.994*	2.661	2.954*	4.299	4.517*
Habits (protect rights)	2.593	2.914*	2.616	2.764*	3.588	3.695

*Denotes means, within rows, that are *not* significantly different from each other, for each dependent variable, at alpha < 0.01.

Study Three: Relational De-escalation, Self-Monitoring and Gender

Methods and procedures

One hundred and twenty-four males and 173 females completed a survey that provided them with a hypothetical scenario of a relational problem, and which asked them first, to indicate their reactions to the problem and, second, had them write an essay concerning what they would do in the given situation. These essays were coded into typologies of relational de-escalation tactics. Two variables were manipulated when constructing the scenarios: Dependence/Independence in the relationship, and Partner/Actor Attribution of Responsibility for the relational problem. First, the level of intimacy in the relationship was standardised by asking all respondents to imagine they were in a 6-month-old romantic relationship in which 'the two of you have disclosed personal and intimate information to one another, you have seen each other on a regular basis and have met each other's closest friends and family members'. We then described the relational partner as one who is either *dependent* on the actor, or *independent*. Attribution of responsibility was manipulated by indicating that one of six specific problems surfaced in the relationship—three occurrences in which the *partner is perceived as responsible for the problem*, and three in which the *actor is likely to accept responsibility for the change* (see Table 4.7, and Braaten, 1987).

We were interested in exploring relational de-escalation in depth, as partners often have incompatible goals in this type of interaction. How actors attain such discrepant goals without violating the expectations and sensitivities of their partners affects perceptions of the communication event and subsequent relational characteristics and satisfaction (Canary & Cupach, in press; Canary & Spitzberg, 1987; Gottmann, 1982). Two factors that can affect the way interpersonal problems are handled are relational dependence and attribution of responsibility. While dependency has been found to lead to integrative/co-operative tactics (Williamson & Fitzpatrick, 1985) it is unclear if having an independent as opposed to a dependent partner would affect the manner in which the actor perceives and deals with a relational problem. Responsibility attributions (i.e. whether the actor or partner is perceived as the primary source of the problem) are related to integrative behaviours when the actor attributes responsibility to the self and to distributive behaviours when the actor attributes responsibility to the partner (Sillars, 1980a, 1980b).

As in the other studies, respondents rated the scenarios in terms of Confidence of Success (five items, alpha = 0.694); Anticipated Persistence (four items, alpha = 0.778); and Familiarity (four items, alpha = 0.888). In this particular study we also had respondents rate the scenarios in terms of the personal importance of three *interactional* goals offered by Clark & Delia (1979). Clark and Delia argue that three types of interactional goals might be pursued in any communication event: Image Maintenance, Relational Maintenance and Instrumental goals. In this study four items were used to measure the importance of Image Maintenance goals (alpha = 0.823; sample item, 'I would be very concerned about the image I presented to the partner in this situation'). Five items were used to measure the importance of Relational Maintenance concerns (alpha = 0.883; sample item, 'I would want to stay friends with the partner in the future'). Four items were used to measure task or instrumental goals (alpha = 0.753; sample item, 'I would be highly motivated to change this situation as soon as possible').

The essays were coded into four general message types; three involved relevant sub-categories. Table 4.8 presents samples of essays

TABLE 4.7 *Descriptions of dependent and independent partner and relational problems in which either partner or actor is responsible (Study Three)*

Dependent
You realise that the dating partner is *not* an independent type of person. He (she) depends on you for advice and opinions. The partner almost always asks for your ideas before making decisions, and hardly ever makes unilateral decisions—that is, the partner hardly ever makes decisions about activities involving you without first talking it over with you. ($M = 3.58$)a*

Independent
You realise that the dating partner is an *independent* type of person. He (she) is *not* dependent on you for advice and opinions. The partner almost never asks for your ideas before making decisions, and the partner will very often make unilateral decisions—that is, the partner will make decisions about activities involving you *without* first talking it over with you. ($M = 6.29$)b*

Partner Responsible
Recently you have become aware of a problem. While things went smoothly when you were first getting acquainted, you realise that the partner now *takes you for granted*. When you first dated, you did fun, spontaneous, things together. Then, the partner started to take things for granted in the relationship and you realised that you were putting more into the relationship than you were getting out of it—you called him/her more than he/she called you, you initiated more things, you gave in to his/her desires more than they did, you helped your partner more than she/he helped you, etc. Romance slipped away. You talked to the partner once about this, and the partner promised to do more. However, the promise lasted only a week or so. Now you are right back to where you were before, *doing all the work and being taken for granted*. ($M = 6.03$)a**

Recently, you have become aware of a problem. While things went smoothly when you were getting acquainted you realise that the dating partner has become increasingly *possessive* of you over the last several months. He/she is very demanding and jealous. The partner wants more and more out of you, wants to know whom you see during the day, and wants you to accede to his/her wants. You do not particularly like to feel *suffocated*. ($M = 6.28$)a**

Recently, you have become aware of a problem. More than one of your friends has told you that the partner has cheated on you. That is, the partner has apparently been seeing another boy (girl) friend on the side for some time. Recently, this other boy (girl) friend of your partner's has revealed their affair to others. ($M = 6.43$)a**

Actor Responsible
Recently, a problem has come up in this relationship. Your partner, after graduation, is planning to take an excellent job offer in town. You, however, have received your best job offer in a town east of here—a job offer that you always wanted to receive. You know your friend, while liking you, wants to stay in town with parents, family and friends. ($M = 5.09$)b**

Continued

TABLE 4.7 *Continued*

Recently, you have become aware of a problem. You realise that you actually do not *love* the partner. That is, when you started dating the two of you did fun, spontaneous, things together. Now, however, things have become more serious than you'd like, and you must admit that you probably let it get too serious. You still like the partner, you have no complaints about the relationship—you simply feel that you are changing, your feelings are changing, and you do not feel as strongly about this partner as you did once. ($M = 5.05$)b**

Recently, you have become aware of a problem. You ran into an old flame at a party recently, and the old flame made it quite obvious that he/she wanted the two of you to get back together. Further, the idea of getting back together with this 'old flame' is very appealing to you. ($M = 5.02$)b**

---

*Rated on a 9-point scale where 1 = Extremely Dependent and 9 = Extremely Independent; a, b significantly differ at $p<0.05$
**Rated on a 9-point scale where 1 = Partner highly responsible and 9 = Actor extremely responsible; a, b significantly differ at $p<0.05$

representing each message type. First, *Emotional Detachment* approaches ($N = 40$) were characterised by a withdrawal of commitment to the relationship and a withdrawal of caring about the partner. All expressions of concern for the partner's needs or concerns were absent from these approaches, but the actors did not explicitly break off the relationship or try to solve a problem. Instead actors adopted a 'wait and see how it turns out' attitude.

De-escalation approaches ($N = 82$) involved the argument that the partner and the actor ought to see less of each other, see other people or generally become less intimate, involved, and committed (see Cody, 1982; Banks *et al.*, 1987). Instances of De-escalation could be distinguished into two relevant sub-categories: Positive Tone and Appeals to Independence. Positive Tone essays expressed a concern for the feelings of the partner and attempted to minimise hurt and rejection. Appeals to Independence essays reported attempts by the actor to explain the break-up as a temporary condition by arguing that the two were too young, not settled sufficiently, etc., to continue to have a relationship as serious as the one that had developed.

Open Discussion tactics were used when the actor proposed having non-emotional discussions with the partner in the hope of solving the problem or establishing a compromise. With the first sub-category of tactic, Integrative Solutions, actors sought to include the partner in an open discussion in determining a course of action which could maintain and/or strengthen the relationship; that is, actors expressed genuine interest in solving the problem and maintaining intimacy (if not, in several cases, in increasing intimacy). A second group of Open Discussion essays was not as integrative—the sub-category Demand Change. Integrative Solutions reflected a motivation on the part of the actor to work together, with the partner equally inclined to compromise to solve the problem. In the Demand Change sub-category actors talked about the problematic behaviour of the partner (or external pressure) and attempted to talk about how the pair of them (or the partner solely) could be effective in changing the partner. The actor did not express interest in giving in for the good of the relationship (see examples in Table 4.8).

Terminate approaches are ones in which the actor would move towards ending the relationship by severing the commitment to it completely. Actors in the Justification sub-category explained their reasons why the two partners should not date any more. An Assertive/ Ultimatum approach conveyed the message that the actor was extremely displeased with the target and that there would be no future for the relationship, the actor forcing the partner to concede that the partner was blameworthy. The assertive tactics coded here were similar to the 'negative identity management' tactics coded in Cody (1982).

Interaction goals

MANOVA results revealed a significant Gender × Self-Monitoring interaction effect (approximate $F(3,279) = 2.65$, $p<0.05$) (due to difference in Image Maintenance concerns: univariate $F(1,281) = 4.58$, $p<0.05$). For females, concern over one's image was not affected by levels of self-monitoring ($M = 2.50$, high self-monitoring; $M = 2.71$, low self-monitoring). For males, low self-monitoring respondents rated image concerns lower in preference ($M = 3.15$) than did high self-monitoring respondents ($M = 2.25$).

Reactions

There was a significant interaction effect for Dependent/Independent × Self-Monitoring (approximate $F(3,279) = 3.66$, $p<0.05$), due to ratings of Confidence (univariate $F(1,281) = 5.27$, $p<0.05$) and Persistence ($F(1,281) = 9.72$, $p<0.01$), and there was a significant Attribution × Dependent/Independent × Gender × Self-Monitoring interaction effect

TABLE 4.8 *Example of essays for each message category (Study Three)*

Open Discussion Messages (N = 100)

Integrative Solution (N = 45)

'I would begin by getting the two of us to sit down and discuss matters in as open and unemotional an environment as could possibly be achieved. I would ask my partner how she felt about our situation and how she would propose to deal with it. At the same time I would express my view of the situation and how I would handle it. Ideally the two of us could reach a compromise that would benefit the two of us.'

Demand Change (N = 55)

'I would sit down and tell them as nicely as possible "to get a backbone", to learn to make their own decisions without the help of someone else, because there might not always be someone there to ask.'

'About being possessive and jealous, I'd tell my partner that we don't own each other and there are some things that we should keep to ourselves because if we display too much to each other, it doesn't make up a healthy relationship. I would tell them that I like my space and I need it in all my relationships because I don't like to feel suffocated.'

De-escalation Messages (N = 82)

Appeal to Independence (N = 45)

'I would try to get out of the relationship. I would tell him that we have become too dependent on each other. And, that both of us need room to explore new things—get out and meet new people. That we both need variety and a change. However, I would still like to see him and still be friends. I would not want it to seem as though I was dropping him for my "old flame".'

Positive Tone (N = 37)

'In this situation I would be inclined to try to end the relationship. I think I would try to explain to my partner that I need some time away from them. Explain that I need more "space" and time to myself. I would be nice. I tell the partner that I do like them and point out good qualities I know and like about them. And how they are an important part of my life. I might try to just slow down the amount of time we spend together by seeing them less and less. I might talk to them about being too serious for this stage in my life, but I still like him. I think the best I could do to help him would be to say good things about him also and say that maybe he needs a break from me also.'

Termination Messages (N = 92)

Assertive/Ultimatum (N = 38)

'I would tell the partner that if she didn't lay off and give me more space, I would end our relationship. I would tell her that I was feeling suffocated and if you don't trust me and always have to know where I am, our relationship stinks.'

Cont'd

TABLE 4.8 *Continued*

Justification ($N = 54$)

'I would explain to her that I felt this sort of one-sided relationship is not fair, nor is it fulfilling. Although her dependence upon me would make me afraid for her if our relationship ended, I think I would be left with no other choice. I would simply tell her that I can no longer go on giving and not receiving and I would tell her to begin seeing other people as I would do the same.'

Emotionally Detached ($N = 40$)

'I would try and tell the partner my feelings. It is usually a mutual feeling. The guy may be acting the way he is on purpose so as to discourage you. I would definitely talk about the problem but I know from experience that you can't change someone. Rather than hurting someone's feelings I would probably let the relationship die out by keeping busy with other things.'

(appproximate $F (3,279) = 3.95$, $p<0.01$) due to ratings of Confidence (univariate $F (1,281) = 9.87$, $p<0.01$) and Persistence (univariate $F (1,281) = 5.50$, $p<0.05$).

Tables 4.9 and 4.10 present the means for confidence and persistence. Low self-monitoring males generally anticipated less confidence than high self-monitoring males, and rated themselves as least confident in episodes involving independent partners who were responsible for relational problems (Table 4.9). The same basic pattern was obtained for ratings of anticipated persistence. Conversely, low self-monitoring males anticipated feeling most confident and persistent when they felt responsible and when the target was independent. The 'principled and honest' low self-monitoring male, then, would be more confident disengaging from a relationship in which he experienced a change in feelings and desires, and in which the

TABLE 4.9. *Mean ratings of confidence of success by gender, self-monitoring, responsibility and partner dependence/independence (Study Three)*

| | Males | | Females | |
	Partner Responsible	Actor Responsible	Partner Responsible	Actor Responsible
High self-monitoring:				
Partner dependent	3.51	3.38	3.36	3.52
Partner independent	3.75	4.86	4.71	4.72
Low self-monitoring:				
Partner dependent	4.15	4.00	4.76	3.87
Partner independent	5.51	3.93	4.28	4.90

partner was independent (thus making it easier to disengage, relative to the dependent partner) (*M*s are 3.93, confidence; and 3.76, persistence). On the other hand, high self-monitoring males projected greater confidence when the partner was dependent on the actor (presumably increasing the actor's power relative to an independent partner); persistence was also more likely (*M*s = 4.24 and 3.05) in the partner-dependent conditions (as well as in the partner dependent/partner responsible condition, see Table 4.10). As opposed to the low self-monitor, high self-monitoring males anticipated least confidence in partner independent/actor responsible relationships (*M* = 4.86; *M* = 4.94 for persistence). In contexts such as these the high self-monitoring male would probably let the relationship 'die off', as some self-monitors rely on Emotional Detachment when they accept responsibility (see below); the self-monitor might find it easier to avoid communicating his desires if the relationship can simply deteriorate and end of its own inertia.

High self-monitoring females also rated episodes involving dependent partners higher in perceived self-confidence and in anticipated persistence, and they rated persistence extremely low in likelihood when the partner was independent and responsible (again, a combination of features which allows the actor to let relationships die of their own accord). Low self-monitoring females generally rated confidence and persistence as more probable when they accepted responsibility for the relational change (but see means in Tables 4.9 and 4.10), and rated persistence extremely unlikely in partner dependent/partner responsible condition. We found (see below) that low self-monitoring actors are likely to adopt Emotional Detachment approaches to relational disengagement when the partner was responsible for problems—and it may be the case that when the

TABLE 4.10. *Mean ratings of persistence by gender, self-monitoring, responsibility and partner dependence/independence (Study Three)*

	Males		Females	
	Partner responsible	*Actor responsible*	*Partner responsible*	*Actor responsible*
High self-monitoring:				
Partner dependent	4.24	3.05	3.98	3.50
Partner independent	4.17	4.94	5.64	4.81
Low self-monitoring:				
Partner dependent	5.27	4.69	6.21	4.26
Partner independent	5.92	3.76	5.13	4.32

partner is responsible low self-monitoring actors might let the relationship slide and adopt a wait-and-see attitude (reduce emotional commitment, and see if the relationship ultimately survives). Although it is an obvious oversimplification of four-way interactions, we conclude that the results partially reflect the motives of the 'principled and honest' low self-monitor: when the low self-monitoring person accepts responsibility for relational changes, he or she is more likely to be persistent and display confidence than when the partner is perceived as responsible (except confidence ratings for females, see Table 4.9). High self-monitoring persons were confident and persistent when their partners were dependent on them.

De-escalation tactics

We anticipated that low self-monitoring actors would use more Emotional Detachment approaches, fewer De-escalation messages (especially Positive Tone), and fewer Open Discussion approaches (especially Integrative Solutions). Logic analyses and multi-table analyses were conducted to assess the impact of self-monitoring on de-escalation tactics. Two significant effects were obtained dealing with self-monitoring. First, there was a significant Attribution of Responsibility × Self-Monitoring Interaction for Emotional Detachment ($\chi^2(1) = 5.10, p<0.05$). When the partner was responsible, low self-monitoring respondents relied more on Emotional Detachment (19%) than did the high self-monitoring respondents (8%). On the other hand, when the actor accepted responsibility for relational changes, high self-monitoring persons relied more on Emotional Detachment (17%) than did low self-monitors (10%). Low self-monitors apparently adopt a more 'powerless' approach by withdrawing emotional feelings when the partner causes problems, but the high self-monitors 'cooled' the relationship when they wanted to change relational definitions.

Self-monitoring was not associated with use of Positive Tone, or with Integrative Solutions. However, self-monitoring was related significantly to the Demand Change sub-category of Open Discussion; there was a significant Gender × Self-Monitoring interaction ($\chi^2 (1) = 3.69, p<0.05$). Females used Demand Change equally at both high (18%) and low (20%) levels of self-monitoring; male high self-monitors relied on this approach more (26%) than did low self-monitoring males (10%). Male high self-monitors expressed a greater desire to persuade the partner to change, relative to other types of actors. Within this framework, high self-monitoring males expressed a greater desire to demand changes in the partner than other types of respondents, and preferred to become emotionally detached from relationships they wanted to change. Low self-monitoring persons became more emotionally detached if their partners caused a problem and low self-monitoring males were least likely to demand changes in their partners.

Summary of Results, and Comparison of Results using Sub-scales

Table 4.11 presents a summary of the results of our three studies, along with summaries of analyses using each sub-scale of the self-monitoring measure. We had hypothesised that high self-monitors would rely on more expressive methods of influence, and we found that (male) high self-monitors in Study One did in fact rate Manipulation of Positive Feelings, Negative Feelings, Referent Influence and Compromise as more characteristic of their typical ways of influencing others (there was also a weaker, yet still significant, correlation for Coercive Influence). In Study Two we summed ratings across goal types and found, for both males and females, that self-monitoring was associated with the same types of influence methods: Referent, Negative Feelings, Positive Feelings, Compromises, and, to a lesser extent, Direct Request and Coercion. In Study Three self-monitoring was not related (as expected) to Positive Tone and Integrative Solutions; however, high and low self-monitors used Emotional Detachment in different ways, and the 'principled and honest' low self-monitor male rarely used the Demand Change form of de-escalation/conflict resolution. Each study, then, indicated that low self-monitoring actors or low self-monitoring *male* actors preferred not to use expressive tactics or to pressure others via manipulation of feelings, relationally oriented messages, coercion, or changing dating partners. In short, low self-monitors declined to manipulate others.

We further expected low self-monitors to react differently from high self-monitors when pursuing interpersonal (as opposed to practical) goals. The results of Study One merely indicated that low self-monitoring males expected to be less successful than other types of actors. Study Two indicated that high self-monitors considered goals easier to imagine and anticipated greater persistence across all types of sampled goals, and high self-monitors rated anticipated success, willingness to enter and familiarity higher in several goals involving interpersonal motives (activities, assistance and relational initiations), as well as an event involving a bureaucrat (in this case, a police officer). (Perhaps the 'principled and honest' low self-monitoring person would not attempt to persuade a police officer if the low self-monitor accepted responsibility for speeding.) In Study Three we found that low self-monitoring males were less concerned with image than other actors, and we found that high self-monitors generally rated confidence and persistence higher when dating partners were dependent (but see above); low self-monitors rated confidence and persistence higher when they accepted responsibility for relational changes.

We raised two questions: (1) Is self-monitoring related to perceptions of events (or is it related primarily to tactical preferences)?; and (2) How do results compare if we rely on the sub-scales of the self-monitoring scale? First, when we rely on the overall self-monitoring measure, it appears that high and low self-monitors do not differ from one another in terms of perceptions of situations. Instead, it is probable that self-monitoring is related to procedural knowledge—in particular, expressive and manipulative behaviours in the pursuit of interpersonal goals. The supplemental analysis using the 18-item inventory (Snyder & Gangestad, 1986) also indicated no significant relationships to situation perceptions, and the same was obtained for Other-Directedness. However, Acting Ability was significantly related to higher ratings of Intimacy, higher ratings of Homophily, lower ratings of Target Dominance and lower ratings of Situation Apprehension; those actors who claim to have acting ability rated themselves as more similar to the targets they influenced and perceived less anxiety about influencing others. Extroversion was also weakly, but significantly, associated with Apprehension ($r = 0.243$), Dominance ($r = 0.166$) and Rights to Influence ($r = 0.161$). Both these sub-scales, however, were more strongly associated with other outcomes (reactions, tactical preferences; see below and Table 4.11).

Snyder & Gangestad (1986) argued that an 18-item measure can adequately assess the self-monitoring construct. We found that the 18-item measure and the 25-item measure produced extremely similar results; in fact, in Study One the correlations are virtually identical. Also, in Study Three, the 18-item measure replicated the interaction effect for Emotional Detachment (high self-monitors used the tactic more when accepting responsibility (14%) than when attributing responsibility to the partner (8%), whereas the low self-monitor employed the tactic differently: self-responsible, 17%; other-responsible, 13%). The sizes of some correlations in Study Two (Table 4.5) changed when employing the 18-item inventory, but all results generally supported the hypotheses concerning expressiveness. The 18-item measure did produce slightly higher alpha coefficients (0.706, 0.728, 0.771) than the 25-item measure (0.690, 0.712, 0.754). Thus, we conclude that the 18-item measure is a viable measure of a *general* self-monitoring construct.

TABLE 4.11 *Summary of results of self-monitoring scale and its subcomponents*

Analysis	Self-Monitoring (25 items)	Acting Ability	Other-Directedness	Extroversion
Study One: Characteristic influence methods	Self-monitoring was related to Referent Influence, Compromise, Positive & Negative Feelings and Coercion (primarily true for males).	Acting ability was related to Positive Feelings for both sexes: for males and females, acting ability was weakly associated with different tactics.	Similar pattern as for acting ability—correlations weaker than relying on total self-monitoring score.	For females, extroversion correlated significantly with Positive Feelings. Weak correlations obtained for males, with four tactics (see Table 4.1).
Study One: Reactions	Low self-monitoring males expected themselves to be less successful than other actors.	High scorers on acting ability rated events as more Familiar, and rated Confidence higher, anticipated Persistence higher, and Willingness to Enter events higher than low scorers.	Other-directedness was not related to reactions.	Extroversion was weakly associated with anticipated Persistence.
Study One: Perceptions	Self-monitoring was not related to Situation Perceptions.	High scorers rated themselves as more similar to their targets (high Homophily, higher levels of Intimacy, lower ratings of Target Intimacy) than low scorers.	Other-directedness was not related to Situation Perceptions.	High scorers on extroversion rated Situation Apprehension lower, Target Dominance lower, and Rights to Persuade higher than introverts.

Study One: Strategy preferences (likelihood of use)	Low self-monitors relied less on Compromise, Referent Influence, Positive Feelings, and Negative Feelings across role relationships.	Acting ability was not related to ratings of preference.	Other-directedness was related to Referent Influence and to Positive and Negative Feelings (replicating, in part, the findings for self-monitoring total score).	Extroversion was related to Rationality—extroverts relied on rationality more than introverts.
Study Two: Characteristic methods of influence	For both males and females, self-monitoring correlated with emotionally based and relationally oriented methods.	Similar pattern of results for self-monitoring were obtained (see Table 4.2.).	For male actors, same pattern of results as acting ability (see Table 4.2.). For females, correlations obtained for three methods (see Table 4.2.)	Extroversion correlated with Avoidance and Rationality for both males and females; different pattern obtained due to gender (see Table 4.2.). High scorers rated Anticipated Persistence Willingness to Enter, and anticipated Persistence higher in probability than did Introverts.
Study Two: Reactions	Self-monitoring correlated with Ease of Image, and Anticipated Success and Willingness to Enter (see Table 4.3.).	High scorers on acting ability rated all goals higher in Familiarity than low scorers; high in reactions (see Table 4.6.); females scoring low on acting rated the Bureaucrat event as harder to imagine than males; males scoring low on acting rated Elicit Support goal harder to imagine.	Other-directedness was related to Familiarity. Also, male low scorers rated Anticipated Persistence lower than high-scoring males. High scorers on other-directedness rated persistence high in two goals: Gain Assistance (strangers) and Initiate Relationship.	

TABLE 4.11 Continued

Analysis	Self-Monitoring (25-items)	Acting Ability	Other-Directedness	Extroversion
Study Two: Tactical preference	Self-monitoring correlated with preferences for Referent Influence, Compromise, Coercion, Negative Feelings, and Direct Requests. Low-scoring males rated Positive Feelings lower in preference than others. Low self-monitoring males also rated Rationality lower in preference in the Give Advice (friend) goal than other actors.	Acting ability correlated with Coercive Influence and with Direct Requests. Low-scoring males rated Negative Feelings lower in preference than males who scored high. High scorers rated Compromise higher in preference in Gain Assistance (friend) and Initiate Relationship goals; high scorers rated Rationality higher in preference in Initiate Relationship goals, and rated Rationality higher in Elicit Support goals. High scorers also rated Referent Influence higher in preference in eight goals, mostly interpersonal ones (see text). Gender and acting ability interacted to influence ratings of Positive Feelings in six goals (see text).	Other-directedness was related to general ratings of Negative Feelings and Referent Influence. Males who scored low rated Direct Requests, Positive Feelings and Coercion lower in preference than other actors; females who scored high rated Compromise higher in Escalate Relationship goals than females who scored low; and males who scored low rated Compromise and Protect Rights (Habits) lower than males who scored high on other-directedness.	Extroversion was not related to Direct Requests, Compromise, or Positive Feelings; but was related to higher ratings of Referent Influence and Avoidance. In four goals (Assistance with friends, professors and strangers, and in Initiating Relationships) extroverts relied more on Positive Feelings. Males who scored low on Extroversion rated Rationality lower in preference in the Give Advice (friend) goal than other actors; and males who scored low on Extroversion rated coercion higher in preference in six goals: Bureaucracy, Give Advice (friend), Assistance (professor), Give Advice (parents) and Escalate Relationship (females scoring high or low on Extroversion did not differ in ratings of coercion, rating the method low in preference).

Study Three: Interactional goals	Low self-monitoring males rated Image concerns lower.	Acting ability was not related to Interactional Goals.	Other-directedness was not related to Interactional Goals.	Extroversion was not related to Interactional Goals.
Study Three: Reactions	Self-monitoring interacted with Gender, Attribution of Responsibility and Dependence to affect ratings of Confidence and Persistence (see text).	Acting ability was not related to Reactions.	Actors scoring high on other-directedness rated Persistence as more probable than other actors.	The complex set of interactions obtained for self-monitoring were replicated for extroversion. Also, female extroverts rated actor-responsible/partner-dependent relationships as more Familiar than other actors in other conditions.
Study Three: Tactical preferences	Low self-monitors withdrew emotions when the partner caused problems; high self-monitors withdrew emotions when they accepted responsibility for relational changes. Low self-monitoring males were least likely to demand changes in the partner than other actors (see text).	Actors scoring low on acting ability used more Assertive tactics (18%) than those who scored high on acting ability (8%). Males who scored low on acting ability were less likely to Demand Change (11%) than males who scored high (23%).	Low scorers on other-directedness used Integrative Solutions at equal rates when partner was responsible (19%) and when actor was responsible (14%). High scorers were more selective—24% used Integrative Solutions when the partner was responsible, 3% when the actor accepted responsibility.	Females used Demand Change with equal frequency at high (16%) and low (22%) levels of extroversion. Males relied more on Demand Change if they scored high on Extroversion (31%), rather than low (7%). Males scoring high on Extroversion were also more likely to attempt Open Discussions (44% vs. 21%, low extroversion; 34% and 37%, high and low females, respectively). Also, male introverts were more likely to Terminate (46%) than extrovert males (20%) (29% and 28% for females, high and low levels of extroversion).

TABLE 4.12 *Differences between actors who score high and low on acting ability by types of events (Study Two)*

Events	Confidence of Success High S–M	Confidence of Success Low S–M	Willingness to enter High S–M	Willingness to enter Low S–M	Persistence High S–M	Persistence Low S–M
Activity—friend	1.754	2.102	1.680	2.057	2.434	2.812
Assistance—friend	2.291	2.909	2.309	2.909	3.251	3.983
Assistance—stranger	2.617	3.097	2.566	3.222	3.371	3.847
Assistance—professor	2.286	2.665	1.971	2.131*	2.263	2.699
Initiate Relationship	2.549	3.136	2.457	3.233	4.103	4.920
Bureaucracy	3.446	4.011	2.806	3.392	3.617	3.886*
Give Advice—parents	3.149	3.358*	2.497	2.483*	2.657	2.636*
Permission—parent	2.217	2.131*	2.206	2.290*	2.789	2.991*
Give Advice—friend	2.623	2.807*	2.360	2.449*	2.871	2.642*
De-escalation	2.486	2.767*	2.429	2.801*	2.543	2.307*
Obligation	1.926	2.114*	1.766	1.960*	1.794	1.687*
Elicit Support (third Party)	2.674	2.949*	2.623	2.989*	2.680	2.761*
Escalation	1.891	1.950*	1.749	1.926*	2.394	2.398*
Protect right (habits)	2.663	2.841*	2.589	2.790*	2.549	2.483*

*Denotes means, within rows, that are *not* significantly different from, for each dependent variable, each other at alpha < 0.01.

TABLE 4.13 *Mean ratings of confidence of success by gender, extroversion, responsibility and partner dependence/independence (Study Three)*

	Males Partner responsible	Males Actor responsible	Females Partner responsible	Females Actor responsible
High extroversion:				
Partner dependent	3.83	3.43	3.41	3.77
Partner independent	4.35	4.54	4.73	4.62
Low extroversion:				
Partner dependent	3.79	4.04	4.95	3.60
Partner independent	4.71	4.28	4.26	5.05

The correlational analyses and MANOVA results using the sub-scales indicated that Acting Ability was, not surprisingly (see Cappella, 1986; Snyder, 1987), the most important contributor to predicting outcomes. However, each sub-scale had some impact: (1) Acting Ability was generally related to perceptions of actors' ability to construct or perform a range of (expressive) behaviours, and to confidence in performing those behaviours; (2) Extroversion was related to the motivation to pursue desired goals actively; and (3) Other-Directedness was related to actors' interest in monitoring the behaviour of others—relying on either emotionally oriented or relational tactics (integrative solutions, referent influence). More specifically, we found the following:

1. Acting Ability was related to situation perceptions and to reactions (but not tactical preferences, in Study One); in Study Two, Acting Ability was strongly associated with emotionally oriented tactics, ratings of Familiarity of goals and to different reactions in six of the goals (see Table 4.12). In Study Three, actors scoring higher on Acting Ability used more Assertive tactics and relied more on Demand Change methods of influence than others. Generally speaking, then, persons who scored high on Acting Ability rated tactics requiring manipulation of emotions higher in likelihood of use, and rated outcomes pertaining to confidence at achieving change higher (i.e. confidence of success, $r = 0.283$, in Study Two).

2. Extroversion was most strongly associated with Avoidance ($r = -0.419$, for males in Study Two), and with general reactions to goals in Study Two: Persistence ($r = 0.290$), Willingness to Enter ($r = 0.287$), Confidence of Success ($r = 0.328$) and Ease of Imagining the situation ($r = 0.251$). Extroversion was only weakly associated with tactical preferences in the first two studies (Tables 4.3 and 4.5). In the third study Extroverts were more likely to attempt Open Discussion or Demand Change tactics while introverted males were more likely simply to terminate a relationship. Complex interactions involving Extroversion indicated that low scores on Extroversion were associated with less confidence, etc. (but see Tables 4.13, 4.14 and 4.15).

3. In our studies Other-Directedness was least important in predicting outcomes, largely due to the fact that its predictive utility was redundant with that of other sub-scales. When Acting Ability correlated with a tactical preference, Other-Directedness did so also (see Tables 4.3 and 4.5). Other-Directedness was virtually uncorrelated with reactions (i.e. $r = -0.06$, -0.05, 0.00 and 0.06, with Ease of Image, Confidence of Success, Willingness to Enter and Persistence, Study Two). One source of unique contribution, however, is in important events like relational disengagements, in which high scorers used more integrative solutions when the partner was responsible for relational dissatisfaction (see Table 4.11). This finding, plus the

TABLE 4.14 *Mean ratings of confidence of persistence by gender, extroversion, responsibility and partner dependence/independence (Study Three)*

| | Males | | Females | |
	Partner Responsible	Actor Responsible	Partner Responsible	Actor Responsible
High extroversion:				
Partner dependent	5.12	3.31	4.20	3.98
Partner independent	4.36	4.74	6.20	4.68
Low extroversion:				
Partner dependent	4.45	4.69	6.28	3.73
Partner independent	5.38	4.03	4.62	4.34

TABLE 4.15 *Mean ratings of familiarity by gender, extroversion, responsibility and partner dependence/independence (Study Three)*

| | Males | | Females | |
	Partner responsible	Actor responsible	Partner responsible	Actor responsible
High extroversion:				
Partner dependent	5.10	4.07	4.71	6.38
Partner independent	4.37	4.85	5.56	5.35
Low extroversion:				
Partner dependent	4.56	5.19	5.59	5.00
Partner independent	5.95	5.44	4.79	5.95

correlations with Referent Influence and other relationally oriented and emotionally based tactics, seems to confirm the general expectation that Other-Directedness has more to do with monitoring the behaviour of relevant others when managing relationships than the constructs of Extroversion and Acting Ability.

How does the self-monitoring inventory predict goal-driven behaviour, manipulative activities and expressiveness? The answer seems to rest in the combination of measures that reflect the drive to achieve the goal (Extroversion), the perceptions of one's ability to construct and perform behaviours (Acting Ability), and one's intention to monitor the behaviour of others.

Conclusion

Snyder (1974) proposed that the 'goals' of self-monitoring concern the ways in which persons control their emotional reactions in self-presentation and expressive behaviours. Our studies indicate that high self-monitors are more expressive than low self-monitors in their tactical appeals to the nature of the relationship and the target's emotions. In addition, Study Three revealed that low self-monitors were more likely to use emotional detachment when the partner was perceived as responsible for the disengagement. Further, these results were mediated by gender. While high and low self-monitoring females were consistent in their reactions, high self-monitoring males tended to be more confident of their success and were more concerned with their images than were low self-monitoring males. Further, high self-monitoring males were more likely than low self-monitoring males to use referent influence, compromise, positive and negative emotional appeals, and coercion (Study One), positive and negative feelings, referent influence, compromise, direct request and coercion (Study Two), and demand for change (Study Three). Also, several other interaction effects primarily involved male participants. This may occur because females have, as a group, a greater sensitivity to standards of expressive appropriateness. Accordingly, self-monitoring would not appreciably affect females' reactions or behaviours as readily as it affects males' reactions and behaviours, especially in terms of the different influence goals females and males pursue (see Cody, Canary & Smith, in press).

An additional concern arises when we note that the self-monitoring sub-scales did not precisely affect behaviour in ways identical to that of the overall measure. While the Acting Ability sub-scale and the total measure displayed similar results, the total measure tapped strategy choice differences better (i.e. higher conditions) while Acting Ability tapped self-in-situation perceptions better (see Table 4.11). These results can be interpreted as *either* confirming or disconfirming the methodological assumptions of the self-monitoring construct (see Snyder & Gangestad, 1986). The basic consistency of our results utilising the total measure leads us to believe that the self-monitoring construct is quite useful in examining differences in goal-directed strategies, but that not all items may be appropriate to assess tactical behaviour. In the study of social influence, Acting Ability served one important function, Extroversion another. Other-Directedness was less relevant to the outcomes studied here, but this does not mean that Other-Directedness would not be useful in studying relational maintenance and decay. Only a few correlations were higher using a sub-scale rather than the general construct (see Tables 4.1 and 4.2). While it is tempting to recommend the use of the sub-scales, this temptation is attenuated by noting the unacceptable coefficients of internal consistency for Extroversion and Other-Directedness (see Note 1: 0.491 to 0.690). The 18-item scale, the 25-item scale, and the Acting Ability sub-scale achieved adequate levels of internal consistency and were significantly related to the hypothesised outcomes. The use of other sub-scales is only justified if improvements in measurement are also offered.

Our results encourage us to continue examining how relevant personality factors interact with goal types to affect episodic perceptions and behaviours. For example, high self-monitors reported greater confidence in their success, willingness to enter various goal situations, and familiarity with goal types that required some type of favour or relational initiation than did low self-monitors (Study Three). This Goal × Self-Monitoring interaction is intuitively appealing, because we can observe how such goals would trigger self-consciousness among low self-monitors. As Snyder & Swann (1975) postulate, if attention is focused on demands of the situation, then corresponding attention to inner states will also increase the likelihood that those inner states will guide behaviour (p.1035). This interpretation is consistent with Neidenthal, Cantor & Kihlstrom (1985), and explains why low self-monitors are more apt to have goals that are consistent with their self-concepts, whereas high self-monitors more readily adapt to a variety of goal types. Additional research on personality and goals is warranted. Elsewhere we report on the effects of gender (Cody, Canary & Smith, in press) and locus of control (Canary, Cody & Marston, 1986; Canary, Cunningham & Cody, 1988) as these personological variables interact with goals to affect strategic behaviour. How other personality variables interact with goal types to affect strategic behaviour remains a very promising area for future research.

Acknowledgement

The authors would like to thank Laura Koekemoer for her assistance in typing this paper.

Note to Chapter 4

1. Items used to measure the Acting Ability sub-scale included items (from the original self-monitoring scale) 5, 8, 18 and 20 (Study One, alpha = 0.726), items 1, 5, 8 and 18 (Study Two, alpha = 0.724) and items 5, 8, 18, 20 (Study Three, alpha = 0.724). Extroversion items included items 1, 14, 21 and 23 (Study One, alpha = 0.491), items 2, 12, 14, 20, 22 and 23 (Study Two, alpha = 0.686) and items 12, 14, 21, 22 and 23 (Study Three, alpha = 0.667). Other-Directedness was measured with items 7, 13, 16, 17 and 19 (Study One, alpha = 0.586), 7, 13, 16, 17 and 19 (Study Two, alpha = 0.629) and items 7, 3, 16 and 19 (Study Three, alpha = 0.690).

5 Persuasive arguments and group influence: research evidence and strategic implications

RENÉE A. MEYERS
Department of Communication, University of Oklahoma, USA

DAVID R. SEIBOLD
Department of Speech Communication, University of Illinois, Urbana, USA

Introduction

Argument and group decision-making

From its beginnings in late nineteenth-century forensics pedagogy, the study of argument has been a rich intellectual tradition in the field of communication. Since the 1970s, this domain has expanded its research horizons to include examination of argument in diverse forms and contexts. Especially notable are investigations of argument in the interpersonal context (Jackson & Jacobs, 1980, 1981; O'Keefe & Benoit, 1982; Trapp, 1983; Trapp & Hoff, 1985; Yingling & Trapp, 1985), efforts to construct theories of argument (Burleson, 1979, 1980a, 1980b, 1981, 1982; Hample, 1980, 1981, 1985; Jackson & Jacobs, 1980, 1981; Jacobs & Jackson, 1981, 1982; Willard, 1976, 1978, 1979, 1981), and attempts to delineate appropriate and generalisable definitions and assumptions (Brockriede, 1975; Leff & Hewes, 1981; McKerrow, 1977; D. O'Keefe,

1977, 1980; Willard, 1976). Most recently the study of *group* argument has also gained prominence. In a critical review of research on the role of argument in groups, Gouran (1985) commented on this newest domain of argument research:

> Although argument as a concept has long been acknowledged for its relevance to interaction in small groups, attention to its general functions and role has been rather limited in research. In fact, only recently has argument begun to attract more than scattered attention. One can speculate as to the reasons for this discrepancy between the acknowledged importance of argument and the paucity of inquiry into its role. Whatever the factors responsible for the inconsistency, it is clear that the period of neglect is coming to an end (p.723).

Recent investigations of group argument in communication have explored such diverse topics as patterns of argument in consensus and dissensus groups (Canary, Brossman & Seibold, 1987; Pace, 1985), argumentativeness as a personality trait of group members (Infante, 1981, 1982; Infante & Rancer, 1982; Infante *et al.*, 1984; Rancer, Baukus & Infante, 1985; Rancer & Infante, 1983), argumentativeness and leadership emergence (Schultz, 1980, 1982, 1983), the functions of argument in group deliberation (Hirokawa & Scheerhorn, 1985), and the argument–polarisation relationship (Alderton, 1981, 1982; Alderton & Frey, 1983, 1986; Boster *et al.*, 1980; Boster & Hale, 1983; Boster & Mayer, 1984; Boster *et al.*, 1982; Hale & Boster, 1987; Mayer, 1985), among other topics.

But the study of group argument is not unique to communication research alone. Recently, organisation behaviourists and decision scientists have turned their attention towards understanding the function of argument in corporate decision-making groups (Cosier, 1978, 1981, 1983; Huff, 1983; Mason, 1969; Mitroff & Emshoff, 1979; Mitroff, Mason & Barabba, 1982; Schwenk & Cosier, 1980; Schweiger & Finger, 1984; Schweiger, Sandberg & Ragan, 1986; Sussman & Herden, 1982). In general, investigators have studied whether utilising structured argument formats (i.e. devil's advocate or planned dialectical enquiry) contributes to higher quality decisions. Results have indicated that utilisation of both dialectical enquiry, a format which involves structured argumentative debate between advocates of a plan and proponents of a counterplan, and devil's advocate, a format which includes detailed criticism of a plan developed and advocated by an expert, are useful for surfacing assumptions and evaluating crucial information in uncertain and ill-structured decision-making situations (Cosier, 1978, 1981).

Finally, social psychologists have also channelled their efforts towards understanding the role of argument in decision-making groups. Especially germane to this chapter is a prominent theoretical perspective on group argument advanced by social psychologists Vinokur and Burnstein (1974). Persuasive Arguments Theory (PAT) predicts group outcomes from the culturally based *cognitive* arguments members generate while making private decision choices *prior* to group discussion. This perspective is especially intriguing for small group communication specialists because PAT proponents contend that group 'discussion is not crucial for producing shifts in individual choices. It is merely one common and effective medium for the exchange of important information regarding the solution of a choice dilemma' (Vinokur & Burnstein, 1974, p. 314).

Research evidence has been generally, albeit not conclusively, supportive of the theory (Burnstein, 1982; Hinsz, 1981; Hinsz & Davis, 1984; Madsen, 1978; Bishop & Myers, 1974; Myers & Lamm, 1976; Vinokur & Burnstein, 1974; Vinokur, Trope & Burnstein, 1975). Today, PAT continues to be reviewed, tested and cited in social psychology literature (Burnstein & Sentis, 1981; Burnstein & Vinokur, 1973, 1975, 1977; Burnstein, Vinokur & Pichevin, 1974; Burnstein, Vinokur & Trope, 1973; Hinsz, 1981; Hinsz & Davis, 1984; Laughlin & Earley, 1982; Madsen, 1978; Vinokur & Burnstein, 1974, 1978a, 1978b; Vinokur, Trope & Burnstein, 1975), and has been the subject of several interdisciplinary review articles on group decision-making processes (Burnstein, 1982; Cartwright, 1971; Davis & Hinsz, 1982; Dion, Baron & Miller, 1978; Myers, 1982; Myers & Lamm, 1976; Pruitt, 1971a, 1971b; Vinokur, 1971).

Overview

Because Persuasive Arguments Theory is the single most prominent theory of *group* argument in the literature today, and more importantly, because PAT explains the argument–group outcome relationship without direct recourse to communication, it serves as a point of departure for three tasks we undertake in this chapter. First, following a review of PAT assumptions and findings, we offer a conceptual and empirical critique of PAT's non-interaction-based orientation to group argument. Our critique and empirical findings lead us to conclude that *interaction* plays a more important role in the determination of group argument than PAT admits. Second, having provided preliminary evidence that persuasive arguments affect group outcomes through their enactment *in interaction*, we next seek to answer the question 'What do these patterns of persuasive arguments look like in interaction?' Research literature from three related areas is examined: (a) mainstream group communication research, (b) interpersonal argument research, and (c) structurational argument research. Finally, we conclude this chapter by speculating on the tactical and strategic implications of argument in group decision-making interaction. Drawing upon research findings just reviewed, as well as our own observations of decision-making interactions, we posit four potential argument strategies which serve to influence group decision outcomes.

Persuasive Arguments Theory

Persuasive Arguments Theory (PAT) was first introduced and tested by Vinokur and Burnstein (1974) and has been widely regarded as one of the most promising perspectives for predicting how groups move from initially diverse opinions to consensus, especially how groups polarise in the direction of the initial group opinion (Myers & Lamm, 1976). PAT is a non-interactional theory of group decision-making that predicts decision outcomes from the cognitive arguments individuals generate prior to discussion. Because it assumes that (a) the primary focus of study should be the *arguer* and (b) arguing is individual information processing which results in cognitive responses or arguments, we have previously distinguished it as a cognitive-informational perspective on argument (Meyers, 1987; Meyers & Seibold, 1985, 1987).

PAT assumptions

Assumptions about argument

PAT assumes that arguments generated in discussion are not significantly different from arguments generated by individuals outside the interactive context (cognitive arguments). PA theorists conceive of argument as group members' 'reasons or considerations' generated in the process of making their private decision choice prior to group discussion (Vinokur & Burnstein, 1974). In a typical PAT investigation, participants are asked to list their 'reasons, considerations, arguments' after making a private individual decision choice concerning how to advise a hypothetical character confronted with a problem dilemma. The participant advises whether to choose an alternative that is less attractive but safe (cautious choice) or one that is more attractive but less likely to succeed (risky choice). (See Appendix to this chapter for examples of decision tasks.) Each participant is instructed to list arguments for both the cautious and risky alternatives to insure adequate evaluation of the decision options.

PAT assumes there exists in any community a standard set of socially derived and culturally specific arguments for any given decision option. Although vague in this regard, PA theorists suggest this set comprises all available arguments (within a given social community) that exist for a decision alternative, and that each individual possesses some or all of these arguments (Burnstein, 1982). PAT's positing of a standard set of arguments undergirds the assumption that individual arguments generated prior to discussion (i.e. cognitively generated arguments) will 'correspond to' or be 'isomorphic with' subsequent discussion-generated arguments (Vinokur, Trope & Burnstein, 1975).

Assumptions about argument influence

PAT proponents Vinokur & Burnstein (1974) contend that an argument's influence is determined primarily by its 'novelty' (or the degree to which an argument is unknown to group members) and 'persuasiveness' (as rated by judges on a ten-point scale ranging from (0) extremely unpersuasive to (9) extremely persuasive). Of the two argument characteristics, Vinokur and Burnstein consider novelty the *sine qua non* of argument influence. PAT researchers predict that novel arguments, if surfaced in group discussion, will stimulate members to reconsider their initial decision choices and opinions. Because members more readily attend to novel stimuli (Feldman, 1966; Taylor & Fiske, 1978), group outcomes will be influenced in the direction of novel arguments. PAT researchers utilise the novelty and persuasiveness ratings of members' cognitively generated arguments to predict outcomes following group discussion. This research strategy implicitly assumes that novelty and persuasiveness ratings determined on arguments *outside* interaction are stable, reliable predictors of argument influence *in* interaction.

In brief, Persuasive Arguments Theory embraces the following assumptions about argument and argument influence: (a) cognitively generated arguments will correspond to discussion-produced arguments; (b) novelty and persuasiveness are crucial predictors of argument influence, and (c) ratings of novelty and persuasiveness determined on cognitively generated arguments will be stable, reliable predictors of argument influence in discussion.

PAT findings

Findings regarding assumptions about argument

Most often cited as evidence for the assumption of correspondence between cognitive and discussion arguments is a study by Vinokur, Trope & Burnstein (1975), in which a set of cognitively generated arguments was collected together with a set of discussion-produced arguments on the same five task situations. After categorising all the arguments and analysing the similarity between the two sets of arguments, Vinokur, Trope and Burnstein concluded that (a) 'the *same* pool of arguments are available before and after discussion' (1975: 137), (b) 'group discussion does not raise considerations (arguments) different from those raised by subjects in their private decisions' (p.137), and (c) 'the two distributions of arguments (private or discussion) were very similar, suggesting that discussion does not elicit new kinds of arguments (e.g. those concerning the value of riskiness or caution *per se*) which have not been considered by subjects privately before the discussion' (p.146).

Findings regarding argument influence assumptions

Two related sets of investigations buttress PA proponents' implicit assumptions regarding argument influence in group discussion. The first set of studies examines whether novelty is directly related to persuasiveness. Vinokur & Burnstein (1978b) had judges rate the 'novelty' and 'persuasiveness' of a set of cognitive arguments. Contrary to expected results, correlations (computed on arguments produced for each of five different problem tasks) revealed *no consistent relationship* between novelty and persuasiveness. The pooled correlation for ratings across all problem tasks was zero, three of the five correlations were insignificant, and three were in the direction opposite of that predicted by PAT. In subsequent analyses, Vinokur & Burnstein (1978b) discovered that argument 'validity' mediated the novelty–persuasiveness relationship. To date, results regarding the novelty–persuasiveness relationship remain tentative.

In a second set of studies PAT proponents utilised a mathematical model incorporating ratings of cognitive arguments' novelty and persuasiveness to predict argument influence on group decision outcomes. In an initial study employing this model, Vinokur & Burnstein (1974) found that a product–moment correlation computed between the model's predictions and actual group outcomes across five problem tasks was quite strong ($r(5) = 0.93$; $p<0.01$). Subsequent research findings have generally supported Vinokur and Burnstein's initial results. Bishop &

Myers (1974) tested a similar model and obtained a correlation of 0.95 ($p<0.05$) between predicted and observed scores across four decision tasks. Similarly, Madsen (1978) found that, in combining data from his experiment and Vinokur and Burnstein's (1974) investigation, the average correlation between predicted and observed values was quite high ($r(7)$ = 0.92; $p<0.01$). Finally, Hinsz (1981) also found Vinokur and Burnstein's model predictions to be a fairly good fit to mean observed values ($r(8)$ = 0.77; $p<0.05$).

While on the surface past studies appear generally supportive of PAT assumptions about argument and influence, from a communication perspective we think their findings warrant closer scrutiny. In the next section, a conceptual and empirical critique of these findings is offered. Theoretical and investigative limitations of the PAT research programme are discussed, and preliminary empirical evidence for the role of *interaction* in determining group argument is advanced.

Critique of PAT assumptions and findings

Critique of correspondence assumption

Because Vinokur, Trope & Burnstein (1975) were only interested in investigating one dimension of argument correspondence—the degree of rationality of cognitive and discussion arguments—we think that conclusions of *general* correspondence between these two sets of arguments may be premature. Hypothesising that these two sets of arguments might more readily discriminate on distinct communication-based dimensions, we investigated whether differences existed in (a) the *number* of arguments produced in the two conditions, and (b) the *content* of arguments generated in the two conditions (Meyers & Seibold, 1987). Our results revealed that discussion arguments were not directly isomorphic with cognitive arguments in number or content. First, the *number* of distinct arguments generated in discussion was significantly greater than the number generated in the cognitive condition. Second, although some overlap existed in the *content* of the two sets of arguments, they also differed on two levels: (a) various cognitive arguments were never produced in discussion, and (b) 'new' arguments emerged in interaction. These results offered preliminary empirical support for a non-correspondence view of cognitive and discussion arguments, and suggested the importance of *interaction* in the production and/or modification of arguments in decision-making group discussion.

Critique of assumptions about influence

From a communication perspective, the PAT assumption that argument influence is predictable from novelty and persuasiveness ratings of cognitive arguments seemed questionable in two respects. First, in light of our findings that cognitive and discussion arguments do not directly correspond, the use of cognitive arguments to predict group discussion outcomes may be a debatable practice. Second, the idea of novelty as an influential variable required further examination because, from an interactional viewpoint, it seemed possible that repetitive and reaffirmed arguments produced by several group members in interaction (i.e. non-novel arguments) might generate greater influence on final decision outcomes. Tests of these hypotheses revealed that (a) novel arguments were *less* persuasive (based on judges' ratings) than non-novel arguments in discussion, and (b) the PAT model incorporating cognitive argument novelty ratings was a generally poor predictor of outcomes following group discussion, especially at the group level of analysis (Meyers, 1987). Only when this model was modified to include more interaction-based elements—discussion arguments, number of arguments, and member collaboration—did correlations between predicted and observed values improve.

Taken together, these tests offer preliminary evidence of the moderating effect of *interaction* in the argument–group outcome relationship. Although more research is necessary to draw firm conclusions about the interaction–outcome link, our initial findings indicate that argumentative interaction is not merely a display of members' cognitive arguments, but that group outcomes are a product of how arguments are produced, modified, extended, and otherwise influenced *in* group interaction.

Having produced initial evidence that persuasive arguments affect group outcomes through their enactment in interaction, the next section of this chapter seeks to answer the question 'If interaction makes a difference, what do these patterns of persuasive arguments look like *in interaction*?' First, mainstream group communication research is reviewed for insights into influence patterns and argument structures in group discussion. Second, research on interpersonal argument is examined for evidence of the character of argument in *interpersonal* contexts. Finally, recent structurational research on group argument is explicated as a means of wedding these two sets of research findings within a theoretical framework that posits communication as a centralising force.

Persuasive Arguments and Interaction

Findings from group communication research

Mainstream group communication research offers indirect evidence of argument patterns and structures in interaction. Although much of this research lacks strong theoretical underpinnings, findings indicate how various patterns of group discussion affect such outcome factors as decision quality, group consensus and choice shifts. These investigations lay the groundwork for examining more thoroughly structures of interactive *argument* in group decision-making discourse.

Interaction patterns and decision quality

Research on the communication–decision quality relationship has established that group interaction which results in high quality decisions is characterised by non-disruptive, organised and procedurally helpful statements (Leathers, 1969, 1970, 1972). Hirokawa (1980a, 1980b, 1982a, 1982b, 1983) and Hirokawa & Pace (1983) have shown that higher quality decisions are preceded by (a) rigorous examination and agreement upon criteria for the decision, and (b) systematic examination of the validity of assumptions, opinions, inferences, facts and alternative choices. Other research has revealed that certain types of communicative patterns can hinder rather than enhance group decision efforts. Gouran (1981, 1982, 1983, 1984, 1986) discovered that group inferences often function to promote patterns of collectively shared errors that lessen decision quality. Finally, Courtright (1978) found that interaction patterns which exhibit a 'lack of disagreement' increase the chances for 'groupthink' and poorer quality decision outcomes.

Interaction patterns and group consensus

Research which examines the relationship between interaction structures and group consensus/dissensus has shown that groups who achieve consensus not only exhibit more agreement and less randomness (Giffin & Ehrlich, 1963; Gouran & Geonetta, 1977; Lumsden, 1974; Saine & Bock, 1973), but are also characterised by less opinionatedness, more objectivity (Gouran, 1969; T. Hill, 1976) and fewer redundant statements (Kline & Hullinger, 1973). In addition, orientation behaviours (goal-facilitating statements that use facts, make helpful assertions, and lessen tension) are consistent patterns found in consensus groups (Gouran,

1969; Kline, 1972; Knutson, 1972; Knutson & Holdridge, 1975; Knutson & Kowitz, 1977).

Interaction patterns and group shifts

In research on communication–risky shift relationships, Cline & Cline (1979) found that cautious-shift groups were characterised by more agreement than risky-shift groups, and members of risky-shift groups more readily offered information than did participants in cautious-shift groups. In a second study in which diffusion of responsibility was examined as a viable explanation of group shifts, Cline & Cline (1980) again found differences in interaction patterns between the two types of groups. They examined group members' acceptance of personal responsibility (use of personal references—'I' statements) versus their diffusion of responsibility (use of group or other-oriented references—'you', 'we', and 'they' statements). Results showed that discourse patterns differed between risky- and cautious-shift groups with cautious-shift groups characterised by more 'I' statements and risky-shift groups emitting more 'you' statements. Although these differences were small in size, Cline & Cline (1980) concluded that risky-shift group interaction patterns were more likely to display communication aimed at diffusing responsibility than were cautious-shift groups.

In other research on the interaction–group shift link, Alderton & Frey (1983) discovered that the direction of arguments emitted during initial and final stages of group discussion reflected the direction of final group shifts. Finally, Boster and colleagues (Boster & Mayer, 1984; Boster et al., 1980) found that the source of the argument (especially if a member of the majority) played a role in how group members perceived and accepted arguments in group discussion. Group members perceived risky and cautious arguments to be of highest quality if advocated by a majority of group participants.

Taken together, this body of findings from mainstream group communication research reveals some of the various patterns and structures which interaction displays in group decision-making discussion. On the simplest level, these studies provide glimpses into two broad categories of patterns: (a) those aimed at accomplishing the task, and (b) those directed at cultivating and establishing relationships. Findings revealed that groups vary in the way the task is represented in group discussion (depending upon members' choice of facts, opinions, inferences and assertions), as well as in the way those representations are examined and validated (i.e. systematic examination of opinions and alternative choices, rigorous investigation of decision criteria, non-randomness (or random-ness), among other formats). Similarly, these findings hint at ways in which members cultivate and establish relationships through interaction to achieve necessary convergence on a final outcome (i.e. expressed agreement, less opinionatedness, use of terms such as 'we', 'you'). It appears that both task and relationship interaction patterns are important influences on final decision outcomes, and we return to these categories in our subsequent discussion of the strategic implications of persuasive arguments in interaction.

In the next section, we examine research on *interpersonal* argument in an effort to gain insight into argument patterns in dyadic influence attempts. Two consistent interaction patterns—disagreement and reason giving—characterise much interpersonal argument (Meyers, 1987; Trapp, 1983). Findings regarding each of these patterns are reviewed.

Interpersonal argument research findings

Patterns of disagreement

Much past research indicates that patterns of overt *disagreement* characterise much interpersonal argument. O'Keefe & Benoit (1982) asserted that 'displays of overt opposition are part of every argument and that the relationship of opposition such displays create make other displays of opposition relevant' (p.162). Similarly, Trapp (1983, 1986; Trapp & Hoff, 1985) has indicated that argument occurs when two or more parties intentionally engage in disagreement. In an assessment of general characteristics which define both paradigm and peripheral cases of argument, Trapp (1983, 1986) found the presence of disagreement among participants to be one distinguishing characteristic of argumentative interpersonal discourse. Similarly, Martin & Scheerhorn (1985) found that ordinary actors view argument as 'hostility laden discourse', and Jacobs & Jackson (1981, 1982; Jackson & Jacobs, 1980) have consistently contended that argument stems from the occurrence of disagreement in a communicative system that prefers agreement. Finally, Gouran (1985) indicated that much past group research has viewed argument as disagreement-relevant discourse.

Patterns of reason-giving

Past research on interpersonal argument has documented the existence of patterns of reason-giving in disputative discourse (Meyers,

1987). Trapp (1983) indicated that along with disagreement, a second important characteristic of interpersonal argument is reason-giving:

> From the data I have examined, I believe interpersonal argument can be generally described by two characteristics. The first characteristic is disagreeing . . . The second characteristic of interpersonal argument involves the process of reason-giving. In general, this process of comparing views of reality allows us to view argument as an attempt to move our views of reality from a position of disagreement to a position of agreement. (p.527).

Trapp & Hoff (1985) found that in serial interpersonal arguments members utilise reason-giving techniques to evaluate differences. They discovered that reason-giving in such situations is a process of discovering similarities and attempting to change dissimilarities. Similarly, Yingling & Trapp (1985) asserted that 'disagreement and reason-giving are clearly involved in the process of hashing out differences with respect to mutual incompatibilities' (p.623).

Additionally, research has identified reasoning activities as an important element of *group* argument. Pace (1983) found that subjects typically listed 'good reasons' offered in the course of group discussion as a primary motivation for opinion evaluation. Hirokawa & Scheerhorn (1985) suggested that one of the primary functions of argument is to clarify individuals' reasoning processes. They state that 'arguments presented by group members can . . . function to *clarify the reason(s) underlying their [members'] decisional preferences*' (p.739). Recently, Leff & Hewes (1981) defined argument, in its most general sense, as a 'series of propositions offered as reasons to resolve a doubtful issue' (p. 773). Similarly, a definition of argument as reason-giving propositions framed Alderton & Frey's (1983) investigation of argumentation in decision-making groups. Finally, even PAT proponents conceive of arguments as members' reasons for a given decision choice (Vinokur, Trope & Burnstein, 1974).

The consistent finding that disagreement and reason-giving characterise interpersonal argument provides preliminary insight into the way argument is patterned in interpersonal influence attempts. Similar to findings from mainstream group communication research, interpersonal argument also exhibits both a task and relationship dimension. Reason-giving is aimed at achieving agreement on a single solution, at changing another's opinion, at removing dissimilarities between arguers, at accomplishing the task. On the other hand, the level and type of disagreement expressed often functions to create, maintain or alter the relationship between participants. In the next section, a final body of research findings is reviewed. Preliminary findings from the structurational research programme both provides unique insights and serves to reinforce previous findings regarding argument patterns and structures in group interaction.

Structurational argument research

The structurational perspective on argument derives from Giddens' theory of structuration (1971, 1972, 1974a, 1974b, 1976, 1977, 1979, 1984), and has been explicated in detail elsewhere (Meyers, 1987; Seibold & Meyers, 1986; see also Poole, Seibold & McPhee, 1986). Within this theoretical perspective, group argument is conceived as a social practice (Seibold & Meyers, 1986). From this perspective, arguments are both systems (observed patterns of interaction) and structures (the unobservable generative rules and resources that enable argument).

> As systems, arguments are observable patterns of interaction manifest in discursive claiming and reason-giving during deliberations about simple or controversial matters of fact, value, or action . . . Undergirding these systems, however, are argument structures—the rules and resources that enable the production (and reproduction) of arguments. These rules and resources include culturally appropriate and sanctioned ways of disputing that competent interactants must master to produce arguments . . . (Seibold & Meyers, 1986: 147)

Argument systems and structures serve to produce and reproduce each other. 'Argument systems are produced in interaction through interactants' knowledgeable and skillful (but perhaps unreflective and unarticulated) use of particular rules and resources—a process that in turn reproduces those structures and makes them available as future resources' (Seibold & Meyers, 1986: 148). In short, arguments are both the medium and outcome of group interaction.

Argument patterns in group interaction

To date, research within the structurational perspective has produced preliminary glimpses into the character of argument and its role in the structuration of group decisions. In an initial effort to understand argument as a social practice, Seibold et al. (1981) reported a qualitative analysis of argument in the extended discourse of a four-person group attempting to reach a consensual verdict for a legal case. Consistent with a structurational research approach, they reviewed three prominent, representative theories of argument—Jackson & Jacobs (1980), Perelman & Olbrechts-Tyteca (1969), and Toulmin (1958b)—and developed separate coding schemes consistent with the tenets of each theoretical perspective. Results of coding the data with each separate scheme revealed interesting features of group argument. Two distinct patterns emerged. First, argument was goal-oriented, structured, organised, and aimed at achieving the group's task. Results from the Toulmin and Perelman/Olbrechts-Tyteca schemes indicated that what appeared on the surface as incoherent and disjointed interaction was actually a global progression of claims, elaborations, amplifications, and moves toward final convergence on a single goal. Second, the Jackson & Jacobs (1980) scheme indicated how arguments escalate and are jointly produced in interaction, especially how individual members are linked to each other in and through argument. Seibold et al. (1981) have called this 'tag-team' arguing in which members flesh out implicit arguments and supply backing for each other's statements.

Building on this initial research effort and other related findings within the structurational programme (Canary, Ratledge & Seibold, 1982; Seibold, Canary & Tanita-Ratledge, 1983), a coding scheme consistent with the structurational conception of argument as system and structure was advanced. Ratledge (1986) recently tested the scheme's reliability with results demonstrating moderate reliability across coders. Utilising that coding scheme, Canary, Brossman & Seibold (1987) have provided further evidence of the character of argument in decision-making groups. They found four broad categories of argument structures: (a) *simple* arguments used to support another single arguable; (b) *compound* arguments that extend an aspect of a simple argument, embed an argument within another argument, or construct a parallel structure to make dual points in a single sequence; (c) *eroded* arguments that collapse due to delivery failure or disassembling by the author or other group members; and (d) *convergent* arguments that use another's position in the construction of a single argument through agreement with others or joint production of the point (tag-team arguing).

These initial efforts from the structurational research programme reveal the structured nature of argument and reinforce the ways in which argument is patterned around task and relationship dimensions. Members utilise argument to change opinions, to win adherence, to move towards a single task solution. In the process of arguing, members create, maintain and dissolve relationships through agreement/disagreement, disassembling others' arguments, and mutual support. Both the task and relationship dimensions of argument have strategic properties capable of influencing final group outcomes. In the next section, we speculate on ways in which members strategically utilise argument at both the task and relationship level to achieve certain outcomes. We consider the various forms argument-as-strategy takes in group discussion and the implications of those tactics for group influence in general.

Strategic Implications of Argument

In explicating a structurational research agenda for the study of group decision-making, Seibold, Poole & McPhee (1980) delineated three levels of group interactions: (a) the *valence* of the message, (b) its quality as *argument*, and (c) the *influence strategy* it evidences (p.11). Although each of these message levels serves to advance preferences in group decision-making interaction, influence strategies are the most complex of the three levels. Typically they embody combinations of valenced statements and persuasive arguments, and are aimed at establishing clear linkages between group members and given decision proposals. Seibold, Poole & McPhee (1980: 14) explain:

> Whereas message valence and argument are decision specific, strategic interaction usually entails speakers' attempts at linking *members* more directly to preferred proposals . . . For example, group members' interaction strategies (e.g., coalition formation or negotiation) will consist of patterns of more specific messages— each with their valence and some measure of argument—involving person-oriented persuasive tactics such as threat, ingratiation, moral appeals, bartering, invoking past debts, and so forth.

Drawing upon Seibold, Poole and McPhee's conception of strategy, we speculate next on the ways in which argument may be used in group interaction to link members more directly to preferred proposals. We posit two broad categories of argument strategies: (a) those aimed at interpretation of task and (b) those concerned with formation of interpersonal relationships. We have chosen to categorise argument-as-strategy along the task and relationship dimensions because past group research has typically honoured these distinctions (Bales, 1950; Bales & Strodtbeck, 1951; Poole, 1983; Poole & Doelger, 1986). We assume that strategic argument links members to given decision proposals by (a) convincing individuals to accept a standard interpretation of task, and/or (b) cultivating interpersonal coalitions among group members.

In the next section we utilise this task/relationship distinction to explicate more fully specific group argument influence strategies. The strategies we advance are preliminary, emanating from our own observations of decision-making groups and a larger qualitative analysis of 45 group discussions (Meyers, 1987). We caution the reader to consider these findings in that light, and to recognise that future testing is required if the validity and generalisability of these data are to be fully realised.

Strategic argument and interpretation of task

Poole & Doelger (1986) posit that group members enter group discussion either sharing a common interpretation of the task or possessing divergent interpretations. As group discussion unfolds, interaction displays individuals' varying task interpretations. The search for consensus involves attaining agreement on a single (although not necessarily correct) task interpretation. Argument is the medium through which members promote their own task interpretation, challenge others' interpretations, and suggest compromises between divergent interpretations. Argument serves to link members to a standard representation of task and ultimately to given decision proposals.

We propose two ways members utilise argument to promote a given task interpretation: (a) extended elaboration of their own task interpretations, and (b) repetitive testing and questioning of others' task interpretations.

Extended elaboration

Our observations and analyses indicate that group members attempt to link others to decision outcomes via extended elaboration of their task interpretations. These extended elaborations typically take the form of real or hypothetical narratives. The narratives evolve from evidence woven together to produce a story that recreates and enlivens the teller's interpretation. *Real* narratives describe personal experiences of the arguer or experiences of significant others in the arguer's life which resemble the task situation. *Hypothetical* 'what if' dramas ask resistant group members to imagine themselves in the task situation.

The example delineated below, taken from our discussion data, is representative of how extended elaboration is employed to attain agreement on a given task interpretation. In this excerpt, group members are trying to decide whether Mr N., who is in poor health, should

(a) have a risky heart operation, or should (b) try to change life habits that are ingrained and very important to him. (See Appendix for a complete description of this group task.) Neither option *guarantees* a longer life, but either has the potential to prolong his life. Three of five group members (Chris, Kathy and Gail) believe that Mr N. should (and easily could) change his life habits. Notice in the excerpt below how Meg tries to change their task interpretation and promote her interpretation by recounting a real-life story about her father, who faced a similar crisis.

Chris: Just think how much we change our lifestyles all the time anyway.

Kathy: I can't . . . yeah, yeah.

Chris: To adapt to . . .

Gail: Yeah, I really think that nowadays a lot of people, especially 45-year-old men, you know, smoking and drinking, the whole bit. A lot of people are changing, a lot of people are changing their lifestyle.

Meg: OK, except that I looked at it, um, my dad had a problem with his heart and he was supposed to change, you know, a ton, and he did for a while. And then, you know, he's on medication for it, and if you're not feeling any pain or anything, you're gonna try and get away with as much as you possibly can. Like having a beer here and there when you're not supposed to drink at all. And you're gonna think little things like that don't add up, but they will. Nobody, I don't know anybody who completely changes everything.

In this excerpt, Meg uses extended elaboration to promote her task interpretation. Her strategy creates a vivid, real, illustrative argument aimed at getting resistant members to understand and more fully accept her interpretation of the task, and subsequently, her decision solution. Such extended narratives establish the teller's credibility and stimulate the listener to consider similar situations or family members with identical problems. They are designed to get members to construct linkages between themselves and the subsequent decision proposal.

Questioning and testing

An equally tenable strategy for promoting one's own task interpretation, noted in our analysis of discussion transcripts, was repetitive testing of others' interpretations. Diligent questioning of others' assumptions and assertions slowly erodes alternative interpretations until the only solution left standing is the decision proposal of the challenger. In the excerpt below, members are discussing whether Mr C., who is having severe stomach pains, could reschedule his flight if he cancels his trip at the last minute. (See Appendix for a complete description of this group task.) Notice how Annette and Kurt continually challenge each other's interpretation of the task. Annette questions Kurt's interpretation that 'Mr C. can easily reschedule his flight'. Kurt is determinedly sceptical of Annette's interpretation that if 'Mr C. misses his flight he will be unable to reschedule'.

Kurt: Money is money, and I don't think he'd miss his flight.

Annette: He might, he might already. Maybe this is the only time he can go. Maybe this is the only time this year, or the next year and a half he can go on vacation.

Mark: Exactly, I agree.

Kurt: I don't think that's obvious.

Missy: No way.

Annette: He'll miss his flight. He won't be able to reschedule his flight if he's going overseas.

Kurt: But look, it's his vacation now. Perhaps, you know, he could die.

Annette: Doesn't sound like he's going to die.

Throughout this entire excerpt Annette denies the validity of Kurt's statements and Kurt is equally resistant to Annette's interpretation. As members test and question possible task interpretations, they force the group's argument into even more complex realms of reasoning, challenging members to re-evaluate their present task interpretation in light of new evidence. This strategy produces scepticism and a context ripe for opinion change. It attempts to link members to decision proposals by changing, or devaluing, currently held task interpretations.

In sum, securing acceptance of a given task interpretation via (a) elaborated sequences of argument that form realistic stories and narratives and/or (b) repetitive questioning and testing of others' arguments for a given task interpretation are two possible strategies members utilise to achieve convergence on a single decision proposal. In addition to these task-related strategies, argument also functions strategically in the interpersonal realm to move the group towards its goal. This second type of argument-as-strategy is detailed next.

Strategic argument and interpersonal coalitions

The formation of interpersonal subgroups in decision-making discussions can function to influence the group's final decision. Much past research has substantiated the power of majority coalitions in small group discussions. For example, Davis (1973) reported considerable support for majority rule as a predictor of group outcomes. Boster and colleagues have demonstrated that arguments expressed by the majority are more positively evaluated and thereby have a qualitatively stronger effect on opinion change (Boster & Mayer, 1984; Boster *et al.*, 1980). In addition, some recent research indicates that even minority members may successfully influence the group's decision if they band together to produce a strong coalition with a single voice (Nemeth, 1977, 1982; Nemeth, Swedlund & Kanki, 1974; Nemeth & Wachtler, 1974). In light of these previous findings, we posit two interpersonal-based argumentative strategies designed to influence decision choices by creating powerful coalitions: (a) repetitive agreement among like others, and (b) supportive tag-team arguing.

Repetitive agreement among like others

One strategy which members use to link others interpersonally to decision proposals is to support and encourage arguments similar to their own. In group discussion, members quickly discover others' points of view and decision preferences. Like-minded members typically band together by expressing verbal (and nonverbal) agreement. This creates a perception of unity and strength that outsiders may find difficult to ignore. In time, resistant members may feel pressure to conform to the subgroup's position even if they do not agree with its task interpretation. As witnessed in the excerpt below, this strategy of interpersonal agreement is utilised to establish convergence among three of the five group members in this discussion group. In this case, group members are deciding whether Mr C., who awoke with severe stomach pains, should go on his long awaited vacation or should go to the hospital (see Appendix for a complete description of the decision task).

> **Joe:**   I thought that he should just go check into the hospital . . .
> **Sue:**   Exactly.
> **Joe:**   Just because it could ruin his trip. I mean, if it gets any worse, it's going to ruin his trip. And, you know, you can look at the problems of having to get medical care overseas. He can always change his plans and catch a plane the next day. I don't think it would distract him that much.

Sue: Right.
Chris: And you know, your health is nothing to mess around with. And like you said, overseas. You never know what kind of medical attention . . .
Sue: Yeah, I know.
Chris: Yeah.
Sue: Yeah.

Repetitive agreement and unquestioning support for others' arguments creates a coalition that moves members towards the subgroup's decision choice. Early formation of interpersonal relationships via consistent agreement serves to frame and inform the remainder of the group discussion. Outsiders (i.e. members who disagree with the coalition's stance) may feel tremendous pressure to conform, may fail to question the subgroup's arguments for fear of verbal/nonverbal disdain, or may seek refuge in silence or adaptation. For whatever reason, it seems plausible that repetitive agreement and consistent support for certain arguments creates influential interpersonal networks that function to link members to decision proposals.

Tag-team arguing

Seibold *et al.* (1981) first noticed this strategic form of argument in their research on argument coding schemes. In a qualitative analysis of one decision-making group's discourse, Seibold *et al.* (1981) found that group members formed interpersonal relationships and coalitions through argument. They labelled this joint construction of argument as 'tag-team' argument.

> Even this qualitative analysis of a single group points up ways in which actors relate to each other through argument. For example, certain types of (weak) argumentative stances were met with scorn and ridicule. Too, argument development was both facilitated and hindered through interpersonal dynamics. The 'tag team' phenomenon we have alluded to demonstrates the ways in which group members flesh out implicit argument acts and, in particular, supply backing for others' statements. (Seibold *et al.*, 1981: 21)

More recently, Canary, Brossman & Seibold (1987) reaffirmed the occurrence of the tag-team strategy in an analysis of argument structures of four decision-making groups. They discovered that, especially in consensus groups, members would 'team up' to form a single argument. They posited that 'the joint construction of an argument is persuasive to others as it presents a unified view of what supporters consider reasonable' (p.15). Similarly, we noticed tag-team arguing in our own data. The excerpt below, taken from our own group discussions, represents one example of how arguments are jointly produced in interaction to create a perception of unified support. Note how Sue adds to Lynn's argument and then is similarly reinforced by Lynda. Each addition makes the argument stronger and creates a more formidable case.

> **Lynn:** I know because I've had that feeling when I've gotten on a plane, right before something like that. And you really, you do get nervous before and stuff like that. But the only thing that led me to believe otherwise is that the pain has gotten more severe in the last few minutes. And that just seemed to me like maybe there is something radically wrong, and he should just check it out.
>
> **Sue:** And another thing that got me is it, it said here that he awoke in the morning with the pain. Now even though you're scared of planes, would you wake up in the morning and have pain like that?
>
> **Lynda:** No, I think the pain stage would begin just with the nervous stage.
>
> **Sue:** Yeah, the nervous stage when you're boarding the plane.

Tag-team arguing may well produce a stronger influence on decision outcomes than any single argument can muster. At the very least, it produces a perception of unity and support for the subgroup's preferred decision goal.

Clearly, both interpersonal and task-related argument strategies are important for convergence achievement. In this chapter, we have posited, and offered limited support for, four possible group decision-making argument strategies. How these task- and interpersonally-oriented strategies are related in group interaction, how they support or contradict each other, how they contribute to, or hinder, vigilant decision-making behaviour remain questions for future research.

Conclusion

We began this chapter by questioning the adequacy of a prominent non-interactional theory of group argument to describe group discussion processes and predict argument–decision outcome relationships. The ensuing conceptual and empirical critique suggested that Persuasive Arguments theorists are overlooking a significant component of the group decision-making process—interaction. We intimated that interaction plays a mediating, if not moderating, role in the determination of final group outcomes, and reviewed related group communication and interpersonal argument research findings to produce a preliminary picture of persuasive argumentation processes in group interaction. This review pointed up the ways in which argument functions in both task-related and interpersonal capacities to determine final group outcomes. Finally, we speculated on how argument links members to specific decision proposals—how it is used strategically to influence final decision outcomes.

We end this chapter by calling for renewed efforts among communication scholars to develop theoretical frameworks for investigating and analysing argument in group decision-making interaction. As Gouran (1985) stated: 'Although argument as a concept has long been acknowledged for its relevance to interaction in small groups, attention to its general functions and role has been rather limited in research.' We join with him in arguing that it is time for this period of neglect to come to an end.

Appendix: Descriptions of Group Tasks

Mr C.

Mr C. is about to board a plane at the airport at the beginning of his overseas vacation. Although he has been looking forward to this trip for some time, he is troubled because he awoke in the morning with a severe abdominal pain. Because he has never flown before, he thinks that the pain may simply be an upset stomach brought on by anticipation of the flight. Although he is not far from a hospital where he knows he will obtain quick attention, he realises that a visit to the hospital will cause him to miss his flight which in turn will seriously disrupt his vacation plans. The pain has gotten more severe in the last few minutes.

Imagine you are advising Mr C. Check the *lowest* probability you would consider acceptable for Mr C. to board the plane.

Mr C. should board the plane if the chances are at least:
—1 in 10 that his abdominal pain will *not* become more severe during the trip. (Mr C. should board the plane even if there is a very small chance that his abdominal pain will *not* become more severe.)
—2 in 10 that his abdominal pain will *not* become more severe during the trip.

—3 in 10 that his abdominal pain will *not* become more severe during the trip.
—4 in 10 that his abdominal pain will *not* become more severe during the trip.
—5 in 10 that his abdominal pain will *not* become more severe during the trip.
—6 in 10 that his abdominal pain will *not* become more severe during the trip.
—7 in 10 that his abdominal pain will *not* become more severe during the trip.
—8 in 10 that his abdominal pain will *not* become more severe during the trip.
—9 in 10 that his abdominal pain will *not* become more severe during the trip.
—10 in 10 that his abdominal pain will *not* become more severe during the trip. (Mr C. should *not* board the plane unless it is certain that his abdominal pain will *not* become more severe.)

Mr N.

Mr N., a 45-year-old accountant, has recently been informed by his physician that he has developed a severe heart ailment. The disease would be sufficiently serious to force Mr N. to change many of his strongest life habits—reducing his work load, drastically changing his diet, giving up favourite leisure time pursuits. The physician suggests that a delicate medical operation could be attempted which, if successful, would completely relieve the heart condition. But its success could not be assured, and in fact, the operation might prove fatal.

Imagine you are advising Mr N. Check the *lowest* probability that you would consider acceptable for Mr N. to have the operation.

Mr N. should have the operation if the chances are at least:
—1 in 10 that the operation will be successful. (Mr N. should have the operation even if there is a small chance that the operation will be successful.)
—2 in 10 that the operation will be successful.
—3 in 10 that the operation will be successful.
—4 in 10 that the operation will be successful.
—5 in 10 that the operation will be successful.
—6 in 10 that the operation will be successful.
—7 in 10 that the operation will be successful.

—8 in 10 that the operation will be successful.
—9 in 10 that the operation will be successful.
—10 in 10 that the operation will be successful. (Mr N. should *not* have the operation unless it is certain that the operation will be successful.)

6 The hidden costs of persistence

DAVID KIPNIS
Department of Psychology, Temple University, Philadelphia, USA

STUART M. SCHMIDT
Industrial Relations and Organizational Behavior Department, Temple University, Philadelphia, USA

GREGG BRAXTON-BROWN
Department of Marketing, School of Business, Pepperdine University, Culver City, California, USA

The Hobbesian assumptions that we are programmed by our desires, and by our dependence on other people to satisfy our desires, provide a framework for understanding influence acts. If we accept these assumptions, then it follows that everyone must exercise influence and power on a day-to-day basis. Failing this, desires must be abandoned. Thus it is not a question for debate as to whether people exercise power. What needs to be understood is how people get their way—the tactics used to influence others, how and when these tactics are used, and what happens then. This chapter is about what happens then; that is, the consequences of exercising influence.

In particular this chapter will examine the consequences of using upward influence in organisations (Kipnis, Schmidt & Wilkinson, 1980; Porter, Allen & Angle, 1981; Schilit & Locke, 1982). This is the process by which employees attempt to gain compliance from their managers or someone at a higher organisational level than themselves. Upward influence is an essential aspect of one's organisational behaviour and is said to contribute substantially to individual effectiveness (Kanter, 1977; Pelz, 1952; Schilit, 1986).

The Use of Influence—A Brief Review

Recent studies of verbal influence strategies have focused on several related questions. The first asks if it is possible to describe parsimoniously the seemingly unending numbers of verbal tactics used by people to influence others. Based on factor-analytic and multiple classification techniques, from two to four dimensions have been found to describe the range of verbal influence strategies used in interpersonal relations (Cody, McLaughlin & Jordan, 1980; Falbo, 1977; Falbo & Peplau, 1980; Kipnis & Cohn, 1979). Using the same analytic techniques, up to seven dimensions of influence have been identified in organisational settings (Kipnis, Schmidt & Wilkinson, 1980); presumably organisations provide their members with a broader array of potential means to cause behaviour in others.

Based on a series of factor-analytic studies of verbal influence strategies in organisations (Kipnis, Schmidt & Wilkinson, 1980), the first two authors of this chapter have constructed three scales, which describe the type and amount of influence used by organisational members to influence their subordinates, colleagues or superiors. These scales are collectively called the Profile of Organisational Influence Strategies (POIS).[1] The POIS measures the following dimensions of influence: Reason, Friendliness, Assertiveness, Coalitions, Higher Authority, and Bargaining. When measuring the use of influence with subordinates, a seventh dimension is added to measure the use of Sanctions. The POIS is used to measure influence in the research described in this chapter.

A second question examines the circumstances under which individuals choose to invoke one or another of the strategies isolated through analytic techniques. Not surprisingly, the choice of tactics is found to be guided by an array of social and personal forces. Among these forces are the balance of power between the influencing agent and the target person, the reasons why the agent wants to exercise influence, cognitive factors relating to the agent's beliefs about his or her own competence, the agent's expectations that he or she can successfully influence the target person, the degree of intimacy between agent and target, and the setting in which influence occurs (Fitzpatrick & Winke, 1979; Kipnis & Schmidt, 1983; Marwell & Schmitt, 1967a; Miller *et al.*, 1977; Porter, Allen & Angle, 1981; Schmidt & Kipnis, 1984). It is of interest that contingency theories of leadership have identified several of the above factors as important in guiding a leader's choice of influence tactics. Thus, for instance, Fiedler suggests that a leader's relations with followers, and the leader's power in the setting, determine the effectiveness of the leader's influence tactics (Fiedler, 1967).

A third question in the study of influence asks about the consequence for the target person of using various verbal strategies. This is a major question asked about influence by social scientists. The goal here is to identify circumstances under which target persons accept or resist specific attempts to change their behaviour (e.g. Cialdini, 1984, 1988). At times, this question is extended to examine how target persons evaluate themselves and/or the influencing agent, as a consequence of being the target of influence (e.g. French & Raven, 1959).

What is conspicuously missing in the research literature is information about whether the use of influence feeds back to the influencing agent. It is possible that agents' use of influence can change their own behaviour, as well as the behaviour of the target of influence. At a minimum, one obvious consequence is that agents should be satisfied when they get their way, and dissatisfied when they don't. People whose wish is somebody else's command are usually described as 'happy as kings'.

This chapter discusses several consequences for the influencing agent of using different influence styles. The consequences assessed are the effects of using different styles of influence on interpersonal relations and on subjective symptoms of stress. Since the research on which this chapter is based is drawn from organisational studies, the specific consequences that are discussed are concerned with the relation between influence styles and their effects on (1) performance evaluations and (2) employees' feelings of job and personal stress. Before examining these consequences, two short digressions are made. The first digression examines motivations involved in exercising influence; the second describes our recent attempts to describe how people use 'mixes' of influence tactics.

Why bother to influence others?

The answer, as social philosophers from Thomas Hobbes to Emerson (1962) have observed, is that we are dependent on others for most things, material, non-material, psychological and spiritual. Out of this dependency, then, arises the impulse to cause behaviour in others. Further, the more we want from others, and/or the more we believe they are unwilling to give us what we want, the more likely we are to exercise influence. It has also been observed that as our wants remain unfulfilled, people escalate to using many different kinds of tactics. If the balance of power favours them, they use harsher tactics. If not, they escalate by using weaker tactics, such as crying, acting nice, and begging (Kipnis, 1976). In either case, escalation increases pressure on the target person to comply.

In short, influence strategies represent our attempts to control the world, and the people in it. One suspects that the more people try to influence others, the less effective they are. Cartwright (1965), for instance, has noted that people who are truly powerful give the appearance of exercising very little influence. This is because many of their needs are anticipated by others, and for the rest, they rely on simple requests to get their way.

Influence styles

Everyday observations suggest that people vary in the extent to which they use available strategies to influence others. Some persons use hardly any forms of influence, remaining passive and quiet. Others seem to use the same strategy of influence regardless of what they want, or of the issues involved. Still others appear to use complex mixes of tactics to get their way, such that if one tactic fails others are invoked. These persons appear to refuse to take 'no' for an answer.

Unfortunately, there has been very little research designed to identify empirically 'mixes' of influence strategy usage, or the consequences of using such 'mixes'. In a pioneering paper, however, Perreault & Miles (1978) reported an extensive study of the choice of individual influence strategy mixes between dyads in complex organisational systems. In their study, more than 1,200 organisational employees described how frequently they used each of five tactics to influence a given target person. The tactics included the use of one's formal authority, expertise, referent power (ingratiation), external control impression management, and internal control impression management. A hierarchical cluster analysis of the frequency of use of these tactics identified five distinct clusters of people, who were similar in their reliance on the use of different mixes of the five influence tactics. These mixes consisted of people who were non-influencers, who relied on expertise, who used referent tactics, who relied on their formal positions, and who used multiple strategies of influence.

In the research on which this chapter is based, we also grouped respondents in terms of their pattern or 'mix' of influence use. Our respondents were three sets of employees, including blue-collar and clerical employees, supervisors, and chief administrators of hospitals.

Each group used the Profile of Organisational Influence Strategies (POIS) to describe how they influenced their immediate superiors using the six upward influence strategies of Assertiveness, Friendliness, Reason, Higher Authority, Bargaining and Coalitions.

The POIS scores were subjected to a K-Means cluster analysis (Dixon, 1983). This cluster analysis found four meaningful clusters, which mirror the first four found by Perreault and Miles and are labelled as follows: *Shotgun* (employees who used all available tactics to get their way with their superiors); *Ingratiator* (employees who had high scores on the use of the strategy of Friendliness, and average scores on the remaining strategies); *Tactician* (employees who had high scores on the strategy of Reason, and average scores on the remaining strategies); and *Bystander* (employees who had below average scores on all strategies). In this chapter we will describe the consequences of exercising influence for each of these four types.

Some Consequences of Using Influence

After those two digressions, we can now return to describing possible consequences for the influencing agent of exercising influence. Described below are four outcomes that we have looked at in relation to the above pattern of influence usage.

Social relations with the influencing agent

Relations from the target's point of view

It is generally agreed that there is a relation between impression management strategies and how people evaluate the influencing agent (Schlenker, 1980). For instance, persons who adopt an ingratiating style of influence are found to be liked better by others than persons who rely on coercion and demanding tactics of influence (French & Raven, 1959; Jones, 1964). Indirect support for this generalisation was most recently reported by Arffa & Strube (1986), who found that Type A personalities were associated with less harmonious relations with others than Type B's. Presumably Type A's antagonise by their continual attempts to influence and control people.

This line of reasoning suggests that persons who use a Shotgun style of upward influence may be disliked by their superiors. This is because people who continually attempt to influence others, who refuse to take 'no' for an answer, are often considered bothersome. We thought that this prediction would be particularly true for Shotgun women. Several writers suggest that women are punished by men for being assertive: that at a minimum they are evaluated less favourably than their assertive male counterparts (e.g. Costrich et al., 1975; Muehlenhard, 1983). This should mean that male supervisors evaluate female Shotgun employees less favourably than male Shotgun employees.

We examined these possibilities using two samples of employees. As a measure of like–dislike, we used performance appraisals of each employee by his or her boss. In the first sample 59 blue-collar and clerical workers (37 males and 22 females) completed the POIS, describing how they influenced their immediate supervisors.[2] Supervisors independently evaluated each employee's performance on scales measuring the employee's ability to (a) work independently, (b) work co-operatively, (c) solve problems, (d) carry out orders, (e) his or her potential for promotion, and (f) overall job performance. These evaluations were summed into an employee performance evaluation score.

The second sample consisted of 113 entry level supervisors, 59 males and 54 females, average age 30 years. They had been employed for an average of three years in various entry level managerial positions in such diverse fields as engineering, accounting, sales, computers and personnel management. This sample also used the POIS to describe how they influenced their superiors. Their superiors independently evaluated their performances on a form similar to that used in the clerical and blue-collar sample.

In Table 6.1 we show the average performance evaluations of male and female employees in the two samples. The findings for the supervisor sample are based on evaluations given by male superiors. The findings from these two samples were fairly consistent. We expected that people who refused to take 'no' for an answer would not be liked too well. More particularly, we expected that these Shotgun employees would receive low performance evaluations from their bosses. As can be seen, our expectations were confirmed. In both samples, male and female employees classified as Shotguns received unfavourable performance evaluations. No support was found, however, for the prediction that Shotgun women would be evaluated any differently by male superiors than Shotgun men: both male and female Shotgun employees were given equally low ratings. It seems clear, then, that assertive women in these samples were not punished more than assertive men for their outspoken styles of influence.

TABLE 6.1 *Relation between employee influence styles and supervisor's performance evaluations*

| | Workers | | Supervisors[a] | |
	Male	Female	Male	Female
Shotgun	24.0	32.3	30.1	32.1
Ingratiator	29.4	41.5	32.7	35.9
Bystander	30.1	30.2	34.7	36.2
Tactician	32.7	31.0	36.0	33.3
F Tests:	Style × Gender ($p<0.05$)		Style ($p<0.05$)	

Note: High scores denote more favourable evaluations.
[a] Based on the evaluations of male superiors.

Who did receive the best performance evaluations? Here traditional stereotypes emerged. Higher performance evaluations were given to male (as opposed to female) Tacticians in both samples. In contrast, higher performance evaluations were given to female Ingratiators in the worker sample, and to female Ingratiators and Bystanders in the supervisor sample. Clearly male employees in these samples were valued for their use of reason to persuade, and women were not. One can only speculate whether the reverse of this pattern would occur if women were doing the evaluating. That is, would women supervisors give high evaluations to male Ingratiators and female Tacticians?

In summary, the findings are consistent with the widespread belief that a contentious interpersonal influence style promotes dislike. Perhaps the contribution of our approach is in extending the link between influence style and social relations to the area of performance evaluations within organisations. It is encouraging to find that Cody & McLaughlin (1988) reported a somewhat similar pattern of findings in their study of influence styles in traffic courts. These researchers found that traffic violators (mostly male), who used strong and assertive tactics to persuade judges of their innocence, were usually found guilty by the judges. Traffic violators who used reason and logic to persuade were more often found innocent by these same judges.

Relations from the point of view of the agent

So far we have suggested that a strong and demanding style of influence breeds dislike for the influencing agent. In this section we shall examine the extent to which a strong and demanding style of influence breeds dislike for the target person.

The ways in which the use of influence can transform the powerholder's evaluations of others has been called the metamorphic effect of power. This view of power argues that the successful use of power can alter the agent's view of self and others, simply as a consequence of 'causing' behaviour in others (Kipnis, 1976, Chapter 9). Metamorphic effects can be understood by examining (1) the kinds of influence tactics that are used and (2) the attributions of the powerholder concerning who controls the target person's behaviour: the target person or external forces including the powerholder.

It is theorised that the successful use of strong tactics, such as are found in the Shotgun style, increases the powerholder's sense of control over the target person. For instance, if a manager said to any employee 'I insist you do as I say', and the employee subsequently complied, a reasonable inference by the manager is that his or her orders caused this subsequent compliance. Such an inference is less likely to be made if the manager said (and meant) 'Here's what I would like you to do, but you decide for yourself'. Compliance subsequent to this second tactic is more likely to be attributed by the manager to the employee's own decision.

As a general rule, strong tactics are seen as forcing compliance. As a result, the target is not seen as a free agent. Another consequence of the successful use of strong tactics concerns evaluations of the target person by the powerholder. These evaluations become less favourable when the target person is seen as externally controlled. To illustrate, in a recent experimental simulation of organisations (Kipnis et al., 1981), business students were appointed as leaders of small groups and instructed to act as either authoritarian or democratic leaders. Authoritarian leaders chose to use strong and controlling tactics in which all decisions were made by themselves. Democratic leaders chose to use rational tactics to influence. They also delegated decision-making powers to group members. At the end of the work period, authoritarian leaders reported that group members were externally controlled; that is, they were less likely than democratic leaders to attribute group members' performance to 'group members' motivations to perform well'. Further, authoritarian leaders evaluated the task performance of group members less favourably than democratic leaders.

Other examples of the metamorphic effects of power are found in studies among dating and married couples (Kipnis et al., 1976; Kipnis &

Cohn, 1979). Based on factor analyses of influence tactics used in these relations, it was found that there were links between the use of strong and controlling tactics (I make the other person miserable; I get angry and demand that he or she give in), attributions of control of the partner, and the amount of love expressed for the partner. That is, the use of strong tactics was associated with control of decision-making power in the relationship, with less affection, less satisfaction with sexual relations, and less favourable evaluations of partners than was true for couples who shared power equally, and who used rational tactics.

The apparent explanation for these less favourable evaluations is that the behaviour of the target person, no matter how excellent, is seen as guided by the powerholder's orders rather than by the abilities and motivations of the target person. Hence the target person is given little credit for anything he or she does. In general our society values competence, self-control and autonomous behaviour. The use of directive and controlling influence tactics is directly aimed at reducing these forms of independent behaviour; thus their use creates the relatively lasting belief in influencing agents that targets of influence are incompetent and worse.

Income

So far we have shown that an agent's influence style has direct consequences for the kinds of social relations that emerge between target persons and the agent of influence. In keeping with the chapter's focus on upward influence, we also asked whether influence tactics might affect employees' salaries. We reasoned that since salary reflects the individual's job performance, which we have seen was considered unsatisfactory among men classified as Shotguns, it is likely that male Shotgun employees would receive lower salaries than male Tacticians.

Data to test this relation were based on the responses of 108 male chief executive officers (CEOs) of for-profit and not-for-profit hospitals. The CEOs managed hospitals that contained between 100 and 300 beds. These CEOs used the POIS to describe how they influenced their managers, defined as their Board of Directors, Board of Trustees, or in the case of for-profit hospitals, the person to whom the hospital administrator reported. It was found that CEOs with Tactician patterns of influence earned significantly more ($73,240) than CEOs with Shotgun patterns ($56,000), Ingratiators ($53,000), and Bystanders ($60,270). In this instance, then, non-emotional forms of influence were linked to a recognised benchmark of organisational success—money.

Stress and influence

In addition to causing stress in others, the use of a Shotgun style may cause the influencing agent to experience personal stress. This conjecture is based on the well-documented findings that persons who continually strive to control their worlds, and who express hostility in their relations with others (i.e. Type A personalities), are vulnerable to physical and psychological stress symptoms (Ganster, in press; Mayes, Sime & Ganster, 1984; Osipow & Spokane, 1984). It was previously pointed out that influence strategies represent ways to control people and events. If this is true, it follows that the use of both stronger influence tactics and a broader array of tactics should be associated, on the one hand, with measures of Type A personality, and on the other hand, with measures of stress. Influence, then, may mediate between the goal of controlling others and the experience of personal stress. Deluga (1986), for example, found that organisational members who were stressed by high levels of role conflict attempted to influence others using many different tactics (i.e. a Shotgun style).

To test these ideas, the 108 CEOs (described above) were sent a second questionnaire eight months after providing information about their incomes and answering the POIS. The second questionnaire contained scales to measure job and personal stress experiences. Eighty-seven of the original 108 CEOs returned this questionnaire.

The Personal Stress scale contained two sets of items to measure psychological stress and physiological stress. The Psychological Stress scale asked about experiencing symptoms of tension, anxiety, general nervousness; periods of irritability or anger; periods of depression, feeling blue or helpless; periods of impatience, feeling frustrated. Responses to these questions were summed to give a measure of Psychological Stress. The Physiological Stress scale asked about the following health-related problems: severe headaches; difficulty in sleeping, exhaustion, or severe fatigue at the end of the day; shortness of breath, excessive coughing; high blood pressure; heart disease. Items in this scale were also summed.

The Job Stress scale contained three sub-scales measuring Work Pressure, Role Ambiguity, and Role Conflict. The first two sub-scales were developed by Insel & Moos (1974), and the last by Rizzo, House & Lirtzman (1970). Because of the high intercorrelation between the three scales they were combined in an index called Job Stress.

In Table 6.2 we show the average scores of CEOs on measures of job stress, physical symptoms and psychological symptoms. What we found was that CEOs with an active, assertive style of exercising influence reported the highest levels of subjective stress. That is, Shotguns were bothered most by tensions arising from their work, as well as from personal tensions, such as anger, the inability to sleep, and other psychological symptoms of stress. The same pattern was found for reports of physical stress symptoms, although not at a statistically significant level. Persons who relied on the use of reason and logic to persuade, i.e. Tacticians, reported the least amount of job and personal stress.

TABLE 6.2 *The relation between influence styles and measures of stress*

	Job Stress	Physical symptoms	Psychological symptoms
Shotgun	44.45	11.25	12.65
Ingratiator	37.55	10.65	10.15
Bystander	35.26	11.00	10.71
Tactician	32.00	8.64	8.55
F Tests:	Cluster $(p>0.05)$	$(p$ ns$)$	Cluster $(p>0.05)$

Note: High scores indicate high levels of stress.

Here, then, we have suggestive results that people who use every means possible to get their way, i.e. Shotguns, are vulnerable to symptoms of stress. An over-emphasis on the use of influence, therefore, may be indicative of an urgent need, not only to exercise control, but also of subjective feelings of tension and stress. These outcomes appear to support the previously mentioned suggestion by Cartwright that people who continually seek to exercise influence are not very successful. In addition, the findings suggest the interesting possibility that an individual's influence style may be as predictive of health status as direct measures of the Type A personality.

Morale and influence

We also tested the idea that employees who have a Shotgun influence style would be relatively dissatisfied with their work, because they are considered ineffective in their jobs by their bosses, and are also experiencing high levels of job tension and personal stress. Stress and failure, then, should surely leave Shotguns unhappy with their jobs. To test these ideas, a job satisfaction survey was given to a group of sales representatives for a medical manufacturing firm. We asked them to rate their satisfaction with their pay and benefits, the work itself, opportunities for advancement, the supervision they received, and management policies. The sales representatives also completed the POIS, describing how they influenced their superiors.

What we found was that the more these sales representatives attempted to influence their superiors with the strategies of Assertiveness, Coalitions and Higher Authority, the less satisfied they were with all aspects of their work. While perhaps obvious, these findings document that the more one has to 'work' to convince others to do what he or she wants, the less the satisfaction in the doing.

We also asked each sales representative's immediate superior to fill out the POIS describing the tactics that they used with each subordinate. Again, not surprisingly, we found that the more the boss used Assertiveness to influence a particular sales representative, the lower that representative's job satisfaction ($r = -0.50$). In short, using controlling influence tactics, and/or being the target of such tactics, are prognostic of dissatisfaction and low morale.

Conclusions

We have illustrated in this chapter the various ways in which the use of influence can have consequences for the influencing agent. Further, we have shown that some styles of influence are associated with greater costs to the influencing agent than others. In particular, the Shotgun style of influence was associated with the most negative outcomes for the agent, and a Tactician style with the fewest negative outcomes. That is, Shotguns were associated with a lack of harmony in social relations, with job and personal stress, job dissatisfaction, and low incomes. Thus people who refuse to take 'no' for an answer, and use strong and controlling tactics, may get their way with others, but must expect to experience problems themselves. Based on these findings, simple common sense suggests that people should avoid the use of Shotgun tactics, as they appear to be associated with personal distress. If everyone used only reason to influence, it seems clear that absolute harmony would exist in the world.

Unfortunately, data from social science research suggest that people cannot simply choose the particular set of tactics that are least costly, i.e. a Tactician style, as a means of influencing others. As we pointed out in the introduction to this chapter, such factors as the balance of power between people, resistance by target persons, the influencing agent's self-confidence, expectations of successfully influencing, what the agent wants, how strongly he or she wants it, and more, all serve to guide the choice of tactics. Such factors as these may leave the individual with little choice but to use a Shotgun style.

Nevertheless, the findings reported here challenge common stereotypes that success makes substantial use of directive and controlling influence behaviours. Indeed, the belief that one should vigorously and persistently exercise influence has given rise to a number of training programmes that teach this theme. For instance, programmes as diverse as neurolinguistic programming and contingency leadership training agree that people should actively seek to cause behaviour in others. Frequently it is suggested that when one strategy of influence fails, others should be used in rapid succession until compliance is gained. While the use of such influence may overcome target resistance, the findings of this study suggest that training programmes would do well to point out the costs associated with a Shotgun style. Among the costs described here are subjective experiences of stress and job dissatisfaction, as well as that of being seen and evaluated unfavourably by significant others.

We conclude with the caveat that (with the exception of the section on the metamorphic effects of power) the findings reported in this chapter are based on the attempts of less powerful persons (employees) to influence more powerful persons (their bosses). It remains to be seen whether similar results would be obtained when people attempt to influence equals or those with less power than themselves. It also remains to be seen whether these findings can be replicated in other settings in which influence is used, such as marriage or friendship relations.

Notes to Chapter 6

1. The POIS is available from University Associates, San Diego, California.
2. Data for this study were taken from an undergraduate Honours thesis by Marge Pedrick, under the supervision of the first author.

Part II:
Presenting and Defending the Self

7 Strategic self-presentation: an overview

ROBERT M. ARKIN
Department of Psychology, Ohio State University, Columbus, Ohio, USA

JAMES A. SHEPPERD
Department of Psychology, College of the Holy Cross, Worcester, Massachusetts, USA

The term *self-presentation* refers to the process of establishing an identity through the appearance one presents to others. Three decades ago, Erving Goffman stimulated a tradition of research: he noted that it is clearly in a person's 'interests to control the conduct of others', especially conduct that has immediate personal consequences for the individual (Goffman, 1959: 3). Goffman characterised impression management in everyday relations as one common way to accomplish this end. People are acutely aware that others form impressions and use these impressions to guide the course and outcome of social relations. Indeed, M. Snyder (1977) argued that self-presentation, or impression management, is 'the inevitable consequence of social perception' (p.90); by this, he meant that the importance of impression formation in everyday relations implied that people would attempt to manage the impressions made.

The manner in which people plan, adopt and carry out the process of conveying an image of self has grown immensely in scope and sophistication since Goffman first generated interest in the topic. Taxonomies and models of contemporary research agree that there are many goals people strive to achieve through their presentation of self. Research has provided evidence for a host of subtle and sophisticated strategies people undertake to realise these goals.

The purpose of this chapter is to provide a brief overview of contemporary research on self-presentation. Today, one can hardly scan a journal in social psychology without seeing some insightful account or intriguing demonstration of the ways in which people behave to create impressions on others. Increasingly, the same is true in the fields of sociology and communication. To provide some order to this overview, and to distill the literature to manageable proportions, we will focus on two *self-presentation styles* (Arkin, 1981), and touch on the ways in which adopting one or the other of these styles can facilitate or impede an individual's personal success in interpersonal relations. Our focus in this chapter is also exclusively on *direct* tactics of image management (cf. Cialdini & Richardson, 1980); *indirect* tactics (i.e. conveying an impression of self through information about people and things to which one is merely connected) are the focus of the following chapter (Chapter 8) by Cialdini, Finch, and DeNicholas.

Self-Presentation Styles

We live in a world in which a great deal of what we do is evaluated, both by ourselves and by others, with an eye towards assessing a host of personal qualities (Tedeschi, 1981). For instance, performance on the tennis court, in the classroom, in the concert hall, and across a table for two is scrutinised closely to determine athletic, intellectual, artistic or social competence. In addition to ability, characteristics such as likeability, trustworthiness and reliability are assessed and reassessed on a continuous basis.

An acquisitive self-presentation style

Whether the goal can be superficially described as that of appearing knowledgeable, facile, smooth or productive, the underlying basis of impression management characteristically involves impressing others favourably whenever and wherever possible. The prototype of the effective impression manager is the individual high in 'self-monitoring' (e.g. M. Snyder, 1979). The 'high self-monitor' has 'the flexibility and adaptiveness to cope quickly and effectively with a diversity of social roles . . . [she] can choose with skill and grace the self-presentation and social behavior appropriate to each of a wide variety of social situations' (Snyder, 1979: 102). As described in much greater detail in Chapter 4 of this volume, self-monitoring (Snyder, 1974, 1979) is a trait dimension that represents a combination of self-presentational and self-attentional differences. The high self-monitoring individual is simultaneously sensitive to situational cues to appropriate behaviour and is also skilful at monitoring his or her own expressive behaviour to keep it in accordance with these cues.

Historical perspectives

Actually, William James (1890) anticipated this analysis of self-presentation quite some time ago. James focused on the pervasive nature of an acquisitive brand of self-presentation:

> A man [sic] has as many social selves as there are individuals who recognize him and carry an image of him in their mind . . . But as the individuals who carry the images form naturally into classes, we may practically say that he has as many different social selves as there are distinct groups of persons about whose opinions he cares. He generally shows a different side of himself to each of these different groups. Many a youth who is demure enough before his parents and teachers swears and swaggers like a pirate among his 'tough' young friends. We do not show ourselves to our children as to our club companions, to our masters and employers as to our intimate friends. (1890, Vol. 1: 294)

Similarly, Goffman (1959) drew an analogy between everyday life and the world of the theatre in his 'dramaturgical' approach. For Goffman, borrowing from Shakespeare, 'all the world's a stage, and all the men and women merely players'. According to Goffman (1959), self-presentation is designed to overcome obstacles to smooth encounters and lasting relationships. The goals of the relationship are the multitude of material and social benefits people obtain from affiliating with others.

Among the benefits of affiliation, the quest for social approval or liking was among the first motives posed (Crowne & Marlowe, 1964; Jones, 1964) and is still thought to be one of the primary forces underlying self-presentation (Jones & Pittman, 1982). Individuals who score high on a scale of Need for Approval (Crowne & Marlowe, 1964) tend more than their low-scoring counterparts to engage in socially desirable behaviour. For instance, they (a) tend to report extremely favourable attitudes about dull and boring tasks they must do for the experimenter, (b) tend to conform in response to social pressure, (c) tend to give popular rather than unusual word associations, (d) are less likely to use or report noticing 'dirty' words, (e) are more susceptible to persuasive appeals to change their attitudes, and (f) tend to suppress hostility towards persons who insult or take advantage of them (Crowne & Marlowe, 1964). Each of these behaviours reflects a sort of smoothing over of interpersonal relations; each is an expression of the socially desirable thing to do.

Contemporary perspectives

Jones & Pittman (1982; and Jones, 1964) refer to such approval-based self-presentation as *Ingratiation*. The main goal of the ingratiator is to be seen as likeable. There are many ways this can be accomplished, or course; one common tactic is to give compliments, another is to conform to another person's opinions or to copy or imitate his or her acts (e.g. Jones, 1964). As the saying goes, imitation is the sincerest form of flattery. It is clear that people tend to like other people whose beliefs, attitudes or behaviours are similar to their own (e.g. Byrne, 1971). Ingratiators tend to use both verbal and nonverbal indicators of attentiveness as well as agreement. For instance, the individual seeking to be ingratiating tends to lean forward, nod and agree and smile, ask questions and talk less (Godfrey, Jones & Lord, 1986).

Such flattery—compliments, favours, imitation and attentiveness—must be given with skill and grace, however. Indiscriminate flattery can lead a target individual to suspect ingratiation (Kauffman & Steiner, 1968), and transparent ingratiation produces suspicion and can produce disliking where likeability was sought (Jones & Wortman, 1973). This fine line between promoting 'the attractiveness of one's personal qualities' (Jones & Wortman, 1973) and risking sycophancy is called the 'ingratiator's dilemma' (Jones & Wortman, 1973). Unsuccessful ingratiators appear to be the victims of 'either too much or too little' (Godfrey, Jones & Lord, 1986: 115).

A person can seek to present an identity directed at gaining some immediate or deferred reward through other means as well. In contrast to the goal of affection or attractiveness, sought by the ingratiator, Jones & Pittman (1982) posed the tactic of *Intimidation*; intimidation is designed to induce fear in another and, in turn, to make attempts at social influence more effective. The person who is feared is credible when threats and other forms of coercion are used. That is, by creating an image of being dangerous, the intimidator is in a position to control the course and outcome of social interaction merely by seeming likely to mete out punishment. The ineffective intimidator is the one who seems unable to live up to his or her reputation; the person who is wishy-washy, or blustery and weak, finds that his or her threats are diminished—not enhanced—by tactics of intimidation.

Another tactic, *exemplification* (Jones & Pittman, 1982), can be effective in eliciting imitation in others. For example, the individual who exemplifies the best of work habits (arriving at work early, no coffee breaks, taking work home) projects an image that permits rigid adherence to high standards in evaluating others. By fostering a perception of integrity or moral worthiness, one can also arouse guilt in the target of the influence attempt. In either case, the exemplifier can induce stricter adherence to some desired standard of behaviour. Of course, the exemplifier runs the risk of seeming to be a hypocrite or sanctimonious. As with the ingratiator's dilemma, there is a fine line between the desired reaction (guilt, emulation) and a response that is reactive (feelings of exploitation). Exemplification also requires skill and grace.

Self-promotion is the tactic used as a vehicle to help demonstrate competence, either in terms of some general ability (one's intellect) or some specific skill (playing piano). The goal of this tactic is respect or deference. Self-promotion requires as much skill, grace and sophistication as all the other forms of acquisitive self-presentation described above. For instance, the individual whose shortcomings are known by others may have to acknowledge such weaknesses, but then go on to emphasise other positive characteristics that may not have been apparent (Baumeister & Jones, 1978). There is also the danger of making claims that prove a great mismatch with reality (e.g. Wortman, Costanzo & Witt, 1973), such as when someone fraudulently brags about some athletic prowess.

Individuals can use a variety of tactics to achieve self-promotion (Godfrey, Jones & Lord, 1986); for instance, subjects instructed to engage in self-promotion are likely to draw attention to themselves by using first-person pronouns. In addition, they are more likely to mention or consider mentioning their accomplishments when pursuing self-promotion. In so doing, self-promoters can capture the attention of others and provide evidence of their competence.

Finally, perhaps the most intriguing of these self-presentational tactics described by Jones & Pittman (1982) is *supplication*. The supplicant seeks to demonstrate his or her helplessness. Unlike the self-promoter (who seeks respect), the intimidator (who fosters fear) or the exemplifier (who seeks guilt or hopes for emulation), the supplicant acknowledges weakness and dependence. The supplicant relies on a sense of obligation, or feelings of nurturance, to lead others to treat the supplicant well. Unlike the other self-presentation strategies, then, supplication is not a direct attempt to seek power and therefore influence. It stems from a position of weakness. An individual may feign fatigue, and seek help on a dull task without seeming to be lazy. Being 'poor with one's hands' is a convenient way to avoid the role of Mr Fixit around the house. And knowing little about the specifics of cars can be used to get help with changing the tyre. Recent evidence suggests that, in certain circumstances, people will even 'strategically fail' at some task, lowering others' expectations for satisfactory performance and taking themselves 'off the hook', so to speak (Baumgardner & Brownlee, 1987; Weary, 1988).

Distinguishing assertive and defensive strategies

Jones & Pittman (1982) argue that supplication is distinct from the other strategies of self-presentation in that it is the tactic of last resort. They suggest that, in the hierarchy of choices among tactics of social influence, advertising one's weakness and dependence on another person is perhaps the least desirable means of 'getting one's way' (Cialdini, 1988). Relatively powerless individuals must opt for weaker strategies of influence in general (e.g. Canary, Cody & Marston, 1986), but supplication is an extreme form of acknowledging one's powerlessness. While weak forms of social influence, such as supplication, can achieve the short-term goal, the long-term costs can be substantial. Dependency on powerful others has collateral disadvantages, such as depressive affect (e.g. Ford & Berkman, 1988), beyond the loss in credibility and social power in the long-term course of social exchange. In sum, the tactics of supplication and of self-promotion appear to be incompatible and at odds with one another.

The tactic of supplication seems distinct from the other strategies of self-presentation outlined by Jones & Pittman (1982) in another way as well. It has only a superficial appearance of accomplishing some positive end. Instead, supplication seems more often than not to be focused on avoiding some negative outcome: that is, the weakness and dependence that constitute the supplication strategy is often genuine. An individual is willing to reveal it only because getting help and realising some goal prevents some negative outcome that is very costly. The supplication strategy seems to stem from a position of weakness (cf. Canary, Cody & Marston, 1986), while the other strategies described by Jones & Pittman (1982) tend to stem from a position of strength, and seem to be more clearly acquisitive in nature.

The person well up the social hierarchy may eschew self-presentational tactics altogether. The ultimate power of leadership can mean that it is not important how the subordinate views the leader, 'for the subordinate's opinion of the leader seldom has repercussions' (Snodgrass,

1985: 152). However, the superordinate individual's 'feelings about the subordinate can very well affect the subordinate's tenure, salary, grade, promotions, and so forth' (p. 152). Consequently, the subordinate in any social hierarchy must remain sensitive to the self-presentation he or she attempts as well as to the way the presentation of self is received by superiors. In sum, the role of the subordinate demands great skill and effort devoted to self-protection (associated with lowest levels of power) as well as various forms of self-promotion (associated with moderate degrees of power). By contrast, the person with absolute power need not be sensitive to the opinions or feelings of others at all.

In this section, we have posed a distinction between assertive self-presentation—broadly conceived to include acquisitive self-presentation in the form of ingratiation, intimidation, self-promotion, and other specific tactics—and self-protection. Having posed this distinction, we are now in a position to turn expressly to the topic of self-protection. Increasingly, the typical focus on the successful, facile, smooth and graceful among us has been viewed as an incomplete picture of the topography of self-presentation (e.g. Arkin, 1981; Tedeschi & Norman, 1985). In the sections to follow, we will develop further the idea that assertive and defensive strategies of self-presentation constitute two broad classes of self-presentational behaviour that offer a useful theoretical and empirical framework.

A protective self-presentation style

The polar opposite of the skill of the 'self-monitor' (the prototype of the acquisitive self-presenter described above) could be the carefree existence of the person completely unconcerned with social influence. Such a person could be described as indifferent to the social situation, or unaware of or insensitive to the long-term social consequences of his or her actions. Of course, such an individual might also be characterised as out of touch with social reality, where material and social necessities are meted out in both the short term and the long term by powerful others.

Quite apart from disinterest, or ignorance of the social consequences of one's actions, there is another countervailing force that competes with the desire for social approval and the material and social rewards that approval signifies: the desire to avoid social disapproval. As noted by Snyder and Higgins in Chapter 9 of this volume, one means of avoiding disapproval is by offering an excuse for some inadequate behaviour that has created a social predicament (see also Chapters 10, 11, 12 and 13). Excuses attempt to recast some action as inadvertent, an accident, or as an unintended after-effect. For example, the statement 'I didn't mean to . . . ' is a type of excuse commonly used to divert a powerful party from taking restorative action (Jellison, 1977). Similarly, justifications provide reasons why an apparently negative behaviour should be viewed instead as legitimate, justified, or even good (see particularly Chapter 11). Individuals may cite a higher good, as when a positive end seems to justify an uncomfortable means. Finally, disclaimers are used to deny personal responsibility for an event even before it occurs.

Together, the forms of self-protection listed above constitute ways of diverting superiors and peers from taking some action that is very costly to the individual. When in some predicament, and when anticipating some predicament, a person can present an identity directed at avoiding some specific and rather immediate loss or punishment.

The role of 'state' social anxiety

Being interviewed for a desirable job, going on a first date, or giving a speech before a large and important audience are acts that could make almost anyone feel anxious. Some people—those who are shy (Zimbardo, 1977) or easily embarrassed (Crozier, in press)—may tend to feel anxious in almost any situation in which they might be evaluated. For these individuals, anxiety appears to have more traitlike qualities than it seems to be just a temporary and passing state.

Schlenker & Leary (1982) proposed that a 'state' of social anxiety arises when a person is motivated to make a particular impression on an audience, but doubts he or she is able to do so. In short, if an unsatisfactory evaluative reaction from a subjectively important audience is likely, social anxiety is the result. Naturally, according to this viewpoint an individual must assess the likelihood of achieving a preferred self-presentation, or social anxiety should never occur. Schlenker & Leary (1982) therefore propose that an assessment process is triggered whenever a self-presentational goal is important to the individual, and when some signal indicates that the social performance under way may be undermined. That is, people tend to feel anxious when motivated to impress others favourably, but are in doubt about the outcome. If an assessment indicates that the desired image will be achieved, the initial presentation of self is reinaugurated; that is, the initial acquisitive presentation of self is continued. However, if the assessment indicates that the desired image will not be achieved, the individual must 'make the best of a bad situation' (p. 658). To cope with such a predicament, the individual will adopt a cautious, innocuous, or non-committal presentation of self (Schlenker & Leary, 1982).

The simple principle offered by Schlenker and Leary helps to organise much of what is known about the antecedents of social anxiety. People tend to feel anxious (a) when dealing with powerful, high status others whose impressions matter, (b) when in a novel situation, where the social rules of action are unclear or unknown, (c) when there is a large number of people present, such as a large party or an audience to a speech, (d) when the context is an evaluative one, as when one is trying to make an impression during a first date, (e) when the desired impression one is trying to create involves something important or central to the individual's self-image, as when a student presents his or her senior honours project to the faculty for their consideration (Leary, 1983: 69–97).

In all these instances, people are highly motivated to make particular impressions, ones which have favourable implications, but at the same time are likely to doubt that they can foster the desired impression. The irony Schlenker & Leary (1982) offer is that it is precisely these circumstances (where a favourable presentation of self is most desired) in which doubts about one's self-presentational efficacy are most likely to arise.

The role of 'trait' social anxiety

The shy person has been posed as the prototype of someone inclined to adopt a conservative social orientation (Arkin, 1981). Those who are shy (Zimbardo, 1977), or easily embarrassed (Crozier, in press), tend to feel anxious in almost any situation in which they might be evaluated. To regulate that anxiety, even before it arises, the person who is 'trait' anxious chronically approaches social situations intending merely to avoid social disapproval rather than to seek approval. The term 'protective self-presentation' was coined to characterise this type of social conservatism. The 'protective' individual attempts to create an impression that is merely safe.

In sum, despite the general preference to present oneself in socially desirable ways (in order to engender approval and liking, sustain an interaction, and maximise the likelihood that others will help meet one's social and material needs), for the shy individual the motive to sustain a sense of safety and security (e.g. Sullivan, 1953) often predominates.

That is, when a person weighs the costs of disapproval as high or higher than the rewards of approval or accolades that can follow success, a conservative and safety-oriented style of interpersonal relations can supplant the acquisitive self-presentation style described earlier. In short, 'getting along' becomes pre-eminent over 'getting ahead' (Hogan, Jones & Cheek, 1985; Wolfe, Lennox & Cutler, 1986). For instance, the risk of social disapproval and the desire merely to 'get along' can produce self-censorship and compromise. To illustrate, individuals high in social anxiety, who place great stock in protecting their social image and avoiding disapproval (Arkin, 1981; Schlenker & Leary, 1982), tend to moderate their judgements when they expect to be confronted by someone who holds a different opinion from their own (e.g. Turner, 1977). In so doing, these individuals seize a part of the attitude scale that is normatively and practically unassailable. By appearing to have no attitude at all, one can avoid appearing to have the wrong attitude. Those who have no attitude can be persuaded, but they cannot be attacked.

The protective nature of moderating and self-censoring one's views (cf. Arkin, 1981) is highlighted when attitude moderation is contrasted with attitude polarisation. There are clear acquisitive advantages to holding fast, or even polarising one's judgements. A position towards the pole (on a generally preferred side of an issue) tends to convey the impression that one is knowledgeable, authoritative, expert and well-informed (Jellison & Arkin, 1977). Consequently, interpersonal politics (tactics for gaining, holding and using power in interpersonal relations) would tend to suggest that individuals position themselves towards one or the other end of an attitude dimension if they desire to establish themselves as competent, authoritative or powerful. An exception to this strategy, however, is found among candidates for high level public office who traditionally tend to avoid expressing attitudes or positions that might be interpreted as extreme.

In general, however, in contrast to the individual seeking social power, the person who values getting along as much or more than getting ahead tilts towards a neutral position. This is the safe territory where followers can wait for consensus to emerge. When it does, they seek the safety of numbers and submerge their personal identity within the identity of the group.

Empirical Illustrations of the Self-Presentation Styles Concept

Most attempts at self-presentation reflect an intermixing of both the acquisitive and protective self-presentation styles. Specifically, a given self-presentational act may be undertaken for reasons of self-promotion as well as self-protection. To illustrate the intermixing of the two self-presentational styles, we now focus on two specific self-presentational behaviours (the self-serving bias in causal attribution; and self-handicapping) that could be undertaken to serve either motive. Both conceptually and empirically, however, it is possible to disentangle the two sources of self-presentation, and the following illustrations provide a vehicle for that as well.

The self-serving bias

The process of self-attribution provides a rich illustration of the tug towards self-promotion and the competing appeal of self-protection. The 'self-serving bias in causal attribution' (Weary & Arkin, 1981) is a fairly clear use of attributional principles aimed at protecting, preserving and sustaining, or enhancing, one's image. The 'bias' refers to a rather pervasive tendency to attribute successful outcomes to oneself and failing outcomes to other factors (Weary & Arkin, 1981). Such a bias serves to modulate the link between the 'whatness' and the 'whyness' of things. By denying personal responsibility for a failing outcome, the negative quality of the event is vastly reduced; although the failure has occurred and cannot be reversed (i.e. the 'whatness' is left intact), the implications of the failing outcome in determining others' judgements of one's level of ability is minimised. Put simply, by attributing a failing outcome to some extraneous external cause, one can sever the usual link between performance and evaluation. Commonly, this is referred to as 'excuse-making' (Snyder, Higgins & Stucky, 1983; see Chapter 9 of this volume, by Snyder and Higgins, for empirical and everyday illustrations). By contrast, when one assumes personal responsibility for successful outcomes, the positive quality of the success can be increased by asserting the link between performance and evaluation (i.e. taking personal credit for the successful outcome).

As a self-presentational device, however, the self-serving bias would seem to be an *ad hoc* tool for fine-tuning one's image. A person associates himself or herself with success, and dissociates himself or herself from failure, only after the outcome has been achieved. The outcome, success or failure, reflects well or poorly on the individual. The attributional account is then offered to help the person cope with—or capitalise on—that outcome. That is, the 'self-serving bias' arises when a person is already in a predicament (i.e. a failure has occurred) or enjoys the prospect of basking in further glory (i.e. success has occurred). A more subtle approach would involve the strategic manipulation of a context proactively, so that only desired inferences about personal qualities could be drawn by others.

The most direct way of achieving such a result would be to undertake tasks only when success is assured. Throughout life, people make choices (college major, career, marital partner) that they judge to be surer bets than other options. Indeed, some persons opt for a course that seems predictable (e.g. the military), and forgo control over their destiny in order to ensure certainty about their outcomes (e.g. Burger & Arkin, 1980). However, most persons choose courses of action that constitute a challenge, in which the probability of success and failure are both present (and perhaps near equal). The prospect of success and that of failure may be weighted differently, though, in terms of the value placed on making a favourable impression (consequent to success) and avoiding an unfavourable image (consequent to failure). A heavy stress on avoiding an unfavourable image might foster the self-presentational strategy of 'self-handicapping'.

Self-handicapping

The term 'self-handicapping' refers to a person's attempt to reduce a threat to esteem by proactively seeking or creating inhibitory factors that interfere with performance and thus provide a persuasive causal explanation for potential failure. The introduction of extraneous interfering causal factors obscures the link between performance and evaluation, at least in the case of that potential failure, and mitigates the impact of the failure feedback. As with the self-serving bias phenomenon, the result is that a failure is not viewed as a reflection of low ability or incompetence. Yet, the probability of failure is increased by the introduction of the 'handicap'; in the face of the handicap, success is less likely. To quote those who first studied the phenomenon, the self-handicapper 'reaches out for impediments, exaggerates handicaps, and embraces any factor reducing personal responsibility for mediocrity . . . ' (Jones & Berglas, 1978: 2), even at the cost of making mediocrity more likely.

Regulating 'state' social anxiety

Berglas & Jones (1978) demonstrated self-handicapping first in a laboratory experiment. Participants in this study were informed that they had performed very well on a pre-test measuring intellectual ability. For half of the participants, the items on the pre-test were moderately difficult, leading them to believe that they had a reasonable probability of reproducing their performance on a follow-up test. For the remaining participants, however, the items on the pre-test were predominantly unsolvable. These subjects could not understand how they performed so well on the pre-test and, consequently, were led to doubt their ability to reproduce their performance on the follow-up test. Prior to taking the follow-up test, participants were given a choice between taking a drug that would facilitate test performance (called 'Actavil'), a drug that would interfere with test performance (called 'Pandocrin'), and a neutral drug which was described as likely to have no effect on test performance at all. Ostensibly, they were given the choice because the researchers were interested in the influence of the drugs on intellectual functioning. In fact, the alleged drugs were placebos.

From a self-presentation styles perspective, the participants who believed they had performed very well on a test that actually consisted of unsolvable items had been placed in a predicament. These participants desired to sustain their positive presentation of self through reproducing the successful performance on the re-test. However, because their prior success followed working on unsolvable problems, they doubted their ability to do so. According to Schlenker & Leary (1982), these participants should have experienced 'state' social anxiety. Furthermore, they could have exacerbated their predicament by choosing the facilitating drug, 'Actavil'. They might perform no better in spite of the boost afforded them by the Actavil. Yet, should they choose the interfering drug, 'Pandocrin', they might actually increase the likelihood of failing.

However, choice of the interfering drug provided a path towards reducing the experience of social anxiety and would serve to counteract the interfering effects of the state of social anxiety itself. By choosing to handicap their forthcoming performance these individuals could provide themselves with a non-ability explanation for failure. Should they perform poorly on the upcoming test, their failure would be attributable not to their own shortcomings, but to the debilitating drug instead. With a handicap in place, these subjects would no longer be expected to perform at their previous level. In a sense, the handicap would take them 'off the hook', releasing them to pursue a more obtainable self-presentational goal. The net result would be lowering social anxiety. There is evidence to suggest that social anxiety is reduced by the presence of a handicap; both Leary (1986) and Brodt & Zimbardo (1981) found that socially anxious persons, forced to perform in the presence of a debilitating handicap, were less anxious during the course of a social encounter than their counterparts who were not exposed to the debilitating handicap.

Berglas & Jones (1978) found that participants who had experienced the 'non-contingent success', in which their successful performance was somewhat of a mystery, resolved the conflict by ingesting the interfering 'Pandocrin'. (Those who were more sure of their ability to perform well on the follow-up test more often chose the facilitating 'Actavil'.) By choosing the interfering pill, they were able to mitigate the implications of the failure for spoiling their public image. The pill provided an excuse, should they fail, permitting them to conceal their inadequacy.

Taking a debilitating drug, consuming alcohol and withdrawing effort are all illustrations of self-handicaps. Each of these acts obscures the inference that poor performance is due to incompetence. However, each of these actions reflects an internal 'disposition' that is itself not particularly flattering. The alcoholic, the drug abuser and the chronically slothful individual are all able to protect themselves from the attribution of incompetence. However, the short-term and long-term costs of this type of label (e.g. shame) are little better than an attribution of incompetence. A more strategic self-handicap would set the stage so that a poor performance would be attributable to some *external* impediment, a factor that could not reflect poorly on the handicapper. The most common example in the literature involves the choice of an inordinately difficult goal, or task, for which the likelihood of success is low (e.g. see Arkin & Baumgardner, 1985).

Interestingly, the choice of a very difficult goal or impossible task confers an additional advantage. It is hard not to admire an individual with high aspirations. Consequently, it is possible that a self-presentation strategy such as self-handicapping stems from the desire to promote oneself, rather than to protect oneself. In addition to the admiration one receives for being willing to work under less than ideal circumstances, and the admiration associated with accepting challenges or trying the impossible, there is always the possibility of success. The person who succeeds in spite of a handicap is all the more entitled to the accolades that success ordinarily brings.

Although, in principle, self-handicapping would embody this self-promotive feature alongside its self-protective quality, we suspect that genuine handicaps are rarely sought with an eye towards promoting one's image in this way. People may claim (or, more likely, 'let on') that their successes were achieved in spite of overwhelming odds, but it seems unlikely that people would risk failure (i.e. actually handicap themselves) in order to demonstrate true excellence (i.e. success in spite of the handicap). Handicapping as an acquisitive brand of self-promotion seems likely to occur only when success is already assured. Thus, it seems likely that self-handicapping is predominantly self-protective.

Self-promotion probably takes the form of more direct attempts to establish one's competence, intelligence, knowledge, skills or prowess. The self-promoter may display his or her 'credentialled self' by displaying diplomas, certificates, or plaques of one type or another. Ordinarily, these tactics are employed for some immediate objective, such as obtaining a job. The job application itself constitutes a study in the art of self-promotion. Modesty is a strategy restricted to a very special set of circumstances, such as when the audience already has an image of the actor as competent (Ackerman & Schlenker, 1975) or when the actor fears he or she will be asked to deliver on a more flattering claim in the short term (Wortman, Costanzo & Witt, 1973).

The role of 'trait' social anxiety

In the previous section it was argued that, when performance circumstances are characterised by doubt and uncertainty, people will regulate their anxious feelings by self-handicapping. Given their doubt and uncertainty, it might be anticipated that persons who are chronically high in social anxiety would be prime candidates for self-handicapping. By self-handicapping, socially anxious persons would be able to keep their anxiety feelings in check.

Before discussing self-handicapping and trait social anxiety, it is first necessary to draw a distinction between two classes of self-handicaps. Self-handicaps differ with respect to whether they are 'created' by an individual prior to some performance or exist in some form prior to performance. By 'created', we mean to imply impediments that are set in place or actually fashioned by the individual. Created or constructed handicaps would include such actions as ingesting alcohol or drugs, choosing inhibiting performance circumstances, preparing for some performance to an inadequate degree, etc. In contrast to constructed handicaps are those handicaps that pre-exist either within the individual or in the individual's context, prior to performance. This class of handicaps would include personal disabilities, physical complaints, personal constraints such as test-anxiety, and environmental factors such as loud noise, poor lighting, and the like.

Regarding pre-existing self-handicaps, there is evidence to suggest that socially anxious persons will self-handicap by pre-emptively claiming their anxiety symptoms as an excuse for failure. In one study, for instance, high and low socially anxious undergraduates were instructed that they were to take a test of social intelligence. Some of the participants were led to believe that anxiety symptoms had no effect on test performance, while others were told nothing about the relationship between anxiety symptoms and test performance. An additional group of high and low socially anxious participants also was given no information regarding the relationship between anxiety and test performance; instead, they were provided with instructions that de-emphasised the evaluative nature of the test (Snyder et al., 1985). Prior to taking the test, all participants were provided with an opportunity to report their current level of anxiety.

The researchers found that highly socially anxious participants reported experiencing heightened anxiety symptoms in a setting in which their anxiety could serve as an excuse for poor performance. In the setting in which social anxiety was described as having no effect on performance, and in the non-evaluative setting, socially anxious participants did not report heightened anxiety. Low socially anxious persons did not demonstrate the self-protective strategy in any instance; rather they reported relatively few anxiety symptoms regardless of how the test setting was characterised. To summarise, the study by Snyder et al. (1985) suggests that high socially anxious persons are willing to use their anxiety symptoms strategically as a pre-emptive excuse for failure on an upcoming test.

Although socially anxious persons appear willing to claim their anxiety symptoms as a handicap to an upcoming performance, they seem unwilling to discount personal responsibility for an unsuccessful act by constructing a handicap to performance. In two experiments high and low socially anxious participants were given a choice between listening to performance-enhancing or performance-debilitating music while taking a test measuring intellectual ability (Arkin & Shepperd, 1988). Although low socially anxious persons chose to listen to performance-debilitating music while taking the test, high socially-anxious individuals did not.

The research described above raises an interesting question: why are socially anxious individuals willing to report their anxiety as a handicap (a pre-existing handicap) but not willing to engage in the ostensibly similar behaviour of acquiring an external impediment to performance (a constructed self-handicap)? Both pre-existing self-handicaps and constructed self-handicaps provide a pre-emptive excuse for failure—the handicap itself. Should a person perform poorly in the presence of either a pre-existing or constructed handicap, he or she can assert the handicap as a plausible cause of the failure. Moreover, the two forms of self-handicapping share the added advantage of augmenting ability should the person perform successfully in the presence of the handicap. After all, success achieved in spite of a handicap should be seen as an admirable accomplishment.

Nevertheless, there are several plausible explanations for the inconsistent findings among socially anxious individuals across the two classes of self-handicaps. First, there may be different costs associated with the two forms of self-handicapping. Specifically, the anxious person who reports that his or her debilitating anxiety functions as an obstacle to a successful performance suffers no increased risk of failure by making such a claim. For the anxious person, the probability that failure will ensue as a result of crippling anxiety remains the same regardless of whether the knowledge of this handicap is made public or kept private. Thus, in terms of the impact it has on actual task performance, claiming a pre-existing handicap is a relatively safe venture. Conversely, constructing handicaps, by definition, diminishes the probability that the handicapper will perform successfully. Indeed, the handicaps which are likely to be most persuasive are the same ones that debilitate task performance the most. In short, persons who construct handicaps not only (1) must admit to embracing an action which, if it is to be persuasive as a handicap, is likely to be negatively sanctioned, but also (2) diminish the likelihood that a successful performance on the task will occur. In weighing the costs and benefits associated with constructed self-handicaps, it seems likely that socially anxious persons perceive the increased risk of failure as too costly. Consequently, they resist using this attributional strategy.

A second explanation is also based on the equation of the relative costs associated with internal pre-existing versus constructed forms of self-handicapping. Constructed handicaps subject the handicapper to a very great risk of being caught practising deception. People who construct a handicap run the risk that observers will call their bluff, forcing them to attempt the task again unencumbered by the handicap. With the handicap removed, their true ability (or lack thereof) is laid open to the scrutiny of others. Should they continue to fail in the absence of the handicap, they are left with the cost of the handicap (being perceived as lazy, as a drug or alcohol abuser, etc.) yet denied the benefit of a non-ability attribution made for failure. With internal pre-existing handicaps, the handicapper's bluff can never be called. While an audience may come to doubt the authenticity of a self-handicap that is merely reported, they can never conclusively exclude it as the cause of a failure. Thus, there is less risk associated with internal pre-existing self-handicaps because only the handicapper can know the impact they truly have on performance.

This same argument can be used to explain why socially anxious persons are unwilling to deny personal responsibility for an unsuccessful outcome after it occurs (i.e. make self-serving attributions; Arkin et al., 1980). As with acquiring a self-handicap, citing a cause other than lack of ability as the source of failure raises the spectre of being challenged. Persons who assert extenuating circumstances (e.g. 'my poor performance was due to not having enough time to do my best') as an excuse for failure may be requested to repeat the task with the extenuating circumstances removed. Likewise, they may be faced with the prospect that their excuse will not be judged credible; an excuse is often offered to a more powerful and knowledgeable expert who presumably has a better understanding of what is and is not a viable excuse for failure. It is the resulting embarrassment and the risk of being labelled as one who 'shirks responsibility' that may dissuade socially anxious persons from making self-serving attributions.

The third explanation for the inconsistent findings is that the two forms of self-handicapping may tap different levels of sophistication in knowledge of attributional inference processes. Socially anxious persons are characterised by a focus away from the task and on avoiding disapproval (Baumeister & Steinhilber, 1984). In a sense, they are very much like test-anxious persons (Mandler & Watson, 1966; Wine, 1971). In a test situation, test-anxious persons tend to think not about the test, but rather about such interfering things as how poorly they are performing, the time constraints, the difficulty of the problems, how others have performed, and their level of ability. These interfering thoughts inhibit test-anxious individuals from concentrating on the test problems, and consequently impede performance.

In a similar manner, the inordinate focus of socially anxious persons on social disapproval may interfere with the tendency to make attributional links between behaviours and outcomes. The report of a pre-existing self-handicap (e.g. reporting anxiety symptoms as an impediment to performance in the Snyder et al. study) is a relatively simple means by which the socially anxious person can manipulate the attributions made for a performance. It merely requires that the audience infer the appropriate attribution from the handicapper's verbal report of personal circumstances that debilitate performance. By contrast, constructing a self-handicap (e.g. taking a test while listening to distracting music as done in the Arkin and Shepperd studies) is a more complex strategy, demanding that the handicapper engage in a more sophisticated attributional inference process. It requires that the handicapper not only be cognisant of the fact that a constructed handicap can serve as a persuasive excuse for a potential failure, but also that he or she realise that observers of the handicap can be drawn into making non-ability attributions should failure occur. To summarise, socially anxious persons may fail to draw the conclusion that a constructed self-handicap can provide an excuse for failure on a forthcoming task. Specifically, their intense concern with evaluation may cloud their ability to make the inference that creating a handicap ultimately can result in others making non-ability attributions for failure.

Summary and Conclusions

Our purpose in this chapter has been to provide a selective overview of the self-presentation literature. Particular attention was given to a framework emphasising two opposing styles of self-presentation: (1) an acquisitive style undertaken with the goal of self-promotion, and (2) a conservative style undertaken with the goal of self-protection. The opposing nature of these two styles was examined in terms of the regulation of state social anxiety and the differences between individuals high and low in trait social anxiety.

From both an historical and a contemporary perspective, the literature on self-presentation has been difficult to organise theoretically. Most attempts at placing the literature within a framework have focused on supplying a litany of strategies for presenting the self. Missing from these approaches is some type of organisational scheme. This chapter offers a framework for viewing self-presentation, one which attempts to move towards an analysis of the broader goals realised through self-presentation: self-promotion and self-protection.

8 Strategic self-presentation: The indirect route

ROBERT B. CIALDINI, JOHN F. FINCH and MARALOU E. DE NICHOLAS
Department of Psychology, Arizona State University, Tempe, Arizona, USA

We are known by the company we keep. Or, at least, so goes the wisdom mothers frequently impart to their children in order to discourage associations with the 'bad' kids down the street. They insist that, for most observers, what we do is often less important than whom we do it with. As in many things, mothers are right. Observers do assume that friends are similar to one another (Miller *et al.*, 1966) and that similar people will behave similarly (Read, 1987b). Thus, on the basis of a simple friendship connection, observers may make personality and behavioural attributions that are independent of a person's true traits and actions.

More tellingly, there is evidence to suggest that such attributions will be made on the basis of associations far more rudimentary than even a simple friendship—associations that lack any semblance of causality or intent. Take, for instance, the circumstances of a military messenger in ancient Persia. This courier had special reason to hope for Persian battlefield success. Should he carry news of victory to the emperor, he would be feted royally. Should he bring news of defeat, however, he would be killed, proving the Shakespearean adage that 'the nature of bad news infects the teller'. Scientific evidence in this regard comes from research by Manis, Cornell & Moore (1974), who found that one who transmits information that the recipient favours is liked more than one who transmits information that the recipient does not wish to hear, and that this liking effect occurred even though the transmitter had neither caused nor endorsed the information. Like the imperial messengers of ancient Persia, then, the transmitters in the Manis *et al.* study acquired the valence of the message with which they were merely paired.

Another domain in which observers assume congruence between items that are non-causally connected can be seen in the research of Jones and his co-workers on the *over-attribution* phenomenon. They have repeatedly found a tendency for observers to perceive that the author of a public statement believes what was said, even if the author had no choice in making the statement (Jones & Harris, 1967; Jones *et al.*, 1971; Snyder & Jones, 1974). Apparently, the mere connection between person and statement is enough to incline observers towards a view of the two as alike.

The implication of data of these kinds for those interested in self-presentational processes is straightforward: because observers perceive as similar those things that are connected in even the most basic ways, raw associations can be used in the service of image management.[1] That is, one seeking to enhance public image can do so not only by presenting information about his or her *own* traits, actions and accomplishments but, in addition, about the traits, actions and accomplishments of his or her *associates*. These alternative routes to favourable self-presentation are embodied in Cialdini & Richardson's (1980) differentiation between *direct* and *indirect* image management tactics. The first of these classifications hardly needs any elaboration, as it is the subject of much investigation and the topic of a number of chapters of this volume. It refers to techniques for the favourable, direct presentation of the self. We know considerably less, however, about the category of indirect image management tactics, which refer to techniques for favourable, indirect presentation of the self via information about the people and things to which one is simply connected. It is to this latter category of self-presentational procedures that we will devote the majority of our attention in this chapter.

The Indirect Route

If, as has been suggested so far, we *can* manage our self-presentations indirectly by managing information about our personal connections, a fundamental question arises: *do* we? If yes, then a set of intriguing additional questions becomes relevant concerning why, how, when and for whom we do so. Fortunately, even though the current research on indirect tactics hardly compares in volume to the rich literature on direct tactics, enough evidence exists to provide answers to each of these questions. To address the fundamental issue of whether the indirect route to a favourable impression is systematically used, we can examine an early line of work on something called the MUM effect (Rosen & Tesser, 1970; Tesser, Rosen & Batchelor, 1972; Tesser, Rosen & Tesser, 1971).

The issue of whether indirect tactics occur reliably

Recall that the research of Manis, Cornell & Moore (1974) demonstrated that persons who merely transmit favourable or unfavourable information are liked and disliked, respectively, for it. Experiments on the MUM effect (the tendency to 'keep Mum about Unpleasant Messages') indicate that people are aware of this liking process and attempt to use it to their advantage. After learning of a phone call carrying either positive or negative information for another, participants in those studies regularly sought to transmit the good news personally ('You just got a phone call with great news. Better see the experimenter for the details.') but not the bad ('You just got a phone call. Better see the experimenter for the details.'). It seems as though participants understood implicitly that they would be viewed less favourably if they were connected to bad news, so they acted *strategically* to link themselves only to good news. But, did they really? After all, one could argue that they disclosed the nature of the good news call but not the bad news call because they enjoyed seeing the other person's happy face and wanted to avoid seeing the other's distress. Perhaps strategic self-presentation had nothing to do with it. This interpretational ambiguity raises a crucial conceptual question: are actions that publicly connect a person only to positive things intended to do so for reasons of favourable self-presentation? To answer that question clearly, we need to turn to a different research arena—the sports arena.

The issue of the strategic nature of indirect tactics

Cialdini *et al.* (1976) conducted a set of studies on the phenomenon of basking in reflected glory. They noted that people frequently speak publicly, not of their own attainments, but of their connections to the attainments of others. They noted further that sports fans seem especially susceptible to this tendency, often trumpeting an association with a victorious team, even though they have done nothing—caught a ball, scored a point, made a stop—to bring about the success. Cialdini *et al.* hypothesised that such behaviour could be conceptualised as an attempt at image management: by connecting themselves to positive others, the fans were attempting to share some of the positivity in observers' eyes. To test their hypothesis, the researchers ran an initial experiment in which they examined the inclination of college students to bask in the reflected glory of their university football team's victories by virtue of the clothing they chose to wear afterwards.

They reasoned that if students wanted to build personal prestige through their university connection to a successful team, they would have to find a way to make that connection as visible as possible to observers. One way the students could do so would be to wear clothing that clearly identified their school of attendance. Therefore, at seven universities with powerful football programmes (Arizona State, Louisiana State, Ohio State, Notre Dame, Michigan, Pittsburgh, and Southern California) raters checked the proportion of students wearing apparel that carried school names, insignia, or emblems on the Mondays following Saturday games during one collegiate football season. The results were quite clear in showing that students were significantly more likely to wear school-identifying apparel on Mondays after a team victory than after a loss or a tie. But does this result necessarily signify an attempt on the part of students to manage others' impressions through the visibility of their positive associations? Perhaps not. It might be argued, for example, that the students simply liked their school more after a football team victory and, therefore, were more likely to wear school-linked apparel. To eliminate this sort of alternative explanation, Cialdini et al. conducted a second study.

They argued that if managing public information about one's simple associations is undertaken in the interests of favourable self-presentation, then it ought to be the case that such information management would be especially prevalent among individuals whose prestige had just been publicly jeopardised. In this second study, Cialdini et al. used a different measure than wearing apparel to assess subjects' tendencies to manage information about their connections to a successful or unsuccessful team— the pronouns students used to describe a school team's victory or defeat. It was predicted that college students who were asked to describe a hometeam victory would use the connecting pronoun 'we' more than some distancing pronoun such as 'they', and that this effect would be strongest for those who had recently undergone an image-threatening experience.

To provide some research participants with an image-threatening experience, students at Arizona State University were called on the phone and, under the guise of a survey, were asked a series of questions concerning their knowledge of their school. Half of the participants were told that they had done very poorly on the test of their knowledge, thereby giving them an image-threatening experience; the other participants were told that they had done very well on the test, thereby giving them an image-bolstering experience. Then, all participants were asked to describe the outcome of a certain game that their school's team had played that year. Half of the respondents were asked to describe the outcome of a particular game that their school's team had won and half were asked to describe a game that their school's team had lost. The pronouns participants used in their descriptions were recorded. As predicted, students used the term 'we' to describe a victory significantly more frequently than to describe a defeat (32% versus 18%). And this tendency was decidedly more pronounced among those who had just failed (40% versus 14%) and, consequently, needed an image boost, than among those who had just succeeded (24% versus 22%).

These results offer confirmation of the hypothesis that people will seek to manage their interpersonal regard by *strategically* managing the public perception of their simple connections to positively or negatively toned entities. That is, not only did respondents try to connect themselves through pronoun selection to victories rather than defeats, but they were especially motivated to do so after a public failure of their own. Thus, those persons most needful of positive self-presentation were most likely to engage in a process of drawing selective self-associations, implicating an image-management motive in that process.

The issue of the forms that indirect tactics can take

We have argued to this point that people do systematically seek to associate themselves with positive rather than negative entities in the eyes of observers because these observers tend to see associated objects as alike. The evidence for our contention, however, has come from only a single form of behaviour—the tendency of people to enhance the visibility of their connections solely to positive messages, people and events. If indirect tactics of impression management are truly robust behavioural tendencies, we should expect to see them manifested in a range of situations as variations on a common theme. For instance, besides attempting to strengthen their perceived connections to positively evaluated things, we should see people attempting to strengthen the perceived positivity of those things to which they are already clearly connected. Indeed, this was one of the predictions of a pair of experiments by

Cialdini & Richardson (1980) in which college students were asked to rate their school on an array of evaluative dimensions (quality of the academic environment, social environment, athletic teams, etc.). Before evaluating their school, however, participants were given a test of 'latent creativity' and were provided with manipulated feedback as to their performances on it. In both studies, it was found that the more poorly participants were told (by the experimenter) that they had done, the more positive were their subsequent pronouncements to the experimenter about the quality of their schools. Thus, as in the pronoun study, the more their personal prestige was damaged, the more participants sought to associate themselves with positive things in an observer's eyes. Note, however, that in the present case the specific form of the tactic was different; it involved enhancing the positivity of a clearly associated object rather than enhancing an association to a clearly positive one.

In addition, Cialdini & Richardson (1980) investigated the existence of a third technique of indirect self-presentation—the public 'blasting' of one's rivals. They reasoned that if students tried to increase the perceived quality of their home university for an observer, they might also try to decrease the perceived quality of a rival university for the same reason. That is, one can manage impressions either by looking good to an observer or by arranging for a competitor to look bad. Using the same manipulated 'creativity test' feedback procedure as before, Cialdini and Richardson found that the more poorly participants thought they had done on the creativity task, the more harshly they rated the quality of their university's traditional cross-state rival school. So, after personal failure, Cialdini and Richardson's subjects engaged in both basking and blasting as indirect tactics of self-presentation, asserting the worth of the school to which they were most positively linked and derogating the worth of the school to which they were most negatively linked.

There is yet another general type of indirect tactic worthy of note— the tendency to avoid actively a perceived connection between oneself and some unflattering event or person. In each statement of their general argument, Cialdini and his co-workers (Cialdini *et al.*, 1976; Cialdini, in press; Cialdini & Richardson, 1980; Richardson & Cialdini, 1981) have asserted that the attempt to manage self-presentations through personal associations is not limited to promoting one's links to positive entities; it could also manifest itself in action designed to obscure one's links to negative entities. A study by Snyder, Lassengard & Ford (1986) illustrates this *distancing* effect nicely. Teams worked on a problem-solving task and were given false feedback regarding their performances. Members of one set of teams were told they had done very well on the task;

members of a second set were told they had done very poorly; and members of a third set were given no performance feedback at all. Later, on the way to another task, all participants were given an opportunity to take and wear badges that identified their team membership. As might be expected from the results of the apparel-wearing and pronoun-use studies of basking that we have described, those persons who were associated with the successful teams were the most likely to display the association by taking and wearing a team badge. More relevant to our current concern with distancing, however, is that those associated with the failing teams were by far the least likely to do so. Moreover, Snyder, Lassengard & Ford argued that the size of the distancing effect in their data was larger than that of the basking effect.

The issue of the target of indirect tactics

So far, we have tried to make the case that perceived associations can be used for the purpose of image management and, consequently, that those who use them in this fashion should be viewed as engaging in a type of strategic communication. But, the question remains, 'strategic communication to whom?' We have suggested in our treatment of indirect tactics of image management that the target of the strategic communication is someone in the communicator's social environment. No doubt that is true, as the evidence indicates that people will manage public information about their associations in ways that take into account aspects of the audience (Cialdini et al., 1976, study 3; Cooper & Jones, 1969).

It is interesting to wonder, however, whether others constitute the only audience affected by the presentation of personal connections. That is, it seems conceivable that the self may serve as the target of indirect tactics of favourable self-presentation. There is growing evidence to suggest that *direct* tactics of image management are undertaken for purposes of enhancing or protecting self-concept (see Greenwald & Breckler, 1985, and Schlenker, 1986, for reviews). Should we expect such an 'inner-audience' effect, though, for indirect tactics? Cialdini & Richardson (1980) have argued that we should. They have maintained that, besides generating information about their connections, people are also observers of those connections. Consequently, they may be susceptible to the same tendency that other observers exhibit to perceive connected things as similar and disconnected things as dissimilar. Evidence in this regard can be found in a set of studies by Stotland and his associates, who demonstrated that a person who perceives a similarity with another on one attribute will assume similarity on additional attributes as well (Burnstein, Stotland & Zander, 1961; Stotland & Dunn, 1963; Stotland, Zander & Natsoulas, 1961). Thus, persons may come to see themselves more positively when they can convince themselves that, in some specific way, they are connected to positive things and/or are not connected to negative things.

Following this reasoning, Finch & Cialdini (in press) conducted research to determine whether people would seek to manage their images through a personal connection if there were no public audience to perceive the connection. In this way, they questioned whether indirect image management techniques occur wholly in the interests of interpersonal regard or, additionally, in the interests of self-regard. Specifically, participants in the study were exposed to a profile of the historical figure Grigori Rasputin (the 'Mad Monk' of Russia), in which he was described in exceedingly unfavourable terms. In the process of reading the profile, half of the subjects encountered information indicating that the day and month of Rasputin's birth matched their own. Actually, the experimenters had secretly rigged each profile with this information, which they had obtained from participants' records. These participants, then, thought that they alone knew of their birthdate connection to the evil Rasputin. The other half of the participants encountered no birthdate information in the (otherwise identical) profile and, consequently, perceived no connection with Rasputin. After reading the profile, all subjects rated their opinions of Rasputin.

Finch and Cialdini predicted that participants who perceived a connection with Rasputin would try to manage the connection by boosting their view of Rasputin's character. In two separate experiments, this prediction was supported. Participants who learned privately of a birthdate similarity to Rasputin rated him significantly less negatively than those who did not learn of such a connection. It is important to recognise something else that was noteworthy about the connection besides its private character—its tenuous nature. A birthdate similarity represents an accidental, trivial, and non-causal association. Yet it was powerful and meaningful enough to change the way participants preferred to view the associated entity. This finding lends support to our earlier contention that even links of the most rudimentary sort may be used in the service of image management, because observers tend to respond similarly to things that are associated even in the most rudimentary ways (Heider, 1958). The Finch and Cialdini studies add to and extend the prior research by suggesting that, because people are observers of their own connections, they will systematically manage information concerning these (sometimes elementary) connections in an attempt to delude or impress themselves!

The issue of personality dispositions towards indirect tactics

A final question to be addressed in our consideration of indirect tactics of impression management flows from the evidence indicating that such tactics are most likely to occur after a personal failure experience (Cialdini *et al.*, 1976; Cialdini & Richardson, 1980). Evidence of this sort indicates that the use of self-presentational tactics may be prompted by a desire to restore a diminished image. We may ask, then, whether persons whose *usual* image of themselves is relatively diminished would be especially likely to try to bolster that image by managing information regarding their associations. In other words, would a dispositional tendency to see oneself in failure-like versus success-like terms generate similar data patterns to those produced by acute manipulations of failure and success? Fortunately, as yet unreported data relevant to this question have been collected in a pair of experiments originating from our laboratories.

The pronoun usage study

Recall that one experiment we have already described concerned the tendency of college students to manage their connections to a successful or unsuccessful football team via pronoun selection (Cialdini *et al.*, 1976, study 2). In that study, students were first made to succeed or fail on a test of campus knowledge. They were then asked to describe the outcome of a football game that their university's football team had either won or lost that season. The dependent variable of interest was the pronoun respondents used in their description of the game outcome. Use of the pronoun 'we' was thought to reflect a tendency on the participants' part to associate themselves with the team, whereas use of some other designation such as 'they' was thought to reflect a tendency to insulate themselves from the team. The results indicated, as predicted, a general tendency for respondents to use 'we' more in characterising a team victory than a team defeat (32% versus 18%). Furthermore, this tendency was significantly more pronounced for participants who had been made to fail on the campus knowledge test (40% versus 14%) than for those who had been ensured of success on that test (24% versus 22%).

In the Cialdini *et al.* (1976) study, the campus knowledge test provided a way to affect, situationally, participants' perceptions of their images. In an as yet unreported follow-up study, we chose not to manipulate image but to measure it, and then to expose selected participants (with existing successful or unsuccessful self-images) to the procedures of the pronoun usage study. As a measure of successful versus unsuccessful self-image, we employed the Personal Control Scale (Mirels, 1970) that is derived from the larger Rotter Internal–External Control (I–E) Scale (Rotter, 1966). The Personal Control Scale was developed as a way to distinguish persons who believed that they could successfully control their personal environments from those who believed that they had no mastery over their personal environments. In our pronoun use follow-up study, Introductory Psychology students completed the Personal Control Scale during a mass testing session at the beginning of the academic semester. We then selected students for participation on the basis of their scores. Specifically, we selected four groups of participants: high perception of control, moderately high perception of control, moderately low perception of control, and low perception of control. Later, analyses showed that the two moderate groups did not differ significantly from one another on the dependent variable of the study; consequently, they are combined in all subsequent discussion.

As in the first pronoun usage study, when students were telephoned, they were asked to participate in a brief survey of college students' knowlege of campus events. All agreed and were asked to describe the outcome of a football game their school team had either won or lost that season. In the follow-up study, however, participants were given no acute success or failure experience prior to their description of the outcome of the game; instead, they were simply categorised according to their Personal Control Scale scores as perceiving high, moderate, or low levels of mastery over their personal environments. The results of the study (presented in Table 8.1) are quite consistent with those of the original pronoun usage study. There was a significant overall tendency for

TABLE 8.1 *Pronoun usage as a function of perceived level of personal control and team outcome*

| | Perceived Level of Personal Control | | |
Outcome	High	Moderate	Low
Team victory	64.5% (31)	62.3% (61)	66.7% (21)
Team defeat	58.9% (34)	43.9% (57)	36.8% (19)

Note: Numbers indicate the percentage of 'we' usage per condition. *N*'s are in parentheses.

participants to use the pronoun 'we' to describe a hometeam victory more than to describe a hometeam defeat (63.7% versus 47.3%). Furthermore, this tendency was most visible in participants with a failure-like self-image and was virtually absent in those with a success-like self-image.

The birthdate usage study

Although the Personal Control Scale offers one measure of the disposition to perceive oneself in successful versus unsuccessful terms, it represents a rather narrow such perception, focusing on the dimension of personal control. Therefore, in another as yet unreported study, Cialdini and De Nicholas classified subjects according to a more general measure of overall self-image, the Rosenberg Self-Esteem Scale (Rosenberg, 1965). Cialdini and De Nicholas then decided to investigate the impact of global self-esteem on a new dependent variable designed to reflect the phenomenon of indirect impression management. Finch & Cialdini (1989) showed that birthdate similarity functions as a connection between persons which can spur one member of the pair to try to manage information relative to that connection. In the Finch and Cialdini experiments, participants who discovered that they had the same birthdate as an unsavoury historical figure, Grigori Rasputin, decided that he wasn't so evil after all. In Cialdini and De Nicholas' unreported study using self-esteem, we employed the birthdate connection with Rasputin in a somewhat different way.

On the basis of their scores on the Rosenberg Self-Esteem Scale, participants were categorised as having higher or lower self-esteem. They were then invited by phone to participate in a psychology experiment, to which they came one at a time. Upon arriving at the experimental room, they were given a profile to read that described Rasputin either in very positive or very negative ways. The negative profile characterised him as a power-hungry opportunist, a liar, and a traitor who served himself above all others. The positive profile, by contrast, characterised him as a misunderstood patriot who worked in earnest for his country but who was brought down by malevolent elements within the Russian court. At the beginning of the profile the participants read that Rasputin's day and month of birth matched their own. By the time they had finished reading the profile, then, participants had learned that Rasputin was either a good or bad man and that they shared a birthdate connection with him.

At this point, a second experimenter, naive to the hypotheses, began to ask a series of increasingly focused questions of participants regarding any connections they might see between Rasputin and themselves. In this way, Cialdini and De Nicholas sought to uncover the tendency of participants to try to associate themselves publicly with Rasputin by mentioning the birthdate connection or to dissociate themselves from him by suppressing any mention of the connection. The results are presented in Table 8.2. An overall tendency was found for participants to mention the birthdate connection later in the series of questions when the connection was with the 'bad' Rasputin. However, this tendency was almost entirely accounted for by the special reluctance of lower self-esteem participants to publicise the association.

The two studies of indirect tactics involving dispositional self-concept showed some interesting parallels, both within themselves and with respect to the indirect tactics studies involving situationally induced success or failure experiences. First, both self-concept studies found an overall tendency for people to try to manage information about their associations so that they were perceived to be connected to positive entities and unconnected to negative entities. Such findings are wholly in keeping with a similar tendency found in studies that did not categorise respondents on dispositional dimensions. Second, both self-concept studies determined that those who normally carried an abiding positive self-image were not especially likely to try to enhance that self-image through the selective management of information about their associations. Instead, such indirect image management appeared to fall more clearly in the behavioural province of those persons with a poorer sense of self. This pattern is strikingly similar to that found in studies employing temporary manipulations of personal image (e.g. successes or failures on creativity tasks or knowledge tests), in which participants whose images were threatened by a situational failure were most likely to engage in indirect tactics of self-presentation. A final parallel worthy of note is that, within both of the self-concept studies, the tendency to manage connections strategically

TABLE 8.2. *Speed of mentioning the birthdate connection*

Self-esteem	Rasputin Profile	
	Positive	Negative
Higher	2.92	2.82
	(12)	(17)
Lower	2.17	0.75
	(12)	(12)

Note: Numbers represent speed of mentioning birthdate on a scale of 0–6, with higher numbers reflecting greater speed. *N*'s are in parentheses.

occurred most prominently among persons with lower self-concepts, who attempted to avoid being connected with a negative other rather than attempting to promote a connection to a positive other. Such a relationship suggests that these persons were more motivated towards ego-protection than towards ego-enhancement (cf. Snyder, Lassengard & Ford, 1986).

The issue of future directions for indirect tactics research

At this point, we seem to know quite a bit about indirect tactics of self-presentation. We know that they occur: (1) reliably; (2) strategically; (3) in response to both situational and dispositional experiences of failure; and (4) for the edification of audiences that include the self. Additional questions remain, however. For instance, although the Finch and Cialdini (1989) experiments showed that such tactics were employed for what appeared to be purely intrapersonal reasons, we have not yet examined thoroughly the question of how indirect tactics might differ when the audience is only the self, as opposed to when it also includes others. The rich history of research on impression management (e.g. Tedeschi, 1981) ensures that the concern for positive interpersonal regard will play a prominent role in any self-presentational tactic. It would be interesting to investigate when and how indirect tactics change with shifts from a wholly private to a more public setting. Another direction for future research would be to enquire into the extent to which indirect tactics of image management are functionally distinct from their more direct brethren. That is, it remains to be determined whether indirect tactics work in ways which direct tactics do not, and whether the two classes of image management tactics represent attempts to achieve the same or different personal goals. Whatever the answer, the route to a greater understanding of indirect tactics of self-presentation is likely to be an intriguing one.

Note to Chapter 8

1. Theoretically, such assertions are wholly consistent with Balance Theory, as developed by Heider (1958). According to Heider, because of strains for cognitive balance, observers exposed to even the simplest of connections (termed 'unit' connections) between objects will tend to see the positively linked objects as similar and the negatively linked objects as dissimilar.

9 Reality negotiation and excuse-making: President Reagan's 4 March 1987 Iran arms scandal speech and other literature

C.R. SNYDER and RAYMOND L. HIGGINS
The University of Kansas, Lawrence, USA

> . . . there are reasons why it happened, but no excuses.[1] (US President Ronald Reagan, 4 March 1987)

Introduction

After the release of the Tower Report in late February of 1987, United States citizens awaited President Reagan's response. The subsequent speech of 4 March was preceded by a level of interest and concern that was unequalled in America since Watergate. It was a carefully prepared performance, one that was aimed at lessening the damage of the Iran arms sale scandal and restoring the President's positive image, as well as the viability of his administration.

What was noteworthy about this speech, from our point of view, is that it highlighted several issues. First, here was a man who obviously saw himself as a 'good person', and this 'goodness' was maintained by maximising his linkage to positive acts, and minimising his linkage to negative acts. In other words, he appeared to present himself for evaluation on two dimensions of appraisal—one dimension that pertained to the positiveness of his actions, and another dimension that involved the degree to which he was linked to these actions. President Reagan, like most of us, therefore, appeared through this speech to be reacting to feedback so as to sustain his personal theory of self. This latter process is the essence of what we call reality negotiation, and excuse-making is a prime example of such a process.

In the following pages we will first provide a more detailed consideration of this general reality negotiation process. Included will be an examination of two major dimensions of appraisal, the valence-of-act and linkage-to-act dimensions, and of the way in which people bias feedback so as to preserve their personal self-theories on those dimensions. Excuse-making, as an example of the reality negotiation process on these two dimensions of appraisal, will then be explored. Next, we will analyse President Reagan's 4 March speech in terms of the valence-of-act and linkage-to-act dimensions of appraisal. Finally, we will discuss the adaptiveness of the excuses in this speech in particular, and excuses more generally.

Reality Negotiation and Self

Dimensions of appraisal

Our beginning assumption is that there are two dimensions of appraisal that are established early in childhood, and are carried throughout the adult life span. These two dimensions, shown in Figure 9.1, serve as an interactive matrix against which people evaluate their 'goodness', and react to information that may in varying degrees be relevant to them. A first dimension involves the perceived *linkage* of the person to a particular act or outcome. On this dimension, the person may have no linkage to an act (i.e. no sense of agency or association is present between the person and an outcome), or may increasingly be linked to an act to the point of absolute linkage. The linkage dimension has little meaning in and of itself, however, unless it is crossed with a second dimension, the *valence* of the act with which one is or is not linked. Here, the act may vary from one that is perceived as very negative to one that is very positive.

As can be seen in the upper right quadrant of Figure 9.1, the 'good' self is composed of an overall appraisal that one is linked to positive acts. For a normal person, we would assert that appraisals of most situations

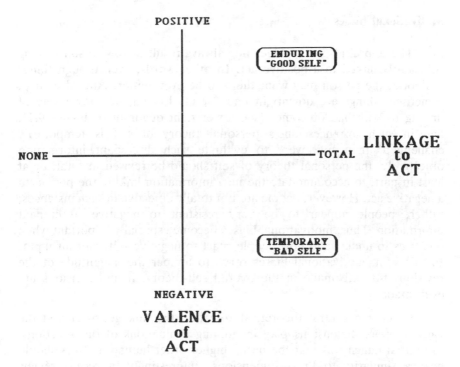

FIGURE 9.1 *The Linkage-to-Act and Valence-of-Act dimensions of appraisal*

result in the person's being somewhat linked to a positive outcome (of varying degrees).[2] Consistent with this latter assertion, people have been shown to report considerable overlap between 'who they are mostly' and how they 'would like to be', but little overlap between 'who they are mostly' and the person they 'hope never to be' (Ogilvie, 1987). Other research shows that people are especially accepting of positive rather than negative feedback (see Markus & Nurius, 1986; Snyder, Shenkel & Lowery, 1977). Additionally, people appear to put themselves in situations in which they believe that they will be linked with positive acts (see Pyszczynski & Greenberg, in press, for related discussion); moreover, people even go so far as to link themselves with the positive acts when there are no legitimate grounds to do so (see Cialdini *et al.*, 1976, for related discussion). Perhaps this 'good self' idea is best captured in the words of William Saroyan (cited in Myers & Ridl, 1979: 89): 'Every man is a good man in a bad world—as he himself knows.'

Motivational biases

The appraisal process does not always result in the person's being sufficiently linked to a positive act. In other words, even though things are good, the person may want them to be even better. And of course, sometimes things are downright bad for us. Indeed, life has a way of linking us with bad outcomes (see lower right quadrant of Figure 9.1), and in such instances one's personal theory of self is temporarily challenged. If people were to evaluate such discrepant information objectively, the personal theory of self should be revised in total, or at least in part, to accommodate the new information linking the person to a negative act. However, people are not totally objective in such instances; rather, people appear to be very resistant to negative, discrepant information. Thus, motivational biases become especially important when one tries to understand how people react to negative self-relevant input. In this vein, motivational biases serve to temper the magnitude of the revisions that are made in the overall self-theory, if any revisions are even made.

Given the central theoretical role that the linkage-to-act and the valence-of-act dimensions play in guiding evaluations of one's actions, our initial hunch was that the basic, higher-order human motives should bear a similarity to these dimensions. Interestingly, a recent review (Taylor & Brown, 1988) suggests that people are motivated to preserve three illusions about themselves. These protective illusions are (1) an unrealistically positive self-evaluation, (2) an exaggerated sense of control, and (3) unrealistic optimism/hope. Further, Taylor and Brown report that these illusions are associated with greater adaptiveness (e.g. enhanced happiness, caring for others, persistence and performance at tasks). What should be emphasised in the present context, however, is that each of these motives can be related to the two basic appraisal dimensions that we have posited. That is, by maximising the positiveness of acts and one's linkage to these acts, or minimising the negativeness of acts and one's linkage to those acts, the person is preserving his or her positive self-evaluation, sense of control and optimism/hope.

Definition and elaboration of reality negotiation process

Reality negotiation is the motivated process of responding to feedback about oneself so as to sustain the person's basic theory of self. By reacting to new, discrepant information through the *negotiated reality* process, the person derives a 'revised' self-view. In a sense, then, revised self-theories are not end-states, but instead, are constantly evolving as one encounters discrepant and nondiscrepant information relevant to the working self-theory. People not only store information about themselves in terms of self-theories, but they are motivated to preserve these theories whenever possible (see, for related discussions, Epstein, 1973; Tedeschi, 1986).

A first point of elaboration in regard to reality negotiation is to emphasise that it is a motivated ('hot') process of reacting to information relevant to one's theory of self. In this reality negotiation process, the person seeks to sustain a personal theory that he or she is linked to positive acts. Whenever possible, the typical person will bias information to preserve this perception. Reality negotiation may occur in the context of protecting oneself against negative feedback (as will be the focus of this chapter), but it may also reflect an enhancing process whereby one attempts to augment the favourable implications of the feedback. That is, although information may be on the positive end of the valence-of-act and the linkage-to-act-appraisal dimensions, people may exaggerate the positiveness and/or linkage as part of the reality negotiating process. Such enhancing reality negotiating processes, like the protecting ones, are fuelled by the underlying biasing motives that are designed to safeguard positive self-evaluation, control and optimism/hope.

The reader may recognise that the enhancing type of reality negotiation process rests within the time-honoured telic theories that emphasise the comparison of the good person experienced now and the imagined ideal person. The ideal self has played a key role in psychoanalytic thinking (e.g. Horney, 1950), adjustment research (Rogers, 1954; Higgins, Klein & Staum, 1985), and recent social psychology theory and research (in which it has been called positive possible self; Markus & Nurius, 1986). In the upper right corner of Figure 9.2, the enhancing reality negotiation processes of increased positiveness of act and linkage to that act are shown. These processes enable the person to be 'pulled' closer to some abstract ideal self that exceeds the normal positive self.

In addition to the enhancing type of negotiated reality described in the previous paragraph, there are also motivational forces to push us away from linkage to bad acts. These forces are also shown in Figure 9.2 (lower right corner). In this latter sense, reality negotiation can operate by diminishing the negativeness of the act, lessening the linkage to the act, or both.

Unlike the more abstract ideal self, we would hold that the negative self is very concrete in nature. That is to say, the negative self or selves

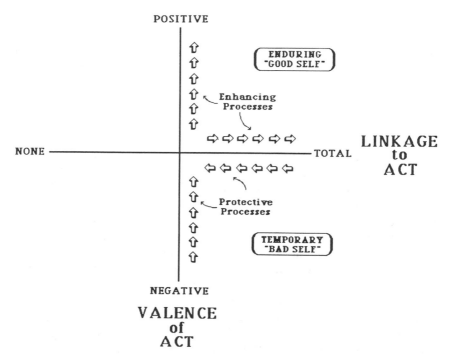

FIGURE 9.2 *Enchancing and protective reality negotiation processes on the Linkage-to-Act and Valence-of-Act dimensions of appraisal*

are activated in specific situations and provide a vivid benchmark from which people seek to distance themselves (in terms of both valence and linkage). Recent research has corroborated the abstract make-up of the ideal self (or selves) and the concrete nature of the negative self (or selves) (Ogilvie, 1987). Because of the vividness of the negative selves, as well as the general aversion to being linked to bad acts, we would argue that the protective reality negotiation processes are more rigorous and potentially have more impact than the enhancing ones. In other words, these protective processes play more of a role in the normal person's coping with feedback than do the enhancing processes.

Although people may bias information to support their personal theories of self, this reality negotiation process must operate within the constraints of external reality as defined by other people (Schlenker, 1980). External reality is defined, in this latter sense, as consensual agreement among other people. Thus, in reality negotiation, we may achieve a biased compromise between what we want to perceive about ourselves and what outside persons will not seriously question. In this latter vein, it may be the case that one of the characteristics of non-adaptive reality negotiation processes is that they do not take external audiences into account (e.g. delusions).

Yet another point of elaboration in regard to the reality negotiation process is that it provides a mechanism not only for determining the shape of the revised self-concept on the appraisal dimensions (as we have described above), but it also controls the rate by which we have to adapt to threatening self-relevant information (Janoff-Bulman & Timko, 1987; Snyder & Higgins, in press). In other words, it allows for a slowing of the change process, thereby facilitating a better formulated revised theory of self. A similar point has been made in philosophy of science (see Popper, 1963), where it has been argued that the conservatism in adopting a new theory actually results in a better, more fully articulated theory.

Overall, reality negotiation is a biased, enhancing or protecting process that operates to achieve a favourable perceived position along the dimensions of valence-of-act and linkage-to-act. The variety of defence mechanisms that have been described over the years all reflect protective reality negotiation processes. And, more to the point of this chapter, excuse-making is a prime example of protective reality negotiation. We turn to an examination of excuse-making next.

Excuse-Making as Reality Negotiation

Definition

Excuse-making is defined, in the present context, as a strategy that protects the personal theory of self by diminishing (1) the perceived linkage between the person and the bad act, and/or (2) the badness of the act. The protective forces of excuse-making, as shown in Figure 9.2, operate on the linkage-to-act and valence-of-act dimensions. These two dimensions of appraisal were inherent in our previous work on excuse-making (see Snyder, Higgins & Stucky, 1983). Additionally, the traditional distinction made between justifications and excuses (see Schlenker, 1980; Scott & Lyman, 1968) can be understood on the basis of badness-of-act and linkage-to-act dimensions. For example, justifications have been described as attempts to minimise the undesirable quality of one's action. In our framework, therefore, justifications reflect strategies that operate on the valence-of-act dimension of appraisal. Excuses, on the other hand, have been previously characterised as attempts to lessen the sense of responsibility for one's bad act. In our framework, such strategies are operating on the linkage-to-act dimension. For our purposes, excuse-making represents the overarching protective process that employs both the linkage-to-act and valence-of-act dimensions.

Initial location on dimensions of appraisal

Excuse-making is ignited in concrete situations where the person experiences, or anticipates experiencing, some relatively high degree of linkage to an act that is bad. A logical first question involves the manner in which the initial sense of linkage to the act and the valence-of-act is determined. In regard to the valence-of-act, we would suggest that a 'bad' act, in general, is 'any action or behavior on the part of a person that falls below the standards that have been established as being typical for that person or people in general' (Snyder, Higgins & Stucky, 1983: 39–40). The act is perceived as increasingly negative the more it falls short of established standards. Further, when the standards for an act become more clear-cut, the potential negativeness of not meeting these standards should also increase (Snyder, 1985b).

The extent of the initial sense of linkage depends on several factors. One such factor is the importance of the activity for one's identity. To the extent that a person has repeatedly performed in a particular performance arena, and has a continued investment in that arena, the sense of linkage will be greater to an act occurring within that context. Also, when the feedback about an act and one's linkage to that act is delivered by an increasingly influential external source (e.g. a high status expert, a powerful other person), then the sense of linkage should be greater (see Becker, 1963, for related discussion). Similarly, the greater the number of external sources that converge to give feedback regarding one's linkage to an act, the stronger the linkage. Finally, the greater the extent to which the external audience has the facts regarding the situation, the greater the linkage to the act.

Overall, the greater the badness of the act and the linkage to the act, the more the person should experience a threat to the positive self-theory. In turn, the greater the threat to self-theory, the stronger should be the excuse-making forces on the dimensions of appraisal. Although it is obviously not the focus of this chapter, it could be argued that the negative act with which one has ultimate linkage is one's death. This consummate threat is one that people appear to defend against their entire lives (see Becker, 1973; Greenberg, Pyszczynski & Solomon, 1986).

The beginning of the excuse-making process

In the initial evaluations on the appraisal dimensions, it can be noted that external audiences, especially if they contain a powerful (e.g. knowledgeable, high status, or decision-making) person or people who are consensual in their feedback, serve to intensify the sense of badness of act and linkage to the act. Such circumstances obviously facilitate the tendency of the transgressing person to aim his or her excuses at the external audience. In other words, from the very start in such instances, the reality negotiation excuse-making process is tailored to the reactions of external audiences. The best example of this type of excuse-making is found in the legal system; the defendant and defence attorney engage in a series of formalised reality negotiations that are aimed at lessening the badness of the act and the linkage to the act in the eyes of the jurists or judges.

Generally, at the beginning of the excuse-making process, the protagonist will select an excuse that appears plausible to the appropriate audiences that may be involved. The audiences include the internal one of the protagonist, as well as an imagined or real external audience with whom the protagonist will have to negotiate. At this point in the sequence, the person may engage in mental simulations (see Kahneman & Tversky, 1982), in which the excuse is presented to the audiences and hypothetical reactions are anticipated. From the internal audience perspective, the protagonist will be predisposed to select the most biased excuse that still reasonably fits the facts; from the external audience perspective, the protagonist will select the excuse that fits the facts *and* has the maximal probability of being accepted. In this latter vein, research has shown that people have accurate ideas regarding what may be a 'good' excuse for external audiences (Tetlock, 1981; Weiner *et al.*, 1987).

Unlike the example of the jury described earlier in this section, in most instances of excuse-making the protagonist does not attend rigidly to external audiences. In many instances in everyday life, excuses are proffered on a more informal basis to ourselves and perhaps a few others in our life sphere. Sometimes, there may be no external audience involved, and thus the protagonist attends only to the internal audience. In many day-to-day failures or disappointments, only the internal audience must be considered in making the excuse.

Overall, the more negative the act may be on the valence-of-act dimension of appraisal, and the greater the linkage to that act, then the probability that external audiences will be involved in the beginning and subsequent excuse-making process is also increased.

Continuing and completing the excuse-making process

Excuses for the internal audience

Given the fact that psychologically healthy people appear to have self-serving biases about themselves (Taylor & Brown, 1988), it should come as no surprise that the excuse-giver is predisposed to believe his or her excuse. Furthermore, unless the excuse-making process is brought into awareness by a salient external audience, it should proceed almost automatically at a low level of awareness. Additionally, excuses take on the status of reasons in our own minds, and a state of self-deception may occur about the whole process. That is, people do not believe that they are making excuses, which have bad connotations, but rather they hold that they have reasons for their actions (Snyder, 1985a). Indeed, the quotation opening this chapter shows that President Reagan employed such thinking in his speech of 4 March 1987.

Such self-deception enables the excuse-maker to avoid having to make an excuse for making an excuse. Thus, the person also avoids the self-focused attention that may actually serve to lessen a sense of psychological adjustment (e.g. Carver & Scheier, 1981; Duval & Wicklund, 1972). In turn, the self-deceptive excuse-maker may focus his or her energies on task relevant stimuli that may facilitate subsequent performance. The net effect may be that the self-deceptive excuse-maker feels better and actually behaves so as to enhance the probability of subsequent success in the performance arena (Snyder & Higgins, in press).

In summary, when the internal audience is the major consumer of excuse-making, the reality negotiation inherent in excuses typically should sustain the person's positive self-theory. As we have noted, this process may have adaptive implications for the excuse-maker.

Excuses for the external audience

Some of the earliest writers (e.g. Scheff, 1968; Scott & Lyman, 1968), as well as more recent theorists (e.g. Schönbach, 1985), have described the alternating process of excuse-making that occurs between the protagonist and the external audience who is the recipient of the excuse. Simply put, the protagonist offers a first excuse; the external audience may or may not accept the excuse; the protagonist revises the excuse; and so on until an excuse is settled on by both the protagonist and the external audience or, more rarely, no agreement is achieved. Typically, some implicit agreement about the badness of the protagonist's act and his or her linkage to that act is obtained. In this context, 'reality' is what the two parties (i.e. the protagonist and the external audience) agree (implicitly or explicitly) about the badness of the act and the protagonist's linkage to that act. As the reader can surmise in the foregoing discussion, it is indeed a reality negotiation process.

   Unlike the excuses that serve only the internal audience of the protagonist, when the external audience becomes involved there is less opportunity for self-deception. Indeed, the protagonist considers what excuse may work best (see previous section), and must continually remain somewhat aware of his or her excuses and the audience's reaction to these excuses. During such circumstances, the protagonist must not only be concerned about the linkage to the original, instigating bad act, but must also attend to the process of doing a good job at excusing.

   Just as excuse-makers are biased to accept their excuses, it may also be the case that external audiences exhibit positive biases in forming perceptions of others (e.g. Schneider, Hastorf & Ellsworth, 1979; Sears, 1983). This latter bias should help the excuse-maker. Further, if the external audience perceives some similarity to the excuse-giver, then the positive perceptual bias should be amplified (Burger, 1981). Additionally, because audiences prefer to refrain from delivering negative feedback to other people (e.g. Tesser & Rosen, 1975), the excuse protagonist may not be confronted in the reality negotiation process. Moreover, if the observers do not interact with the transgressor, the feedback may be ambiguous and difficult for the transgressor to decipher (Goffman, 1955). In turn, the excuse-giver should interpret the ambiguous feedback as being positive (see Jacobs, Berscheid & Walster, 1971, for a similar point).

   The aforementioned process may be tempered by one overriding principle. Namely, the greater the negativeness of the act and the linkage to the act, the less willing external audiences should be to allow a negotiated reality that is biased in favour of the transgressor (Schlenker, 1980). With this latter caveat in mind, however, it is generally accurate to assert that the overall dialogue process between the excuse-giver and the external audience may reflect a collaborative illusion in which the transgressor and the audience typically arrive at a negotiated reality that is maximally benign for the transgressor given the circumstances. This latter point reminds us of the subtitle of our 1983 *Excuses* book— *Masquerades In Search of Grace*. Perhaps a certain grace is allowed through the excuse-making process.

President Reagan's Speech of 4 March 1987

The threat

President Reagan had a dilemma in the last months of 1986, and his problem intensified with the release of the Tower Report in late February of 1987. In terms of the two dimensions of appraisal that we have hypothesised in this paper, 'the act' was bad and the President was being linked to it.

First, consider the act, which appears to have been an arms-for-American hostages transaction with Iran, with the added factor that part of the money obtained from the sale of arms apparently was laundered for aid to the Nicaraguan Contras. In addition to these acts, related issues arose regarding the small amount of information that was being provided by the administration and the length of time it was taking to get such information. The arms-for-hostages aspect of this act was bad because it was antithetical to the policy, both within the American sector and the larger world context, of not bargaining for hostages; moreover, the implementation of aid to the Nicaraguan Contras was not yet approved by the American government, nor were the methods of getting money for the aid acceptable (i.e. the covert sale of arms). The standards of conduct were fairly clear-cut, and they were violated. To make matters worse, the Tower Report succinctly labelled these activities as unacceptable.

Second, the President was experiencing a strong linkage to these actions. Consensually, Americans perceived the President as the architect of these actions. Powerful people, including the authors of the Tower Report, appeared to have 'the facts' and were explicitly tying the President to the actions pertaining to the Iran arms scandal.

The excuse performance

In President Reagan's speech, there are ten excuse episodes. Of these, five appear to operate on the valence-of-act dimension, three

operate on the linkage-to-act dimension, and two address both the valence
and linkage dimensions.

Excuses on the valence-of-act dimension

1. 'The reason I haven't spoken to you before now is this: You
   deserved the truth. And, as frustrating as the waiting has been,
   I felt it was improper to come to you with sketchy reports, or
   possibly even erroneous statements, which would then have to
   be corrected, creating even more doubt and confusion. There's
   been enough of that.'

The obvious concern is the President's delay in responding to this
controversy. By describing this time period as being necessary in order
to 'get the facts', the President's excuse reframes the delay in a more
positive light.

2. 'I'm often accused of being an optimist, and it's true I had to
   hunt pretty hard to find any good news in the board's report.
   As you know, it's well stocked with criticisms, which I'll discuss
   in a moment, but I was very relieved to read this sentence,
   " . . . The board is convinced that the President does indeed
   want the full story to be told".'

Here, the President is repackaging the sale of arms incident in the
context of his general honesty and desire to be truthful.

3. '. . . there are reasons why it happened, but no excuses.'

The President and his speech writer, like the rest of us, intuitively
know that excuses have a bad name. They are the apparent manoeuvres
of less-than-competent people. So the problem is how to use excuses and
yet appear not to use them. The self-deceptive solution, as shown in this
important passage of the speech, is to elevate the President's explanations
to the status of reasons and to assert simultaneously that there are no
excuses involved. Perhaps this was more than mere *self*-deception,
however, given the media reaction of 'President Makes No Excuses'. We
will return to this last point later in this chapter.

4. 'Let's start with the part that is the most controversial. A few
   months ago I told the American people I did not trade arms
   for hostages. My heart and best intentions still tell me that it is
   true, but the facts and evidence tell me that it is not.'

At one level, the President admits that it was an arms-for-hostages
deal, in agreement with the Tower Report, but at another level (his heart
and best intentions), he says that it was not. Implicit in this passage is

the logic that 'it isn't so bad' because the President's 'heart and best intentions' tell him it isn't.

5. 'It's clear from the board's report, however, that I let my personal concern for the hostages spill over into the geopolitical strategy of reaching out to Iran. I asked so many questions about the hostages' welfare that I didn't ask enough about the specifics of the total Iran plan.'

The excuse in this passage reframes the bad outcome as being less pejorative because the whole operation was based on humanitarian concern for the hostages.

Excuses on the linkage-to-act dimension

1. 'First, let me say I take full responsibility for my own actions and for those of my Administration. As angry as I may be about activities undertaken without my knowledge, I am still accountable for these activities.'

The key phrase in this passage is 'As angry as I may be about activities undertaken without my knowledge . . . ' Obviously, even though the President appears to affirm some linkage, he also weakens that linkage by pointing to the actions of subordinates.

2. 'As I told the Tower board, I didn't know about any diversion of funds to the Contras. But as President, I cannot escape responsibility.'

This statement of innocence attempts to distance the President totally from any linkage to the diversion of funds. The use of the verb 'escape' in the second sentence of this extract suggests that the linkage issue obviously was still on the President's mind.

3. 'One thing still upsetting me, however, is that no one kept proper records of meetings or decisions. This led to my failure to recollect whether I approved an arms shipment before or after the fact. I did approve it; I just can't say specifically when.'

By highlighting the fact that there weren't any records, the President distances himself from the situation in general, as well as in the fact that he has forgotten when he approved the arms shipment.

Excuses employing both the valence-of-act and linkage-to-act dimensions

1. 'As the Tower board reported, what began as a strategic opening to Iran deteriorated in its implementation into trading arms for hostages.'

The 'we didn't mean for it to turn out this way' excuse is being employed in this statement. Foreseeability is culpability, but unforeseeability is a good excuse. (It should be noted, however, that the Tower Report stated that the intent was arms-for-hostages 'almost from the beginning'.) This unforeseeability excuse reframes the overall act (i.e. the good beginning and the bad ending) and distances the linkage of the protagonist (i.e. the bad ending from the good beginning).

2. 'You know, by the time you reach my age, you've made plenty of mistakes if you've lived your life properly. So you learn. You put things in perspective. You pull your energies together. You change. You go forward.'

The 'you've made plenty of mistakes if you've lived your life properly' recasts mistake-making as a normal, even adaptive process. Additionally, by introducing the age issue, the President is paradoxically asserting that his age and not the 'real him' has contributed to the mistake. Interestingly, this passage is the last one in the speech, and the excuses appeal for grace in a very human, almost self-effacing manner.

Sequelae of Excuse-Making: The Speech and Beyond

Having examined the excuses that President Reagan gave in his speech, it is appropriate now to consider the 'effects' of this speech upon both Mr Reagan and the external audiences. Unfortunately, one cannot examine the effects of this speech in any causal sense of the word because the best information that we have available can be characterised as sequelae of the speech. In other words, there are certain reported or inferred states that appeared to have followed this speech, but we cannot ascertain the degree of association, much less the causation. Nevertheless, the sequelae of this speech are interesting from a theoretical perspective in understanding the effects of excuses, and these sequelae are consistent with the related empirical literature on the 'effects' (both associational and causal) of excuse-making.

The 'effects' of excuses for the excuse-giver

After the speech, the President appeared to be in better spirits. He reported that he had addressed the relevant issues in this speech, and he expressed a desire to 'get on with things'. Indeed, he immediately initiated a reorganisation of his cabinet and hired a new Chief of Staff. Thereafter, he held his first news conference in months, and he began to make trips outside the White House. Overall, President Reagan appeared to have recaptured his self-described sense of optimism; moreover, he appeared to feel 'back in the saddle'.

Are the apparent personal benefits of excuse-making described in the previous paragraph particular only to President Reagan? We think not. Rather, the relevant literature suggests that there may be esteem and affect benefits, as well as subsequent health and performance benefits associated with excuse-making (Snyder & Higgins, in press). We will explore this literature next.

Esteem and Affect

If excuses are personally functional, then excuse-making should have beneficial effects on a person's self-esteem and affective state. First, consider self-esteem. In the study that is most relevant to our account, McFarland & Ross (1982) gave college females failure feedback on a social judgement task, and thereafter induced half of these women to attribute their failure to their ability and the other half to the difficulty of the task. The women who had the externalising task difficulty excuse reported higher self-esteem than the women who had the more internal ability attribution.

Interestingly, McFarland and Ross also took affect measures in their study, and found that the excuse-condition women reported more positive affect than did the women in the other condition. Similar beneficial effects for excuse-making have also been found for anxiety and hostility measures (Mehlman & Snyder, 1985).

Another set of studies has examined the effect of projection-like excuses on the excuse-giver. In a typical experimental paradigm, the research participants are delivered failure feedback, and are then either allowed, or not allowed, the opportunity to 'project' their failure onto other people (i.e. to note how other people would also fail in the same situation). Such projection excuses implicitly suggest that something in the situation, not the person, is causing the bad performance. Generally, failed persons who are allowed to make projection-like excuses report less anxiety than people who are not allowed to make such excuses (e.g. Bennett & Holmes, 1975; Burish & Houston, 1979; Holmes & Houston, 1971).

Yet another body of 'excuse' research relates to the particular affect of depression. A large number of studies from the reformulated helplessness model (e.g. Abramson, Seligman & Teasdale, 1978) are relevant. In this model, depressive affect is diminished if the person makes external (E), variable (V) and specific (S) attributions for failures. The EVS pattern for failures is a prototypical excuse-making pattern, while the internal (I), stable (S) and global (G) pattern is the classic depressive pattern (Snyder & Higgins, in press).

Many of these learned-helplessness paradigm studies employ between-subject designs to show that non-depressed persons exhibit more of an EVS pattern for failures in comparison to the ISG pattern for depressed persons (e.g. Peterson, Bettes & Seligman, 1982). The cross-sectional nature of these studies naturally lessens the degree to which one can make inferences about the ISG/EVS pattern. In one within-subject study (Peterson, Luborsky & Seligman, 1983), the EVS pattern of attributions for failures has been shown to precede a decrease in depression, and the ISG pattern precedes an increase in depression. Additionally, prospective studies have explored the predictive effects of the ISG/EVS attributional pattern of depression when people undergo a negative, stressful event. These studies show that an EVS as compared to an ISG pattern of attributions relates to less depression when one has confronted a 'failure' experience (e.g. Metalsky et al., 1982; Peterson, Nutter & Seligman, 1982; Rothwell & Williams, 1983).

Health

Beyond the predicted effects of attributional style on depression, the reformulated learned helplessness model suggests that people who exhibit an ISG as compared to an EVS pattern of attributions for bad events may also be at risk of poor health generally; moreover, there may be actual performance decrements for persons with the ISG rather than the EVS pattern. We will address the health results in this section, and the performance results in the next section.

Although no data analyses were presented, Seligman (1986) has reported that older adults with an EVS rather than an ISG attributional pattern evidenced enhanced immune system functioning. In a study of 32 diabetic children, physicians rated the children who perceived their disease as being due to external, variable and specific factors as coping better than children with internal, stable and global attributions (Tennen *et al.*, 1983). It should be noted that the internal attribution in these results varies from the hypothesised results. Another way of measuring health is number of visits to a doctor; in this vein, Seligman (1986) reports that undergraduate students with an EVS pattern of attributions for negative events made half as many doctor appointments as did the undergraduates with an ISG pattern.

Studies employing a 'time machine' methodology are also relevant in the present section. In 'time machine' studies, the attributional content of people's explanations for events in their lives at a given point in time are examined in relation to subsequent life events. An example may help to clarify this methodology. Seligman (1986) examined comments of Hall-of-Fame baseball players (playing between 1900 and 1950) regarding their bad and good performances. The ISG/EVS scores for each player's good and bad games were obtained by analysing quotations attributed to them by newspapers. The variable that Seligman sought to predict was age at death. An EVS pattern for bad games correlated with longevity ($r = 0.26$, $p<0.08$), as did an ISG pattern for good games ($r = 0.45$, $p<0.01$). In two other studies (Elder, Bettes & Seligman, 1982; Seligman, 1986), the EVS attributional pattern for negative life events in the 1940s significantly predicted health in 1970.

Performance

There are several correlational studies performed under the revised learned helplessness (or related) paradigms. These studies suggest that an EVS rather than an ISG attributional pattern for bad events is 'adaptive' in that it relates to better (1) selling (Anderson, 1983; Seligman, 1986); (2) anagram performance (Alloy *et al.*, 1984; Pasahow, 1980); (3) college performance (Seligman, 1986); (4) persistence in getting a manuscript published (Crittenden & Wiley, 1980); and (5) psychotherapy outcomes (Peterson & Seligman, 1981).

Other studies have explored the question of whether excuse-making causes, rather than is merely associated with, improved performance. In this context, one of the most common experimental approaches has been to train people to attribute their failures to lack of effort (an externalising excuse). Persons trained with such excuses exhibit improved performance on the following tasks: (1) psychomotor (Zoeller, Mahoney & Weiner, 1983); (2) anagrams (Andrews & Debus, 1978); (3) reading (Chapin & Dyck, 1976); (4) mathematics (Dweck, 1975); and (5) selling (Anderson, 1983). The aforementioned improvements in performance were obtained with subject populations ranging from grade school to college students.

In addition to these 'lack of effort' excuses, studies have also trained people to make specific rather than global, or variable instead of stable, attributions for failure (e.g. Anderson, 1983; Wilson & Linville, 1982, 1985). Such training also results in enhanced performance on various cognitive achievement tasks.

Overall, the literature suggests that several personal benefits flow from the excuse-making process. Indeed, the excuse-making person may experience benefits relating to esteem, affective state, health and performance. Thus, it would not be unreasonable to assume that President Reagan may have experienced similar effects after his speech of 4 March.

An interesting aspect of this research, at first examination, is that it appears to have focused on excuses that are aimed at lessening the linkage to bad acts. For example, it can easily be seen that the revised learned helplessness model operates along the linkage-to-act appraisal dimension with the EVS/ISG attribution indexes; moreover, it takes as given that these attributions are basically meaningful only when applied to 'bad' acts.

We do know, however, that excuse-makers also actively manipulate the valence-of-act dimension (recall Reagan's speech and the previous brief discussion of justifications). The valence-of-act and linkage-to-act dimensions of appraisals are often intertwined; to the extent to which this is true, there is evidence on the 'effects' of valence-of-act excuses. Thus, excuses that heighten the salience of external causal factors for a bad performance implicitly lessen the negativeness of the performance (Snyder, Higgins & Stucky, 1983). For example, the consensus-raising excuse of projection moves the causal focus to an external factor (i.e. if everyone is performing poorly, it must be something in the situation that is driving the behaviour), but it also lowers the badness of the act (i.e. something that everyone is doing can't be that bad).

The 'effects' of excuses on the external audience

Returning to President Reagan's speech, the first public reactions were generated by the announcers and political analysts from the major television networks. The general tenor of this first wave of evaluations was that President Reagan had given a strong performance. He was seen as being energetic, focused, and responsive to the important issues of this particular dilemma. The next morning the major American newspapers, such as the *New York Times*, ran headlines such as 'President Takes Blame' and 'Makes No Excuses'. These headlines indicated that the President had been successful in portraying the image that he hadn't engaged in simple excuse-making. In subsequent polls regarding the President, his previous ratings, which were at an all-time low, began to climb again. Of course, this may have been a simple regression towards the mean. Again, by turning to the relevant literature, we may gain some insights into the effectiveness of the President's excuses in particular, as well as excuses more generally, on external audiences.

Blaming

By blaming others, the excuse logic is that one's link to a bad act is diminished. Generally, although there is very little literature on this topic, the available evidence suggests that blaming is a poor strategy. In a group task in which there is failure, for example, it has been found that group members increasingly disliked another group member when this latter person took progressively less responsibility (Forsyth, Berger & Mitchell, 1981). In another study with fifth- and sixth-grade children, ratings were made of team members of a losing softball team. The person who was described as blaming the other team for the loss received much lower ratings than the 'no excuse' person on the dimensions of likeability, smartness and goodness (Dollinger, Staley & McGuire, 1981; see also Dollinger & McGuire, 1981).

Foreseeability/Intentionality

Intentionality links an act to its author (see Jones & Davis, 1965). Even children appear to know this basic rule when judging behaviour (see Gruenich, 1982, for review). Additionally, adults know that people's bad actions should be viewed less negatively when there is an increasing lack of foreseeability or intentionality (Darley & Zanna, 1982; Shaw, 1968). In fact, these ideas have been built into our legal systems.

In most of the research on observers' reactions to foreseeability/intentionality-based excuses, the raters know whether the transgressor did or did not foresee or intend the action. While such certainty of intentionality/foreseeability is useful methodology, in the real world the observer does not know the veracity of this information. A study by Weiner et al. (1987) sheds light on this latter question. In this experiment (Weiner et al., 1987, experiment 3), naive participants responded to another participant (actually a confederate) who arrived 15 minutes late. The confederate gave no excuse, a 'bad' (i.e. it was 'controllable') explanation, or a good (i.e. it was 'uncontrollable') explanation. The uncontrollable excuses generated less resentment, anger, dislike, etc.; also, people were more willing to interact with the persons giving the excuses of uncontrollability. (Other experiments by Weiner *et al.* (1987, experiments 1 and 4) also indicate that people intuitively know that a good excuse involves lack of intentionality or controllability.) These studies, taken together, suggest that the social fabric is not severed when lack of intentionality/foreseeability/controllability is invoked as an excuse.

In summary, the literature reviewed above indicates that the effectiveness of excuses on external audiences is a mixed bag, with some excuses clearly being more effective than others. What literature there is available on blaming suggests that it is not a very effective excuse. One could say, in fact, that it is a backfiring excuse in which the excuse-giver runs the risk of compounding the original transgression in using a blaming strategy. Most people may intuitively know this, however, and thus may embed their blaming excuses in a larger general context wherein the blaming is not very salient. For example, this appears to be the case in Mr Reagan's speech in that he does deflect the blame while simultaneously taking some responsibility.

The foreseeability/intentionality studies provide fairly clear-cut evidence that these are 'good' excuses in that they lessen the linkage of the transgressor to the bad act. These excuses may also serve to lessen the negativeness of the act (i.e. an unforeseen or unintentional act is generally perceived as being more benign). What is also noteworthy is that people appear to know that lack of intentionality is a very acceptable excuse for external audiences. This excuse tactic is utilised in Mr Reagan's speech.

Before leaving this section on audience reactions to excuses, a study that clearly involves both the valence-of-act and linkage-to-act dimension is worthy of mention. Riordan (1981) had research participants read newspaper reports (bogus ones) of a US Senator who had committed a transgression (i.e. hired a prostitute or taken a bribe). The Senator either offered an explanation that sought to lessen the badness of the act (e.g. he was conducting an investigation or doing what everyone does), or an explanation that sought to lessen his linkage to the act (e.g. he was drunk, or he was so mad that he lost control). The raters of these vignettes reduced the wrongfulness of the acts when 'badness' explanations were given; moreover, the responsibility for the acts was diminished when the linkage explanations were given. These results indicate that excuse explanations tailored to the valence-of-act or linkage-to-act dimensions 'work' on those very dimensions.

Conclusion

The reality negotiation process in general, and excuse-making in particular, appear to be adaptive in that they often generate benefits. The individual's esteem, ongoing emotional state, as well as his or her health and performance in a variety of arenas, all appear to profit from the excuse-making process. Additionally, audiences are especially willing to 'allow' certain excuses (e.g. excuses involving lack of intentionality). Thus, the successes that Mr Reagan evidently experienced because of his excuse-laden speech are similar to the benefits that most of us obtain when we make excuses for our transgressions. Although excuse-making certainly has a bad reputation, we must know that they 'work'. Could so many users be wrong?

Notes to Chapter 9

1. All of President Reagan's quotes have been taken from the text of the speech as printed in the *New York Times*, 5 March 1987.
2. There is at least one notable group of people who do not appear to appraise themselves favourably in most situations. Namely, depressed people appear to form self-theories in which they are linked to negative acts (Alloy & Ahrens, 1987; Pyszczynski & Greenberg, 1987).

10 Severity of reproach and defensiveness of accounts

PETER SCHÖNBACH and PETRA KLEIBAUMHÜTER
Faculty of Psychology, Ruhr-Universität Bochum, FRG

Look right with us into our domain of discourse: the account episode. This label denotes a model of interaction between an actor and an opponent across four phases:

1. *Failure event*: The actor is, rightly or wrongly, held at least partly responsible by the opponent for a failure event, i.e. the violation of a normative expectation held by the opponent. This can be either an acted offence, or the omission of an obligation.

2. *Reproach phase*: Frequently the opponent reacts to the failure event with some kind of reproach, ranging from a raised eyebrow or a seemingly innocuous why-question to most violent vituperations. However, instead of, or in addition to, a reproach the opponent may also offer other responses such as an expression of sympathy or compassion during this phase, or may genuinely ask without any innuendo why the failure event occurred.

3. *Account phase*: The actor's reaction to the opponent's utterance is often an account in the narrow sense, an excuse or a justification; hence the label 'account phase' for this stage of the interaction. Other prominent types of reactions during this phase are concessions of own responsibility or guilt, or else some direct or indirect refusal to offer an account or an admission of responsibility.

4. *Evaluation phase*: Eventually, either right after the actor's account, concession or refusal, or after some more altercations between the two agents, the opponent will come to an evaluation of any or all of the following: the account or account substitute, the failure event in the light of the account, and the actor's

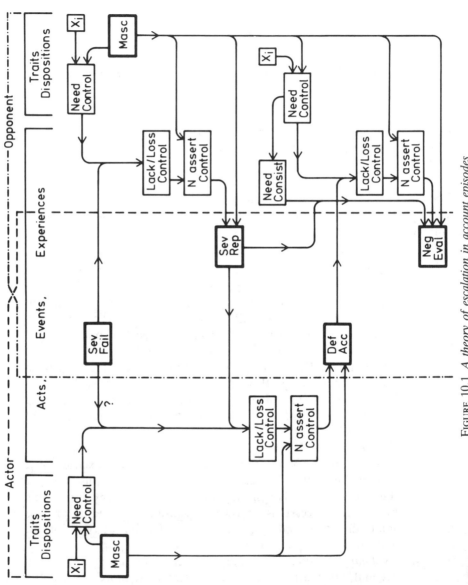

FIGURE 10.1 *A theory of escalation in account episodes*

personality in the light of both failure event and account. Such evaluations mark the end of the account episode, and at the same time the auspices for ensuing events: mitigation or elimination of the conflict engendered by the failure event and continuation or restoration of a viable relationship between actor and opponent; or else escalation of conflict and possibly disruption of the relationship between the two agents of the episode, sometimes including their social environments as well.

Account episodes are integral parts of many different types of social processes at all levels of complexity. Thus they deserve, and require, intensive study. Our basic proposition and question is this: granted that legal and moral norms and institutional provisions exist which facilitate an orderly course and a beneficial accomplishment of account episodes, and granted also that such positive outcomes are indeed often achieved, why do account episodes nevertheless founder in so many cases in which an objective observer would not see a head-on collision of fundamental interests and hence a foundering of the account episode as an inevitable consequence?

To approximate an adequate answer to this question is difficult, mainly because of the sequential nature of account episodes. A multidimensional approach is called for, including the construction of theoretical guidelines and category systems for coding the reactions of the participants in account episodes, as well as a set of empirical studies that are linked by common elements and thus supplement each other. We cannot go into any detail here except to say that an elaborate taxonomy for account phase reactions already exists (Schönbach, 1985) and a corresponding taxonomy for reactions of opponents during the phases of reproach and evaluation is being constructed, and that close to a dozen relevant studies have been conducted so far in our working unit at Bochum University. In this report we shall present just one of them.

Schönbach (1986) developed a theory of conflict escalation in account episodes. Figure 10.1 presents a diagrammatic outline of the theory in order to illustrate just two points: (1) the theory joins its hypotheses in a network of synchronic and diachronic linkages; three of them were selected for testing in the study to be presented and in some co-ordinated investigations, and these hypotheses will be stated and discussed shortly; (2) one basic determinant of the interactions between actors and opponents that is envisaged by the theory may be called 'need for maintaining or regaining an adequate sense of being in control of one's actions as well as of other events in one's social environment'. This control need is seen as operative in both actor and opponent, and furthermore, as being sensitised in both of them beyond average levels in an account episode setting.

An aspect of the theory which does not appear in Figure 10.1 is an assumed reciprocal relationship between need for control and need for positive self-esteem. Hence, all boxes in the diagram standing for 'need for control' and 'lack or loss of control', respectively, may be seen as also containing corresponding levels of need, or lack or loss of self-esteem. An attack on an opponent's sense of control by the failure event, or later in the process by an unsatisfactory account, let alone a refusal, is assumed to lower, at the same time, to some extent the opponent's feeling of self-worth. A derogation of his or her self-esteem implied or made explicit by the failure event or by the actor's account phase behaviour is assumed to lower the opponent's sense of being in control, and this in turn will heighten his or her need to regain control. Corresponding processes are assumed to occur in the actor subsequent to threats stemming from the failure event or the opponent's reproach, directed primarily either at the actor's sense of being in control or else at his or her self-esteem.

Three Hypotheses

1. The greater the severity of a reproach, the more defensive, within limits, will be the actor's reaction during the account phase.

Severity of reproach means primarily the severity of the threat to the actor's sense of control and/or self-esteem implied or explicated by the reproach. The reaction of an actor is called 'defensive' to the extent that it tries to bolster or regain a satisfactory sense of control and/or self-esteem by means which do not, or do not sufficiently, take into consideration the opponent's needs for control and self-esteem.

2. The greater an actor's habitual need for control, the more defensive, within limits, will be his or her reaction during the account phase, given that the opponent's reproach phase reaction has exceeded a threshold value of severity.

Both hypotheses are formulated in ways that predict main effects. However, we also envisage the possibility of interaction effects, i.e. either some acceleration from a combination of high levels of both opponent's severity and actor's needs for control, or else ceiling effects that equalise the reactions of various actors, provided that at least one of the determinants of defensiveness during the account phase is strong. These qualifications with respect to possible interactions also apply to the following, third hypothesis.

3. Account phase reactions of male actors are, on the average, more defensive than the reactions of female actors.

In line with many studies of 'masculinity' versus 'femininity' (e.g. Bem, 1974; Spence & Helmreich, 1978; Runge *et al.*, 1981) we believe that, as a rule, males have higher needs for control than females do. Therefore, the route from 'masculinity' to need for control and thence to defensiveness of account phase reactions is seen as the principal mediator of the relationship stated in our third hypothesis. Two further routes from 'masculinity' to defensiveness of account phase reactions are envisaged as supplementary lines of influence. Considering the stronger average potential of assertiveness among males as compared to females, it seems plausible to assume that even with feelings of lack or loss of control held constant, the average male will act under stronger pressure to assert or reassert control than the average female. Finally, in the light of the comparatively high aggressiveness of males versus females (e.g. Maccoby & Jacklin, 1974), one may expect a male actor to react in a more hostile and rejecting manner than a female one even if their needs to (re)assert control happen to be equally strong. At present we cannot empirically distinguish among those three routes of influence in order to assess their validity, let alone their respective weights. However, we do have evidence pertinent to the more general prediction of hypothesis 3 and shall offer it shortly.

Method

The study to be presented was conducted with 93 female and 92 male teachers as respondents in individual interviews. Each interview started with a questionnaire to be filled in by the respondent. Among 57 Likert-type items with five response alternatives each, 20 items represented a German version[1] of the 'Desirability of Control' scale by Burger & Cooper (1979). These 20 items were interspersed with eight filler items on leisure activities and six items on self-satisfaction adapted from the scales of Hormuth & Lalli (1986) and Bergemann & Johann (1985). This part of the questionnaire was preceded by Heinemann's (1979) German version of the self-consciousness scale constructed by Fenigstein, Scheier & Buss (1975), which need not concern us here.

The core part of the interview consisted of a role-taking task. Each respondent had to imagine being a babysitter who did not notice that the child in his or her care had sneaked into the kitchen and drunk from a bottle containing cleaning fluid, so that it had to be whisked to the hospital by the emergency ambulance. The respondents had to write down in their own words what they would say in response to the reaction of the returning parents of the child. The parents' reaction was systematically varied across three versions: 1. *Neutral Question* (parents ask for an explanation); 2. *Derogation of Self-Esteem* (parents say: 'How could that have happened to you? Apparently you were too much occupied with yourself!?'); 3. *Derogation of Sense of Control* (parents say: 'Why haven't you been able to prevent this? We wouldn't have thought that you would lose sight so easily!').

Two different reproach versions, one mainly attacking self-worth and the other mainly directed at sense of control, were included because of a supplementary tentative hypothesis that specific interactions between type of reproach and moderator variables, such as degree of self-acceptance and need for control, might occur. Our basic assumption of a reciprocal causal relationship between self-esteem and sense of control does not imply a perfect correlation. Hence we thought that persons predominantly concerned with their control competence and only moderately with their self-worth might be more strongly affected by a direct attack on their sense of control than by a primary attack on their self-esteem, and it might be the other way around with persons predominantly concerned with their self-worth. However, no general predictions as to the relative severity and strength of *Derogation of Sense of Control* and *Derogation of Self-Esteem* seemed justifiable. Both versions were, of course, taken to be more severe than the baseline version *Neutral Question*.

The respondents' free answers to the parents' reactions were categorised according to Schönbach's (1985) taxonomy for account phases by two coders[2] working independently. Discrepancies between their codings were subsequently resolved by discussion, and in cases of remaining doubt by the first author. After sufficient initial experience with the material the two coders reached a concordance level of $C = 0.80$, according to Holsti's formula (North *et al.*, 1963: 49), with a new batch of 40 accounts.

Three data levels were then constructed: (1) frequencies of each basic category within relevant groups of respondents; (2) frequencies of each of four superordinate categories, i.e. Concessions, Excuses, Justifications and Refusals, within relevant respondent groups; (3) an index CATCOMB computed by summing, for each respondent, twice the number of Refusal categories in the respondent's account plus the number of Justification categories, minus the number of Excuse categories, minus twice the number of Concession categories plus a constant to avoid negative values. CATCOMB served as an overall measure of defensiveness, amenable to analyses of variance.

Most analyses were carried out with a 3×2 design with the factors *Version of Reproach* and *Gender of Respondent*. In some cases the design was enlarged by dichotomised moderator variables such as control needs and self-satisfaction. These moderator variables, and others, also entered into correlation and regression analyses. A factor analysis of the 20 items of the Burger and Cooper scale of control desirability has produced a meaningful two-factor solution. Factor 1 was composed of nine items with loadings between 0.70 and 0.46; they furnished a sub-scale labelled *Need for Competence and Influence*. A typical item of this sub-scale reads 'I would prefer to be a leader rather than a follower'. Factor 2 was composed of nine items with loadings between 0.65 and 0.35. These items furnished a sub-scale labelled *Need for Constancy and Shielding*. A typical item of this sub-scale reads 'I try to avoid situations where someone else tells me what to do'.

Results

We shall first present distributions of the four superordinate categories and then various mean values on the CATCOMB scale. Refusals, such as a refutation of responsibility by an actor, clearly are most defensive, followed, as a rule, by justifications of one's own behaviour. Excuses which admit some fault or failure but try to minimise one's own involvement in the affair seem to be less defensive than justifications, and concessions of own responsibility or guilt, including expressions of regret, obviously are least defensive of all. We may then expect a weakening of concession tendencies and possibly also of excuse tendencies in all conditions which instigate or foster an actor's defensiveness. Correspondingly we may expect a strengthening of any refusal tendencies and possibly also of some, or all, justification tendencies under those conditions.

Hypothesis 1: Severity of reproach–defensiveness of account

Figure 10.2 shows, according to expectations, that in the two derogation conditions fewer respondents than after a neutral question offered one or more concessionary statements. It turned out that a

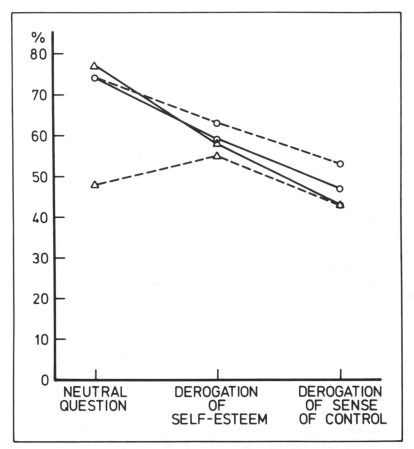

FIGURE 10.2 *Percentages of female (O) and male (△) respondents within each of three reproach settings who offered one or more concessions (—) or excuses (---)*

derogation of the actor's sense of control had a stronger overall effect than a derogation of his or her self-esteem, but the difference between these two conditions is not significant ($X^2 = 2.32$). On the other hand, the difference between the conditions *Neutral Question* (henceforth NQ) and *Derogation of Self-Esteem* (DS) is significant at $p < 0.05$ and the difference between NQ and *Derogation of Sense of Control* (DC) is significant at $p < 0.001$, with male and female data combined.

The data on excuse frequencies in Figure 10.2 show a similar but much less pronounced pattern. None of the differences among the three conditions NQ, DS and DC is significant.

Figure 10.3 presents the corresponding data for justifications and refusals. Clearly, greater proportions of respondents in the two derogation conditions DS and DC offered justifications or refusals (or both) than in the NQ condition. The following significance values corroborate the message of the diagram. For justifications: DS vs. NQ: $p<0.03$; DC vs. NQ: $p<0.002$. For refusals: DS vs. NQ: $p<0.001$; DC vs. NQ: $p<0.001$. Again, no significant differences emerged between DS and DC for male and female data combined. Obviously, however, men and women differed in their refusal tendencies after a derogation of their sense of control. We shall return to this point shortly. For male respondents the difference between refusal percentages in DS and DC is significant at $p<0.03$.

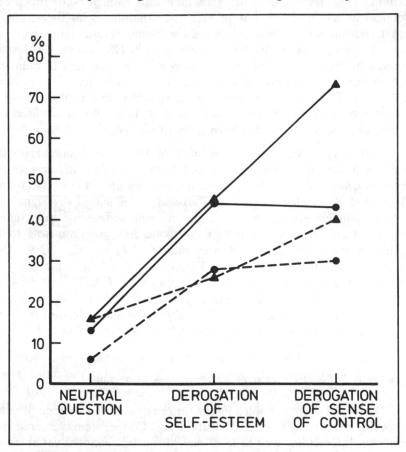

FIGURE 10.3 *Percentages of female (●) and male (▲) respondents within each of three reproach settings who offered: one or more justifications (---) or refusals (—)*

Hypothesis 3: Male actors are more defensive than female actors in account phases

It will be convenient to discuss the data pertinent to this hypothesis first, before turning to hypothesis 2.

Obviously, men and women did not differ in their willingness to make concessions (see Figure 10.2), yet men were clearly less willing than women to offer an excuse ($p<0.05$). This sign of support for hypothesis 3 is corroborated by the data in Figure 10.3. Male accounts included slightly (but not significantly) more justifications than did female accounts. The refusal tendencies of men and women were practically identical in NQ and DS; but in DC, the condition with the strongest threat, female respondents did not show higher refusal rates over and above the level reached by their counterpart in DS, whereas males did so most markedly! The difference between the percentages of men and women in DC who offered one or more refusal statements is significant at $p<0.02$. This interaction between 'masculinity' and control threat is one of the most interesting findings of our study. We shall discuss it further after some more data have been presented.

The CATCOMB means presented in Figure 10.4 summarise the evidence pertinent to hypotheses 1 and 3. In an analysis of variance the factor *Version of Reproach* produced a highly significant ($p<0.001$) main effect, and the factor *Gender of Respondents* a marginally significant ($p<0.10$) main effect. No interaction emerged with this index. Newman–Keuls *a posteriori* tests proved the following contrasts to be significant at $p<0.05$: for female respondents: NQ vs. DS, NQ vs. DC; for male respondents: NQ vs. DC. Figure 10.4 should also facilitate our turning to the remaining hypothesis 2, because the CATCOMB measure is most appropriate for demonstrating the influence of the moderator variables *Need for Competence* and *Need for Constancy* derived from the Burger and Cooper scale for measuring 'Desirability of Control'.

Hypothesis 2: Need for control–defensiveness of account

Both moderator variables just mentioned, as well as a general index of control needs based on all 20 Burger and Cooper items, entered into significant interactions with at least one of our independent variables. In this chapter we shall present by way of example only the effects of *Need for Constancy*. Remember that this index consists of items which are mainly directed at the need to maintain control by shielding against

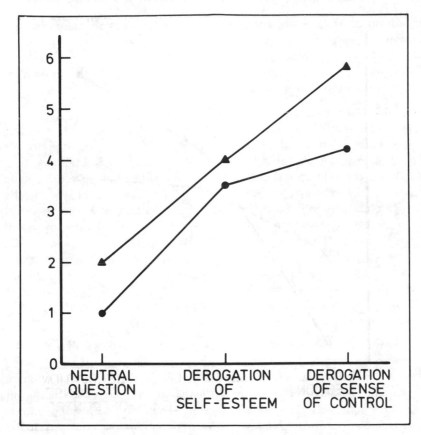

FIGURE 10.4 *Average CATCOMB values of female (•) and male (▲)
respondents within each of three reproach settings*

unwanted external influences and pressures. On this dimension, with a
potential range between 1 and 5 and an overall mean of 3.89, the male
respondents ($M = 3.96$) exceeded the female respondents ($M = 3.91$)
only very slightly and not significantly. Furthermore, high versus low
need for constancy had quite similar effects in men and women on their
respective levels of defensiveness in the three reproach settings. Therefore
the data for men and women were combined in Figure 10.5.

The diagram in Figure 10.5 shows a much steeper gradient of the
CATCOMB means from NQ via DS to DC for respondents with high
constancy needs than for those with low constancy needs. The interaction
between the factors Version of Reproach and Need for Constancy is

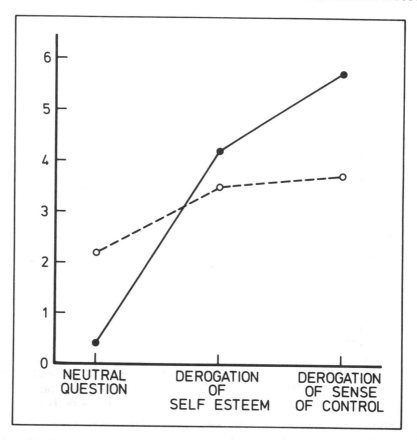

FIGURE 10.5 *Average CATCOMB values of respondents with low (---) and high (—) control needs for constancy, within each of three reproach settings*

marginally significant at $p<0.10$, yet corroborated by significant ($p<0.05$) *a posteriori* contrasts, e.g. NQ vs. DS and NQ vs. DC in the group with high constancy needs.

It should be noted that the lowest degree of defensiveness was manifested by those respondents with high need for constancy who were not confronted with a clear reproach but with a request for an explanation. Apparently this restrained reaction of the parents was particularly reassuring for respondents with high constancy needs. On the other hand, a reproach, especially one which derogated their sense of control, quickly aroused the defences of such respondents. We may take this data pattern as an encouragement and plea for joint consideration of situational and dispositional variables as a basic research strategy wherever feasible.

Discussion

Severity of reproach

The data strongly support the prediction that a reproach with the actor's sense of control or self-esteem as primary target would elicit rather defensive reactions. Particularly noteworthy is the fact that such a reproach apparently not only strengthens an actor's tendency to refute the opponent's charge or justify his or her behaviour during the failure event, but also markedly weakens the actor's readiness to offer some concessions. This very fact may well be especially damaging to the already dim prospects of a beneficial outcome for an account episode marked by a severe reproach.

'Masculinity'

The data also support the hypothesis about the stronger defensiveness of males compared to females, even though one may wish to add some qualifications. Figure 10.4 clearly shows the effect size of Gender of Respondents to be much smaller than the effect of Version of Reproach; the corresponding d-values (Cohen, 1977: 276) are 0.06 and 0.21, respectively. The comparatively weak gender effect in our case may partly be due to the fact that the babysitter situation employed in our study is generally considered a typically feminine domain, therefore our female respondents may have reacted with relatively strong defences to the imputation of a failure in this situation. In a previous study (see Schönbach, 1987) 180 students had to role-play actors after three different failure events. One vignette presented the babysitter situation and the neutral question version of the parents' reaction. Results very similar to ours were obtained in this case, with male students slightly more defensive than female students, offering fewer concessions ($p<0.07$) and more refusals (n.s.). But the difference between corresponding CATCOMB values for males (3.10) and for females (2.88) did not reach significance. In contrast to this weak effect, clear and significant differences between males and females of this very sample emerged, with males being more defensive in a role-playing situation after a breach of trust by the actor ($p<0.001$) and also in a setting after a dubious self-defence ($p<0.061$).

'Masculinity' will probably prove to be a fairly general and comparatively strong factor in future studies with new failure events. We derive some indication for this from two further studies by our working group which are still in progress. However, more important than the demonstration of any main effects of 'Masculinity' may be the modification of defensive account tendencies of male and female actors due to the type of the failure event, the target and the severity of the reproach to be answered, and the type and level of individual control needs! The very high percentage (73%) of male respondents in the DC condition who reacted to the derogation of their sense of control with refusals is a telling point. It may be noted in passing that on various control dimensions, especially those indicating a demand for leadership, our male respondents clearly and significantly exceeded the female respondents. On the sub-scale Need for Competence and Influence the average value for males (M = 3.47) was significantly ($p<0.04$) higher than the average value for females (M = 3.32). A split close to the median on this dimension was exceeded by 65% of the males, but only 46% of the females (X^2 = 6.75, $p<0.01$). These data patterns are also in good accord with our theory.

Need for control

Our second hypothesis, predicting control need effects on defensiveness of accounts, may also be seen as strengthened by our data. However, again, some qualifications are in order. The data pattern obtained with the index Need for Constancy and Shielding, and presented in Figure 10.5, is roughly replicated if we substitute Need for Competence and Influence as a measure of control needs. But in this case the interaction between level of control need and type of reproach is not significant. Furthermore, Need for Competence interacts significantly with Gender of Respondents with respect to the degree of defensiveness manifested in CATCOMB, and there is reason to believe that the feeling of competence control and the need for such control have rather different connotations for men and for women.

Imagine an opponent with ambivalent feelings towards the actor responsible for a failure event: an opponent vexed and hurt by the event, but also interested in mending the rupture caused by the failure in order to maintain a viable relationship with the actor. Before uttering any reproach, this opponent should, among other things, pay attention not only to any general degree of control needs of the actor, but also to his or her hierarchy of specific control needs such as the desire for competence exertion or the desire for constancy maintenance, and last but not least to the individual meanings attached to these specific needs in relation to the actor's degree of self-acceptance and social anxiety. A formidable cognitive and motivational achievement indeed! Yet, we have reason to believe that the very experience of being hurt in his or her self-esteem and sense of being in control will incline the opponent to seek restoration of the diminished self-esteem and sense of control by way of self-serving reproaches that do not pay any heed to the specific control and self-esteem needs of the actor, and are therefore likely to elicit equally unheeding defensive reactions from the actor, which in turn will probably aggravate the opponent's feelings of hurt and vexation.

It is our basic proposition that with these considerations we touch the core of the derailing interactive forces that are responsible for so many foundering account episodes. Further tests of this proposition will be our main concern in future research.

Notes to Chapter 10

1. We are grateful to Delia Nixdorf and Ilona Prystav for having provided a first draft of a German translation of the Desirability of Control scale, which we adopted with minor modifications.
2. The study to be reported was initiated and supervised by Peter Schönbach and conducted by Petra Kleibaumhüter in partial fulfilment of the requirements for a diploma degree in psychology. We gratefully acknowledge the assistance of Gabi Minjoli who took charge of eight of the 185 interviews and acted as a check-coder in categorising the respondents' accounts. Delia Nixdorf, Ilona Prystav and Joachim Studt, diploma students responsible for corresponding studies, joined us in stimulating discussions.

11 Account-giving and the attribution of responsibility: Impressions of traffic offenders

MARGARET L. MCLAUGHLIN and MICHAEL J. CODY
Department of Communication Arts and Sciences, University of Southern California, Los Angeles, USA

KATHRYN FRENCH
Speech Communication Department, University of Southern California, Long Beach, USA

Antaki & Fielding (1981: 49), noting that conclusive evidence of intra-individual stability with respect to moral decision-making has failed to materialise despite repeated investigation (see Blasi, 1980; Forsyth, 1980; Forsyth & Pope, 1984; Haan, 1986; Kurtines, 1986; Turiel & Smetana, 1984), propose that 'for the individual consistency exists with respect to his *representation* of the [moral decision-making] situation and his behavior within it, rather than directly in terms of his behaviors.' Mischel & Mischel (1976: 106) similarly argue that most persons are quite adept at reconciling what would appear to be discrepant moral actions, for example lying in one set of circumstances but telling the truth in another, and thus presenting a uniformly moral self for the world to see. That the self-image benefits from this transformation process goes without saying.

Rest (1984: 26), in his paper on the components of morality, has argued that it is impossible to understand, predict or influence moral behaviour, or even in fact to label the behaviour as 'moral' to begin with, until we know the inner processes that produce the behaviour. Rest claims that there are at least four such processes: (1) making sense of the situation in terms of determining what the possible courses of action are and what their repercussions might be for all persons involved; (2) trying to make a judgement as to what the correct action would be, and comparing possible actions for their goodness-of-fit to ideal standards of conduct; (3) making a choice between 'the right thing' and (usually) social-normative or conventional values (for example, violating the speed limit because everyone else is); and (4) carrying out the chosen course of action. These components are neither serially ordered nor mutually exclusive, but rather each influences 'the other components through feedback and feedforward loops'.

Our interest in this chapter centres on what Rest has referred to as 'defensively re-interpreting the situation', the construction of situation definitions which will provide the greatest possible degree of mitigation for an actor's choice of an ethically or legally dispreferred alternative. The process of defensive reinterpretation is usually initiated at the time a choice among alternative actions is considered, and informs the actor's decision. Its product, an *account* of the situation, may be reactivated, modified or embellished in some fashion when (or if) the actor's conduct is called into question (Blumstein *et al.*, 1974; Cody & McLaughlin, 1985b, 1988; Coleman, 1976; Ditton, 1977; McLaughlin, Cody & O'Hair, 1983; McLaughlin, Cody & Rosenstein, 1983; Rogers & Buffalo, 1974; Schönbach, 1980, 1986; Scott & Lyman, 1968; Semin & Manstead, 1983; Snyder & Higgins, 1986; Sykes & Matza, 1957).

Backman (1985: 264) describes decision-making situations with ethical ramifications as dilemmas with two 'horns', one of which is the threat of negative typification should one's choice be noted and questioned, the other of which is that 'some behaviors required or prohibited by norms' are linked to other significant outcomes. A person might, for example, be loath to park in another's reserved parking spot, for a variety of reasons including the moral knowledge that it is 'not right', yet be unable to locate an alternative spot that would allow him or her to park and make it to an important meeting on time. In current thinking about moral decision-making, particularly in Backman's work, there is an acknowledgement of the importance of the *social construction* of the problematic situation, and the application of rules within a particular situational construction, to the actor's conduct.

The resolution of some moral dilemmas may be more or less fully socially prescribed or scripted (Backman, 1985) such that in making a choice the actor can expect that attributions of culpability, negligence, responsibility, cost, benefit, and so forth will be made in predictable ways. For any given dilemma the actor faces, this means that there are well-known ways to construe this or a similar dilemma as a situation in which the choice made was, if not in fact called for under some moral rule, at least justifiable or excusable given the circumstances.

If an actor is unable to envisage a definition of the situation which will suitably frame the preferred action, that action may be discarded in favour of one for which a more plausible grounding can be constructed. The actor's task is to contextualise the moral dilemma in such a way as to 'blunt the effects of anticipated censure from self and others, either by reducing the strength of the rules operating in the situation or by providing a basis for accounts or explanations' (Backman, 1985: 268). The situational construction which guides the actor's choice in a problematic situation is also likely to emerge later in his or her retrospective attempts to create understanding on the part of others as to why a negatively typified action was undertaken.

Resources Required for the Construction of Accounts

What we mean by a 'resource' is a *knowledge base* to which an actor may have recourse in fashioning a definition of the morally problematic situation which will most favourably frame an action contemplated or already taken. These may include: (1) knowledge of constraints which affect the way in which an account can be fashioned in interaction, encompassing knowledge of conventional goals which might be activated in the recipient during the presentation of a mitigating situation definition; (2) abstract moral principles; (3) situational determinants of the evaluation of conduct; and (4) conventional accounting schemata.

Interactional constraints

Backman (1985: 264) points out that definitions which situate moral actions are worked out collaboratively by interactants, that all parties have a stake in the outcome of these negotiations, and the goals of each party are potent determinants of the definition that will ultimately be reached. Thus an actor in contemplating possible accounts will attempt to assess the (possibly competing) goals and plans of potential evaluators of his or her moral decision-making. For example, as Coleman (1976) has noted, a defendant who has fashioned an elaborate excuse for his conduct may in fact find that the judge, who is required to keep things moving along, may look more favourably upon a brief plea of guilty than a long-winded and time-consuming defence. Similarly, the possibility that an initial account might be rejected by the recipient can prompt the preparation of an alternative or back-up account. If the actor's construction of candidate definitions/explanations of the problematic situation has not been adequately attentive to the possible contingencies, then he or she may have to do considerable bottom-up work in the midst of delivery to produce a suitable frame for the conduct in question.

Abstract moral principles and their application

Backman (1985: 274) has advanced the notion that there is a 'deep moral structure', consisting of concepts such as 'a sense of fair play', 'a sense of decency', 'being for the underdog', and so forth. Kurtines (1986: 787) has done extensive study of the moral principles of *justice*, utility or *benevolence*, and instrumentalism or *pragmatism*. In Kurtines' view, such principles function as schemata which structure and integrate an individual's knowledge of social life and define his or her fundamental value system. Moral schemata also contain propositions regarding the objective features of moral dilemmas and the appropriate application of general principles to particular types of dilemma. According to Kurtines (1986: 786), in situations in which the moral dilemma is to cheat or not, to steal or not, to violate a law or not, any of the three moral principles may be invoked to justify a decision; for example, benevolence for speeding ('my wife was sick and I was rushing her to the doctor') or justice for overparking ('these meters are always taking my quarters, so the city owes me'). In constructing an account of an action, the actor may try to construe the objective features of the situation in such a way as to make his behaviour appear to be, or have been, principled.

The situated evaluation of conduct

Another knowledge base which can be exploited as a resource for reframing the dispreferred action has to do with the situated evaluation of conduct. Relevant concepts include *offence severity* (Blumstein *et al.*, 1974) or *severity of the consequences* (Kurtines, 1986); *negligence, intention* and *responsibility* (Antaki & Fielding, 1981; Fishbein & Ajzen, 1973; Shultz & Wright, 1985); and *fairness* (Messick *et al.*, 1985). All available evidence indicates that conduct is evaluated with reference to the specific circumstances surrounding its occurrence, including the character of the actor(s) and other parties, the perceived characteristics of the setting, and the nature of the action. These judgements constrain the kinds of situational constructions that can be placed on the actor's conduct. Blumstein *et al.* (1974: 558), for example, found that the more a 'failure event' (Schönbach, 1980) was offensive, the more likely it was that the person involved would be evaluated as *unrepentant* and *responsible* for the offence, and the less likely it was for an account to interfere with a judgement 'in the moral abstract'.

McLaughlin, Cody & O'Hair (1983) found that mitigating strategies like admitting one's guilt were normative if one wanted to avoid negative typification for a very severe offence in an interpersonal context (see also Schönbach, 1986). Schultz & Wright (1985) found that equal amounts of responsibility were assigned regardless of whether or not conduct was intentionally harmful or intentionally beneficial, but that persons were held more responsible for negligent harm than negligent benefit. Equal responsibility was assessed for accidental harm and accidental benefit. Their findings suggest that the question of one's own intentions and/or care is a pivotal issue to consider in the development of accounts of questionable conduct.

Several scholars have highlighted the importance of concepts like *merit, need* (Alves & Rossi, 1978; Backman, 1985; Kurtines, 1986) and *fairness* in their discussions of moral judgement. Alves & Rossi (1978) found that considerations of need and merit often conflicted, and that judgements of fairness were influenced by characteristics of the judged (sex, education, occupation) as well as characteristics of those judging. Messick *et al.* (1985: 489) found strong support for an *egocentric bias* in judgements of fairness, such that persons tended to evaluate their own behaviours as more fair than those of other persons. Kurtines (1986) found that both situation-specific merit and need were significant predictors of the distribution of rewards and punishment and the assignment of responsibility.

Both Backman (1985) and Haan (1986) have suggested additional factors which may affect the evaluation of conduct, and as a consequence the kind of accounts the actor can construct to frame it; they include characteristics of the situation such as the degree of ambiguity (Backman, 1985), the 'obviousness/subtlety of issues' (Haan, 1986), and properties of the setting in which the conduct is undertaken (Backman, 1985). To this list we might add features of the setting in which the account would most probably be delivered. For example, the evaluator of the re-framed conduct might be more likely to find it acceptable if the account is delivered outside the hearing of others.

Conventional strategies for excusing and defending conduct

A number of scholars have proposed taxonomies of accounts (Cody & McLaughlin, 1985b; Harré, 1977; McLaughlin, Cody & O'Hair, 1983; McLaughlin, Cody & Rosenstein, 1983; Scott & Lyman, 1968; Schönbach, 1980, 1985; Sykes & Matza, 1957). The most detailed is probably Schönbach's (1985, 1987), which lists conventional topical realisations of *conceding, excusing* (denying responsibility but acknowledging harm), *justifying* (acknowledging responsibility but denying harm), and *refusal* (denying guilt, the right of the other to reproach, or denying that the event in fact occurred). For example, in constructing an excuse the actor might plan to claim that s/he undertook the questionable conduct while disabled or overwhelmed in some way, or that s/he was not solely responsible, or that external circumstances interfered with his or her effort to do 'the right thing'.

In constructing a justification the actor might plan to claim that the conduct at issue was not seriously offensive, was more morally correct than some other action, was dictated by higher loyalties, and so forth. Thus negative typification for speeding in a school zone, for example, might be staved off by claiming that there were no children present at the time, or that had the driver not been speeding, she would have been late in picking up her own child, and the child would have been upset, and so on. In constructing a refusal, the actor accused of running a red light might flatly deny guilt, or claim that in fact it was another car which had run the red light, or assert that the light was still yellow at the time that s/he crossed the intersection, and so on.

The Account as a Basis for Attribution

Our interest in this chapter is in the differential effect of conventional forms of accounts on attributions about the actor made by account recipients, specifically attributions about the *moral character* of the author of the account. Participants in our study were presented with transcribed courtroom statements made by defendants in cases involving traffic violations. The defendants' statements varied with respect to the type of account given. After reading the statements, our respondents were asked for their impressions of each defendant with respect to his/her responsibility or blameworthiness for the event, his or her truthfulness to the Court, his or her intention to violate the law, and the extent to which his or her driving behaviour was influenced by dispositional or situational factors.

Respondents also evaluated the severity of each offence and rated the likelihood that the defendant had in fact been penalized by the Court.

Our previous work on accounts (Cody & McLaughlin, 1985b, 1988; McLaughlin, Cody & O'Hair, 1983; McLaughlin, Cody & Rosenstein, 1983) has lent considerable support to the notion that types of accounts may vary with respect to the degree of mitigation they represent. In interpersonal situations, an actor who concedes (admits guilt) or uses an excuse is more likely to have his/her account honoured and the reproach for the untoward conduct withdrawn, whereas *aggravating* account types such as justification or refusal tend to result in reinstatement of the original reproach and a lack of honouring. More aggravating accounts leave the hearer with the feeling not only that the offender is unrepentant, but that the offender was in fact fully responsible for the questionable conduct.

These general claims, however, must be amended for non-interpersonal contexts in which the recipient of an account for some untoward behaviour is a representative of an institution. In two studies, one of patrolman/driver encounters (Cody & McLaughlin, 1985b) and the other of courtroom statements by traffic offenders (Cody & McLaughlin, 1988), we have found that concession (guilt admission) tends to result in negative typification in the form of ticketing, fines, and other penalties. Excuses, which we have found in several studies (including the patrolman/driver study) to be not only commonplace but also relatively well received, were, in the courtroom, likely to be followed by the imposition of a penalty in about 75% of the cases (Cody & McLaughlin, 1988) and were not significantly more effective than flat denials in avoiding penalty. Although the precise nature of the results obtained by the different forms of accounting behaviour has varied considerably as a function of context, we have rarely failed to find a significant effect for account type regardless of the circumstances and regardless of how the 'effect' of the account has been measured: oral evaluations (McLaughlin, Cody & Rosenstein, 1983); ticketing/not ticketing (Cody & McLaughlin, 1985b); or imposition of a penalty (Cody & McLaughlin, 1988). Our expectation is that the current data set will show similar trends. Thus we anticipate that *there will be a significant difference in impressions of defendants formed as a function of the type of account used in their statements to the Court* (Hypothesis 1).

With respect to specific perceptions of the personal characteristics and predicted courtroom outcomes of defendants, we anticipate the following:

(a) *Likelihood that the defendant was penalized by the Court.* In our **study of the** actual outcomes of defendants (Cody & McLaughlin, 1988), we found that *logical proofs* (a form of refusal in which the defendant demonstrates that s/he could not have committed the offence in question) was significantly less likely than all other account types to result in a penalty, whereas concessions (guilt admissions) almost invariably did. *Excuses* and *denials* (a form of refusal in which the offence is flatly denied) were significantly less likely than *justifications* or *challenges* (a form of refusal in which the credibility of the arresting officer is attacked) to result in imposition of a penalty. We expected that a similar ordering with respect to likelihood of penalty would be generated by our respondents after they read transcripts of the defendants' accounts.

(b) *Offence attributable to the defendant's personal traits.* We anticipated that dispositional attributions would be greatest when defendants used justifications and excuses. In a justification the actor often discloses personal goals, motives and values which he places above the strict letter of the law and which led him to the questionable conduct. In an excuse the actor may detail personal failings or impairments which interfered with his desire to 'do the right thing'. Account forms like logical proofs or challenges call somewhat less attention to the personality and character of the actor.

(c) *Offence was intentional.* We anticipated that attributions of intent to violate the law would be greatest for defendants using justifications, inasmuch as they usually attempt to minimise the seriousness of their offences and/or offer good reasons for having done what they did (e.g. 'if I hadn't run the red light I would have been hit from behind'). We expected that use of excuses would be least likely to result in attributions of intentional offence: a frequent theme in excuses is that the offender exercised care; that s/he did not mean for it to happen.

(d) *Offence due to the circumstances.* We anticipated that situational attributions for defendant behaviour would be highest when the defendant made excuses (i.e. cited extenuating circumstances). (We did not anticipate that the dispositional ((b) above) and situational attributions would be opposing; Reeder & Spores (1983: 739) note that one may believe that a person engaged in wrongdoing because the circumstances were conducive to it, and simultaneously believe that a 'good' person would not have been unduly influenced by those circumstances.)

(e) *Defendant was to blame.* As noted earlier, Shultz & Wright (1985) have demonstrated that for harmful outcomes (as opposed to beneficial ones), persons are held responsible for their actions whether the actions were intentional or simply the result of carelessness (negligence). Consequently, an excuse that 'I just got distracted because the children were fighting in the back seat and I lost track of my speed for a minute' will probably do no more to ward off an attribution of blameworthiness than would a justification ('I was in a hurry because I was late for work and my boss was already annoyed with me'). Because both excuse and justification call attention to the character and motives of the defendant, they should be more likely to lead to attributions of personal responsibility for the offence than would account strategies which focus explicitly elsewhere (on the arresting officer, in the case of a challenge; on the plausibility of the charge, in the case of logical proofs).

(f) *Defendant was dishonest in Court.* Judgements about the truthfulness of an account doubtless are far more influenced by the specific details of the defendant's narrative which lend it (or do not) coherence and plausibility. However, as Reeder & Spores (1983) note, there is a tendency for untoward actions in one context to generate correspondent attributions about how the actor's character would manifest itself in other contexts. Therefore accounts which are encouraging of dispositional attributions about the actor, such as excuses and justifications, should be more likely than other types of accounts to produce the kind of negativity effect (Kanouse & Hanson, 1972) that would carry over to judgements of the defendant's honesty.

Methods

Respondents

Respondents were 176 undergraduates enrolled in upper- and lower-division communication courses at the University of Southern California and California State University, Fullerton.[1] Respondents were offered additional course credit for participating.

Stimulus materials

Participants responded to a questionnaire which asked them to make judgements of the character and intentions of defendants accused of traffic offences. Judgements were to be made on the basis of accounts given by the defendants to the Court. Stimulus materials for the questionnaire consisted of 20 accounts given by defendants appearing in traffic courts in the greater Los Angeles area (Cody & McLaughlin, 1988). The accounts were obtained by undergraduate observers who worked in pairs at four locations to write down the statements made by defendants with respect to a variety of traffic offences such as speeding, reckless driving, illegal parking, driving 'under the influence', running a red light, and making an illegal left turn. In addition to transcribing the statements made during the defendant's hearing, observers also made collaborative ratings of the defendant on a variety of scales including concreteness of account, nonverbal expression of regret, and politeness. Observers had trained to a median reliability of 0.80 on tape recordings of the half-hour television show, *The People's Court*. Three coders sorted the 375 defendant accounts obtained in the study into one of six categories: (1) concession; (2) challenge; (3) denies offence; (4) logical proofs; (5) justify; and (6) excuse. Inter-coder agreement averaged 89%, and ranged from 83% for justification to 98% for concessions. A description of each category and a representative defendant account is given in Table 11.1.

For the present investigation, two examples each of the two most common offences, running a red light and speeding, were selected from each of five account categories, excluding concession. Concession accounts were not used because they were usually extremely brief ('Guilty, Your Honour') and virtually always led immediately to a penalty. Examples were chosen only if (1) the observers had provided a clear indication of the precise nature of the offence (55 mph in a 35 mph zone, 25 mph in a 15 mph zone, etc.); and (2) it was the defendant's first moving violation, according to the record available to the judge and noted by the observers.[2] The 20 accounts so selected, ten for running a red light and ten for speeding, are given in Table 11.2.

In Part I of the questionnaire, respondents rated *severity of the offence* in the abstract; that is, they judged the seriousness of 'running a red light', 'driving at 55 mph in a 35 mph zone', etc., against two rating scales: 'the violation for which the defendant was cited was very serious' (7) to 'not at all serious' (1) and 'the violation for which the defendant was cited was a severe offence' (7) to 'not an offence at all' (1). In Part II of the questionnaire, respondents were provided with the 20 accounts in one of two randomly ordered series, and after each account were asked to provide a written answer to the question, 'what is your impression of the defendant?'[3] In Part III of the questionnaire, the 20 accounts were again presented in one of two randomly ordered series along with a set of 7-step Likert-type rating scales designed to measure perceptions of (1) the *likelihood that the defendant was penalised* by the Court ('I think the Court did impose a penalty on the defendant' and 'I think the defendant was not penalised by the Court'); (2) the *influence of the defendant's personality* on the driving behaviour for which s/he was cited ('the defendant's driving behaviour was influenced by his/her personality' and 'the defendant's driving behaviour does not reflect the kind of person s/he is'); (3) the extent to which the *defendant intended to violate the law* ('the defendant didn't mean to violate the law' and 'the defendant

TABLE 11.1 *Category definitions and representative accounts of oral arguments in court*

Account type	Representative example
1. *Concession*: Plea of guilty or no contest.	'Guilty, Your Honour.'
2. *Challenge*: Defendant argues against charge on grounds that arresting officer was inexperienced, unprofessional, not competent, and/ or not impartial.	'I might have been going 60, but I was not going anything like 70. I think the officer added those extra miles on just to make me more upset.'
3. *Denies Offence*: Defendant asserts that offence did not take place. May dispute officer's judgement but does not attack his charâcıer, motives or integrity.	'The light may have been yellow, but it was not red when I made the turn. . . . The officer's view was obstructed by other cars.'
4. *Logical Proofs*: Defendant makes arguments to the effect that the offence could not have occurred, or that s/he could not have committed it, or that there is room for doubt. (Often assisted by physical evidence.)	'Your Honour, I can't be guilty because they painted the kerb red after I parked there. . . . Here are papers from the city showing that the kerb was painted the day I got ticketed.'
5. *Justify*: Defendant argues that there were good reasons for committing the offence, or attempts to minimise the offence. Accepts responsibility but denies harm.	'I left my curling iron on, and was rushing to get home to turn it off before the house burnt [*sic*] down.'
6. *Excuse*: Defendant admits that the offence occurred/did harm but denies reponsibility on the grounds of impairment, obstruction by others, circumstances, etc.	'There was a car to the left of me, and the pedestrian was on the west side; the car on my left was ahead of me, therefore obstructing my view.'

Source: Cody & McLaughlin (1988)

TABLE 11.2 *Stimulus materials: twenty accounts given by defendants in traffic court*

Account type	Account

1: *Running a red light*

Challenge

The defendant stated that the yellow light was too short. The defendant stated that there was another car adjacent to his/her own car when he/she crossed the intersection.

Challenge

The defendant stated that there was no way she/he could have run the red light. The defendant asked why the police officer did not stop the driver nearby who was making an illegal left hand turn.

Deny Offence

The defendant stated that she/he did not deserve a ticket. The defendant stated that he/she did stop at the stop light; it was just that his/her car was the first to go when the light turned green.

Deny Offence

The defendant stated that there was no way that the officer could have seen him/her. She/he stated that the light was red, so she/he slowed down, then it turned green so she/he kept going.

Logical Proofs

The defendant stated that there were not one but two signal lights at the intersection. The defendant stated that the police officer's estimate of how far the defendant was behind the limit line when the light turned yellow could be anywhere from 60' late to only 30' late. According to the defendant, the vehicle code says to stop at the limit line when there is one; since the line was faded and couldn't be seen, there practically was none. The defendant stated that there was a lot of doubt involved.

Logical Proofs

The defendant stated that she/he went through a caution light, not a red light. The defendant stated that a motorcycle had come into the left lane next to him/her. The police officers had asked the people on the motorcycle who ran the red light. The defendant stated that the car that went through the light turned into a wholesale outlet. The people on the motorcycle came up to him/her, according to the defendant, saying they were sorry. The defendant stated that she did not

cont'd

TABLE 11.2 *Continued*

Account type	Account
	understand why they were apologising. When the police officer asked him/her why he/she was stopped, the defendant stated that she/he had not been able to answer because it did not seem that he/she had done anything wrong.
Justify	The defendant stated that she/he had been pulled over for running a red light, but that it was yellow when she/he went through it. The defendant stated that there was a car following closely behind and it would have hit the defendant's car had she/he come to a quick stop. The defendant stated that she/he did not have to increase his/her speed in order to make it through the light.
Justify	The defendant stated that he/she just followed the one car in front of his/hers. The defendant stated that she/he was aware that there was a police car nearby, and did not believe that she/he would have done anything illegal knowing that the police would observe it.
Excuse	The defendant stated that he/she wasn't so far into the intersection when the light was red. The defendant stated that she/he had just moved here from out of state, and was driving a new car. The defendant stated that she/he wasn't trying to jump the red light; that there was an incline on the street and the car didn't make it.
Excuse	The defendant stated that his/her view of the signal light was obstructed by a truck.
2: *Speeding*	
Challenge	(The defendant was charged with driving at 37 mph in a 25 mph zone) The defendant stated that he/she was a good tax-paying citizen. The defendant stated that the area in which he/she was ticketed was a speed trap.
Challenge	(The defendant was charged with driving at 66 mph in a 55 mph zone) The defendant took issue with the police officer's estimate that he had paced the

Continued

Account type	Account
	defendant for about one-half mile. The defendant stated that the traffic was heavy, not light, as the officer claimed. The defendant stated that she/he was not speeding. According to the defendant, the officer did not ask for the car registration when the defendant was pulled over. Further, according to the defendant, when the officer asked for the defendant's driver's licence, the officer did not notice that the defendant gave him his/her California I.D. by mistake. The officer did not run a check on the 'licence', according to the defendant. The defendant stated that he/she thought the officer was confused about what he saw, and perhaps mistook the defendant's car for another he had seen speeding.
Deny Offence	(The defendant was charged with driving at 58 mph in a 45 mph zone) The defendant stated that he/she was not driving at 58 mph but rather at 45 mph. The defendant stated that he/she was going at a moderate speed, and that it was not dangerous for the zone. The defendant stated that there were other cars in the area when the officer clocked him/her.
Deny Offence	(The defendant was charged with driving at 35 mph in a 15 mph zone) The defendant stated that he/she was in a temporary 25 mph speed zone before he/she got to the 15 mph speed zone due to the slide area. The defendant stated that the police officer entered an incorrect location on the ticket; the defendant stated that he/she had in fact only been driving at 25 mph in a 25 mph zone.
Logical Proofs	The defendant was charged with driving at 65 mph in a 55 mph zone) The defendant stated that new tyres can change the speed of the speedometer. The defendant stated that she/he bought new tyres in December. The defendant pointed out that the citation had been issued in early January.
Logical Proofs	(The defendant was charged with driving at 35 mph in a 25 mph zone) The defendant stated that he/she could

Contd

TABLE 11.2 *Continued*

Account type	Account
	not have been speeding because he/she had just come to several complete stops at stop signs. She/he stated that her/his daughter had been the victim of a hit and run, and therefore she/he would never speed.
Justify	(The defendant was charged with driving at 50 mph in a residential zone) The defendant stated that she/he was late for work, and that she/he was very familiar with the neighbourhood and she/he knew where to look for the children.
Justify	(The defendant was charged with driving at 78 mph in a 55 mph zone) The defendant stated that he/she entered the freeway in the slow lane going at 55 mph. It was 8.00 at night and the traffic was heavy. According to the defendant, the traffic was moving quickly, about 75 mph, and she/he was afraid of getting rear-ended because the other cars were following so closely. The defendant stated that his/her car was made of plastic. The defendant stated that she/he speeded up to move into a lighter traffic area, going with the flow of traffic to avoid being hit from behind.
Excuse	(The defendant was charged with driving at 75 mph in a 55 mph zone) The defendant stated that she/he was driving a new car that was shipped from Europe. According to the defendant, it doesn't show your speed in mph, it shows it in kilometres. The defendant stated that he/she did not know how fast he/she was going. Therefore, according to the defendant, she/he stayed with the flow of traffic.
Excuse	(The defendant was charged with driving at 40 mph in a 25 mph zone) The defendant stated that someone else was parked in his/her designated space at work and she/he was late for an appointment because he/she had to drive around looking for a place to park.

intentionally broke the law'); (4) the extent to which the *defendant's driving behaviour was not due to circumstances* ('the defendant's driving behaviour reflects the circumstances s/he was in at the time' and 'the defendant's driving behaviour was not influenced by the situation'); (5)

the extent to which the *defendant was to blame* for the traffic offence ('the defendant was responsible for the traffic violation for which s/he was cited' and 'the defendant is not to blame for the traffic offence for which s/he was cited'); and (6) the extent to which the *defendant was dishonest in his/her account* ('the defendant told the truth to the Court' and 'the defendant was dishonest in what s/he told the Court'). Scales for variables (2) and (4) were adapted from Reeder & Spores (1983). Responses to each pair of scales were averaged to form an index of each of the six variables. Higher mean scores correspond to more of the property.

Results

Separate analyses were conducted for each of the two offence types. Our preliminary examination of the 'speeding' data indicated that offence severity varied considerably across the levels of the accounts factor, whereas the description of the offence was constant for all the 'running a red light' cases.

Alpha coefficients for the six dependent variables and the intercorrelations among the variables are presented in Table 11.3 ('running a red light' data) and Table 11.4 ('speeding' data). Reliability was satisfactory for all six variables across both conditions. The cell means for each of the dependent variables are given in Tables 11.5 and 11.6. Alpha reliability for offence severity was 0.915.

TABLE 11.3 *Intercorrelations and alpha coefficients for six dependent variables, 'running a red light' data set*

Variable	Penalty	Personality	Intentional	Not situation	Blame	Dishonest
Penalty						
Personality	0.24***					
Intentional	0.25***	0.12				
Not situation	−0.00	−0.41***	0.25***			
Blame	0.50***	0.23***	0.30***	0.08		
Dishonest	0.18**	−0.03	0.47***	0.33***	0.31***	
Alpha	0.95	0.84	0.80	0.70	0.80	0.86

*$p<0.05$; **$p<0.01$; ***$p<0.001$

TABLE 11.4 *Intercorrelations and alpha coefficients for six dependent variables, 'speeding' data set*

Variable	Penalty	Personality	Intentional	Not situation	Blame	Dishonest
Penalty						
Personality	0.32***					
Intentional	0.26***	0.16*				
Not situation	0.04	−0.34***	0.19**			
Blame	0.57***	0.24***	0.21**	0.14*		
Dishonest	0.12*	−0.11	0.29***	0.33***	0.17*	
Alpha	0.94	0.85	0.83	0.68	0.80	0.88

*$p<0.05$; **$p<0.01$; ***$p<0.001$

TABLE 11.5 *Account type cell means for six dependent variables, 'running a red light'*

Variable	Challenge	Deny offence	Logical proofs	Justify	Excuse	M
Penalty	4.03	3.50[ab]	3.05	3.40[b]	3.69[a]	3.53
Personality	3.47[ab]	3.34[bcd]	3.14[ef]	3.30[adfg]	3.26[ceg]	3.30
Intentional	3.12	2.81[ab]	2.51[c]	2.63[bcd]	2.78[ad]	2.77
Not situational	2.73[abc]	2.74[cde]	2.73[bef]	2.49[g]	2.57[adfg]	2.65
Blame	3.90[a]	3.44[b]	3.03	3.35[b]	3.79[a]	3.50
Dishonest	2.91[ab]	2.83[bc]	2.49[d]	2.33[d]	2.73[ac]	2.66
M	3.36	3.11	3.33	2.92	3.14	

Note: Within rows, means with common superscripts are not significantly different, $p<0.001$.

'Red light' cases

Data were submitted to a one-way multivariate analysis of variance for repeated measures (BMDP4V) with *account type* as the independent variable and *likelihood that the defendant was penalised, influence of the defendant's personality, defendant intended to violate the law, defendant's driving behaviour was not due to circumstances, defendant was to blame*, and *defendant was dishonest in his/her account* as the dependent variables. (Reeder & Spores (1983) make a strong case for the use of within-subjects

TABLE 11.6 *Account type cell means for six dependent variables, 'speeding'*

Variable	Challenge	Deny offence	Logical proofs	Justify	Excuse	M
Penalty	3.60^{ab}	3.56^{ac}	3.55^{bc}	4.16^d	4.01^d	3.77
Personality	3.45^{ab}	3.18^c	3.32^{bcd}	3.76	3.48^d	3.44
Intentional	3.07^a	2.80^b	2.75^b	3.64	3.09^a	3.07
Not situational	2.88^{ab}	2.77^{bc}	2.94^{ac}	2.46^d	2.37^d	2.68
Blame	3.63^{ab}	3.43^{bc}	3.64^{ac}	4.18^d	4.04^d	3.78
Dishonest	2.58^{abc}	2.82^{de}	2.31^{cef}	2.76^{bdf}	2.48^a	2.69
M	3.20	3.09	3.17	3.49	3.24	

Note: Within rows, means with common superscripts are not significantly different, $p<0.001$.

designs in studies in which respondents are asked to make evaluations of moral character.)

There was a significant multivariate main effect for account type, $F(3.83, 669.40$, Huynh–Feldt adjustment$) = 41.88$, $p = 0.000$. Hotelling's T^2 was 196.63, $F(4,172) = 48.31, p = 0.000$. Impressions of the defendants on a linear combination of the six dependent variables differed significantly as a function of the type of account given, confirming Hypothesis 1 for the 'red light' data. Significant univariate main effects were obtained for *likelihood that the defendant was penalised*, $F(3.59, 628.9) = 42.33$, $p<0.0000$; *influence of the defendant's personality*, $F(4,700) = 8.53$, $p<0.0001$; *defendant intended to violate the law*, $F(3.92, 685.96) = 20.69$, $p<0.0001$; *defendant's driving behaviour was not due to circumstances*, $F(3.90, 683.32) = 7.47$, $p<0.0001$; *defendant was to blame*, $F(3.73, 652.86) = 48.38$, $p<0.0001$; and *defendant was dishonest in his/her account*, $F(3.79, 663.76) = 26.56$, $p<0.0001$.

With respect to the perceived likelihood of receiving a penalty, users of challenges were regarded as significantly more likely, and users of logical proofs significantly less likely, than **users** of all other account types to have a penalty imposed upon them. This was consistent with expectations. Unexpectedly, users of challenge were significantly more likely to have the offence attributed to personal traits than were users of logical proofs, and, although excuse and justification were about equally likely to lead to this dispositional attribution, they were not, as predicted, generally more likely to do so than challenges, denials and logical proofs.

Users of challenge were significantly more likely to be perceived as intentional offenders than any other category of defendant (an unanticipated finding), whereas the use of logical proofs was least associated with attributions of intentional wrongdoing. Excuses and justifications, unexpectedly, did not differ with respect to attributions of intentional wrongdoing. Results for the circumstances variable were not particularly striking, although users of justification were significantly less likely to be targets of the attribution of situational influence than users of challenges, denials or logical proofs. Excuses did not differ significantly from justifications with respect to the attribution of situational influence.

Users of logical proofs were significantly less likely than users of any other account type to be held responsible for the offence. Users of challenge and excuse were significantly more likely to be blamed for the offence than defendants who used the other categories, but, contrary to our expectations, users of justification had a comparatively lower likelihood of having responsibility attributed to them than users of excuse. Finally, defendants who used challenges, excuses, and denials were perceived as being dishonest relative to users of justification and logical proofs. We had anticipated greater attributed dishonesty for justification and less for challenges and denials.

'Speeding' cases

The 'speeding' data were submitted to a one-way multivariate analysis of variance for repeated measures (BMDP4V), with *account type* as the independent variable and *likelihood that the defendant was penalised, influence of the defendant's personality, defendant intended to violate the law, defendant's driving behaviour was not due to circumstances, defendant was to blame*, and *defendant was dishonest in his/her account* as the dependent variables. There was a significant main effect for account type, $F(3.91, 683.85$, Huynh–Feldt adjustment) $= 22.41$, $p =0.000$. Hotelling's T^2 was 85.2568, $F(4,172) = 20.95$, $p=0.000$. Impressions of the defendants on a linear combination of the six dependent variables differed significantly as a function of the type of account given, confirming Hypothesis 1 with respect to the 'speeding' data.

Offence severity was not a factor controlled in the study; in fact, data obtained when respondents rated the severity of defendants' offences in the abstract (prior to reading their accounts) indicated that severity might be a confounding variable. Among the speeding offences, the mean rated severity of those for which defendants used challenge was 3.31; for denial of offence, 4.65; for logical proofs, 3.19; for justification, 5.72; and for excuses, 5.06.

The variability of the severity ratings across account categories dictated that offence severity be used as a covariate in the repeated measures ANOVAs on the six dependent variables. However, in none of the six analyses did severity contribute significantly to prediction of the dependent variable beyond what could be explained by account type: *likelihood that the defendant was penalised*, $F(1,699)$ for covariate = 0.45, $p<0.50$, $F(4,699)$ for account type = 15.01, $p<0.0001$; *influence of the defendant's personality*, $F(1,699)$ for covariate = 1.18, $p<0.227$, $F(4,699)$ for account type = 23.04, $p<0.0001$; *defendant intended to violate the law*, $F(1,699)$ for covariate = 0.05, $p<0.83$, $F(4.699)$ for account type = 30.91, $p<0.0001$; *defendant's driving behaviour was not due to circumstances*, $F(1,699)$ for covariate = 0.40, $p<0.53$, $F(4,699)$ for account type = 17.42, $p<0.0001$; *defendant was to blame*, $F(1,699)$ for covariate = 0.37, $p<0.54$, $F(4,699)$ for account type = 26.72, $p<0.0001$; *defendant was dishonest in his/her account*, $F(1,699)$ = 1.82, $p<0.18$, $F(4,699)$ for account type = 9.12, $p<0.0001$. Inasmuch as there were no significant effects for severity as a covariate, the cell contrasts were done on the unadjusted means.

All of the univariate main effects for account type were significant. As expected, users of logical proofs were regarded as significantly less likely to have been penalised than persons using excuses and justifications. As expected, justification was significantly more likely to result in the offence's being attributed to the defendant's personal characteristics than any other account type. Excuses, although ranked immediately after justifications on this variable, were not significantly more likely than challenges or logical proofs to evoke dispositional causal attributions.

Defendants who denied the offence or who used logical proofs in their accounts were perceived to be less likely to have intentionally violated the law, whereas those using justification were significantly more likely than users of any other type of account to be perceived to have deliberately broken the law, as anticipated. There was little real variation among account categories with respect to attributions about the influence of circumstances. As expected, blame was most likely to be placed with defendants who justified or made excuses for their driving behaviour. Finally, although there was not a great deal of variability across categories with respect to attributed dishonesty, the defendants using excuses were rated as significantly less likely than defendants using denials, logical proofs, or justifications to be trying to deceive the Court. This finding was counter to expectations.

Discussion

Strong support was found for the claim that impressions of a defendant's moral responsibility for a traffic offence varied as a function of the type of account given by the defendant to the Court. This finding held across two of the most common kinds of traffic offence, running a red light and speeding. Significant effects for type of account were obtained for all of the dependent variables measured: the likelihood that the defendant was penalised; the likelihood that the defendant's personality influenced his or her driving behaviour; the probability that the defendant intentionally broke the law; the probability that the defendant's driving behaviour was a product of the circumstances at the time; the extent to which the defendant was to blame; and the probability that the defendant was dishonest in his/her account. Perceptions of the defendant did not appear to be influenced by the severity of his/her offence beyond what could be explained by the type of account given.

With respect to the imposition of a penalty, respondents were reasonably accurate in their assessments. Logical proofs, which Cody & McLaughlin (1988) found to result in a penalty in only 25% of their 375 cases, were rated by respondents in the present study as least likely, across offence types, to have led to a penalty. Cody and McLaughlin found that the use of challenges and justifications resulted in the imposition of a penalty in about 91% of their cases. Respondents in the present study rated justifications as most likely to lead to a penalty in the speeding data, and challenge as most likely in the running a red light data. However, across conditions, *excuses* had the highest mean rated likelihood of penalty, whereas in the Cody and McLaughlin study excuse was significantly *less* likely to result in a penalty than either challenges or justifications.

With respect to the attribution of a personality influence on the defendant's driving behaviour, we had anticipated that dispositional causal attribution was most likely to occur for justifications and excuses, inasmuch as they focus attention on the values and character of the defendant more than the refusal account types like challenge or logical proofs. In fact, justification did produce the highest attribution of the offence to the defendant's personal traits for the speeding data, and the highest mean scores across offence types, as we would expect, but generally there was not a great deal of variability on this factor.

For attributions to the defendant of intentional wrongdoing, we had expected that justifications would produce the highest scores and excuses the lowest. Although use of justification was significantly more likely to produce high attributed intent than any other account type in the speeding data, challenge was most likely to do so in the red light data. Excuse was only comparatively low on attributed intent in the red light data set and actually yielded high ratings of defendant's intentional wrongdoing for the speeding data.

As anticipated, the use of excuse produced the greatest causal attribution of the offence to 'the circumstances' for the speeding cases. In the red light data, use of justification was most likely to produce a situational causal attribution. Mean scores for justifications and excuses on this variable across account types were roughly equal (Ms =2.475 and 2.470, respectively).

Consistent with predictions, justification and excuse were both highly and about equally likely to result in the defendant's being blamed or held responsible for the offence, but for the speeding data only. For the red light data, challenge and excuse produced higher ratings of attributed responsibility.

With respect to attributions of honesty, our findings were completely counterhypothetical. We had expected that excuses and justifications, which frequently have the effect of focusing attention on the character and goals of the account-giver, would produce an attributional set to generalise from the defendant's observable wrongdoing in the one domain (traffic) to projectable wrongdoing in another (the Courtroom). However, the refusal strategies (logical proofs, denials, and challenges) were highest in rated dishonesty of defendant's account, across offence types. One possible explanation is that our respondents were of the school of thought which holds that if one is accused of something, s/he must be guilty, or at least have done *something* wrong; therefore, if one admits *neither* responsibility (as in an excuse) *nor* harm (as in a justification), then one must be lying.

As the above account indicates, there was greater support for the predicted orderings of the account types with respect to the dependent variables in the speeding data than in the red light data set. The reader will note from the mean dependant variable score at the bottom of Tables 11.5 and 11.6 that the means for the five account types are remarkably consistent across offence types with the exception of justification. This appears to be a function of the particular examples chosen. The justification category for the speeding data contains the anomalous example described in Note 2; further, the two defendants give particularly unappealing accounts of themselves. The justification examples had more personal detail than are given by the defendants in the corresponding category for the red light data.

One item of further interest is the failure of the severity variable to add significantly to the explanation of perceptions of the defendant beyond what account type could explain. A possible interpretation is that there is some sort of consistent isomorphism between severity of offence and type of account. Some offences are less 'deniable' than others, particularly when one's accusers have physical evidence at hand (radar, breathalyser results, etc.), and in such cases the alternatives available for a defence are considerably reduced: challenges, logical proofs and denials have much less utility. Some offences, however, such as running a red light or speeding in a low mph zone without radar, offer the creative offender a wider variety of options with which to reply to the charge. What is most suggestive in the present data set (which contains far too few examples per category for a thorough investigation of the severity/ account type relationship) is that offence severity *in the moral abstract* was rated highest for those cases in which the defendants actually used excuses and justifications and lowest for those in which they used refusals (logical proofs and challenges, excluding denials). This would indicate that as an offence becomes more severe (say, 25 mph over the speed limit as opposed to 5 or 10), it becomes less deniable. The defendant may hold out little hope that s/he will be found not guilty, and so must direct all of his or her efforts toward mitigation. We hope to explore this thesis in some depth in a re-analysis of the Cody and McLaughlin (1988) data.

One other interesting finding in our study was that some attributions came more easily than others to our respondents, as evidenced by the mean scores for the dependent variables across account types (see Tables 11.5, 11.6). Respondents seemed reasonably willing to attribute offences to defendants' personal characteristics and to hold them responsible for their offence, but were noticeably reluctant to make situational causal attributions or to draw conclusions about the truthfulness of the defendants' accounts. As noted earlier, it is probable that judgements of honesty or dishonesty are more a function of specific narrative components not available in our transcribings of defendants' accounts than they are of some sort of general negativity effect created by a single instance of the defendant's wrongdoing.

The disinclination to indict 'circumstances' as a factor in the defendant's being cited for a traffic offence requires a different explanation. There is the obvious one, of course: people are more likely to give dispositional accounts of others' behaviours and situational accounts of their own. There is another possibility, however. One will note, first, in Tables 11.3 and 11.4, that the causal attribution variables for person and situation are negatively correlated with each other (the latter variable was coded so that high scores corresponded to a judgement that a driver's behaviour was *not* influenced by situational factors). As we commented earlier, Reeder & Spores (1983: 739) have argued that one may explain behaviour primarily in terms of situational factors, but still be convinced that only a weak, immoral or foolish person would allow himself to be ruled by those factors. Reeder and Spores found that 'situational demands did little to relieve . . . [a] person of responsibility for her actions' (p. 742). Respondents may have simply been reluctant to grant situational factors equal status as a causative agent on the grounds that, as drivers themselves, they have encountered similar circumstances from time to time and have either stayed within the law or managed (mostly) to escape its long arm.

This study was the fifth in a series of reports aimed at uncovering relationships between strategic message choices and communicators' outcomes in the management of social and legal predicaments. As on previous occasions, the actor's selection of a technique for dealing with charges of untoward behaviour was a significant factor in determining the reception of his or her 'defensive re-interpretation' of a problematic situation.

Notes to Chapter 11

1. The authors acknowledge with gratitude the assistance of Shannon LoVette and Dan Canary with the data collection. An earlier version of this paper, without data, by the first and third author, was presented at the annual meeting of the Speech Communication Association, Chicago, 1987.
2. For one of the categories, justification, there was only one case of a speeding offence for which the defendant was a 'first offender', and the observers recorded the precise nature (in mph) of the violation. Consequently, to complete the design with a first offender defendant in the speeding/justification cell we were obliged to use a case for which the only offence recorded by the observers was 'speeding in a residential zone'.
3. An analysis of the open-ended descriptions of the defendants will be presented elsewhere.

12 Explaining events or explaining oneself?

CHARLES ANTAKI
Department of Psychology, University of Lancaster, UK

What I should like to do in this chapter is to puzzle over the kind of things people say when they use the word 'because'. On the face of it, the use of a word like 'because' (or 'since' or 'for' and so on) is a manifestly obvious one. If John says 'Jane was late because there was an accident on the motorway', there seems really not a great deal to ponder over. John is stating two states of affairs, and claiming a causal relationship between them. What, however, if he says 'Jane was late because she should have been there at lunchtime'? Clearly a rather different story is being told, and, if we had to describe it, we should say that John is explaining not Jane's lateness but, rather, his warrant in claiming that her actions counted as 'being late'. In the first case, John was explaining an event; in the second, he was explaining himself.

On the face of it, the two senses of 'because' in this crude sketch are quite distinct; but, as I shall be hoping to show in the chapter, finding ready examples in natural speech is far from simple. The reasons are not merely 'methodological' in some technical sense. They involve us in some difficult decisions to do with the legitimacy of traditional social psychology on the one hand and discourse analysis on the other. In trying to fathom what speakers are up to, we shall get into some rather murky and controversial waters.

Perhaps the best place to start is to say a little about the traditional social psychological attitude towards explanation and accounting. The social psychological tradition I have in mind is what is generally called 'attribution theory'. As readers will no doubt know, this approach (it has long been acknowledged not to be a 'theory' in any recognisable sense) is one of the most popular and influential in cognitive social psychology.

Its record in the citation indices, for example, put it ahead even of such a perennial favourite as research on attitudes, the premier social psychological construct for 50 years. Its basic ideas have now been thoroughly assimilated by generations of psychology students and researchers, and can be simply put. One is that people search for explanations of events in their world. That is certainly reasonable enough. The second is that such explanations are matters of choices among causal candidates; that, though less obvious, is an arguable position. Thirdly, and this is where we shall be concentrating most of our attention, attribution theory takes it that an attribution is an attribution is an attribution; that the form, function and force of the explanation is entirely unaffected by the explainer's context, the nature of the audience, or any match or mismatch between the two.

An example will help flesh out what I mean. One classic path of research in attribution theory has been to track down the kind of information people use when they make an attribution. If you happen across a newspaper report of a woman biting a dog, you will ask yourself, according to the theory, whether she has bitten other dogs, has bitten this dog before, and whether other people have bitten this dog. Assuming the usual answers to these questions, you will conclude that the woman's behaviour is unique, and you will agree that the cause of the behaviour is something to do with her peculiarities. Now of course I have used a trite example, and have hardly given attribution theory the best advertisement it could have; yet the form of explanation in this little vignette is essentially the form of explanation in any attribution theory or experiment that one could care to describe. Three things characterise the explanation ('something to do with the woman's peculiarities'): it is thoroughly circumscribed by the description of the event it is meant to solve; it is wholly divorced from the context of the explainer (the newspaper) and the audience (you as reader); and it is quite non-negotiable.

Suppose, then, that we approached an ordinary, everyday conversation with this view of explanations. We would be looking for statements in which speakers simply and clearly responded to a fully specified event with a brief and economical causal report. Of course, there are cases where we will find something reasonably like this; it will happen whenever the questioner wants to constrain the explainer wholly into a given framework of answer, even to the point of only being able to agree or disagree. In the courtroom, for example, counsel for the prosecution will ask the defendant: 'And will you tell the court why, knowing that it was fully loaded, that it had a hair trigger, and that the victim was standing only two feet away from you, you pointed the gun directly at him?' However, such questions and requests for explanations are unlikely to be the norm in most ordinary discourse. Although we might be able to think of some language games where such a relationship is the case and where an exchange such as the caricature above is permissible, it is not normally the case that one speaker has the authority so closely to constrain the other.

In less limiting circumstances, one would expect to see a freer range of explanations in which speakers themselves defined the event or issue they wanted to explain, and in which they had *carte blanche* over choice of explanatory language. When this is possible—as it usually is in routine conversation—then one can expect to see the variety of explanatory form that I alluded to in the introduction to this chapter. In free speech, perhaps the most obviously different class of explanation from a constrained attribution is the statement of the kind we saw above: 'Jane was late because she should have been there at lunchtime.' What is going on in such a statement? One reading is partly what the grammarians call the 'indirect reason' (Quirk *et al.*, 1987). Quirk *et al.* limit this to 'a motivation for the implicit speech act of the utterance' and an example would be 'Are you going to the shops? Because we've run out of bread'. The speaker is giving a reason for raising a certain matter in a certain way. As Draper (in press) would say of this example, although the need for bread 'caused' the question, the real issue is that without the explanation the hearer would probably be nonplussed by the utterance, not knowing the speaker's intention; the business about the bread is necessary because it communicates what the speaker is 'really after' in the sense that it gives the listener a fair idea of what is contingent on their response (now they know, for example, that if they say 'no', they could be accused of not helping with the shopping, or of being to blame for there being no sandwiches in the morning, and so on).

The other way one could interpret a 'because' statement other than as a justification of a speech act is to think of it as a defence of some more or less controversial assertion that needs some kind of justification (or, in Toulmin's terms (Toulmin, 1958a) some 'warrant' or 'backing') before it is likely to be accepted by the assembled company. An example of the former would be something like 'It was hilarious, because I didn't know he was a vicar at the time', and, of the latter, something like 'United won because I heard it on the radio'.

Given that we cán intuitively imagine this kind of variety among 'because' forms in talk, what literature can we turn to for some empirical data on their prevalence? Surprisingly, the attribution literature is rather light on studies of verbatim talk. In a recent review (Weiner, 1985), 17 studies were described which made some use of ordinary language. Of these, only eight used talk (as opposed to essays, newspaper reports and the like). Of the eight, six were studies of what respondents said when they failed at a laboratory task and one was the transcript of a formal parole-board. This leaves only one study (Nisbett, Harvey & Wilson, 1979) that actually uses transcripts of informal conversations (including 'singles bar conversations . . .[and] a picnic for lower socioeconomic status senior citizens'). This sounds most interesting, but we have to rely on a rather incomplete secondary account of it in Nisbett & Ross (1980), since it is unpublished. So far as it goes, we learn that people make a lot of attributions, and that they can reasonably be coded along standard attributional lines. However, the authors consciously set out to identify explanations as attributions, so will not necessarily have been sensitive to other ways of interpreting what their singles bar customers and senior citizens were up to.

Examining Linguistic Corpora

There exist many large corpora of ordinary conversation in the linguistics literature, and we can turn to one of them to take a broader look at causal connectives.

If we want to look at a causal connective, Altenberg (1980) tells us that 'because' is the most popular in English usage. Among the others, Quirk et al.'s authoritative grammar (1987) lists since, so, for, as, in order to, by virtue of, in the light of, in view of, owing to and due to, together with more elliptical expressions such as seeing that and in case. In fact, as has been pointed out elsewhere (e.g. Draper, 1987) explanations can be recognised perfectly well with no linguistic marker whatsoever (for example: 'Jane will get here before the others; she's got a faster car'), so even this list is a bit misleading.

Furthermore, the list given by Quirk et al. is rather formal and has an RP style which may not generalise well to other linguistic groups. It is perhaps worth noting that in a study of families in Leeds (Munton & Antaki, 1987) we found that, although the standard connectives were indeed the most common, there were also many non-standard formulations which were nevertheless quite clear as explanation markers. In the transcripts of ten families' conversations with a therapist (lasting on average an hour each), the most common connective was 'because' (accounting for 29% of all explanations); next was 'so' (18%), then 'if' (13%). 'If' does not appear in Quirk *et al.*'s listing, but makes sense when the speaker is explaining a hypothetical event:

> But Andrew didn't have that opportunity you see, he didn't get an apprenticeship, so, er, if he'd worked a little harder he may have got one.

The conditional is being used to report a cause of at least a hypothetical event. Still more non-standard was the use of 'when' which in some families was the second most preferred explanatory marker. This usage was often found in a narrative style, though with an explanatory implication:

> you know, the danger and that upsets him when you shout quickly like that, and I mean it's difficult to make them understand what's wrong and I think that's when they get upset, when you can react in a way that an adult can understand but not a little kiddie.

Interestingly enough, although 'because' was usually the single most common connective, the majority of explanations in most families' transcripts was made up of a collection of individual terms, for example, the terms 'put it down to', 'with being' and 'else' which are shown in these extracts:

> **Mother:**   I think you can put that [child's irregular sleep pattern] down to growing, can't you really?
>
> **Father:**   Well we could put it down to teething or stomach ache or something.

> Well, I say it's [his tiredness] also with being woken up during t'night.

> I always had to be in at the right time, else I'd be punished for it.

All this goes to show that in explanations, one cannot be too dogmatic; although 'because' is certainly a common marker, it is far from being the only one, and it may have features not shared by others.

Because

Nevertheless, we can make a start in our survey by collecting together a corpus of 'because' statements and seeing what emerges. In this we have been greatly helped by the existence of the Lancaster–Oslo–Bergen (LOB) corpus, collected by Svartvik and Quirk and their co-workers (Svartvik & Quirk, 1980). This is a corpus of spoken English from a variety of sources. The part that we shall be using is the 40 conversations (all in all, about 200,000 words) that the researchers unobtrusively recorded. The speakers were all educated native English speakers in Britain, mostly in middle-class professions such as lecturing, medicine, accountancy and so on. No claim is made that their style is generalisable to other sociolinguistic groupings.

The procedure we followed was quite simple. The corpus is held on a computer file, and on instruction, it printed out each appearance of the word 'because' (or its contraction 'cos'), together with 20 lines of context. The transcript includes such paralinguistic features as pauses, intonation and so on, and a parallel key tells one something about the speakers (namely their gender, age to within five years, profession where known, and venue of the interaction—for example over coffee at work, or at a dinner party and so on). The corpus yielded 666 'because' or 'cos' items, roughly 17 per conversation. The piece below shows three examples of 'because'. The paralinguistics are not reproduced, and the emphasis is merely to identify each appearance of 'because'.

> **A:** . . . may have been this was from the Chirk people that told me, perhaps it was, it's much more recently than that—may have been Ivor Bond told me, *because* they also know who the head of this . . .
>
> **B:** Oh, I haven't heard anything—well, Mallet is hopping mad about all this *because* Mallet sees a hundred and fifty thousand pounds for a building and various other things down the drain. What I think he doesn't realise is that it's very largely *because* he's been building, erm, this kind of peripheral thing in Appleby.

The first thing to note from this example, as has often been noted before, is just how unintelligible discourse is when taken out of context. There is no doubt that this is a severe problem for any work with transcribed texts for which one does not have some insight, either from the participants, or as a participant oneself, as to what is going on. We shall return to this later.

It became clear that, as coders, we had to read not only the short context extracted from the corpus, but also read the statements in sequence—that is to say, all the items from conversation 1 (from which the examples above come) were read together as they were being coded. This certainly helped, although there were still many occasions on which the topic of conversation was obscure, and little confidence was possible in coding.

When the topic of the utterance was clear the coding could proceed to try to identify clear examples of, on the one hand, causal reports and, on the other hand, justifications of speech acts and of assertions. The easiest of these to identify were the justifications of speech acts, as in this example from the corpus:

> Darling, why don't you go and see *Shampoo*!, because it's a sharp satire on sex and politics.

This counts as a speech act in so far as the ostensible question ('why don't you . . .') has its force as a recommendation for action. The 'because' phrase serves to give warrant to the recommendation, in this case by revealing certain aspects of the recommended behaviour which are (presumably) likely to be attractive to the recommendee. Such uses of 'because' were generally easy to spot, often being marked by a rhetorical question as above, or as in this example:

> Did I see him in that pub? Because I've got no memory at all . . .

Although the speech acts were fairly clear, uses of 'because' as causal reports and as justifications of assertions were only easy to identify at the extremes, of which the statements below are examples.

> But I stayed behind, because th.. the sergeant at the [ka..rr] of the Ulster Constabulary dealing with the case said: 'Sir, just hang your fire for a minute'.

Here the speaker is simply reporting the cause of his behaviour (staying behind) by revealing the legitimate orders of a powerful other (a policeman). That, in ordinary talk, would certainly count as a cause of behaviour.

> But then, chemistry's funny, isn't it, because I remember when they came round to give us a speech about what you could do for the war effort, there was very little they could think of that you could do with chemistry.

The assertion that something not normally marked as peculiar is 'funny' almost inevitably requires warranting, since it carries such a clear implication of deviant personal judgement. Here it is difficult to resist the interpretation that the speaker is motivated to defend his assertion, and that the force of the 'because' clause is to offer evidence that backs up his controversial claim.

Grey Areas

The majority of cases were far from being so straightforward. How, for example, should one interpret a case like this?

It's a bit difficult doing it in a public phone-box, because I find it very hard to write things down in a public phone-box, and anyway one always runs out of twopences.

In one interpretation, the speaker is merely reporting a cause of the difficulty; in another interpretation, the speaker is defending the assertion that the thing is difficult, by revealing two clear pieces of evidence of awkwardness.

One way to guide us through the problems of choosing between the causal interpretation and the more discourse-oriented justificatory account is to use the device of a 'gradient of confidence'. This is due to Leech & Coates (1979), and is best described with an example. Take the verb *can* which, like *because*, has a number of meanings. *Can* might be permission (as in 'you can go out if you eat your dinner first') and might be possibility (as in 'you can get downtown on the number 87 bus'). Between the two poles of this dichotomy there is what Leech and Coates call a gradient of confidence in what the speaker means. For example, the sentence 'she can eat all she wants' might be possibility or permission, just as, in our case, 'it's difficult because it's awkward' might be causal report or justification. Leech and Coates propose that where there is this kind of ambiguity, the interesting question becomes the identification of what it is that separates one meaning from another—which criteria help move a statement along the gradient of confidence between one pole and the other. Take this spectrum of *can* examples:

You *can* start the revels now.

The allowance *can* be paid to a woman over 60 years of age only if her husband was not receiving a retirement pension.

We *can't* expect him to leave his customers.

How, then *can* I help other people impose a ban in which I do not believe?

You *can* look fit as a fiddle and yet be bloodless. (Leech & Coates, 1979: 83)

Leech and Coates identify a criterion (which they call 'restriction') which will move a statement up the gradient: the most restricted use of *can* corresponds to the most confident classification of permission ('You can start the revels now'), and the least restricted corresponds to the most confident classification of *can* as a possibility ('You can look as fit as a fiddle and yet be bloodless').

The point of Leech and Coates's procedure is to suggest that what we can do is lay out our grey examples on what seems, intuitively at least, to be some sort of spectrum, and try and find criteria that will move a statement positively into one camp or another. Inevitably, this will involve us in the kind of argument about, on the one hand, the social psychological account and, on the other, the discourse interpretation that I mentioned earlier in the chapter.

Cause of Event and Cause of Thinking the Event is the Case

Take the simple (hypothetical, for the moment) statement:

She's at home because her phone's engaged.

Here the post-because clause cannot have brought about the state of affairs that is being reported. This gives us a secure feeling that what is being said must be meant as a warrant for the claim. On the other hand it might be pointed out that the 'because' clause *is* a cause: it is a cause of the speaker's thinking that something is the case. All we need say here, I think, is that if this is what cause means then it is indistinguishable from warrant in our sense. A truly causal statement (in the social cognition, attribution theory sense) would be one which was meant to report not the cause of someone's thinking that something is the case, but that something brought the case about. In our example above, it would be something like:

She's at home because she's ill.

It must be said, though, that there are cases in which the status of the 'because' clause is far from clear. The difficulty is in being able to tell whether what is in the 'because' clause is or is not genuinely meant to stand as a cause of the event or of the assertion. For example:

I've got a new television studio which has to be run in and, um, luckily he's quite good at that, 'cos he used to run *Open Door* for the BBC.

It might be that the programme *Open Door* was a reliable training ground for studio-directors, causing them to rise above the laxer standards of programmes elsewhere. In that sense that statement would be equivalent to saying something like 'He's good at his job because of his earlier training' or, more clearly, 'His time at *Open Door* made him good at his job'. Both are ways of expressing what we should recognise as a clear causal report.

On the other hand, suppose that what the speaker meant was 'I know that he's likely to be good at running in my new studio, because I have evidence of his abilities—namely that he once ran *Open Door* for the BBC'. The same information about the programme as a training ground is being mobilised, but this time with a rather different end. Here it is to convince or persuade the audience that the speaker is warranted in his judgement that the director is a good one.

Metacognitions

One way of reinterpreting the question is to say that the decision hinges on whether or not one could assume that the speaker thinks that her/his assertion *requires* justification. That is to say, the decision hinges on what we are willing to guess the speaker knows about her/his listeners. This suggests a spectrum with the least controversial statements being at the causal pole, while most controversial ones appear at the justificatory pole.

A moment's thought will show that if we want to pursue this line of reasoning, we shall have to move towards a consideration of the audience, and jettison the idea of a simple spectrum of statements as such. The idea of treating the statement as the unit of analysis rather falls into the social-cognition trap of assuming that all there is about the attribution is in its surface form. On the contrary. If the important criterion is what the speaker thinks the audience thinks, then the spectrum is not in varieties of statement, but rather in the varieties of audience. One statement will mean quite different things to different audiences. Suppose Linda said to Alan:

The kids had a good time in Spain because there was lots of sun.

This would be a causal report or a warrant, depending on whether Linda can assume one of two things: (i) That Alan does not know whether or not the kids had a good time, but can be assumed to know that Linda's kids are likely to enjoy the sun. In this case (if, for example, Linda and the kids have just got back, and Alan knows the kids reasonably well), then Linda can use the information about the sun directly to back up her claim that the kids enjoyed it. In a more defensive mood, she might even say 'Of course they enjoyed it: they had the sun, didn't they?' (ii) That Alan knows that the kids had a good time (perhaps Linda had just said so), but does not know why. If so, then Linda need not offer any defence that they did, in fact, have a good time; she can offer the information about the sun as a direct cause of their enjoyment, not of her assertion that they enjoyed it.

In this reading, what is important is the metacognitive awareness that exists between interactants. The more confidently the speaker can assume that the event is known to the listener, the less need there will be to defend it, and, consequently, the more the 'because' clause will be offered in a spirit of simple reportage. We can try using that rule of thumb on an example from the corpus:

> Oh, it's lively all right, because I've never given the same lecture twice.

Assume that the speaker has previously established that her lectures are indeed lively, and the statement becomes a causal one. Assume that she has not, and it looks more like a justification of the term 'lively'. Returning to an earlier example (see p. 275),

> It's a bit difficult doing it in a public phone-box, because I find it very hard to write things down in a public phone-box, and anyway one always runs out of twopences.

We can see that, again, if we assume that the speaker has satisfactorily established that the thing *is* difficult, what follows is a report of two causes of its being so; if not, then what follows is offered as proof of difficulty.

One can carry on multiplying examples of this type; we say to ourselves 'if the speaker believed such-and-such, then what they say must mean so-and-so'. The question that now faces us is right at the heart of our practice as researchers. How can we tell what the speaker assumes her/his audience knows? This is the murkiness that I mentioned we should be led into at the outset of the chapter.

Going Beyond the Social Cognitions

The tenor of social cognition work over the past 20 years has been to apply to social psychology the methods, and the theoretical language, of cognitive psychology. The standard interpretation of this is that social psychologists were jealous of the prestige that cognitive psychologists seemed to enjoy and, although they would occasionally indulge in worries over methods and results, such crises would pass without too much alteration to their belief in the positivist way. The positivist way, the standard account runs, is to treat the person as an information processor and to search for better models of the way in which data from the world are translated into personal action. The hallmarks of this way of thinking are, in research, the emphasis on control and prediction: highly structured set-ups (the classic example being, of course, the laboratory experiment), rigorously constrained response language (questionnaires, or, in more extreme cases, Likert-type response scales) and carefully manipulated variables, preferably well-screened from the respondents' consciousness.

These are common enough observations to make about cognitive social psychology. The astounding thing is to recall that the forerunners of modern day social cognitivists were as far away from this kind of thinking as it was possible to be. The early social psychologists were clear that the abstract consideration of the structure of cognition, including its interactive nature, should precede the study of any particular cognition; but the advice of Wundt and Ichheiser went largely unheeded. By contrast, this kind of recommendation found favour in sociological traditions more at ease with a broader, socially distributed, account of cognition. G.H. Mead's crystallisation of Ichheiser's self–other theory located cognitions in the space between interactants, rather than inside any one interactant's head. According to this early way of thinking, the single individual's psyche was an uninterpretable, perhaps even an unintelligible, construct. The mind, as a necessarily social object, needed to be reflected in other minds and to be aware, or be capable of being aware, that it was subject to this outside gaze.

Crudely speaking, the tension this leaves us with is between seeing the person's speech as, on the one hand, a product of an internal process, best understood as self-sufficient information processing and, on the other, a necessarily social construct which is uncompleted and uninterpretable without a context. If one tries to interpret a transcript with the former view, one is inevitably going to see the speakers' behaviour as the manifestation of internally held accounts or explanations which, in a sense, are launched blindly into the social world; if you take the other view, then you might well be unwilling to say anything about how the individual represents her or his world internally, but you will be reasonably at ease with speculating on the interpersonal function that their explanation is meant to fulfil. At one extreme, one could, on this latter view, wholly discount the person in the interaction, and deal only with the discourse at the level of the dyad or group, treating what is said as the product of a socially distributed cognitive system.

This enterprise has its advantages; it takes us away from any misleading focus on the statement or its nominal source, and orients us to the context of its reception. Take this longer extract from the corpus, in which two women start out by talking about a play that A went to see:

A: I said nah, let's go and see it . . . and it was quite funny, we really quite enjoyed it in fact.
B: Oh, *Time Out*'s never right.
A: No. [both laugh]
A: We .. we had already agreed that it wasn't a good thing to go by, but . . .
B: Yeah . . . so you've been seeing him a lot?
A: [coughs] No, about once a week.
B: Is it all sort of fast and furious?
A: No, it's definitely not fast and furious. He's the laziest bugger I've ever come across, I think.
B: [laughs]
A: Whenever we do anything, I have to go and meet him at the pub outside the hospital, and I hate meeting people in pubs . . . and even more, I hate walking into th.. hospital one.
B: Mm . . . yeah.
A: Four thousand people all watching who you're meeting.
B: Yeah.
A: And then we went for this . . . went to the theatre . . . we went for a meal afterwards at . . . erm, oh, place in Baker Street.

In this extract, the account that B initially asks for (B: yeah . . . so you've been seeing him a lot?) is met initially with something of a disclaimer by A (A: [coughs] no, only about once a week). But B presses on with a more direct question (B: is it all sort of fast and furious?), which is put in a form which requires a direct answer from A. The account that A gives is then emphatic, and raises a laugh from B, who allows her to move smoothly away from the report on the relationship to a statement about pubs and then further away onto restaurants. It is tempting to read the text as being the joint product of A's evasiveness and B's tolerance: A's discourse is less than clearly related to the ostensible account that B requires, yet B does not press the point: hence the clipped and elliptical form of explanation, which nevertheless seems to satisfy them both. Compare that with the fuller accounting in this conversation between a senior (S) and a junior (J) academic:

S: I'd like to be frank with you. Since you were here last . . .
J: erm
S: When you were interviewed for a job here
J: hm hm
S: I've heard from a number of sources that you have said in a [3 or 4 syllables unintelligible] that you think that you did not get the job because of me.
J: Oh no, I have never said that—in fact I went to great pains . . . will be perfectly frank with you: I went to great pains to put it about quite publicly that you were the one who was in fact supporting me in the interview with Professor Pitt.
S: I find it very strange that . . .
J: No I have certainly not. That is one, that is one charge on which I am absolutely not guilty.
S: Well I'm glad to hear it because . . . you are
J: Absolutely not guilty
S: You are absolutely right saying that
J: You . . .
S: I was the one who supported you . . .

Note how the senior academic led up to his challenge in his first two turn-takings, and how he half-repeated it after the junior's initial vociferous denial. The entire episode is a compact version of the kind of account sequence that Schönbach (1980) has shown can be modelled with a sophisticated system, though here it is fairly easy to see what is going on. The challenge is direct and the junior's account is equally unequivocal. There are one or two interesting points in the dialogue, however, where only the completion of one speaker's turn by another makes sense of the discourse. S says 'I find it very strange that, er, people, . . .', at which point J breaks in and says 'No, I have certainly not. That is one, that is one charge on which I am absolutely not guilty'. This seems an over-emphatic response to what, out of context, is merely S reporting his state of mind, and yet the joint, confrontatory nature of the episode makes a different sense of it. Presumably the metacognitions at work are something like the following: J knows that S understands that his (S's) report of his puzzlement would be understood by J as revealing that J's initial statement was insufficient to set S's mind at rest. With this appreciation of what S actually has in mind, J can proceed with the account that is being implicitly called for, and can raise further evidence in support of his claim that he did nothing improper. It might also be the case that S wanted to restate his challenge in less forthright terms: the statement 'I've heard [it] from a number of sources' may itself be taken as being S's warranting of his own claims.

Choosing an Approach

Clearly the persuasiveness of the analysis I have been suggesting depends a great deal on how amenable one is to the use of interpretation in understanding explanation. The gradient of confidence on which a statement might move is one that has to be anchored at each end by categories that are, ultimately, the researcher's invention and, equally, the criteria that one chooses to use to make statements migrate closer to one category or another are a matter of interpretative choice. It is hard to see how any researcher's subjective account of the gradient and the criteria could ever be put to empirical validation in the sense that psychologists are familiar with. This is as true for single statements of 'because' as it is for the longer accounting extracts above. If one wanted to say that the speaker is using what looks like a causal statement as a warrant for some claim that she or he is making, all one can do is point to the criteria one is using and see if they are reasonably persuasive.

In the case I have been arguing, the rule of thumb seems to be that if the speaker seems to think that the audience needs convincing of an assertion, then the 'because' clause is a warrant; if not, then it is a cause. Beneath this rule of thumb lies the choice of which approach to discourse one is willing to take. On the one hand, there is the atomic, response-oriented social cognition theory, and on the other, there is the discourse tradition friendlier to function and the role of context. The former, as I have been arguing, is less flexible about interpretation than the latter, since its conception of cognitions as non-negotiable representations of internal information processing leaves little room for analysis of jointly constructed discourse. The latter is certainly more friendly towards that way of thinking about accounts and, crucially, is more in keeping with a tradition of acknowledging the essentially metacognitive nature of social cognition. If we are to get behind 'because', that may be the preferred mode of analysis.

13 Accounting: Societal implications

JERALD M. JELLISON
Department of Psychology, University of Southern California, Los Angeles, USA

Understanding why we do what we do is an abiding human concern. Pondering the reasons for people's actions provides a vocation for professional social scientists and an avocation for people-watchers everywhere. Speculations about the causes of human behaviour fill countless pages of scientific journals and popular magazines.

Perhaps because of the existence of so much common-sense wisdom about the reasons people do what they do, the scientific theories often stand in marked contrast to these everyday accounts. It is the particular task of psychologists to explain human behaviour and at times it seems as though psychologists have almost gone out of their way to develop explanations that go beyond common sense. Examples here might include theories about the mysteries of the unconscious, complicated theories of personality, and the mathematical theories of learning. It is as though the non-obvious nature of the explanations serve as proof of the legitimacy and importance of this scientific approach to human behaviour.

After nearly a century of avoiding common-sense conceptions, social psychologists have lately made these everyday explanations a central research concern. While acknowledging that such explanations may be incomplete, or 'wrong', they are important because people believe they are true. Presumably people make many important life judgements about themselves and others based on these common-sense theories of action.

Recognising the central role these conceptions play in guiding people's decisions, researchers began systematically to analyse the everyday theories people use to explain the causes of human behaviour. The initial topic of interest was how people developed attributions for the causes of their own, and other people's, actions (Heider, 1958; Jones & Davis, 1965). For the most part this early research examined the explanations people developed for their own private use in understanding reality, rather than the public explanations they gave to others.

More recently the communication of explanations to others has evolved into a separate topic of interest. Using terms such as accounts, justifications and excuses, the explanations people publicly give to others has become an independent area of enquiry. The present volume is testimony to the vitality of this research. These public explanations are most frequently given after an individual has committed an action that is deemed socially inappropriate and therefore incurs disapproval; such interpersonal accounts are designed to avoid blame for misdeeds, and may actually precede the commission of an error. Research on self-handicapping (Arkin & Baumgardner, 1985; Jones & Berglas, 1978) suggests that people actively create conditions which both increase the chances of their own failure and can then be used to account for any implication of personal inadequacy.

The concept of accounting has been used broadly to include four very different strategies whose similarity derives from the common goal of mitigating criticism and punishment for inappropriate action (Schönbach, 1980). These include: admitting the error in a concession; denying the act occurred; seeking justification by redefining the action as legitimate or acceptable; and offering excuses which provide an exculpatory explanation for the action. This chapter focuses primarily on the latter process of providing causal explanations but will include accounts offered for both socially acceptable and unacceptable actions.

Rather than examining the details of how people offer explanations, an attempt will be made to place this accounting process in a larger societal context. This will involve a shift of perspective away from individuals in particular situations to a more general cultural level. The goal is to explore some of the larger consequences of the explaining process. Before beginning this general exploration, it will be useful to explicate the issues that societies must confront with regard to the public explanation of behaviour. This analysis will depend on two key assumptions. First, it is assumed that each society has a vested interest in how people account for their own behaviour. Second, because of this vested interest, societies attempt to shape their members' behaviour to conform to what are considered good accounting practices. To understand the reasons for these interests, it is important to clarify the general purposes which accounts serve.

Responsibility and the Accounting Process

The goals of the scientific enterprise usually include explanation, prediction and control. The practice of scientific analysis involves the development of theoretical explanations which are then tested according to their capacity to predict accurately and effectively control outcomes. An explanation's value depends upon its capacity to help us predict and control.

Applying the same reasoning to everyday explanations of behaviour suggests that explanatory accounts also serve to help people predict and control each other's behaviour. It is easy to see that if you fully understand the reasons for a person's past behaviour, then you should have an improved capacity to predict his future actions. For example, knowing someone lied in order to obtain a sum of money suggests that in the future he or she will also be dishonest. Conversely, the fact that a person refused to lie, despite the opportunity to obtain a substantial sum, implies that he or she will also be honest in the future.

While the role that explanations play in enabling people to predict one another's behaviour is relatively straightforward, explanations can be related to the goal of control in at least two different ways. At the most simple level, if the reasons for a person's past actions are known, one can arrange similar conditions and produce the same behaviour in the future. Continuing the above example, by offering the first individual a sum of money one could get him to lie on one's behalf. Stated more generally, accurate explanations can suggest ways that enable a person to shape other people's behaviour more efficiently.

Explanations also get implicated in the process of social control in a more subtle way. This second connection is of greater importance to society as a whole, because it involves the concept of responsibility. Responsibility is a complicated notion usually involving (1) a person's action; (2) the reasons why the person committed the action; and (3) the possible assignment of praise, blame, and other rewards or punishments. While the second of these elements, the reasons for an action, will be the object of primary discussion, let us begin by clarifying the first and third elements.

Each social group designates some behaviours as desirable and others as undesirable. While the content of such lists of positive and negative actions varies from one group to another, every society seems to make such distinctions. Committing one of these highly valenced actions induces others to assess whether the individual is 'responsible' for the action. The judgement that someone is responsible carries with it the possibility that he or she deserves to be rewarded or punished. When someone is held responsible for the commission of a undesirable action, he or she may be subjected to a variety of socially administered punishments. An individual judged responsible for a negative act may be publicly condemned. He or she may be required to make restitution, and in the case of criminal acts may suffer incarceration or even loss of life.

Although the concept of responsibility is often discussed only in relation to undesirable actions, it also applies to the commission of socially approved actions. Being judged responsible for performing a desirable action can result in a variety of positive consequences. On a personal level the individual may experience pride or other good feelings, and socially, people may reward him or her with words of praise, expressions of gratitude, awards or more tangible benefits.

These socially mediated punishments and rewards serve the important function of helping mould future behaviour. Individuals and societies try to encourage desirable behaviour in others with rewards, and they attempt to discourage undesirable behaviours with punishments. These socially applied consequences also send a message to other members of the society, in addition to the immediate recipient; the punishments warn of the dangers of committing undesirable actions, and the rewards signal the benefits associated with acting in a socially valued manner.

This use of rewards and punishments to shape future behaviour rests upon the judgement that the individual was responsible for the actions committed. And that judgement depends heavily on the reasons for the action, and whether or not the action was intentional or unintentional: this is the third element of the concept of responsibility. An individual is held responsible when the action is judged to have been caused by forces within his or her volitional control. People are not held responsible for unintended actions on the assumption that the crucial causal forces are outside the person's control. For example, an individual who deliberately violates a law is punished more severely than one who accidentally violates the same law.

The idea of intentionality rests largely on a distinction between causal factors that are internal to the individual and causal forces whose locus is in the external environment. The internal factors include such things as the individual's desires, values, beliefs, needs and personal attributes which are assumed to determine the individual's choices. The concept of choice implies that the behaviour was under the individual's internal volitional control. By way of contrast, an individual might engage in exactly the same action solely as the result of non-volitional forces, which are often external. This would be the case if the action resulted from bad luck, social pressure or coercion, a lack of awareness, physical attributes of the body, or other factors outside the person's control. If such causal forces are judged to be beyond the person's volitional control, then the action would be deemed to be involuntary and the individual would be held less responsible.

Because of the importance of this issue of volitional control in judgements of responsibility, the accounting process tends to centre around the question of whether the person's action was caused by internal psychological factors or non-volitional factors. The greater the degree to which the action is explained in terms of internal, or volitional, causal forces the greater is the assignment of responsibility. The nature of the supposed causes of an action directly and dramatically affects the magnitude of the punitive and rewarding consequences. Censure for committing a socially undesirable action is far greater if the action was caused by internal forces than by external factors. Since the size of these socially mediated consequences depends so heavily on whether the cause was internal or external, both the individual actor and any involved social observers have a stake in the nature of the account that is proclaimed and socially accepted.

If the individual can successfully deny responsibility for an action because the action was *not* intentional, then he or she may be able to avoid any punishment. If such an explanation is accepted, then the members of the society would not be able to punish the individual. More importantly, society would be denied the opportunity to shape the actor's future behaviour.

Accounts: the individual actor's interests

Individuals' actions tend to be guided by the general principle of minimising punishments and maximising rewards. This principle has direct relevance to the kinds of accounts individuals should give for their own behaviour; it suggests different strategies for accounting for positive and negative actions. Individuals should explain their own socially desirable actions in terms of internal factors—by doing so, they will be held responsible and are more likely to receive possible socially mediated benefits. Conversely, undesirable actions should be accounted for in terms of external factors, so as to avoid responsibility and minimise punishment.

There is so much evidence that individuals do generally follow this pattern of differential explanations for their desirable and undesirable actions, that the phenomenon has been labelled the *self-serving bias* (Bradley, 1978). The self-serving bias refers to the tendency of individuals to give internal explanations for their positive actions and external explanations for their negative actions. Following such a pattern of explanations is obviously in the individual's immediate self interest, but what are the consequences of such a bias in explanations for society at large?

Accounting: society's interests

The issue of socially accepted explanations for behaviour bears on the capacity of members of the society to shape and control individuals' future action. Rewards and punishments are employed to modify behaviour but can only be legitimately applied when the individual is judged to be responsible for his or her actions. And, since people are only responsible for actions which are explained in terms of internal causal factors, a society's interests in social control are best served when individuals explain their behaviour in terms of internal factors.

For a society, it is advantageous to have individuals account for both positive and negative actions in internal terms. Such explanations imply the individual is responsible for all his or her actions and can therefore be legitimately rewarded or punished. The rewards given out following positive actions serve the social goal of encouraging the repetition of such behaviour in the future; the administration of punishments to those responsible for committing negative actions serves to discourage socially unacceptable behaviour in the future.

In the case of positive actions the interests of society and the individual converge on the utilisation of internal explanations. Internal accounts imply the individual is responsible for his good actions. The individual benefits by receiving the social rewards, and in administering these rewards, society can encourage more similar actions in the future. However, the two sets of interests diverge when it comes to accounting for socially unacceptable behaviour. It is often in the individual's self-interest to account for his or her negative actions in terms of external forces, in order to avoid being judged responsible and being punished. If such external accounts are accepted by the members of the society, then they cannot legitimately punish the individual for negative action. If individuals could escape punishment by simply claiming all of their undesirable actions were caused by external forces, then the society would be severely hampered in its attempt to discourage a repetition of negative actions. Such a lack of punishment may actually encourage undesirable action, as the individual usually derives many direct benefits from the action without incurring unpleasant sanctions or costs.

Clearly, if individuals could avoid responsibility by easily giving such external accounts, social control would be seriously damaged. Given society's strong interest in holding individuals responsible for their action, most societies promulgate norms or rules dictating the preferred form that all accounts should take.

The Norm of Internality

One such general accounting rule has been identified as the Norm of Internality (Jellison & Green, 1981). This norm prescribes that individuals should account for their actions in terms of internal volitional forces. By pressuring individuals to implicate internal psychological factors as causal, the society can then hold the individuals responsible and legitimately use rewards and punishments to control future actions.

These internal factors involve many psychological entities that are assumed to play a part in decision making. One such set of factors involves values, attitudes and beliefs: examples of related accounts might be:

I had to act in accord with my *conscience*.
I did it because I *believed* it was the best thing.
I *decided* that's what I was going to do.

Also acceptable as internal causes are certain psychological needs, wants and desires.

I *wanted* to do the right thing.
I *intend* to do it.
I did it because I *needed* some support and attention.
I did it out of *revenge*.

Personality traits, moods and attributes such as self-esteem may also be accepted as plausible internal explanations:

That's just the *kind of person* I am.
I'm very *assertive* person, so naturally I did it.

Such explanations are acceptable so long as they imply that the personal attribute causing the action was within the individual's control.

Emotions and personal feelings are also often considered to be plausible internal explanations. Therefore an individual might comply with the Norm of Internality by accounting for an action by saying:

I did it because I *felt* like it.
I had a *gut feeling* that it was what I should do.
I did it out of *love*.

The kinds of internal psychological factors that fit the Norm of Internality are those which imply that the behaviour was under volitional control: such internal explanations legitimate holding the individual responsible. Explanations framed in terms of either internal or external factors which could exculpate the individual are inconsistent with the norm.

The entire range of excuses (Jellison, 1977; Snyder & Higgins, 1986) which implicate the individual's environment, therefore, are not deemed normatively acceptable. These unacceptable explanations include: blaming other people ('I'm only following orders'); the weather ('What do you expect on a miserable day like today?'); equipment ('If the machine hadn't broken this never would have happened'); one's physical body ('I have a hormone imbalance'); or supernatural forces ('The devil made me do it').

The existence of the Norm of Internality in American society has been demonstrated in several ways. Using Rotter's I–E scale, which contains pairs of internal and external explanations for behaviour, people were asked to evaluate different patterns of responses made by other persons. Stimulus persons who indicated a highly internal pattern of responses received considerable social approval, while disapproval was heaped on those who indicated an external pattern of responses (Jellison & Green, 1981). These findings illustrate another manifestation of this norm, the phenomenon of both the social praise given to explanations which are consistent with the norm and the social condemnation accorded explanations which are inconsistent with the norm's prescriptions.

In a related study people were asked to create a socially favourable impression in other persons who would read their responses to the I–E scale. Thus, the only way to manage one's impression was by the pattern of responses on the I–E scale. When attempting to get others to like them, people overchose the internal explanations. But, when instructed to create a socially undesirable impression, people chose the external responses. It would be interesting to confirm whether the same results would be obtained in other societies and cultures.

Granting the existence of this general Norm of Internality, it is interesting to examine the extent to which it is obeyed. One of the initial generalisations to emerge from the research on attribution process was called the Fundamental Attribution Error (Jones, 1979). The Fundamental Attribution Error refers to the tendency of observers to over-attribute the cause of an actor's behaviour to internal factors to the relative neglect of potential external causal factors. Although derived from laboratory experiments, this basic attributional bias was assumed to be exemplified in many everyday phenomena such as that of blaming the victim. For example, the victims of rape are often seen as inwardly wanting to be raped, and welfare recipients are perceived as intentionally avoiding employment. While these far-ranging observations in part corroborate the existence of the Norm of Internality, they focus on the accounts people give for the behaviour of others and not for their own actions.

In practice, individuals seem to maintain a double standard regarding this norm. They expect others to give internal explanations, and they themselves rely on internal explanations to explain the actions of other persons. This tendency stands in stark contrast to the way in which people account for their own actions. They use internal explanatory accounts for their own positive, but not negative, actions. When their own actions are socially unacceptable, people attempt to establish external accounts in order to avoid responsibility and possible punishment.

In sum, there is a continuing conflict between the vested interests of individuals and society at large over the kind of accounts that are given for socially undesirable actions. The social control problems that centre around the issue of responsibility and the attendant punishments would seem to affect every society. It would be informative to know whether non-Western societies employ other accounting rules, or use alternative mechanisms for assigning responsibility and punishment in order to negotiate this conflict and still exert social control over an individual's actions.

Societal Implications of the Norm of Internality

Although invoked to force individuals to assume responsibility for their actions, the Norm of Internality may have some larger consequences which are unintended and undesirable. One of those added effects could have direct implications for the activities of social scientists.

Scientific explanations of human action

There is a striking similarity between the professional activity of psychological researchers and the everyday actions of individuals. While the average person is uniquely concerned with accounting for his or her own actions, psychologists, especially social psychologists, are in the business of accounting for the social behaviour of all human beings. Despite the difference in the size of the field of enquiry, both the professional and the lay person are concerned with explaining human behaviour.

Scientific explanations of human behaviour are framed in terms of formal theories and concepts. Psychologists have created a great number of these theories designed to provide a scientific basis for explaining human action. These theories are assumed to represent an objective and unbiased account of reality; this claim to objectivity adds to the social importance of the explanations. To protect this supposed objectivity, attempts are made to remove political, economic and social considerations from influencing a social scientist's analyses.

The Norm of Internality, which serves social interests so well when applied to everyday explanations, could have most undesirable consequences if it also affected the scientific explanations produced by scientists. The Norm could potentially create an 'internal bias' in psychological theories. If the Norm did impinge on the professional activity of psychologists, then they would be expected to place a great deal of emphasis on internal psychological and volitional causes rather than external environmental factors.

There is no precise way to assess the possible existence of such a normative bias, but it might be instructive to survey the general nature of explanatory concepts favoured in social psychological theories. One approach is simply to list the kinds of theoretical accounts psychologists seem to rely on most heavily and to compare roughly the degree of fit between these theoretical concepts and the dictates of the Norm of Internality.

Values, attitudes and cognitions

The theoretical constructs of attitudes and values have been historically recognised as cornerstones of social psychology. Values continue to be viewed as important determinants of behaviour (Rokeach, 1973), and despite the inconsistencies in the empirical literature (Wicker,

1969) it is still assumed that attitudes cause behaviour (Ajzen, 1985; Fishbein & Ajzen, 1975).

The recent concern with cognitive mechanisms (Fiske & Taylor, 1984) is an extension of older concepts about beliefs, expectancies and attitudes. The underlying assumption is that the individual's cognitions more or less directly affect behaviour. In some versions, the values and cognitions become part of the process of making a choice and behaviour results from that decision.

The concepts of cognition, belief, attitude and value all locate the cause of action clearly within the individual's psyche, and within the individual's control. This set of scientific causes is therefore perfectly consistent with the dictates of the norm.

Personality

The significance of the concept of personality as a common explanation is demonstrated by the fact that there are several major journals which are devoted to research on personality. Whether talking about traits, states, factors or structures, the underlying assumption is that an individual's personality exerts an important causal force on behaviour selection. Although there are debates about how much an individual's personality constrains or causes behaviour, the locus of causality is always viewed as residing *inside* the psyche.

Needs

Psychological needs and motives represent another common explanatory mechanism. The list of mental needs has become almost embarrassingly long. A few familiar examples from the beginning of an alphabetical list should illustrate this point. There are needs for: achievement, affiliation, approval, belonging, consonance, consistency, competence, certainty, and free choice (aka reactance). All of these higher-level needs are assumed to be intra-psychic, rather than physiologically based, and that assumption makes them congruent with the Norm of Internality.

Self-esteem

The concept of self-esteem has become the most popular general explanation for a wide variety of behaviours (Wylie, 1974). Even such contradictory patterns of behaviour as obesity and anorexia, or masochism and sadism, are interpreted as resulting from the same cause—low self-esteem. The general notion of self-esteem is multidimensional and is variously conceived as a set of beliefs, or feelings, which may take the form of a personality trait, psychological need or self-reflective attitude. In all cases, however, the causal mechanism is clearly located within the psyche.

While this list is not all-inclusive, it suggests that the major causal concepts extant in social psychology are all congruent with the Norm of Internality. While this evidence doesn't prove the existence of an internal bias, it is consistent with such an interpretation. Other suggestions about the possible biasing role of the Norm of Internality can be gleaned from several conceptions which have had an extremely broad acceptance inside and outside of psychology.

Maslow's (1954) conception of a hierarchy of human psychological needs has had a continuing appeal as shown by the frequency with which it is cited in basic psychology and management textbooks. As originally proposed, human needs were grouped into five levels in ascending order. The two lowest levels include the physiological needs related to the physical maintenance and perpetuation of the organism. Although the locus of the physiological needs is inside the individual, their physiological basis is inconsistent with the dictates of the Norm of Internality. In sharp contrast, the three so-called higher level sets of needs clearly have a psychological base, which implies volitional control.

It is interesting to speculate about the possibility that the Norm of Internality affected Maslow's conception. The two 'lower' levels contain the non-psychological needs which are assumed to be outside volitional control; in contrast, the needs included at the 'higher' levels are said to have an intra-psychic basis. Could the elevation of these psychological needs to the *top* of the hierarchy be a subtle manifestation of the norm? A related phenomenon is the emphasis on the importance of 'intrinsic', rather than extrinsic, motivation in achievement behaviour (Deci, 1975).

In conjunction with the concept of self-esteem, Rotter's notion of an Internal–External personality factor has been widely used to interpret a variety of complex social actions. The idea is that people can be differentiated according to whether they are disposed to view the locus of causality for their own actions as being internal or external to themselves. Many forms of therapeutic intervention are directed at improving the individual's sense of internal control (Davison & Neale, 1986).

Violations of the Norm of Internality

The Norm of Internality not only condones internal explanations, it also condemns external explanations. This condemnation of non-internal explanations suggests that bias in scientific explanations may also take the form of eschewing external explanations. This reasoning raises questions concerning the existence of plausible, non-internal explanations which psychologists have been reluctant to endorse.

Behaviourism

Behaviouristic explanations represent an obvious example of a systematic conceptual approach which emphasises the importance of external consequences as the cause of behaviour. According to a behaviouristic analysis behaviour is to be explained in terms of the reinforcement contingencies in the organism's environment (Skinner, 1953, 1974). Such an approach shifts the locus of causality out of the individual's volitional control and is therefore not consistent with the Norm of Internality.

Behaviouristic explanations are generally judged as either wrong, suitable only to lower animal forms, or as explaining only 'elementary' responses (Zimbardo, 1988). There have been attempts to introduce behaviouristic conceptions into social psychology (Staats & Staats, 1958) but such efforts have not been successful. Even in the applied field of business management, behaviourism is judged to be inadequate for explaining 'complex' human behaviour (Porter, Lawler & Hackman, 1984).

What is the source of this condemnation and minimisation? Although social scientists who attempt to explain social behaviour have seen behaviouristic accounts as insufficient for supposedly scientific reasons, it seems possible that such condemnation could have partially resulted from the influence of the Norm of Internality.

Behaviour Genetics

Recently the behaviour geneticists have begun to attempt to explain complex social behaviour (Wilson, 1975). While genes are clearly located inside the organism, they have a neuro-physiological base, rather than a psychological one. This strictly biological emphasis implies that actions are largely outside the individual's volitional control, and is therefore inconsistent with the Norm of Internality.

Not surprisingly, genetic explanations do not receive much attention in social psychological journals or textbooks. When genetic influences are mentioned, the usual reference is to the behaviour of non-human animals. Only the discussion of aggression regularly includes genetic influences, and even here, social and psychological factors are seen as playing a more important causal role. Again the question arises as to whether this reaction by social psychologists is rational, or rationalisation.

Conformity

Several conceptions within social psychology carry a largely negative connotation, and it is interesting to note the extent to which they involve external causation. The phenomenon of conformity was a popular topic of research in the 1950s (Asch, 1955) and continues to be included as an important chapter in contemporary textbooks. Conformity refers to actions that result from external social pressure, real or imagined; this external locus of causality is usually contrasted with the notion of internalised attitudes as a cause of behaviour. Given the obvious emphasis on external forces associated with conformity, it is not surprising that the concept of conformity occupies an ignoble place in the pantheon of social psychological phenomena. While acknowledging the existence and importance of conformity, every textbook more or less explicitly suggests that only weak individuals (those with low self-esteem) *allow* conformity pressures to dictate their choices.

This negativity is most apparent in the characterisation of persons who complied in Milgram's (1974) studies of obedience. As if to demonstrate graphically the evils of conformity, Milgram constructed an environment of social pressure that induced participants to keep inflicting potentially lethal doses of electric shock to a person who had apparently just suffered a heart attack.

Conformity simply refers to behaviours that result from external social pressure; it is not necessarily the case that all such behaviours are negative. Pro-social actions, such as altruism and helping, also result from conformity. Yet in the research on conformity processes, it is only negative behaviours, those that make the individual look inferior or incompetent, that are the focus of study. Could the Norm of Internality have influenced social psychologists to attribute positive actions to internalised attitudes, while external social pressure is used to account for negative behaviours?

Impression management

Since the 1970s a few social psychologists have been using the notion of self-presentation or impression management (Schlenker, 1980; Tedeschi,

1981) to explain human action. The basic assumption of this approach is that a person's actions are guided by an attempt to create a favourable impression in others; thus the proximal cause is external social approval of other persons, as opposed to one's own internal evaluation of self. Originally proposed by Goffman (1955, 1959) over three decades ago, it took another 20 years for experimental social psychologists to begin to utilise the construct's explanatory power. Despite the far-reaching implications of impression management, the concept has failed to gain significant attention within social psychology.

The one exception to this general lack of interest in impression management is a related concept of self-monitoring (M. Snyder, 1987). Self-monitoring is conceived as a *personality* dimension, and refers to the extent to which individuals pay attention to the effects their actions are having on external observers. As with all personality traits, there is a test which differentiates persons low in self-monitoring from those who are high self-monitors. Although identified with self-presentation, self-monitoring actually derives its explanatory power from the concept of personality. It is hardly surprising that low self-monitors are portrayed as more healthy and stronger than high self-monitors (Snyder, 1987).

Summary

Two societal aspects of the accounting process have been discussed. First, the role that accounts play in the assignment of responsibility seems to have led Western societies to develop The Norm of Internality. This norm dictates that individuals should publicly attribute both their positive and negative actions to internal psychological causes. This norm helps to legitimate society's use of rewards and punishments to shape its members' future behaviour.

Although primarily reflected in the explanations given by the average member of society, the Norm of Internality may also affect the kinds of explanation professional social scientists develop to explain social behaviour. A review of the major explanatory concepts employed in social psychological theory was consistent with the idea of an 'internal bias' in so-called scientific explanations for social behaviour. The Norm of Internality also condemns external accounts, and it appears that social scientists are not favourably disposed towards theoretical explanations that emphasise external causal factors.

There seems to be a trend towards the increased use of genetic, neurological and bio-chemical explanations for behavioural phenomena.

If the science of psychology develops a set of theoretical explanations which emphasise non-volitional factors, then what will happen to the acceptance of internal explanations in everyday life? Will such explanations no longer be treated as valid in the accounting process? If this occurs, then societies will have to develop new ways to justify the use of rewards and punishments to control behaviour.

The possibility of the widespread acceptance of non-volitional accounts also raises questions about the importance of individuals and the species *homo sapiens*. As Skinner (1974) has pointed out, the 'dignity of man' is widely assumed to rest on the assumption that human behaviour is caused by that most internal of causes—motivated free choice. One possibility is that judgements about a person's worth will be based less on the reasons for an action and more on its consequences.

Part III:
Conclusion

14 Self-presentation and social influence: An interactionist perspective

JAMES T. TEDESCHI
Department of Psychology, State University of New York at Albany, USA

Introduction

This essay will be a speculative attempt to create an overarching edifice or outline to incorporate various factors associated with communication, social influence and impression management, with some excursions into a theory of self. The strategy is to work from factors known to be associated with enhancing the effectiveness of influence, relate these factors to self-presentational behaviours, and along the way show where the processes examined by the authors of the chapters of this book fit into the scheme. Almost all of the contributors to this book represent an interactionist approach to social psychology. In this approach human behaviour is framed within interaction goals. Power and influence are considered to be ubiquitous to social actions. A skeleton of a theory of social influence will be presented to suggest how impression management concerns and self-esteem are derivative from and integral to the social influence process.

In this scheme it will be shown how characteristics of the source impact on the effectiveness of social influence. Through instrumental learning and modelling people develop a concern for acquiring these characteristics. Self-presentation strategies are devised and carried through to construct a set of identities or reputational characteristics which serve as power bases to attempt influence. Short-term self-presentation tactics are used to embellish and protect these identities.

The individual's desire to control social interaction is directly associated with the development of self-esteem. Because the individual wants to be effective in influencing others, success in doing so not only gains interpersonal objectives but provides feedback about the general ability to influence others. Positive self-esteem is associated with optimism for success in future influence attempts and encourages a person to try them; negative self-esteem is associated with failure in the use of positive forms of influence and may lead a person to use negative forms of influence, such as threats and punishments.

The scheme presented in this chapter may be artificially separated into three areas of study: (1) factors that contribute to the effectiveness of influence attempts—a focus on the target of influence; (2) impression management strategies adopted to acquire identities that make influence effective—a focus on the prospective source; and (3) the feedback loops through which self-esteem is established, enhanced or diminished. These areas are seldom treated as an integrated whole, but rather have their own theoretical and research traditions. The sketch provided herein is intended to direct and encourage research to provide integrative bridges between the areas and to fill in many of the details now missing in the description of various aspects of the influence process.

An Interactionist Perspective in Social Psychology

An interactionist perspective in social psychology focuses upon the contemporaneous factors that converge to elicit actions taken in interpersonal contexts. Kurt Lewin (1951) argued for an interactionist approach as opposed to the history-of-the-organism approach represented by learning, developmental, and personality theories. Lewin argued that only factors that co-exist at a given moment affect decisions made by the person. If dispositions or learning affect actions, they must be represented by some process at the time actions take place. A focus on a slice of time just prior to action, rather than recapitulation of a reinforcement history or specification of the relationship of a child with his or her mother during a critical stage of development, places the emphasis of both theory and research on situational factors in determining human actions. In the context of social action the relevant question to ask is: what are the most pressing social goals for the actor?

Kipnis, Schmidt and Braxton-Brown in their chapter of this volume were quite explicit in stating that the problems of power and influence are ubiquitous in human relationships. If it is assumed that some form of psychological egoism is fundamental to human conduct, then people are largely (if not exclusively) motivated to obtain positive consequences and avoid negative outcomes. The sticky conceptual problems with various concepts of 'reinforcement' can be put aside for a while in favour of an empirical law of effect, and motivation can be left open-ended with some variation of the minimax principle. The point here is that people want some outcomes and do not want others. Kipnis *et al.* argue that most of the outcomes desired by a person are controlled or mediated by other people.

Consider what people want: wealth, status, power, respect, love, security and health. These goals cannot be achieved independently of other people. Others must mediate or provide the money, resources, position, love, and health care that a person desires. Suppose I sat under a Banyan tree and waited for someone to come along and give me wealth, power, or love. It is unlikely that such a Good Samaritan would arrive in a reasonable length of time. That is why there is still plenty of room under the Banyan trees. Most of us realise that if we want wealth, we must do something to convince people who have or control wealth to give it to us. Similarly, if we want love, we must make ourselves lovable to the relevant target person(s), and if we want respect, we must somehow either earn it or con others into believing that we merit it. The upshot is that most human actions occur in the context of interdependence of outcomes and the desire to affect how those outcomes are distributed. This interpersonal context of social actions makes power and influence salient and probably ubiquitous to human interaction. Actors must either forgo seeking to affect outcomes, thereby giving up the realistic possibility of achieving them, *or* actors must take the bull by the horns, foray out into the social world, and assertively try to influence the course of behaviour of significant others.

The mainstream of experimental social psychology focuses upon intra-psychic, largely cognitive, factors that mediate the actions of individuals. In Chapter 13 Jellison explained the tendency of social psychologists to make internal attributions for behaviour as due to a control mechanism ubiquitous to social units. He firmly plants the Fundamental Attribution Bias into a sociological context. After all, why should social psychologists, as differentiated from other members of society, be exempt from the influences of the societies to which they belong? We must be careful not to fall into a logical trap, however. Just because we can trace the origins of a theory to social factors does not imply that it is false. On the other hand, the history of imputing social actions to instincts, propensities, motives, traits, attitudes, and various kinds of software-type cognitive processes has not been especially enlightening. A strictly environmental approach associated with a radical behaviouristic position has likewise not yielded a rich web of theoretical explanations. The mainstream position is that behaviour probably is a function of interactions between environmental forces and intra-psychic events. The chapter in this volume by Smith *et al.*, which reports an investigation of high and low self-monitors, represents the mainstream approach. The complex results consisting of statistical interactions between goals, personality trait, and sex of subjects yield no clear implications for basic theory. The absence of powerful and convincing theories of mechanisms demonstrating this form of inner–outer interaction allows us to suggest that there is something wrong with how both the inner and outer events are represented in contemporary theories.

In his chapter Antaki provides a strong argument challenging the cognitive orientation of social psychologists. He insists that ordinary discourse is framed in the context of audiences and within social contexts. Cognitions have social origins and social purposes, and are not simply built-in units that function only to serve the needs of an inner person (i.e. the Self). Furthermore, speech acts or statements by a person are interpreted by mainstream social psychologists as basic units of analysis. As a consequence the social functions of such verbal behaviour in both thought and social interactions are obfuscated. The most recent example of an asocial cognitive perspective is attribution theory, in which the ways ordinary people attribute responsibility and explain human actions are the chief concerns. Antaki argues that these processes cannot be understood apart from the actions, audiences and social contexts that frame these processes. In other words, expectations about future interactions and consequences shape the way the individual assigns responsibility and explains own and other's actions. Antaki is clearly an interactionist. He has given us one important example of the difference the perspective makes for developing theory and research to explain cognitions, speech acts and other social actions.

In their path-breaking chapter in this volume, Bisanz and Rule attempt to establish that people have persuasion scripts. They provide preliminary evidence to show that scripts are framed within types of influence strategies and mediate compliance-gaining behaviours. Five strategies are identified: (1) asking, (2) self-oriented methods, (3) dyad-oriented methods, (4) appeals to social principles, and (5) negative tactics. The rank-ordering by subjects of how frequently people in general would use these strategies confirmed the assertion of Tedeschi & Bonoma (1977) that coercion is typically a method of last resort.

Story schemas which were canonical with this rank-ordering were more easily recalled than those which were either atypical or randomly ordered with respect to persuasion scripts. Thus, a story in which asking occurred first and negative tactics last were more easily reconstructed than stories in which these elements were presented in the opposite order. The availability and strength of scripts of influence strategies is directly related to perceptions of frequency of use of various forms of influence. This evidence, while only indirect and correlational, is consistent with the Bisanz and Rule hypothesis that scripts mediate influence attempts. Greene's chapter proposes a theoretical strategy that coincidentally is adopted by Bisanz and Rule. Cognitive theories tend to postulate that people cognitively represent categories of actions to be taken and adopt rational strategies by making choices which are appropriate to goals, constraints and opportunities. Such theories contain the flawed assumption of an isomorphism between memory and behaviour. Greene is insistent that three processes must be addressed: (1) how procedural information is represented; (2) how these procedural elements are selected from memory; and (3) the utilisation of information once selected. The interactionist frame given to cognitive theory by Bisanz and Rule has clearly addressed the first two processes.

Interactionist explanations have been provided for a wide range of phenomena originally explained in terms of intra-psychic processes. For example, the forced compliance situation was devised and refined to produce a reliable attitude change following commitment by subjects to counter-attitudinal behaviour. While originally developed to demonstrate the effects of a postulated process of cognitive dissonance, tinkering was necessary to obtain the desired attitude change consistently. It is now generally accepted that interactionist concerns with social responsibility, blame, and appearance of consistency over time are crucial for causing the so-called dissonance effect.[1] Festinger's (1957) original formulation that pure intra-psychic processes related to intolerance for cognitive inconsistency produces attitude change is no longer accepted by researchers in the area. Similar considerations have been brought to light with regard to psychological reactance, anticipatory attitude change, the transgression–compliance relationship, foot-in-the-door and door-in-the-face effects, and many other social psychological phenomena (Baumeister, 1982).

The Target of Social Influence

Morgenthau (1969) has defined power as any action taken by one party (P) which affects another party (W). This definition does not assume that P intends or is aware of the implemented power or that W is aware of it. Careful examination of this formulation indicates that Morgenthau's concept of power is synonymous with interpersonal causation. That is, P's action causes W to feel, think, act, or be different in some other way than would have been the case in the absence of P. While this is not the place to point out all the problems with various notions of power (see Tedeschi & Bonoma, 1972), the Morgenthau formulation does point in the direction of examining the many ways people have of affecting one another's behaviour.

A number of speculative typologies and factor analytic studies have provided a rich repertoire of actions that an actor can perform to influence others (cf. Tedeschi, Schlenker & Bonoma, 1973). Among the modes of influence that have been identified are threats, promises, persuasion, exhortation, modelling, a myriad of impression management behaviours, control over reinforcements/punishments and information, and the expression of emotions. The tendency of social psychologists has been to treat each form of influence as part of a miniature theory rather than attempt to construct a Grand Theory. Furthermore, with the exception of impression management theory and to some extent the study of leadership, the focus of most social influence theory has been on factors that make influence more effective. Much less attention has been given to the study of the source's choice of targets and modes of influence. This concentration on studying what makes a target comply, conform, change attitudes or in some other way act in a manner consistent with the desires of the source of influence has been rather thorough in uncovering facilitating factors. These facilitating factors can be grouped in terms of source characteristics, methods of presentation, and target characteristics. It is important in this chapter only to examine source characteristics since they form the power bases for specific influence attempts. Furthermore, as we shall see, concern for reputational characteristics is central to much social behaviour.

Tedeschi and his colleagues (Tedeschi, Bonoma & Schlenker, 1972) proposed a theory to organise the factors that facilitate influence and explain how the target decides to respond to it. A depiction of the theory is shown in Figure 14.1. At the far left are source characteristics, which are presumed to be objective in the sense that they can be estimated or measured independently of the target's perceptions of them. The characteristics depicted probably do not exhaust the possibilities, and which are operative at any time may be some function of the social context.

The decision by a target person who responds to an influence attempt is binary: yes or no, comply or not comply, change attitudes or do not change attitudes. Of course the target might choose to take flight or leave the field, but this would be a form of non-compliance and is not a third alternative. It is postulated that source characteristics affect the target's estimate of the probability that a current influence communication is true or reliable. For purposes of easy communication this probability estimate will be referred to as *believability*.[2] All else being equal, the more believable a communication, the more likely it is the target will comply with it.

The truthfulness or honesty of the source represents a history of the goodness of fit between the source's communications and events. To some extent truthfulness can be measured. For example, if a source warns target persons about future negative events, the proportion of times the predictions are correct can be taken as a measure of truthfulness. Statements involving contingencies can be considered true or false only when the appropriate contingencies are fulfilled. If a threatener demands

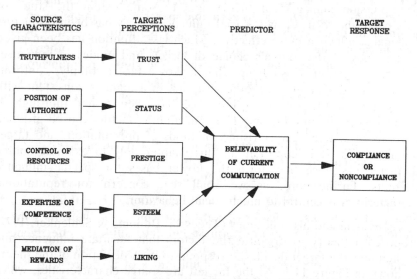

FIGURE 14.1 *Schematic of source characteristics, target perceptions, believability and compliance to influence attempts*

compliance and the target tenders it, then the punishment that was made contingent upon non-compliance will not be administered. Under these conditions the truthfulness of the threatener is untested—it cannot be determined whether the threatener would have punished the target had the latter not complied.

This scheme is deliberately simplified and omits communications that are not tied in any direct way to external events or observable behaviours. In his chapter, Dillard identifies three dimensions of influence messages which might affect the way a target reacts: (1) directness, or how clear the source is about what he wants the target to do; (2) positivity, or the explicitness of outcomes associated with compliance or non-compliance by the target; and (3) logic, or the use of evidence and reason by the source. In their chapter Meyers and Seibold suggest that extended narratives help establish the teller's credibility. Target audiences probably also analyse communications in terms of consistency with past statements, coherence, logic, and so on, but we will omit those considerations here.

The target's perceptions of the source's characteristics are not assumed to be isomorphic but may be biased by misinformation, value incongruencies or other factors. For present purposes it is not necessary to detail these processes of person perception, although the fact that social psychologists have tended to ignore these processes should not escape comment. The target's perception of the source's truthfulness may be a simple average over various verifiable speech acts. Threats, promises, warnings and other kinds of speech acts may be lumped together by the target in calculating an overall index of truthfulness. On the other hand, the importance or significance of the events, the kind of relationship that exists between source and target, and the negativity versus positivity of events may cause people to give different weights to categories in calculating a Truthfulness Index for a particular other person. So little is known about this process that it may even be the case that separate indices are maintained by target persons of the truthfulness of various forms of speech acts. Thus, there may be separate Truthfulness Indices for threats, promises, warnings, statements of facts, etc.

People are concerned about their reputation for truthfulness and honesty. It is not just a matter of letting the chips fall where they may. If others perceive a person as dishonest and untruthful, the effectiveness of influence will be undermined. Target persons will not believe the threats, promises or persuasive communications of a source who has a reputation of not following through on threats or promises or of being dishonest in the use of persuasion.

A major self-presentation concern of many people is to construct a reputation of truthfulness and honesty. Tedeschi, Schlenker & Bonoma (1971) argued that this self-presentational concern is an underlying mechanism for manifestations of attitude change in the forced compliance situation. The participants in such experiments need to feign attitudinal consistency with counter-attitudinal behaviour or else lose credibility in the eyes of the experimenter. An interesting feature of this hypothesis is the proposal that participants need to lie in order to appear truthful—an example of what Arkin refers to as 'Protective' self-presentation.

One factor that must be considered by a target of influence is the probability that the source's current communication is truthful. Whether it is true or not will not be known until the interaction sequence is completed. In effect the target must make a prediction concerning the truthfulness of the current communication. One basis for making predictions about future behaviour is the track record of the relevant person. What has been the pattern of behaviour engaged in by that person in the past? The Truthfulness Index (either a general one or one specific to the kind of speech act under consideration) may be directly extrapolated and used as a probability value in predicting the truthfulness of the current influence communication.

The expertise or competence of the source is acknowledged by most social psychologists as enhancing the effectiveness of persuasive communications. French & Raven (1959) postulated expertise as a general basis of power and not as confined to any particular influence mode. Indeed, Tedeschi found in an unpublished study that expertise mediated compliance to threats in a mixed-motive game. Tedeschi, Schlenker & Bonoma (1973) suggested that expertise strengthens (authenticates) the believability of a source's current influence communication, while lack of expertise weakens (de-authenticates) believability. Another way of saying this is that expertise, or lack of it, biases the way a target person assigns a probability to the truthfulness of the current influence communication. But although the source may have the credentials for expertise, such as diplomas, certificates, licences and degrees, the target person may not *perceive* the source as being an expert.[3] To distinguish between the factors that instantiate a person as somehow being an expert, and the target's perception, we refer to the latter as esteem. Esteem is the granting of respect for another's expertise or competence.

If power is defined in terms of potential to influence, then to acquire a reputation for expertise and to be esteemed by others is to gain in social power.[4] Lasswell & Kaplan (1950) postulated that people invest time, energy and resources to acquire power. A person may make major investments in acquiring expertise. Just as money can be used to buy what a person wants, so can a reputation for expertise. Once acquired and maintained, expertise can be used to get what a person wants from other people. The series of actions that are involved in gaining expertise may be considered a form of self-construction (Baumeister, 1982) or as strategic impression management behaviours (Tedeschi & Melburg, 1984).

Theory and research have established that an individual's position of authority in a group or organisation enhances the effectiveness of influence attempts (French & Raven, 1959; Tedeschi, Lindskold & Rosenfeld, 1985). The examination of the basis, scope and legitimacy of authority has occupied scholars from many areas of expertise (e.g. Freidrich, 1963). For present purposes it will suffice to state that appointment or election or seizure of positions of authority does not assure the occupants that others will legitimise their authority. It is therefore necessary to distinguish between the position of authority held by a person and the granting of legitimacy by others. In Figure 14.1 the target's granting of authority to the source is referred to as a perception of status. Within the limits of the role occupant's perceived scope of legitimate authority, the target suspends personal judgement and tenders obedience to requests from the source. Perceived status may also augment the effectiveness of more direct forms of influence by an authority, although coercive means may undermine the legitimacy of the authority.

There is early recognition by the developing individual that possession of authority is an important basis of power. Freud (1914) and Adler (1927) clearly recognised the envy small children have for the authority and power possessed by their parents. Bandura & Huston (1961) found that children imitated high status permanent teachers more than lower status substitute teachers. Everyday observation indicates that some individuals make a considerable investment in the self-constructive task of climbing the ladder of authority. Once again, we see that the knowledge of what makes influence effective, probably observed and emulated in the socialisation process, feeds back into the self-construction strategies of individuals.

The possession and/or control of material and social resources makes influence more effective, probably because target persons assume the source can apply the resources to reward or punish the target or because it is assumed the source has unusual access to information and third parties. As is the case with the other bases of power, the target's perception of the source is critical for the outcome of the influence process. Crude measurements of the resources controlled by the source in terms of monetary value, votes, jobs, missiles or warheads can be made independently of the perceptions of the target person. But it is possible that the target can under- or over-estimate the resources controlled by the source or the willingness of the source to use the available resources for purposes of influence. For this reason it is important to distinguish between the resources controlled by the source and the target's perception. In Figure 14.1 the latter is referred to as prestige. The greater the prestige of the source, the higher the believability a target will assign to the current influence communication of the source, and hence the more likely it is that compliance will occur.

It does not pay to be overly modest about the amount of resources one controls. People can afford to be modest only when assured that others attribute high prestige to them (Ackerman & Schlenker, 1975). It is more likely that people will boast about and exaggerate the amount of their resources to induce perceptions of high prestige by others. Acquisition of monetary wealth or political capital may preoccupy the individual, who seeks to enhance his or her ability to influence others from this power base.

The last source characteristic (or power base) shown in Figure 14.1 refers to a history of reinforcing/punishing actions by the source *vis-à-vis* the target person. People tend to like those who reward them and dislike those who punish them. This deliberately oversimplified view of the development of attraction is sufficient for present purposes, although the separation of the history of interactions from the perception of the source by the target acknowledges that the relationship is not monotonic. The evidence regarding the influence process is unambiguous in showing that liking for the source leads target persons to be more compliant to positive forms of influence, while disliking may produce more compliance to coercive forms of influence (Tedeschi, Lindskold & Rosenfeld, 1985). Perhaps liking causes the target to make benign attributions about the motives of the source. Liking may be associated with perceived trustworthiness of the source (Hovland, Janis & Kelley, 1953) which, in turn, induces the target to trust (i.e. rely on) the source's current influence communication.

Most people attempt to maintain friendly relationships with others. Goffman (1971) argued that 'demeanour' is a rule of social life. Audiences tend to accept publicly the identity an actor presents. Rules of courtesy are followed to smooth the course of social interactions. In other words, people try to avoid conflict and are typically co-operative in their relationships with others.

Psychologists have long been interested in the antecedents of attraction. An equally interesting but usually unasked question is why people want to be liked. Attractiveness, like money in the bank, is an important basis of power (cf. French & Raven, 1959). People may be strongly motivated to act to benefit others so that they will be liked. The view offered here is that whether they are aware of it or not, pro-social actors are engaged in an investment strategy directed towards accumulation of power over those they benefit.

The development of an identity as a likeable or friendly person is a task of self-construction. A more directly manipulative use of self-presentational behaviour to gain foreseeable or immediate advantages has been referred to by Tedeschi & Melburg (1984) as tactical behaviours, while actions devoted to gaining desired identities that serve as power bases for a wider range of benefits are referred to as strategic actions. Tactical and strategic self-presentations can be either defensive or assertive in nature. A schematic of this classification is shown in Table 14.1. For example, the assertive tactic of ingratiation is intended to induce liking in a target, which in turn is expected by the actor to mediate particular and foreseeable positive outcomes. Strategic self-presentational behaviour is typically not aimed towards gaining direct influence over others, but rather is directed towards developing long-term identities; they are acts of self-construction and have only a general connection with particular influence interactions. Conflicts may occur between the tactical and strategic concerns of the individual. Expedient attempts to gain immediate advantages through ingratiation tactics could be incompatible with the strategic goal of gaining a reputation as a likeable person.

The model presented in Figure 14.1 depicts how source characteristics, taken one at a time, impact on a target's decision to comply or not to comply with influence communications. Sources come bundled with some configuration of *all* of these characteristics. It is therefore important to establish the laws of combination of source characteristics with respect to the way a target calculates the probability associated with a current influence communication. Little or nothing is known about this process.

The recognition that many factors interact with one another in the influence process led Smith *et al.* in their chapter to propose a typology including eleven goals of actors in the influence process, ranging from obtaining permission and giving advice to changing opinion and enforcing

TABLE 14.1 *Classification of tactical and strategic self-presentational behaviours*

Behaviour	Tactical	Strategic
Assertive	Expedient behaviours to establish identity that mediates short-term rewards.	Actions taken to build identities that serve as power bases.
	Example: Ingratiation	*Example*: Expertise
Defensive	Behaviours intended to protect and maintain a desired identity.	Negative reputation resulting from over-use of assertive and/or defensive tactics.
	Example: Accounts	*Example*: Untrustworthy

obligations. According to Smith *et al.*, actors tend to have standard sets of goals, and the frequency with which goals are pursued depends on the role relationships involved. The pursuit of goals is guided by situational perceptions, including actor–target intimacy, target dominance, right to persuade, anticipated target resistance, situational apprehension, and magnitude and duration of personal and relational consequences. For example, a goal to gain permission from a parent is characterised by high intimacy and high target dominance, short-term relational consequences, and low level of apprehension.

Self-Presentation and Social Influence

Self-presentation is a form of social influence in which actors attempt to control the identities audiences attribute to them. We have seen that a desire to control the actions of others motivates the individual to invest time, energy and resources in constructing identities that enhance the ability to influence others. Any communication or action conveys information about the actor to audiences. Schneider (1981) has distinguished between desired and intended identities projected by actors (i.e. primary self-presentations) and unintended and perhaps undesired identities (i.e. secondary self-presentations).

In their theory of self-presentation, Jones & Pittman (1982) focused on identities fostered by actors that are intended to induce emotions of liking, fear, sympathy or respect, which, in turn, tend to mediate desired behaviour by the target audience. The focus of the assertive or acquisitive behaviours referred to by Jones and Pittman as ingratiation, intimidation, self-promotion, exemplification and supplication is some short-term and specifiable outcome that can be mediated by the target (or audience). Cialdini *et al.* (in this volume) describe a number of tactical manoeuvres taken by people to be associated with positive entities, and to dissociate from negative ones.[5] It might be assumed that success in linking to positive entities produces short-term enhancements of esteem, status or prestige. For example, a person who sits next to the Emperor may be perceived as possessing high status. Similarly, the protective or defensive actions referred to by Arkin and by Cialdini *et al.*, such as accounts, self-handicapping, blasting and apologies, are directed to preventing or changing an undesired identity. While these assertive and defensive behaviours typically are directed to short-term interaction goals and hence may be considered tactical in nature, they tend to have long-term (strategic) consequences for the actor's reputation. And, as we have seen, an actor's effectiveness in influencing others is directly associated with his or her reputation.

Tedeschi & Norman (1985) borrowed from Bandura's modelling theory to propose that children observe successful models and imitate them. Successful models, according to social influence theory, are those who are perceived as truthful, likeable, high in status and prestige, and are esteemed for their expertise. Children not only imitate the specific behaviours of the models but also attempt to emulate their reputational characteristics. The ability to delay gratification is important because expedient actions taken to obtain immediate reinforcements might lead to negative reputations for the person. For example, lying, cheating or intimidating others might gain the objectives of the person for the moment, but over a period of time such behaviours contribute to a negative reputation. Tactical and strategic goals often conflict. A wise investor, who has a long-term perspective, an ability to delay gratifications, and a belief that important reputational characteristics can be achieved, will chalk up lost expedient opportunities as part of the costs of gaining the bases of power that will help mediate more interpersonal profits in the long run. The kinds of influence attempted by a source may change the target's perceptions of the source. In this cybernetic system feedback loops are created as a result of a specific influence episode. For example, a threat which turns out to be a bluff or a promise that is not kept would lower the truthfulness index assigned to the source by the target. This consequence of being untruthful reduces the believability of subsequent influence communications and therefore lowers the probability of compliance by the target person.

The use of coercion or the failure to fulfil a promise also decreases the target's liking for the source, thereby lowering the degree of trustworthiness attributed to the source on subsequent influence occasions. Feedback loops may also work in a more benign fashion. If a source issues a warning and it turns out to be both accurate and useful, the source's credibility and likeability would both be increased. The target's esteem for the source's competence might also increase.

In their chapter, Kipnis *et al.* focus on the consequences for actors who use different styles of upward influence within organisations. They identified four styles of upward influence within organisations: (1) Bystander; (2) Ingratiator; (3) Tactician; and (4) Shotgun. The first two types are self-explanatory; the Tactician is subtle and plays by the rules, and the Shotgun is very assertive in using many forms of influence. Research established that employees identified as Tacticians earned the most money, while those classified as Shotguns received the worst evaluations from their supervisors and suffered most from stress. There is a problem of interpretation with these correlational data, however. Perhaps persons who suffer greater stress are induced by their frustrations to engage in more assertive tactics. Or, there may be a vicious cycle between stress and frustrations in the workplace and the Shotgun approach to influence. The important point here is that there are positive and negative consequences to using influence that are separable from the outcomes the source is most directly trying to achieve.

This sketch of the influence process suggests that self-presentation and direct influence attempts form a sort of one-two punch. First, develop important reputational characteristics, then attempt influence. A source must also calculate the costs and gains associated with the modes of influence that can be used. Part of the costs of influencing others is the prior investment in gaining the reputational characteristics that enhance effectiveness. The actor may also accumulate costs associated with the opportunity to use influence, such as those associated with inflicting punishments or providing promised rewards. Other costs may be inflicted by the target person through retaliation or withdrawal of promised rewards.

The feedback loops from type of influence attempted through the target's perceptions of the source may be associated with other costs of attempting influence. For example, failure to punish a target for non-compliance to a threat or reneging on a promise would lower the perception of the source's truthfulness and might also affect other perceptions. Decreased truthfulness reduces the source's base of power for subsequent influence attempts. Punishing non-compliance or providing promised rewards may be costly to the source but such actions constitute an investment in bolstering a reputation for truthfulness (and resolve). This investment should enhance the effectiveness of future influence attempts.

In his chapter in this volume, Dillard distinguishes between the primary goals associated with social influence and secondary goals associated with the impact on the source's subsequent identities of using influence. According to Dillard the source of influence is concerned about how the use of influence impacts on personal resources, relationships with others, and the course of interaction. The attention of actors is not confined to the narrow goal associated with a single influence episode, but includes the wider scope of the general impact on overall social power. Actors may try to use influence modes or seek goals that are perceived by others as undesirable, antinormative, wrong, or puzzling and follow their action by self-presentations to avoid the negative impact on their identities. An important category of such protective or defensive self-presentations are accounts, which are explanations that actors give for their behaviour. Explanations may be necessary to protect or defend a desired identity when a person's actions are evaluated negatively by others.

Accounts may take the form of excuses or of justifications. *Excuses* are explanations through which a person denies responsibility for the consequences associated with behaviour. The person may deny having an intent to produce the consequences, and claim ignorance, misinformation, mistake, inadvertence, and so on. The actor may also offer excuses that deny volition or control over his own behaviour, such as in cases of insanity, illness, drugs or strong emotions. If the actor's excuses are effective, audiences should believe them, and whatever blame and responsibility might have been judged as appropriate would be mitigated or removed. In this way negative aspersions on one's identities or reputation may be controlled or removed. *Justifications* are explanations through which the individual accepts responsibility for the consequences of his actions, but provides reasons to avoid blame and/or penalties from other people. The reasons given in justificatory explanations serve to show that the good associated with the action outweighs the harm, or that the action followed some important social norm. Thus, a person may justify using animals in medical research on the grounds that the results will help people, or, killing another person may be justified as being in self-defence.[6]

In the chapter by Schönbach and Kleibaumhüter, an offering of an account is considered as part of episodes involving four phases: (1) the actor performs an offensive act or omits to fulfil an obligation; (2) reproach either occurs or is expected; (3) an excuse, justification, concession or refusal to offer an account occurs; and (4) audiences will evaluate the actor in terms of both phases (1) and (3). Acceptance of accounts by audiences is presumed by most social psychologists to mitigate responsibility for negative actions.

McLaughlin *et al.* suggested in their chapter that excuses and justifications, as opposed to other kinds of replies to a reproach, may draw attention to questions of motivation or personality and hence increase the likelihood of negative attributions to the actor. The evidence they obtained in traffic court provided partial support for their counter-intuitive hypothesis. For example, the use of justifications by drivers whose alleged offence was speeding led observers to attribute more intent to them for wrong-doing, to blame them more, and to assign their offences to personal traits, but these findings did not extend to driving through a red light. Interactions between the type of offence, the type of attributional question asked, and the kind of explanation offered by the alleged offenders allow few firm conclusions. These complexities will have to be unravelled in future research.

In their chapter, Snyder and Higgins develop the motivational bases of excuses and justifications. They argue that justifications operate on a valence-of-act dimension to lessen the perceived negativity of the actor's conduct, while excuses are used to sever linkage-to-act *and* reduce the negative valence of the action. The actor's sense of linkage-to-act will increase as a function of three factors: (1) the importance of the activity for one's identity; (2) the impactfulness of sources of feedback about the act; and (3) knowledge of facts by an external audience.

Accounts are social influence attempts. Snyder and Higgins view excuse-making as a type of bargaining process: (1) a source offers an excuse, (2) it may not be fully accepted, and (3) some modifications of the excuse are made until the audience accepts it. The agreement may include an acknowledgement (confession) by the actor of wrong-doing. Felson (1982) has suggested that challenges to one's identity, involving the rejection of excuses and justifications and the admonitions associated with blame, may lead to an escalation of conflict and the use of punishments by one or both parties. Indeed, Felson has shown that the failure of one of the parties to offer accounts for questionable conduct is an important factor distinguishing between physical assaults and homicides.

Accounts serve to buttress, reinforce, maintain and defend an actor's reputation when the actor engages in conduct that may be negatively evaluated by others. These explanations for behaviour reduce, limit or remove the costs associated with negative actions. In an indirect sense accounts are power-maintenance tools devoted to mitigating any damage to reputational characteristics (i.e. identities) that are important in the influence process.

In their chapter, McLaughlin, French and Cody argue that the process of defensive explanation of negative behaviours evaluated in traffic court may be initiated at the time the actor chooses among alternative courses of behaviour. This initial account can then be reactivated, modified or embellished when and if needed following the action. From an influence perspective it makes sense that the actor should consider the value and probability of costs before choosing a course of action, including the probable effectiveness of cost-limitation tactics such as in the use of accounts. A similar process was found in a study of the use of threats (Tedeschi et al., 1970). A threatener used fewer threats when the costs of imposing punishments for non-compliance were increased. Actual use of punishments was not affected by amount of costs. Clearly, subjects calculated the probable costs of using threats before transmitting them.

The class of self-presentational behaviour referred to as accounts is essentially a set of influence communications. The goal of the actor is to defend, maintain or enhance a power-related identity in the eyes of a target audience. The factors that affect the success of other forms of influence could therefore be expected to function in much the same ways with the use of accounts. The source characteristics shown in Figure 14.1 can be hypothesised as contributing to the believability of accounts. According to this proposed theory, a target is more likely to believe the account of a source who is or has been assigned a high truthful index, has been granted status and/or esteem, is perceived as having high prestige, and is liked;[7] however, in a preliminary test of this theory of accounts Melburg, Lesser & Tedeschi (1984) found that the excuses of a lower status nurse were more believed than identical excuses from a higher status physician.

The disconfirmation of the expected direct relationship of status and believability is interesting because it suggests that it is more difficult to absolve oneself from responsibility when one is *more* powerful. As Thibaut & Riecken (1955) found in a classic experiment, observers are more likely to make internal attributions for behaviour when the actor is powerful than when the actor is weak. The implication of these findings is that as compared to the impact of source characteristics on such influence modes as threats, promises and persuasion on believability, the opposite effects occur with the use of accounts. However, this implication would hold only for those source characteristics that would be related to attributions of personal control. Holding a position of authority, possessing expertise, or having control over resources are source characteristics most clearly associated with control over others. From these considerations it would be predicted that the accounts of low status, low prestige, and less competent sources would be more believable to a target than accounts from sources who are high on these characteristics.

The postulated mediation of believability of accounts by attributions of responsibility suggests a positive impact of attraction on believability of accounts. The research on interpersonal attraction indicates that observers mitigate the responsibility for a negative action by a liked person but make stronger internal attributions when a disliked person performs the same action (Dion, 1972). Given this attributional bias in favour of actors who are liked we can predict a direct relationship between a target's liking for an actor and believability of the actor's accounts.

We have seen that status, esteem and prestige may decrease believability of accounts, while liking may increase believability. There are no *a priori* grounds for predicting how combinations of these source characteristics would affect the believability of accounts. Would a target believe the account of a source who had high status and prestige but is liked? The case study reported by Snyder and Higgins is indirectly related to this question. The tendency of the American people to accept the accounts of President Reagan and the deflection of responsibility for negative actions away from him, euphemistically referred to by the press in terms of a 'teflon presidency', indicates that liking for an actor may override other characteristics in mediating the believability of accounts.

In summary, it is hypothesised that defensive self-presentational behaviour serves the purpose of reducing the costs associated with influence. The effectiveness of accounts, like other forms of influence, is a function of many factors, including the characteristics of the source. Thus, accounts, which are influence communications intended to protect identities, are themselves made more or less effective by the identities of the actor. In this cybernetic system of action, feedback from action consequences to identities, and back again from identities to action—both self-presentational behaviours and direct use of influence—affect the individual's perception of self.

Self-Esteem and Social Power

The self may be defined as the person's theory regarding his or her identities (Epstein, 1973). A self-theory serves to provide some consistency and unity to the behaviour of the individual. A desire to appear honest to others (i.e. to *be* honest) connects the inhibition of lying in one situation to the fulfilment of promises in another situation. The organisation of assertive and defensive self-presentations to acquire, enhance, maintain and protect power-related identities would be impossible without the regulation, motivation and evaluation provided by some overall guidance system, such as the self. The self is defined in interpersonal contexts and cannot exist apart from others. The perception of self is framed in the context of interpersonal relationships, objectives and consequences. The motivation for action is external; other people partially control the outcomes desired by the actor. Which identity is relevant in an interaction sequence depends on the relationships, goals, constraints and opportunities existent in the specific situation.

Actors perceive and evaluate their own behaviours. These evaluations, referred to as self-esteem, affect the actor's theory of self. Many psychologists have postulated that people have a basic need to evaluate themselves favourably and to avoid negative self-esteem. The master motive of social actions is thus firmly planted inside the person. Tedeschi & Norman (1985) tried to avoid postulating a basic need for positive self-esteem by proposing that self-esteem is derivative from concern for social power. In this formulation positive self-evaluation is associated in an indirect way with the facilitation of social influence and favourable outcomes. Successful assertive self-presentations imply increments in one or more bases of power, which, in turn, facilitate the effectiveness of subsequent influence attempts.

This link between increments of power and self-esteem may be more clearly understood in terms of its development. Small children observe models who are successful in gaining interaction goals and imitate relevant behaviours (Bandura, 1977). More importantly, children also aspire to develop identities similar to those they perceive as important to the model's success. This constitutes the development of an ideal self. The maturing individual engages in self-presentations in a manner intended to construct a real self that approximates the ideal self. If reflective appraisals confirm the self-presentations, the individual in effect has been granted an increment of power, which, like money, can be converted into effective influence and future rewards. The attainment of rewards is associated with positive emotions. The association of rewards to influence and of successful influence to power bases (i.e. identities) is proposed as a learning mechanism for a secondary drive (or generalised reinforcer) for positive self-esteem. A lowering of self-esteem results from an increase in the discrepancy between ideal and real self, a decrement in one or more of the individual's power bases, and a loss of effectiveness in gaining interpersonal objectives.

The above conjectures about the development and functioning of self-esteem in the flow of social interactions is consistent with the theory of accounts proposed in the chapter by Schönbach and Kleibaumhüter. They state that a basic determinant of the course of interactions is 'the need for maintaining or regaining an adequate sense of being in control of one's actions. . .' Their theory explicitly assumes a reciprocal relationship between need for control and need for positive self-esteem. Lowered self-esteem will incline the individual to seek restoration of the diminished self-esteem and in ways that ignore the needs and sensitivities of the audience. Such defensive actions, in turn, elicit equally insensitive and negative behaviours from others and a course of escalating conflict is set. This sequence of behaviours is a major source of human aggression (Tedeschi, 1984; Felson, 1982).

Conclusion

An interactionist view places social behaviour in the frame of the goals, problems and tactics of individual actors. Because other people mediate most of the rewards or punishments likely to be experienced by the individual, the implications for all behaviour in terms of power and influence are probably common to all social interactions. A major criticism of mainstream cognitive psychologists is that they fail to place the phenomena they study in a social context. Indeed, it is sometimes difficult to discern what is social about what they study. An interactionist perspective requires theory construction focused on factors that impact on the influence process. The authors of this volume have concentrated their efforts on developing one or another aspect of the influence process. The scheme presented in this chapter was developed to provide an overview of the general processes in which the more specific details can be placed.

Strategic self-presentational behaviour is directed towards building power bases. The investments involved in enhancing power may be independent of actual attempts to influence others. However, attempts to use influence have feedback effects on the perceptions that others have of the actor and may enhance or detract from power bases (i.e. identities). Actors use supplementary tactical self-presentations, such as accounts, to save face, and to protect and enhance desired reputational characteristics.

There is a general lack of theory and research on the factors that affect the choice of influence target and mode by actors. If there is a rather large number of people who can provide a particular reward, why does the actor choose one rather than another? An associated and interdependent question is: why does the source choose one form of influence rather than another? Furthermore, we can be rather confident that self-presentational tactics are used in tandem with specific forms of influence. Jones & Pittman (1982) referred to intimidation as a set of tactics intended to induce fear in a target person. We could hypothesise that intimidation tactics increase the believability of threats and hence tend to accompany coercive forms of influence.

The scheme offered in this chapter points to many gaps in our knowledge and hence may serve as a guide to future theory development and research. Development of the idea that self-esteem is a mechanism associated with social power might take the form of research on the socialisation process or an extension of modelling theory. We need to know a great deal more about the process of person perception as it relates to power bases. The conflict that sometimes occurs between the immediate gains of tactical self-presentations and the delayed and more general rewards associated with strategic self-presentations would be an entirely new area for research. These and many other issues raised by an interactionist perspective deserve more attention than they are receiving at present by the scientific community. The contributors to this book are pioneers in examining some of these questions.

Notes to Chapter 14

1. For a detailed analysis of the evolution of research in the forced compliance situation, see Tedeschi & Rosenfeld (1981).
2. Tedeschi, Bonoma & Schlenker (1972) and Tedeschi, Schlenker & Bonoma (1973) have proposed the more formal language of decision theory for these

relationships. For present purposes we can avoid this technical language.

3. Whether a person is or is not considered an expert, independent of any one person's judgement of the matter, may to some considerable extent also rest upon social consensus.

4. In meritocracies expertise is a very important basis for social power and it should not be surprising that need-achievement motivation is a dominant behaviour pattern in such societies (McClelland, 1961). Need-achievement motivation represents an investment in acquiring the power basis of expertise and consists of strategic impression management (Tedeschi, Lindskold & Rosenfeld, 1985).

5. Schlenker (1980) enunciated a Law of Association whereby actors attempt to link themselves to positive symbols, organisations, and/or other people, and dissociate from negative entities.

6. Tedeschi & Riess (1981) proposed typologies of excuses and justifications and explain their role in assignment of blame and responsibility, punishment and retribution, and protecting identities (face-saving).

7. We must distinguish between public and private acceptance because there are strong social norms associated with avoiding open and public conflict and criticism of others (cf. Goffman, 1959; Schlenker, 1980). Research undertaken to test the hypotheses derivable from this framework will need to use a bogus pipeline technique or other means to induce subjects to divulge their private reactions to accounts offered to them.

References

ABBOT, V., BLACK, J.B. and SMITH, E.E. 1985, The representation of scripts in memory. *Journal of Memory and Language* 24, 179–99.

ABELSON, R.P. and LALLJEE, M. in press, Knowledge structures and causal explanation. In D. HILTON (ed.), *Contemporary Science and Natural Explanation: Commensense Conceptions of Causality*. London: Harvester Press.

ABRAMSON, L.Y., SELIGMAN, M.E.P. and TEASDALE, J.D. 1978, Learned helplessness in humans: Critique and reformulation. *Journal of Abnormal Psychology* 87, 49–74.

ACKERMAN, B. and SCHLENKER, B.R. 1975, *Self-presentation: Attributes of the Actor and Audience*. Paper presented at the 83rd annual meeting of the American Psychological Association, Chicago.

ADLER, A. 1927, *The Practice and Theory of Individual Psychology*. New York: Harcourt, Brace and World.

AJZEN, I. 1985, From intentions to actions: A theory of planned behavior. In J. KUHL and J. BECKMAN (eds), *Action Control*, pp. 11–39. New York: Springer-Verlag.

ALDERFER, C.P. 1969, An empirical test of a new theory of human needs. *Organizational Behavior and Human Performance* 4, 142–75.

ALDERTON, S.M. 1981, A processual analysis of argumentation in polarizing groups. In G. ZIEGELMULLER and J. RHODES (eds), *Dimensions of Argument: Proceedings of the Second Summer Conference on Argumentation*, pp. 693–703. Annandale, VA: Speech Communication Association.

——1982, Locus of control-based argumentation as a predictor of group polarization. *Communication Quarterly* 30, 381–7.

ALDERTON, S.M. and FREY, L.R. 1983, Effects of reactions to arguments on group outcome: The case of group polarization. *Central States Speech Journal* 34, 88–95.

——1986, Argumentation in small group decision-making. In R.Y. HIROKAWA and M.S. POOLE (eds), *Communication and Group Decision-Making*, pp. 157–74. Beverly Hills, CA: Sage.

ALLOY, L.B. and AHRENS, A.H. 1987, Depression and pessimism for the future: Biased uses of statistically relevant information in predictions for self and others. *Journal of Personality and Social Psychology* 52, 366–78.

ALLOY, L.B., PETERSON, C., ABRAMSON, L.Y. and SELIGMAN, M.E.P. 1984,

Attributional style and the generality of learned helplessness. *Journal of Personality and Social Psychology* 46, 681–7.

ALLPORT, D.A. 1979, Conscious and unconscious cognition: A computational metaphor for the mechanism of attention and integration. In L. NILSSON (ed.), *Perspectives on Memory Research: Essays in Honor of Uppsala University's 500th Anniversary*, pp. 61–89. Hillsdale, NJ: Erlbaum.

ALTENBERG, B. 1980, Causal linking in spoken and written English. *Studia Linguistica* 38, 20–69.

ALVES, W.M. and ROSSI, P.H. 1978, Who should get what? Fairness judgments of the distribution of earnings. *American Journal of Sociology* 34, 541–64.

ANDERSON, C.A. 1983, Motivational and performance deficits in interpersonal settings: The effect of attributional style. *Journal of Personality and Social Psychology* 45, 1136–47.

ANDERSON, J.R. 1976, *Language, Memory and Thought*. Hillsdale, NJ: Erlbaum.

——1981, Concepts, propositions, and schemata: What are the cognitive units? In J.H. FLOWERS (ed.), *Nebraska Symposium on Motivation 1980: Cognitive Processes*, pp. 121–62. Lincoln, NE: University of Nebraska Press.

——1982, Acquisition of cognitive skill. *Psychological Review* 89, 369–406.

——1985, *Cognitive Psychology and its Implications (2nd edn)*. New York: Freeman.

ANDREWS, G.R. and DEBUS, R.L. 1978, Persistence and the causal perception of failure: Modifying cognitive attributions. *Journal of Educational Psychology* 70, 154–66.

ANTAKI, C. and FIELDING, G. 1981, Research on ordinary explanation. In C. ANTAKI (ed.), *The Psychology of Ordinary Explanations of Social Behaviour*, pp. 27–55. London: Academic Press.

ARFFA, M.B. and STRUBE, M.J. 1986, Social relations and Type A Behavior. *Journal of Applied Social Psychology* 16, 277–86.

ARKIN, R.M. 1980, Self-presentation. In D.M. WEGNER and R.R. VALLACHER (eds), *The Self in Social Psychology*, pp. 158–82. London and New York: Oxford University Press.

——1981, Self-presentation styles. In J.T. TEDESCHI (ed.), *Impression Management Theory and Social Psychological Research*, pp. 311–33. New York: Academic Press.

ARKIN, R., APPELMAN, A. and BURGER, J.M. 1980, Social anxiety, self-presentation and the self-serving bias in causal attributions. *Journal of Personality and Social Psychology* 38, 23–35.

ARKIN, R.M. and BAUMGARDNER, A.H. 1985, Self-handicapping. In J.H. HARVEY, W. ICKES and R.F. KIDD (eds), *New Directions in Attribution Research*, Vol. 3, pp. 169–202. Hillsdale, NJ: Erlbaum.

ARKIN, R.M. and SHEPPERD, J.A. 1988, *The Role of Social Anxiety in Self-Presentational Self-Handicapping*. Unpublished manuscript, University of Missouri, Columbia.

ASCH, S.E. 1955, Opinions and social pressure. *Scientific American* 193, 31–5.

BACHMAN, J.G., BOWERS, D.G. and MARCUS, P.M. 1968, Bases of supervisory power: A comparative study in five organizational settings. In A.S. TANNENBAUM (ed.), *Control in Organizations*, pp. 229–38. New York: McGraw-Hill.

BACKMAN, C.W. 1985, Identity, self presentation, and the resolution of moral dilemmas: Towards a social psychological theory of moral behavior. In

B.R. SCHLENKER (ed.), *The Self and Social Life*, pp. 261–89. New York: McGraw-Hill.

BALES, R.F. 1950, *Interaction Process Analysis: A Method for the Study of Small Groups*. Cambridge, MA: Addison-Wesley.

BALES, R.F. and STRODTBECK, F.L. 1951, Phases in group problem solving. *Journal of Abnormal and Social Psychology* 46, 485–95.

BANDURA, A. 1977, *Social Learning Theory*. Englewood Cliffs, NJ: Prentice-Hall.

——1986, *Social Foundations of Thought and Action*. Englewood Cliffs, NJ: Prentice-Hall.

BANDURA, A. and HUSTON, A.C. 1961, Identification as a process of incidental learning. *Journal of Abnormal and Social Psychology* 63, 311–18.

BANKS, S.P., ALTENDORF, D.M., GREENE, J.O. and CODY, M.J. 1987, An examination of relationship disengagement: Perception of break-up strategies and outcomes. *Western Journal of Speech Communication* 51, 19–41.

BAUMEISTER, R.F. 1982, A self-presentational view of social phenomena. *Psychological Bulletin* 91, 3–26.

BAUMEISTER, R.F. and JONES, E.E. 1978, When self-presentation is constrained by the target's knowledge: Consistency and compensation. *Journal of Personality and Social Psychology* 36, 608–18.

BAUMEISTER, R.F. and STEINHILBER, A. 1984, Paradoxical effects of a supportive audience on performance under pressure: The home field disadvantage in sports championships. *Journal of Personality and Social Psychology* 47, 85–93.

BAUMGARDNER, A. H. and BROWNLEE, E. 1987, Strategic failure in social interaction: Evidence for expectancy disconfirmation processes. *Journal of Personality and Social Psychology* 52, 525–35.

BAXTER, L.A. 1979, Self-disclosure as a relationship disengagement strategy: An exploratory investigation. *Human Communication Research* 5, 215–22.

BAXTER, L.A. and WILMOT, W.W. 1984, 'Secret tests': Social strategies for acquiring information about the state of the relationship. *Human Communication Research* 11, 171–201.

BEACH, L.R. 1985, Action: Decision implementation strategies and tactics. In M. FRESE and J. SABINI (eds), *Goal Directed Behavior: On the Concept of Action in Psychology*, pp. 123–33. Hillsdale, NJ: Erlbaum.

BECKER, E. 1973, *The Denial of Death*. New York: Free Press.

BECKER, H. 1963, *Outsiders*. New York: Free Press.

BELL, R.A. and DALY, J.A. 1984, The affinity-seeking function of communication. *Communication Monographs* 51, 91–115.

BEM, S.L. 1974, The measurement of psychological androgyny. *Journal of Consulting and Clinical Psychology* 42, 155–62.

BENNETT, D.H. and HOLMES, D.S. 1975, Influence of denial (situation redefinition) and projection on anxiety associated with a threat to self-esteem. *Journal of Personality and Social Psychology* 32, 915–21.

BERGEMANN, N. and JOHANN, G.K. 1985, Zur Erfassung von Selbstakzeptanz und Akzeptanz Anderer: Eine deutschsprachige Version der Berger-Skalen. *Diagnostica* 31, 119–29.

BERGER, C.R. 1985, Social power and interpersonal communication. In M.L. KNAPP and G.R. MILLER (eds), *Handbook of Interpersonal Communication*, pp. 439–99. Beverly Hills, CA: Sage.

——in press (a), Planning and scheming: Strategies for initiating relationships.

In P. McGHEE, R. BURNETT and D. CLARKE (eds), *Accounting for Relationships: Social Representations of Interpersonal Links*. London: Methuen.

——in press (b), Planning, affect and social action generation. In R.L. DONOHEW, H. SYPNER and E.T. HIGGINS (eds), *Communication, Social Cognition, and Affect*. Hillsdale, NJ: Erlbaum.

BERGER, C.R. and BELL, R.A. 1987, *Plans and the Initiation of Social Relationships*. Paper presented at the annual meeting of the International Communication Association, Montreal.

BERGLAS, S. and JONES, E.E. 1978, Drug choice as self-handicapping strategy in response to noncontingent success. *Journal of Personality and Social Psychology* 36, 405–17.

BERKOWITZ, L. and DANIELS, L.R. 1964, Affecting the salience of the social responsibility norm: Effects of past help on the response to dependency relationships. *Journal of Abnormal and Social Psychology* 68, 275–81.

BERSCHEID, E. and PEPLAU, L.A. 1983, The emerging science of relationships. In H.H. KELLEY, E. BERSCHEID, J.H. HARVEY, T. HUSTON, G. LEVINGER, E. McCLINTOCK, L.A. PEPLAU and D.R. PETERSON (eds), *Close Relationships*, pp. 486–504. New York: W.H. Freeman.

BETTINGHAUS, E.P. and CODY, M.J. 1987, *Persuasive Communication* (4th edn). New York: Holt, Rinehart and Winston.

BISANZ, G.L. 1982, Knowledge of persuasion and story comprehension: Developmental changes in expectations. *Discourse Processes* 5, 245–77.

BISANZ, G.L. and RULE, B.G. 1987, *The Psychological Validity of The Persuasion Schema: Memory for Texts on Persuasion*. Paper presented at the annual meeting of the Canadian Psychological Association, Vancouver.

——1989, Gender and the persuasion schema: A search for cognitive invariants. *Personality and Social Psychology Bulletin* 15, 4–18.

BISHOP, G.D. and MYERS, D.G. 1974, Informational influence in group discussion. *Organizational Behavior and Human Performance* 12, 92–104.

BLACK, J.B. and BOWER, G.H. 1980, Story understanding as problem solving. *Poetics* 9, 223–50.

BLASI, A. 1980, Bridging moral cognition and moral action: A critical review of the literature. *Psychological bulletin* 88, 1–45.

BLUMSTEIN, P.W., CARSSOW, K.G., HALL, J., HAWKINS, B., HOFFMAN, R., ISHEM, E., MAURER, C.P., SPENS, D., TAYLOR, J. and ZIMMERMAN, D.L. 1974, The honoring of accounts. *American Sociological Review* 39, 551–66.

BOOTH, A. 1972, Sex and social participation. *American Sociological Review* 37, 183–92.

BOSTER, F.J., FRYREAR, J.E., MONGEAU, P.A. and HUNTER, J.E. 1982, An unequal speaking linear discrepancy model: Implications for the polarity shift. In M. BURGOON (ed.), *Communication Yearbook 6*, pp.395–418. Beverly Hills, CA: Sage.

BOSTER, F.J. and HALE, J.L. 1983, *Social Comparison and the Polarity Shift*. Paper presented at the annual meeting of the International Communication Association, Dallas.

BOSTER, F.J. and MAYER, M.E. 1984, *Differential Argument Quality Mediates the Impact of a Social Comparison Process on the Choice Shift*. Paper presented at the annual meeting of the International Communication Association, San Francisco.

BOSTER, F.J., MAYER, M.E., HUNTER, J.E. and HALE, J.L. 1980, Expanding the persuasive arguments explanation of the polarity shift: A linear discrepancy model. In D. NIMMO (ed.), *Communication Yearbook 4*, pp. 165–76. Beverly Hills, CA: Sage.

BOWER, G.H. 1978, Experiments on story comprehension and recall. *Discourse Processes* 1, 211–31.

BOWER, G.H., BLACK, J.B. and TURNER, T.J. 1979, Scripts in memory for text. *Cognitive Psychology* 11, 177–220.

BRAATEN, D. 1987, *The Impact of Attribution of Responsibility, Dependence/ Independence and Gender on the Selection of Relational Conflict Tactics.* Unpublished doctoral dissertation, University of Southern California, Los Angeles.

BRADLEY, G.W. 1978, Self-serving biases in the attribution process. A re-examination of the fact or fiction question. *Journal of Personality and Social Psychology* 36, 56–71.

BRIGGS, S.R., CHEEK, J.M. and BUSS, A.H. 1980, An analysis of the self-monitoring scale. *Journal of Personality and Social Psychology* 38, 679–86.

BROCKRIEDE, W. 1975, Where is argument? *Journal of the American Forensic Association* 13, 179–82.

BRODT, S.E. and ZIMBARDO, P.G. 1981, Modifying shyness-related social behavior through symptom misattribution. *Journal of Personality and Social Psychology* 41, 437–49.

BROWN, P. and LEVINSON, S. 1978, Universals in language usage: Politeness phenomena. In E. GOODY (ed.), *Questions and Politeness: Strategies in Social Interaction*, pp. 56–289. Cambridge: Cambridge University Press.

BRUCE, B. and NEUMAN, D. 1978, Interacting plans. *Cognitive Science* 2, 195–234.

BURGER, J.M. 1981, Motivational biases in the attribution of responsibility for an accident: A meta-analysis of the defensive-attribution hypothesis. *Psychological Bulletin* 90, 496–512.

BURGER, J.M. and ARKIN, R.M. 1980, The role of prediction and control in learned helplessness. *Journal of Personality and Social Psychology* 38, 482–91.

BURGER, J.M. and COOPER, H.M. 1979, The desirability of control. *Motivation and Emotion* 3, 381–93.

BURGGRAF, C.S. and SILLARS, A.L. 1987, A critical examination of sex differences in marital communication. *Communication Monographs* 54, 276–94.

BURGOON, J.K. 1978, A communication model of personal space violations: Explication and an initial test. *Human Communication Research* 4, 129–42.

BURISH, T.G. and HOUSTON, B.K. 1979, Causal projection, similarity projection, and coping with threat to self-esteem. *Journal of Personality* 47, 57–70.

BURLESON, B.R. 1979, On the analysis and criticism of arguments: Some theoretical and methodological considerations. *Journal of the American Forensic Association* 16, 112–27.

——1980a, *Argument and Constructivism: The Cognitive-Developmental Component.* Paper presented at the annual meeting of the Speech Communication Association, New York.

——1980b, The development of interpersonal reasoning: An analysis of message strategy justifications. *Journal of the American Forensic Association* 17, 102–10.

——1981, A cognitive-developmental perspective on social reasoning processes. *Western Journal of Speech Communication* 45, 133–47.

——1982, *Foundations for the Study of Argument: Assumptions and Contributions of the Cognitive-Development Perspective*. Paper presented at the annual meeting of the Central States Speech Association, Milwaukee.

——1984, Age, social-cognitive development, and the use of comforting strategies. *Communication Monographs* 51, 140–53.

BURNSTEIN, E. 1982, Persuasion as argument processing. In H. BRANDSTATTER, J.H. DAVIS and G. STOCKER-KREICHGAUER (eds), *Group Decision Making*, pp. 103–24. New York: Academic Press.

BURNSTEIN, E. and SENTIS, K. 1981, Attitude polarization in groups. In R.E. PETTY, R.M. OSTROM and T.C. BROCK (eds), *Cognitive Responses in Persuasion*, pp. 197–216. Hillsdale, NJ: LEA Publishers.

BURNSTEIN, E., MILLER, H., VINOKUR, A., KATZ, S. and CROWLEY, J. 1971, Risky shift is eminently rational. *Journal of Personality and Social Psychology* 20, 462–71.

BURNSTEIN, E., STOTLAND, E. and ZANDER, A. 1961, Similarity to a model and self-evaluation. *Journal of Abnormal and Social Psychology* 62, 257–64.

BURNSTEIN, E. and VINOKUR, A. 1973, Testing two classes of theories about group induced shift in individual choice. *Journal of Experimental Social Psychology* 9, 123–37.

——1975, What a person thinks upon learning he has chosen differently from others: Nice evidence for the persuasive arguments explanation of choice shifts. *Journal of Experimental Psychology* 11, 412–26.

——1977, Persuasive argumentation and social comparison as determinants of attitude polarization. *Journal of Experimental Social Psychology* 13, 315–32.

BURNSTEIN, E., VINOKUR, A. and PICHEVIN, M.F. 1974, What do differences between own, admired, and attributed choices have to do with group induced shifts in choice? *Journal of Experimental Social Psychology* 10, 428–43.

BURNSTEIN, E., VINOKUR, A. and TROPE, Y. 1973, Interpersonal comparison versus persuasive argumentation: A more direct test of alternative explanations for group induced shifts in individual choice. *Journal of Experimental Social Psychology* 9, 236–45.

BUSCH, P. and WILSON, D.T. 1976, An experimental analysis of salesman's expert and referent bases of social power in the buyer–seller dyad. *Journal of Marketing Research* 17, 3–11.

BYRNE, D. 1971, *The Attraction Paradigm*. New York: Academic Press.

CANARY, D.J., BROSSMAN, B.G. and SEIBOLD, D.R. 1987, Argument structures in decision-making groups. *Southern Speech Communication Journal* 53, 18–37.

CANARY, D.J., CODY, M.J. and MARSTON, P. 1986, Goal types, compliance-gaining and locus of control. *Journal of Language and Social Psychology* 5, 249–70.

CANARY, D.J., CUNNINGHAM, E.M. and CODY, M.J. 1988, An examination of locus of control and goal types in managing interpersonal conflict. *Communication Research* 15, 426–46.

CANARY, D.J. and CUPACH, W.R. in press, Relational and episodic characteristics associated with conflict tactics. *Journal of Social and Personal Relationships*.

CANARY, D.J., RATLEDGE, N.T. and SEIBOLD, D.R. 1982, *Argument and Group Decision-Making: Development of a Coding Scheme*. Paper presented at the annual meeting of the Speech Communication Association, Louisville, KY.

CANARY, D.J. and SPITZBERG, B.H. 1987, Appropriateness and effectiveness perceptions of conflict strategies. *Human Communication Research* 14, 93–118.

CANTOR, N. and KIHLSTROM, J.F. 1987, *Personality and Social Intelligence.* Englewood Cliffs, NJ: Prentice-Hall.

CANTOR, N. and MISCHEL, W. 1977, Traits as prototypes: Effects on recognition memory. *Journal of Personality and Social Psychology* 35, 38–48.

——1979a, Prototypes in person perception. In L. BERKOWITZ (ed.), *Advances in Experimental Social Psychology*, Vol. 12, pp. 3–52. New York: Academic Press.

——1987b, Prototypicality and personality: Effects on free recall and personality impressions. *Journal of Research in Personality* 13, 187–205.

CANTOR, N., MISCHEL, W. and SCHWARTZ, J. 1982a, Social knowledge: Structure, content, use and abuse. In A.H. HASTORF and A.M. ISEN (eds), *Cognitive Social Psychology*, pp. 33–72. New York: Elsevier/North-Holland.

——1982b, A prototype analysis of situations. *Cognitive Psychology* 14, 45–77.

CAPPELLA, J.N. 1986, Violations of distance norms: Reciprocal and compensatory reactions for high and low self-monitors. In M. MCLAUGHLIN (ed.), *Communication Yearbook 9*, pp. 359–76. Beverly Hills: Sage.

CAPPELLA, J.N. and GREENE, J.O. 1982, A discrepancy-arousal explanation of mutual influence in expressive behavior for adult–adult and infant–adult interaction. *Communication Monographs* 49, 89–114.

CARTWRIGHT, D. 1965, Influence, leadership, and control. In J.G. MARCH (ed.), *Handbook of Organization*, pp. 1–47. Chicago: Rand-McNally.

——1971, Risk taking by individuals and groups: An assessment of research employing choice dilemmas. *Journal of Personality and Social Psychology* 20, 361–78.

CARVER, C.S. and SCHEIER, M.F. 1981, *Attention and Self-Regulation: A Control-Theory Approach to Human Behavior.* New York: Springer.

——1982, Control theory: A useful conceptual framework for personality—social, clinical and health psychology. *Psychological Bulletin* 92, 111–35.

——1983, A control-theory approach to human behavior, and implications for the problems in self-management. In P.C. KENDALL (ed.), *Advances in Cognitive-behavioral Research and Therapy*, Vol. 2, pp. 127–94. New York: Academic Press.

CHAPIN, M. and DYCK, D.G. 1976, Persistence in children's reading behavior as a function of N length and attribution retraining. *Journal of Abnormal Psychology* 85, 511–15.

CIALDINI, R.B. 1984, *Influence.* New York: Morrow.

——1988, *Influence: Science and Practice* (2nd edn). Glenview, IL: Scott-Foresman.

——in press, Indirect tactics of impression management: Beyond basking. In R. GIACALONE and P. ROSENFIELD (eds), *Impression Management in the Organization.* Hillsdale, NJ: Erlbaum.

CIALDINI, R.B., BORDEN, R.J., THORNE, A., WALKER, M.R., FREEMAN, S. and SLOAN, L.R. 1976, Basking in reflected glory. Three (football) field studies. *Journal of Personality and Social Psychology* 34, 366–75.

CIALDINI, R.B. and RICHARDSON, K.D. 1980, Two indirect tactics of image management: Basking and blasting. *Journal of Personality and Social Psychology* 39, 406–15.

CLARK, R.A. 1979, The impact of self-interest and desire for liking on the selection of communicative strategies. *Communication Monographs* 46, 257–73.

CLARK, R.A. and DELIA, J.G. 1976, The development of functional persuasive skills in childhood and early adolescence. *Child Development* 47, 1008–14.

——1979, Topoi and rhetorical competence. *Quarterly Journal of Speech* 65, 187–206.

CLINE, T.R. and CLINE, R.J. 1979, Risky and cautious decision shifts in small groups. *Southern Speech Communication Journal* 44, 252–63.

——1980, A structural analysis of risky-shift and cautious-shift discussions: The diffusion-of-responsibility theory. *Communication Quarterly* 28, 26–36.

CODY, M.J. 1982, A typology of disengagement strategies and an examination of the role intimacy, reactions to inequity and relational problems play in strategy selection. *Communication Monographs* 49, 148–70.

CODY, M.J., CANARY, D.J. and SMITH, S.W. in press, Compliance-gaining goals: An inductive analysis of actor's goal-types, strategies, and successes. In J. DALY and J. WIEMANN (eds), *Communicating Strategically*. Hillsdale, NJ: Erlbaum.

CODY, M.J., GREENE, J.O., MARSTON, P., O'HAIR, H.D., BAASKE, K.T. and SCHNEIDER, M.J. 1986, Situation perception and message strategy selection. In M.L. McLAUGHLIN (ed.), *Communication Yearbook 9*, pp. 390–420. Beverly Hills, CA: Sage.

CODY, M.J. and McLAUGHLIN, M.L. 1985a, The situation as a construct in interpersonal communication research. In M.L. KNAPP and G.R. MILLER (eds), *Handbook of Interpersonal Communication*, pp. 263–312. Beverly Hills, CA: Sage.

——1985b, Models for the sequential construction of accounting episodes: Situational and interactional constraints on message selection and interaction. In R.L. STREET, Jr and J.N. CAPPELLA (eds), *Sequence and Pattern in Communicative Behavior*, pp. 50–69. London: Edward Arnold.

——1988, Accounts on trial: Oral arguments in traffic court. In C. ANTAKI (ed.), *Analysing Lay Explanation: A Casebook of Methods*, pp. 113–26. London: Sage.

CODY, M.J. and McLAUGHLIN, M.L. in press, Interpersonal accounting, In H. GILES and P. ROBINSON (eds), *Handbook of Language and Social Psychology*. London: Wiley.

CODY, M.J., McLAUGHLIN, M.L. and JORDAN, W. 1980, A multidimensional scaling of three sets of compliance-gaining strategies. *Communication Quarterly* 28, 34–6.

CODY, M.J., WOELFEL, M.L. and JORDAN, W. 1983, Dimensions of compliance-gaining situations. *Human Communication Research* 9, 99–113.

COHEN, J. 1977, *Statistical Power Analysis for the Behavioral Sciences*. New York: Academic Press.

COHEN, P.R. and PERRAULT, G.R. 1979, Elements of a plan-based theory of speech acts. *Cognitive Science* 3, 177–212.

COLEMAN, R.V. 1976, Court control and grievance accounts: Dynamics of traffic court interactions. *Urban Life* 5, 165–87.

COOPER, J. and JONES, E.E. 1969, Opinion divergence as a strategy to avoid being miscast. *Journal of Personality and Social Psychology* 13, 23–30.

COSIER, R.A. 1978, The effects of three potential aids for making strategic decisions on prediction accuracy. *Organizational Behavior and Human*

332 REFERENCES

Performance 22, 295–306.

——1981, Dialectical inquiry in strategic planning: A case of premature acceptance? *Academy of Management Review* 6, 643–8.

——1983, Research notes and communications: Approaches for the experimental examination of the dialectic. *Strategic Management Journal* 4, 79–84.

COSTRICH, N., FEINSTEIN, J., KIDDER, L., MARECEK, J. and PASCALE, L. 1975, When stereotypes hurt: Three studies of sex role reversals. *Journal of Experimental Social Psychology* 11, 520–30.

COURTRIGHT, J.A. 1978, A laboratory investigation of groupthink. *Communication Monographs* 45, 229–46.

CRITTENDEN, K.S. and WILEY, M.G. 1980, Causal attributions and behavioral response to failure. *Social Psychology Quarterly* 43, 353–8.

CROWNE, D.P. and MARLOWE, D. 1964, *The Approval Motive*. New York: Wiley.

CROZIER, R. in press, *Shyness and Embarrassment*. Cambridge: Cambridge University Press.

DARLEY, J.M. and ZANNA, M.P. 1982, Making moral judgments. *American Scientist* 70, 515–21.

DAVIS, J.H. 1973, Group decisions and social interaction: A theory of social decision schemes. *Psychological Review* 80, 97–125.

DAVIS, J.H. and HINSZ, V.B. 1982, Current research problems in group performance and group dynamics. In H. BRANDSTATTER, J.H. DAVIS and G. STOCKER-KREICHGAUER (eds), *Group Decision Making*, pp. 1–20. New York: Academic Press.

DAVISON, G. and NEALE, J.M. 1986, *Abnormal Psychology: An Experimental Clinical Approach*. New York: Wiley.

DE BEAUGRANDE, R. 1980, The pragmatics of discourse planning. *Journal of Pragmatics* 4, 15–42.

DECI, E.L. 1975, *Intrinsic Motivation*. New York: Plenum.

DELUGA, R. 1986, *Job Tensions and the Use of Influence*. Paper presented at the annual meeting of the Eastern Psychological Association, Boston.

DETURCK, M.A. 1985, A transactional analysis of compliance-gaining behavior: Effects of noncompliance, relational contexts, and actors' gender. *Human Communication Research* 12, 54–78.

DILLARD, J.P. 1987, *Influence Goals in Close Relationships*. Unpublished manuscript, Department of Communication Arts, University of Wisconsin, Madison, WI.

DILLARD, J.P. and BURGOON, M. 1985, Situational influences on the selection of compliance-gaining messages: Two tests of the Cody–McLaughlin typology. *Communication Monographs* 52, 289–304.

DILLARD, J.P. and HUNTER, J.E. 1987, *On the Use and Interpretation of the Emotional Empathy Scale, the Self-Consciousness Scale, and the Self-Monitoring Scale*. Unpublished manuscript, University of Wisconsin-Madison.

DILLARD, J.P., SEGRIN, C. and HARDEN, J.M. 1987, *Goals and Interpersonal Influence*. Paper presented at the Third International Conference on Language and Social Psychology, Bristol.

DION, K. 1972, Physical attractiveness and evaluation of children's transgressions. *Journal of Personality and Social Psychology* 24, 207–13.

DION, K., BARON, R. and MILLER, N. 1978, Why do groups make riskier decisions than individuals? In L. BERKOWITZ (ed.), *Group Processes*, pp. 227–99.

New York: Academic Press.

DITTON, J. 1977, Alibis and aliases: Some notes on the 'motives' of fiddling bread salesmen. *Sociology* 11, 233–56.

DIXON, W.J. (ed.) 1983, *BMDP Statistical Software*. Berkeley, CA: University of California Press.

DOHERTY, W.J. and RYDER, R.G. 1979, Locus of control, interpersonal trust, and assertive behaviour among newlyweds. *Journal of Personality and Social Psychology* 37, 2212–39.

DOLLINGER, S.J. and McGUIRE, B. 1981, The development of psychological-mindedness: Children's understanding of defense mechanisms. *Journal of Clinical Child Psychology* 10, 117–21.

DOLLINGER, S.J., STALEY, H. and McGUIRE, B. 1981, The child as psychologist: Attributions and evaluations of defensive strategies. *Child Development* 52, 1084–6.

DOUGLAS, W. 1983, Scripts and self-monitoring: When does being a high self-monitor really make a difference? *Human Communication Research* 10, 81–96.

DOWLING, W.J. and ROBERTS, K. 1974, The historical and philosophical background of cognitive approaches to psychology. In E.C. CARTERETTE and M.P. FRIEDMAN (eds), *Handbook of Perception. Vol. I: Historical and Philosophical Roots of Perception*, pp. 243–54. New York: Academic Press.

DRAPER, S. 1987, Understanding everyday explanation. *Proceedings of the Alvey Workshop on Explanation*, pp. 54–72. Guildford, England: Surrey University.

——in press, What is going on in everyday explanations? In C. ANTAKI (ed.), *Analysing Lay Explanation: A Casebook of Methods*. London: Sage.

DUCK, S. 1985, Social and personal relationships. In G.R. MILLER and M.L. KNAPP (eds), *Handbook of Interpersonal Communication*, pp. 655–86. Beverly Hills, CA: Sage.

DUVAL, S. and WICKLUND, R. 1972, *A Theory of Objective Self-Awareness*. New York: Academic Press.

DWECK, C.S. 1975, The role of expectations and attributions in the alleviation of learned helplessness. *Journal of Personality and Social Psychology* 31, 674–85.

ELDER, G., BETTES, B.A. and SELIGMAN, M.E.P. 1982, Unpublished data, Cornell University. Cited on p. 368 of C. PETERSON and M.E.P. SELIGMAN (1984), Causal explanations as a risk factor for depression: Theory and evidence. *Psychological Review* 91, 347–74.

ELLIOTT, G.C. 1979, Some effects of deception and level of self-monitoring on planning and reaction to a self-presentation. *Journal of Personality and Social Psychology* 37, 1282–92.

EMERSON, R.M. 1962, Power–defense relations. *American Sociological Review* 27, 31–41.

EMMONS, R.A., DEINER, E. and LARSEN, R.J. 1986, Choice and avoidance of everyday situations and affect congruence: Two models of reciprocal interactionism. *Journal of Personality and Social Psychology* 51, 815–26.

EPSTEIN, S. 1973, The self-concept revisited: Or a theory about a theory. *American Psychologist* 28, 212–21.

FALBO, T. 1977, A multidimensional scaling of power strategies. *Journal of Personality and Social Psychology* 35, 537–47.

FALBO, T. and PEPLAU, L.A. 1980, Power strategies in intimate relationships. *Journal of Personality and Social Psychology* 38, 618–28.

FELDMAN, S. (ed.) 1966, *Cognitive Consistency*. New York: Academic Press.

FELSON, R.B. 1982, Impression management and the escalation of aggression and violence. *Social Psychology Quarterly* 45, 245–54.

FENIGSTEIN, A., SCHEIER, M.F. and BUSS, A.H. 1975, Public and private self-consciousness: Assessment and theory. *Journal of Consulting and Clinical Psychology* 43, 522–7.

FESTINGER, L. 1957, *A Theory of Cognitive Dissonance*. Stanford, CA: Stanford University Press.

FIEDLER, F.E. 1967, *A Theory of Leadership Effectiveness*. New York: McGraw–Hill.

FINCH, J.F. and CIALDINI, R.B. 1989, Another indirect tactic of (self-) image management: Boosting. *Personality and Social Psychology Bulletin* 15, 222–32.

FINCHEM, F.D. 1985, Outcome valence and situational constraints in the responsibility of attributions of children and adults. *Social Cognition* 3, 218–33.

FISHBEIN, M. and AJZEN, I. 1973, Attribution of responsibility: A theoretical note. *Journal of Experimental Social Psychology* 9, 148–53.

——1975, *Belief, Attitude, Intention and Behavior*. Reading, MA: Addison-Wesley.

FISKE, S.T. and TAYLOR S.E. 1984, *Social Cognition*. New York: Random House.

FITZPATRICK, M.A. and WINKE, J. 1979, You always hurt the one you love: Strategies and tactics in interpersonal conflict. *Communication Quarterly* 27, 3–11.

FORD, C.E. and BERKMAN, M. 1988, Women, dependency and depression. In S.S. BREHM (ed.), *Seeing Female: Social Roles and Personal Lives*, pp. 91–100. Westport, CT.: Greenwood Press.

FORSYTH, D.R. 1980, A taxonomy of ethical ideologies. *Journal of Personality and Social Psychology* 39, 175–84.

FORSYTH, D.R., BERGER, R.E. and MITCHELL, T. 1981, The effects of self-serving vs. other-serving claims of responsibility on attraction and attribution in groups. *Social Psychology Quarterly* 44, 59–64.

FORSYTH, D.R. and POPE, W.R. 1984, Ethical ideology and judgments of social psychological research. *Journal of Personality and Social Psychology* 46, 1365–75.

FOWLER, C.A. and TURVEY, M.T. 1978, Skill acquisition: An event approach with special reference to searching for the optimum of a function of several variables. In G.E. STELMACH (ed.), *Information Processing in Motor Control and Learning*, pp. 2–40. New York: Academic Press.

FREIDRICH, C.J. 1963, *Man and His Government*. New York: McGraw-Hill.

FRENCH, J.R.P. Jr and RAVEN, B. 1959, The bases of social power. In D. CARTWRIGHT (ed.), *Studies in Social Power*, pp. 150–67. Ann Arbor, MI: University of Michigan, Institute for Social Research.

FRESE, M. and SABINI, J. (eds) 1985, *Goal Directed Behavior: On the Concept of Action in Psychology*. Hillsdale, NJ: Erlbaum.

FREUD, S. 1914, *Psychopathology of Everyday Life*. London: Unwin.

FURNHAM, A.F. 1988, *Lay Theories: Everyday Understanding of Problems in the Social Sciences*. Oxford: Pergamon.

FURNHAM, A. and CAPON, M. 1983, Social skills and self-monitoring processes. *Personality and Individual Differences* 4, 171–8.

GABREYANA, W.K. and ARKIN, R.M. 1980, Self-monitoring scale: Factor structure and correlates. *Personality and Social Psychology Bulletin* 6, 13–22.

GALLISTEL, C.R. 1980, *The Organization of Action: A New Synthesis.* Hillsdale, NJ: Erlbaum.

GANSTER, D.C. in press, Type A behavior and occupational stress. *Journal of Occupational Behavior Medicine.*

GARDNER, H. 1987, *The Mind's New Science: A History of the Cognitive Revolution.* New York: Basic Books.

GIDDENS, A. 1971, *Capitalism and Modern Social Theory.* New York: Cambridge University Press.

——1972, *Emile Durkheim.* New York: Cambridge University Press.

——(ed.) 1974a, *Positivism and Sociology.* London: Heinemann.

——1974b, *The Class Structure of the Advanced Societies.* New York: Harper and Row.

——1976, *New Rules of Sociological Method.* New York: Basic Books.

——1977, *Studies in Social and Political Theory.* New York: Basic Books.

——1979, *Central Problems in Social Theory.* Berkeley, CA: University of California Press.

——1984, *The Constitution of Society: Outline of the Theory of Structuration.* Berkeley: University of California Press.

GIFFIN, K. and EHRLICH, L. 1963, The attitudinal effects of group discussion on a proposed change in company policy. *Speech Monographs* 30, 377–9.

GODFREY, K.K., JONES, E.E. and LORD, C.G. 1986, Self-promotion is not ingratiation. *Journal of Personality and Social Psychology* 50, 106–15.

GOFFMAN, E. 1955, On face-work: An analysis of the ritual elements in social interaction. *Psychiatry: Journal for the Study of Interpersonal Processes* 18, 213–31.

——1959, *The Presentation of Self in Everyday Life.* Garden City, NY: Doubleday.

——1967, *Interaction Ritual.* Garden City, NY: Doubleday-Anchor.

——1971, *Relations in Public.* New York: Basic Books.

GOODCHILDS, J.D., QUADRADO, C. and RAVEN, B.H. 1975, *Getting One's Way.* Paper presented at the meeting of the Western Psychological Associations, Sacramento, California.

GOTTMAN, J.M. 1982, Emotional responsiveness in marital conversations. *Journal of Communication* 32, 108–20.

GOURAN, D.S. 1969, Variables related to consensus in group discussions of questions of policy. *Speech Monographs* 36, 387–91.

——1981, Cognitive sources of inferential error and the contributing influence of interaction characteristics in decision-making groups. In G. ZIEGELMULLER and J. RHODES (eds), *Dimensions of Argument: Proceedings of the Second Summer Conference on Argumentation,* pp. 728–48. Annandale, VA: Speech Communication Association.

——1982, *A Theoretical Foundation for the Study of Inferential Error in Decision-Making Groups.* Paper presented at the Conference on Small Group Research, Pennsylvania State University.

——1983, Communicative influences on inferential judgments in decision-making groups: A descriptive analysis. In D. ZAREFSKY, M.O. SILLARS and J. RHODES (eds), *Argument in Transition: Proceedings of the Third Summer*

Conference on Argumentation, pp. 667–84. Annandale, VA: Speech Communication Association.

——1984, Communicative influences on the decisions related to the Watergate cover-up: The failure of collective judgment. *Central States Speech Journal* 35, 260–9.

——1985, A critical summary of research on the role of argument in decision-making groups. In J.R. Cox, M.O. Sillars and G.B. Walker (eds), *Argument and Social Practice: Proceedings of the Fourth SCA/AFA Conference on Argumentation*, pp. 723–36. Annandale, VA: Speech Communication Association.

——1986, Inferential errors, interaction, and group decision-making. In R.Y. Hirokawa and M.S. Poole (eds), *Communication and Group Decision-Making*, pp. 93–112. Beverly Hills, CA: Sage.

Gouran, D.S. and Geonetta, S.C. 1977, Patterns of interaction in decision-making groups at varying distances from consensus. *Small Group Behavior* 8, 511–24.

Graesser, A.C. 1981, *Prose Comprehension: Beyond the Word*. New York: Springer-Verlag.

Green, S.G. and Mitchell, T.R. 1979, Attributional processes of leaders in leader–member interactions. *Organizational Behavior and Human Performance* 23, 429–58.

Greenberg, J., Pyszczynski, T. and Solomon, S. 1986, The causes and consequences of a need for self-esteem: A terror management theory. In R.F. Baumeister (ed.), *Public Self and Private Self*, pp. 189–212. New York: Springer-Verlag.

Greene, J.O. 1984a, A cognitive approach to human communication: An action assembly theory. *Communication Monographs* 51, 289–306.

——1984b, Evaluating cognitive explanations of communicative phenomena. *Quarterly Journal of Speech* 70, 241–54.

——1987, *The Ecology of Communication: An Action-Production Approach to the Processes of Person–Situation Interaction*. Paper presented at the annual meeting of the International Communication Association, Montreal.

——in press, Cognitive processes: Methods for probing the black box. In C.H. Tardy (ed.), *Methods and Instruments of Communication Research: A Handbook for the Study of Human Interaction*. Norwood, NJ: Ablex.

Greene, J.O. and Cody, M.J. 1985, On thinking and doing: Cognitive science and the production of social behavior. *Journal of Language and Social Psychology* 4, 157–70.

Greene, J.O., Smith, S.W. and Lindsey, E. 1988, *Memory Representations of Compliance-Gaining Strategies and Tactics*. Paper, Speech Communication Association, New Orleans, Louisiana.

Greene, P.H. 1982, Why is it easy to control your arms? *Journal of Motor Behavior* 14, 260–86.

Greenwald, A.G. and Breckler, S.J. 1985, To whom is the self presented? In B. Schlenker (ed.), *The Self and Social Life*, pp. 126–45. New York: McGraw-Hill.

Grice, H.P. 1975, Logic and conversation. In P. Cole and J. Morgan (eds), *Syntax and Semantics: Volume 3, Speech Acts*, pp. 41–58. New York: Academic Press.

Gruenich, R. 1982, Issues in the developmental study of how children use intention and consequence information to make moral evaluations. *Child Development* 53, 29–43.

HAAN, N. 1986, Systematic variability in the quality of moral action, as defined in two formulations. *Journal of Personality and Social Psychology* 50, 1271–84.

HABERLANDT, K. 1980, Story grammar and reading time of story constituents. *Poetics* 9, 99–118.

HABERLANDT, K., BERIAN, C. and SANDSON, J. 1980, The episode schema in story processing. *Journal of Verbal Learning and Verbal Behavior* 19, 51–86.

HALE, C.L. 1987, A comparison of accounts: When is a failure not a failure? *Journal of Language and Social Psychology* 66, 117–32.

HALE, J.L. and BOSTER, F.J. 1987, *A Test of Persuasive Argument, Social Comparison, and Dual Process Models of Choice Shifts*. Paper presented at the annual meeting of the International Communication Association, Montreal, Canada.

HAMILTON, V.L. 1978, Who is responsible? Toward a *social* psychology of responsibility attribution. *Social Psychology* 41, 316–28.

HAMILTON, V.L., BLUMENFELD, P.C. and KUSHLER, R.H. 1988, A question of standards: Attributions of blame and credit for class acts. *Journal of Personality and Social Psychology* 54, 34–48.

HAMPLE, D. 1980, A cognitive view of argument. *Journal of the American Forensics Association* 17, 151–8.

——1981, The cognitive context of argument. *Western Journal of Speech Communication* 45, 148–58.

——1985, A third perspective on argument. *Philosophy and Rhetoric* 18, 1–22.

HARRÉ, R. 1977, The ethogenic approach: Theory and practice. In L. BERKOWITZ (ed.), *Advances in Experimental Social Psychology*, Vol. 10, pp. 284–314. New York: Academic Press.

HAYES-ROTH, B. and HAYES-ROTH, F. 1979, A cognitive model of planning. *Cognitive Science* 3, 275–310.

HAZELTON, V., HOLDRIDGE, W. and LISKA, J. 1982, *Toward a Taxonomy of Compliance-Resisting Communication*. Paper presented at the annual meeting of the Western Speech Communication Association, Denver.

HECKHAUSEN, H. and KUHL, J. 1985, From wishes to action; The dead ends and short cuts on the long way to action. In M. FRESE and J. SABINI (eds), *Goal Directed Behavior: The Concept of Action in Psychology*, pp. 134–60. Hillsdale, NJ: Erlbaum.

HEIDER, F. 1958, *The Psychology of Interpersonal Relations*. New York: Wiley.

HEINEMANN, W. 1979, The assessment of private and public self-consciousness: A German replication. *European Journal of Social Psychology* 9, 331–7.

HIGGINS, E.T., KLEIN, R. and STRAUM, T. 1985, Self-concept discrepancy theory: A psychological model for distinguishing among different aspects of depression and anxiety. *Social Cognition* 3, 51–76.

HIGGINS, E.T., McCANN, C.D. and FONDACARO, R. 1982, The 'communication game': Goal-directed encoding and consequences. *Social Cognition* 1, 21–37.

HILL, C.A. 1987, Affiliation motivation: People who need people . . . but in different ways. *Journal of Personality and Social Psychology* 52, 1008–18.

HILL, T.A. 1976, An experimental study of the relationship between opinionated leaders and small group consensus. *Communication Monographs* 43, 246–57.

HINSZ, V.B. 1981, *Persuasive Arguments, Group Polarization and Choice Shifts*.

Unpublished master's thesis, University of Illinois, Urbana-Champaign.

HINSZ, V.B. and DAVIS, J.H. 1984, Persuasive arguments theory, group polarization, and choice shifts. *Personality and Social Psychology Bulletin* 10, 260–8.

HIROKAWA, R.Y. 1980a, A comparative analysis of communication patterns within effective and ineffective decision-making groups. *Communication Monographs* 47, 312–21.

——1980b, *Group Communication and Problem-Solving Effectiveness: An Investigation of Procedural Functions.* Paper presented at the annual meeting of the International Communication Association, Minneapolis, Minnesota.

——1982a, Group communication and problem-solving effectiveness I: A critical review of inconsistent findings. *Communication Quarterly* 30, 134–44.

——1982b, Consensus group decision-making, quality of decision, and group satisfaction: An attempt to sort 'fact' from 'fiction'. *Central States Speech Journal* 33, 407–15.

——1983, Group communication and problem-solving effectiveness II. *Western Journal of Speech Communication* 47, 59–74.

HIROKAWA, R.Y. and PACE, R. 1983, A descriptive investigation of the possible communication-based reasons for effective and ineffective group decision-making. *Communication Monographs* 50, 363–79.

HIROKAWA, R.Y. and SCHEERHORN, D.R. 1985, The functions of argumentation in group deliberation. In J.R. COX, M.O. SILLARS and G.B. WALKER (eds), *Argument and Social Practice: Proceedings of the Fourth SCA/AFA Conference on Argumentation*, pp. 737–46. Annandale, VA: Speech Communication Association.

HOBBS, J.R. and EVANS, D.A. 1980, Conversation as planned behavior. *Cognitive Science* 4, 349–77.

HOFFMAN, C., MISCHEL, W. and MAZZE, K. 1981, The role of purpose in the organization of information about behavior: Trait-based versus goal-based categories in person cognition. *Journal of Personality and Social Psychology* 40, 211–25.

HOGAN, R., JONES, W. and CHEEK, J.M. 1985, Socioanalytic theory: An alternative to armadillo psychology. In B.R. SCHLENKER (ed.), *The Self and Social Life*, pp. 175–98. New York: McGraw-Hill.

HOLMES, D.S. and HOUSTON, B.K. 1971, The defensive function of projection. *Journal of Personality and Social Psychology* 20, 208–13.

HORMUTH, S.E. and LALLI, M. 1986, *Eine skala zur erfassung der bereichsspezifischen selbstzufriedenheit.* Unpublished manuscript, Psychologisches Institut der Universität Heidelberg.

HORNEY, K. 1950, *Neurosis and Growth.* New York: Norton.

HOVLAND, C.I., JANIS, I.L. and KELLEY, H.H. 1953, *Communication and Persuasion.* New Haven, CT: Yale University Press.

HOWARD, J.A., BLUMSTEIN, P. and SCHWARTZ, P. 1986, Sex, power, and influence tactics in intimate relationships. *Journal of Personality and Social Psychology* 51, 102–9.

HUFF, A.S. 1983, A rhetorical examination of strategic change. In L.R. PONDY, P.J. FROST, G. MORGAN and T.C. CANDRIDGE (eds), *Organizational Symbolism*, pp. 167–83. Greenwich, CT: JAI Press.

HUNTER, J.E. and BOSTER, F.J. 1987, A model of compliance-gaining message selection. *Communication Monographs* 54, 63–84.

INFANTE, D.A. 1980, Verbal plans: A conceptualization and interpretation. *Communication Quarterly* 28, 3–10.

——1981, Trait argumentativeness as a predictor of communicative behavior in situations requiring argument. *Central States Speech Journal* 32, 265–72.

——1982, The argumentative student in the speech communication classroom: An investigation and implications. *Communication Education* 31, 141–8.

INFANTE, D.A. and RANCER, A.S. 1982, A conceptualization and measure of argumentativeness. *Journal of Personality Assessment* 46, 72–80.

INFANTE, D.A., TREBING, J.D., SHEPHERD, P.E. and SEEDS, D.E. 1984, Relations of argumentativeness to verbal aggression. *Southern Speech Communication Journal* 50, 67–77.

INFANTE, D.A. and WIGLEY, C.J. 1986, Verbal aggressiveness: An interpersonal model and measure. *Communication Monographs* 53, 61–9.

INSEL, P. and MOOS, R. 1974, *Work Environment Scale*. California: Consulting Psychologist Press.

INSTONE, D., MAJOR, B. and BUNKER, B.B. 1983, Gender, self-confidence, and social influence strategies: An organizational simulation. *Journal of Personality and Social Psychology* 44, 322–33.

JACKSON, S. and JACOBS, S. 1980, Structure of conversational argument: Pragmatic cases for the enthymeme. *Quarterly Journal of Speech* 66, 251–65.

——1981, The collaborative production of proposals in conversational argument and persuasion: A study of disagreement regulation. *Journal of the American Forensic Association* 18, 77–90.

JACOBS, L., BERSCHEID, E. and WALSTER, E. 1971, Self-esteem and attraction. *Journal of Personality and Social Psychology* 17, 84–91.

JACOBS, S. and JACKSON, S. 1981, Argument as a natural category: The routine grounds for arguing in conversation. *Western Journal of Speech Communication* 45, 111–17.

——1982, Conversational argument: A discourse analytic approach. In J.R. Cox and C.A. WILLARD (eds), *Advances in Argumentation Theory and Research*, pp. 205–37. Carbondale, IL: Southern Illinois University Press.

JAMES, W. 1890, *The Principles of Psychology*, Vols. 1 & 2. Cambridge, MA: Harvard University Press (1983).

JANOFF-BULMAN, R. and TIMKO, C. 1987, Coping with traumatic events: The role of denial in light of people's assumptive worlds. In C.R. SNYDER and C.E. FORD (eds), *Coping with Negative Life Events: Clinical and Social Psychological Perspectives*, pp. 135–59. New York: Plenum.

JELLISON, J.M. 1977, *'I'm sorry I didn't mean to' and Other Lies We Love to Tell*. New York: Chatham.

JELLISON, J.M. and ARKIN, R.M. 1977, Social comparison of abilities: A self-presentational analysis of decision-making in groups. In J.M. SULS and R.L. MILLER (eds), *Social Comparison Processes*, pp. 235–58. Washington, DC: Hemisphere.

JELLISON, J.M. and GREEN, J. 1981, A self-presentation approach to the fundamental attribution error: The norm of internality. *Journal of Personality and Social Psychology* 40, 643–9.

JOHNSON, P. 1976, Women and power: Toward a theory of effectiveness. *Journal of Social Issues* 32, 99–110.

JONES, E.E. 1964, *Ingratiation*. New York: Appleton, Century.

——1979, The rocky road from acts to dispositions. *American Psychologist* 34,

107–17.

JONES, E.E. and BERGLAS, S. 1978, Control of attributions about the self through self-handicapping strategies: The appeal of alcohol and the role of underachievement. *Personality and Social Psychology Bulletin* 4, 200–6.

JONES, E.E. and DAVIS, K.E. 1965, From acts to dispositions: The attribution process in person perception. In L. BERKOWITZ (ed.), *Advances in Experimental Social Psychology*, Vol. 2, pp. 219–66. New York: Academic Press.

JONES, E.E. and HARRIS, V.A. 1967, The attribution of attitudes. *Journal of Experimental Social Psychology* 3, 1–24.

JONES, E.E. and PITTMAN, T. 1982, Toward a general theory of strategic self-presentation. In J. SULS (ed.), *Psychological Perspectives on the Self*, Vol. 1, 231–63. Hillsdale, NJ: Erlbaum.

JONES, E.E., WORCHEL, S., GOETHALS, G.R. and GRUMET, J.F. 1971, Prior expectancy and behavioral extremity as determinants of attitude attribution. *Journal of Experimental Social Psychology* 7, 59–80.

JONES, E.E. and WORTMAN, C. 1973, *Ingratiation: An Attributional Approach.* Morristown, NJ: General Learning Press.

KAHNEMAN, D. and TVERSKY, A. 1982, The simulation heuristic. In D. KAHNEMAN, P. SLOVIC and A. TVERSKY (eds), *Judgement under Uncertainty*, pp. 201–8. Cambridge: Cambridge University Press.

KAIL, R.V., Jr and BISANZ, J. 1982, Cognitive strategies. In C.R. PUFF (ed.), *Handbook of Research Methods in Human Memory and Cognition*, pp. 229–55. New York: Academic Press.

KANOUSE, D.E. and HANSON, L.R. 1972, Negativity in evaluations. In E.E. JONES *et al.* (eds), *Attribution: Perceiving the Causes of Behavior.* Morristown, NJ: General Learning Press.

KANTER, R.M. 1977, *Men and Women in the Organization.* New York: Basic Books.

KAUFFMAN, D.R. and STEINER, I.D. 1968, Conformity as an ingratiation technique. *Journal of Experimental Social Psychology* 4, 400–14.

KEARNEY, P., PLAX, T.G., RICHMOND, V.P. and McCROSKEY, J.C. 1984, Power in the classroom IV: Alternatives to discipline. In R. BOSTROM (ed.), *Communication Yearbook 8*, pp. 724–46. Beverly Hills: Sage.

KELLERMAN, K. and JARBOE, S. 1987, Conservatism in judgement: Is risky shift-ee really risky, really? In M.L. McLAUGHLIN (ed.), *Communication Yearbook 10*, pp. 259–82. Newbury Park, CA: Sage.

KELLEY, H.H. 1967, Attribution theory in social psychology. In D. LEVINE (ed.), *Nebraska Symposium on Motivation*, Vol. 15, pp. 192–241. Lincoln, NE: University of Nebraska Press.

——1971, Causal schemata and the attribution process. In E.E. JONES, D.E. KANOUSE, H.H. KELLEY, R.E. NISBETT, S. VALINS and B. WEINER (eds), *Attribution: Perceiving the Causes of Behavior*, pp. 151–74. Morristown, NJ: General Learning Press.

KERR, B. 1983, Memory, action, and motor control. In R.A. MAGILL (ed.), *Memory and Control of Action*, pp. 47–65. Amsterdam: North-Holland.

KIPNIS, D. 1976, *The Powerholders.* Chicago: University of Chicago Press.

——1984, The use of power in organizations and in interpersonal settings. In S. OSKAMP (ed.), *Applied Social Psychology Annual*, Vol. 5, pp. 179–210. Beverly Hills, CA: Sage.

KIPNIS, D., CASTELL, P., GERGEN, M. and MAUCH, D. 1976, Metamorphic effects of power. *Journal of Applied Psychology* 61, 127–35.

KIPNIS, D. and COHN, E. 1979, *Power and Affection*. Paper presented at the meetings of the Eastern Psychological Association, Philadelphia, PA.

KIPNIS, D. and SCHMIDT, S. 1983, An influence perspective on bargaining. In M. BAZERMAN and R. LEWICKI (eds), *Negotiating in Organizations*, pp. 303–19. Beverly Hills, CA: Sage.

KIPNIS, D., SCHMIDT, S., PRICE, K. and STITT, C. 1981, Why do I like thee: Is it your performance or my orders? *Journal of Applied Psychology* 66, 324–7.

KIPNIS, D., SCHMIDT, S. and WILKINSON, I. 1980, Intraorganizational influence tactics: Explorations in getting one's way. *Journal of Applied Psychology* 65, 440–52.

KLINE, J.A. 1972, Orientation and group consensus. *Central States Speech Journal* 23, 44–7.

KLINE, J.A. and HULLINGER, J.L. 1973, Redundancy, self-orientation, and group consensus. *Speech Monographs* 40, 72–4.

KLINGER, E. 1985, Missing links in action theory. In M. FRESE and J. SABINI (eds), *Goal Directed Behavior: The Concept of Action in Psychology*, pp. 134–60. Hillsdale, NJ: Erlbaum.

KNUTSON, T.J. 1972, An experimental study of the effects of orientation behavior on small group consensus. *Speech Monographs* 39, 159–65.

KNUTSON, T.J. and HOLDRIDGE, W. 1975, Orientation behavior, leadership, and consensus: A possible functional relationship. *Speech Monographs* 42, 107–14.

KNUTSON, T.J. and KOWITZ, A.C. 1977, Effects of information type and levels of orientation in consensus achievement in substantive and effective small-group conflict. *Central States Speech Journal* 28, 54–63.

KUHL, J. 1985, Volitional mediators of cognition-behavior consistency: Self-regulatory processes and action versus state orientation. In J. KUHL and J. BECKMAN (eds), *Action Control*, pp. 101–28. New York: Springer-Verlag.

KURTINES, W.M. 1986, Moral behavior as rule governed behavior: Person and situation effects on moral decision making. *Journal of Personality and Social Psychology* 50, 784–91.

LASSWELL, H.D. and KAPLAN, A. 1950, *Power and Society*. New Haven, CT: Yale University Press.

LAUGHLIN, P.R. and EARLEY, P.C. 1982, Social combination model, persuasive arguments theory, social comparison theory, and choice shift. *Journal of Personality and Social Psychology* 42, 273–80.

LEARY, M. 1983, *Understanding Social Anxiety*. Beverly Hills, CA: Sage.

——1986, The impact of interactional impediments on social anxiety and self-presentation. *Journal of Experimental Social Psychology* 22, 122–35.

LEATHERS, D. 1969, Process disruption and measurement in small group communication. *Quarterly Journal of Speech* 55, 287–300.

——1970, The process effects of trust-destroying behavior in the small group. *Speech Monographs*, 39, 166–73.

——1972, Quality of group communication as a determinant of group product. *Speech Monographs* 39, 166–73.

——1981, Small group communication research in the 1980s: Conceptualization and methodology. *Communication* 10, 3–16.

LEDDO, J. and ABELSON, R.P. 1988, The nature of explanation. In J.A. GALAMBOS,

R.P. ABELSON and J.B. BLACK (eds), *Knowledge Structures*, pp. 103–22. Hillsdale, NJ: Erlbaum.

LEECH, G. and COATES, S. 1979, Semantic indeterminacy and the modals. In S. GREENBAUM, G. LEECH and J. SVARTVIK (eds), *Studies in English Linguistics: For Randoloph Quirk*, pp. 209–30. New York: Longman.

LEFCOURT, H.M. 1982, *Locus of Control: Current Trends in Theory and Research* (2nd edn). Hillsdale, NJ: Erlbaum.

LEFCOURT, H.M., MARTIN, R.A., FICK, C.M. and SALEH, W.E. 1985, Locus of control for affiliation and behaviour in social interactions. *Journal of Personality and Social Psychology* 48, 755–9.

LEFF, M.C. and HEWES, D.E. 1981, Topical invention and group communication: Towards a sociology of inference. In G. ZIEGELMULLER and J. RHODES (eds), *Dimensions of Argument: Proceedings of the Second Summer Conference on Argumentation*, pp. 770–89. Annandale, VA: Speech Communication Association.

LENNOX, R. and WOLFE, R. 1984, Revision of the Self-monitoring Scale. *Journal of Personality and Social Psychology* 46, 1349–64.

LEVENSON, H. 1976, Multidimensional locus of control in sociopolitical activities of conservative and liberal ideologies. *Journal of Personality and Social Psychology* 33, 199–208.

LEVY, D.M. 1979, Communicative goals and strategies: Between discourse and syntax. In T. GIVON (ed.), *Syntax and Semantics. Vol. 12: Discourse and Syntax*, pp. 183–210. New York: Academic Press.

LEWIN, K. 1951, *Field Theory in Social Science*. New York: Harper and Row.

LICHTENSTEIN, E.H. and BREWER, W.F. 1980, Memory for goal-directed events. *Cognitive Psychology* 12, 412–45.

LINDSEY, A.E. and GREENE, J.O. 1987, Social tendencies and social knowledge: Self-monitoring differences in the representation and recall of social knowledge. *Communication Monographs* 54, 381–95.

LIPPA, R. 1976, Expressive control and the leakage of dispositional introversion–extroversion during role-played teaching. *Journal of Personality* 44, 541–59.

LOCKE, E.A., SHAW, K.N., SAARI, L.M. and LATHAM, G.P. 1981, Goal-setting and task performance: 1969–1980. *Psychological Bulletin* 90, 125–52.

LUMSDEN, G. 1974, An experimental study of the effect of verbal agreement on leadership maintenance in problem-solving discussion. *Central States Speech Journal* 25, 270–6.

MACCOBY, E.E. and JACKLIN, C.N. 1974, *The Psychology of Sex Differences*. Stanford; CA: Stanford University Press.

MACKAY, D.G. 1982, The problems of flexibility, fluency, and speed–accuracy tradeoff in skilled behavior. *Psychological Review* 89, 483–506.

——1983, A theory of the representation and enactment of intentions. In R.A. MAGILL (ed.), *Memory and Control of Action*, pp. 217–30. Amsterdam: North-Holland.

MADSEN, D.B. 1978, Issue importance and group choice shifts: A persuasive arguments approach. *Journal of Personality and Social Psychology* 36, 1118–27.

MANDLER, G. and WATSON, D. 1966, Anxiety and the interruption of behavior. In C.D. SPIELBERGER (ed.), *Anxiety and Behavior*, pp. 263–88. New York: Academic Press.

MANDLER, J.M. 1978, A code in a node: The use of a story schema in retrieval. *Discourse Processes* 1, 14–35.

——1983, Representation. In J.H. FLAVELL and E.M. MARKMAN (eds), *Cognitive Development*, Vol. 3, pp. 420–94. New York: Wiley.

MANDLER, J.M. and DEFOREST, M. 1979, Is there more than one way to recall a story? *Child Development* 50, 886–9.

MANDLER, J.M. and GOODMAN, M.S. 1982, On the psychological validity of story structure. *Journal of Verbal Learning and Verbal Behavior* 21, 507–23.

MANDLER, J.M. and JOHNSON, N.S. 1977, Remembrance of things parsed: Story structure and recall. *Cognitive Psychology* 9, 111–51.

MANIS, M., CORNELL, S.D. and MOORE, J.C. 1974, Transmission of attitude-relevant information through a communication chain. *Journal of Personality and Social Psychology* 30, 81–94.

MARKUS, H. and NURIUS, P. 1986, Possible selves. *American Psychologist* 41, 954–69.

MARTENIUK, R.G. and MACKENZIE, C.L. 1980, Information processing in movement organization and execution. In R.S. NICKERSON (ed.), *Attention and Performance VIII*, pp. 29–57. Hillsdale, NJ: Erlbaum.

MARTENIUK, R.G. and ROMANOW, S.K.E. 1983, Human movement organization and learning as revealed by variability of movement, use of kinematic information and fourier analysis. In R.A. MAGILL (ed.), *Memory and Control of Action*, pp. 167–97. Amsterdam: North-Holland.

MARTIN, R.W. and SCHEERHORN, D.R. 1985, What are conversational arguments? Toward a natural language user's perspective. In J.R. COX, M.O. SILLARS and G.B. WALKER (eds), *Argument and Social Practice: Proceedings of the Fourth SCA/AFA Conference on Argumentation*, pp. 705–22. Annandale, VA: Speech Communication Association.

MARWELL, G. and SCHMITT, D.R. 1967a, Dimensions of compliance-gaining behavior: An empirical analysis. *Sociometry* 30, 350–64.

——1967b, Compliance-gaining behavior: A synthesis and model. *Sociological Quarterly* 8, 317–28.

MASLOW, A. 1943, A theory of human motivation. *Psychological Review* 50, 370–96.

——1954, *Motivation and Personality*. New York: Harper and Row.

MASON, R.O. 1969, A dialectical approach to strategic planning. *Management Science* 15, 403–12.

MAYER, M.E. 1985, Explaining choice shift: An effects coded model. *Communication Monographs* 52, 92–101.

MAYES, B., SIME, W.E. and GANSTER, D.C. 1984, Convergent validity of Type A behavior pattern scales and their ability to predict physiological responsiveness in a sample of female public employees. *Journal of Behavioral Medicine* 7, 83–108.

McCANN, C.D. and HIGGINS, E.T. 1987, *Goals and Orientations in Interpersonal Relations: How Intrapersonal Discrepancies Produce Negative Affect*. Paper presented at the annual meeting of the International Communication Association, Montreal, Canada.

McCLELLAND, D.C. 1961, *The Achieving Society*. New York: Van Nostrand.

McCLELLAND, J.L. and RUMELHART, D.E. 1985, Distributed memory and the representation of general and specific information. *Journal of Experimental Psychology: General* 114, 159–88.

McCROSKEY, J.C. 1982, Oral communication apprehension: A reconceptualization. In M. BURGOON (ed.), *Communication Yearbook 6*, pp. 136–70. Beverly Hills, CA: Sage.

McFARLAND, C. and ROSS, M. 1982, Impact of causal attributions on affective reactions to success and failure. *Journal of Personality and Social Psychology* 43, 937–46.

McKERROW, R.E. 1977, Rhetorical validity: An analysis of three perspectives on justification. *Journal of the American Forensics Association* 13, 133–41.

McLAUGHLIN, M.L., CODY, M.J. and O'HAIR, H.D. 1983, The management of failure events: Some contextual determinants of accounting behavior. *Human Communication Research* 9, 208–24.

McLAUGHLIN, M.L., CODY, M.J. and ROBEY, C.S. 1980, Situational influences on the selection of strategies to resist compliance-gaining attempts. *Human Communication Research* 1, 14–36.

McLAUGHLIN, M.L., CODY, M.J. and ROSENSTEIN, N.E. 1983, Account sequences in conversations between strangers. *Communication Monographs* 50, 102–25.

McLAUGHLIN, M.L., LOUDEN, A.D., CASHION, J.L., ALTENDORF, D.M., BAASKE, K.T. and SMITH, S.W. 1985, Conversational planning and self-serving utterances: The manipulation of topical and functional structures in dyadic interaction. *Journal of Language and Social Psychology* 4, 233–51.

McNICOL, D. and STEWART, G.W. 1980, Reaction time and the study of memory. In J.M.T. BREBNER and A.T. WELFORD (eds), *Reaction Times*, pp. 253–307. London: Academic Press.

McQUILLEN, J.S. 1986, The development of listener-adapted compliance-resisting strategies. *Human Communication Research* 12, 359–75.

McQUILLEN, J.S., HIGGENBOTHAM, D.C. and CUMMINGS, W.C. 1984, Compliance-resisting behaviours. In R.N. BOSTROM (ed.), *Communication Yearbook 8*, p. 747–62. Beverly Hills: Sage.

MEHLMAN, R.C. and SNYDER, C.R. 1985, Excuse theory: A test of the self-protective role of attributions. *Journal of Personality and Social Psychology* 49, 994–1001.

MELBURG, V., LESSER, J. and TEDESCHI, J.T. 1984, *Remedial Impression Management Tactics*. Paper presented at the 55th Meeting of the Eastern Psychological Association, Baltimore, Maryland.

MESSICK, D.M., BLOOM, S., BOLDIZAR, J.P. and SAMUELSON, C.D. 1985, Why are we fairer than others? *Journal of Experimental Social Psychology* 21, 480–500.

METALSKY, G.L., ABRAMSON, L.Y., SELIGMAN, M.E.P., SEMMEL, A. and PETERSON, C. 1982, Attributional styles and life events in the classroom: Vulnerability and invulnerability to depressive mood reactions. *Journal of Personality and Social Psychology* 43, 612–17.

MEYERS, R.A. 1987, *An Interactional Test of Persuasive Arguments Theory and an Alternative Structurational Perspective*. Unpublished doctoral dissertation, University of Illinois, Urbana, IL.

——in press, Testing Persuasive Argument Theory's predictor model: Alternative interactional accounts of group argument and influence. *Communication Monographs*.

MEYERS, R.A. and SEIBOLD, D.R. 1985, *Vinokur and Burnstein's Persuasive Arguments Theory: A Test of Assumptions*. Paper presented at the Annual Meeting of the Speech Communication Association, Denver, CO.

——1987, Interactional and non-interactional perspectives on interpersonal argument: Implications for the study of group decision-making. In F.H. VAN EEMEREN, R. GROOTENDORST, J.A. BLAIR and C.A. WILLARD (eds), *Argumentation: Perspectives and Approaches*, pp. 205–14. Dordrecht-Holland: Foris Publications.

——1987, *Persuasive Arguments Theory Assumptions: An Empirical Test and Alternative Perspective*. Paper presented at the Annual Meeting of the International Communication Association, Montreal.

MICHENER, H.A. and SUCHNER, R.W. 1972, The tactical use of social power. In J.T. TEDESCHI (ed.), *The Social Influence Processes*, pp. 239–86. Chicago: Aldine.

MILGRAM, S. 1974, *Obedience to Authority*. New York: Harper and Row.

MILLER, G.A., GALANTER, E. and PRIBRAM, K.H. 1960, *Plans and the Structure of Behavior*. New York: Holt.

MILLER, G.R., BOSTER, F.J., ROLOFF, M.E. and SEIBOLD, D.R. 1977, Compliance-gaining message strategies: A typology and some findings concerning effects of situational differences. *Communication Monographs* 44, 37–51.

MILLER, G.R., DETURCK, M.A. and KALBFLEISCH, P.J. 1983, Self-monitoring, rehearsal and deceptive communication. *Human Communication Research* 10, 97–118.

MILLER, N., CAMPBELL, D.T., TWEDT, H. and O'CONNELL, E.J. 1966, Similarity, contrast, and complementarity in friendship choice. *Journal of Personality and Social Psychology* 3, 3–12.

MIRELS, H.L. 1970, Dimensions of internal versus external control. *Journal of Consulting and Clinical Psychology* 34, 226–8.

MISCHEL, T. 1975, Psychological explanations and their vicissitudes. In W.J. ARNOLD (ed.), *Nebraska Symposium on Motivation*, Vol. 23, pp. 133–204. Lincoln, NE: University of Nebraska Press.

MISCHEL, W. and MISCHEL, H.N. 1976, A cognitive social-learning approach to socialization and self-regulation. In T. LICKONA (ed.), *Moral Development and Behavior: Theory, Research, and Social Issues*, pp. 84–107. New York: Holt, Rinehart and Winston.

MITROFF, I. and EMSHOFF, J.R. 1979, On strategic assumption-making: A dialectical approach to policy and planning. *Academy of Management Review* 4, 1–12.

MITROFF, I., MASON, R.O. and BARABBA, V.P. 1982, Policy as argument—A logic for ill-structured decision problems. *Management Science* 28, 1391–1404.

MORGENTHAU, H. 1969, *Politics among Nations* (5th edn). New York: Knopf.

MUEHLENHARD, I. 1983, Women's assertion. In V. FRANKS and E.D. ROTHBLUM (eds), *The Stereotyping of Women*, pp. 153–71. New York: Springer.

MUNTON, A. and ANTAKI, C. 1987, *Explanatory Constructs in Discourse about Family Problems*. Unpublished manuscript, University of Lancaster, England.

MURNINGHAM, J.K. and CASTORE, C.H. 1975, An experimental test of three choice shift hypotheses. *Memory and Cognition* 3, 171–4.

MURRAY, H.A. 1938, *Explorations in Personality*. New York: Oxford University Press.

MYERS, D.G. 1982, Polarizing effects of social interaction. In H. BRANDSTATTER, J.H. DAVIS and G. STOCKER-KREICHGAUER (eds), *Group Decision Making*, pp. 125–61. New York: Academic Press.

MYERS, D.G. and BISHOP, G.D. 1970, Discussion effects on racial attitudes. *Science* 169, 778–9.

MYERS, D.G. and LAMM, A. 1976, The group polarization phenomenon.

Psychological Bulletin 83, 602–27.

MYERS, D.G. and RIDL, J. 1979, Can we all be better than average? *Psychology Today* 12, 89–98.

NEIDENTHAL, P.M., CANTOR, N. and KIHLSTROM, J.F. 1985, Prototype matching: A strategy for social decision making. *Journal of Personality and Social Psychology* 48, 575–84.

NELSON, K. 1978, How children represent knowledge of their world in and out of language: A preliminary report. In R.S. SIEGLER (ed.), *Children's Thinking: What Develops?*, pp. 255–73. Hillsdale, NJ: Erlbaum.

NEMETH, C. 1977, Interactions between jurors as a function of majority vs. unanimity decision rules. *Journal of Applied Social Psychology* 7, 38–56.

——1982, Stability of faction position and influence. In G.H. BRANDSTATTER, J.H. DAVIS and G. STOCKER-KREICHGAUER (eds), *Group Decision Making*, pp. 185–213. New York: Academic Press.

NEMETH, C., SWEDLUND, M. and KANKI, B. 1974, Patterning of the minority's responses and their influence on the majority. *European Journal of Social Psychology* 4, 53–64.

NEMETH, C. and WACHTLER, J. 1974, Creating the perceptions of consistency and confidence: A necessary condition for minority influence. *Sociometry* 37, 529–40.

NEWELL, A. 1973, You can't play 20 questions with nature and win: Projective comments on the papers of this symposium. In W.G. CHASE (ed.), *Visual Information Processing*, pp. 283–308. New York: Academic Press.

——1980, Reasoning, problem solving, and decision processes: The problem space as a fundamental category. In R.S. NICKERSON (ed.), *Attention and Performance VIII*, pp. 693–718. Hillsdale, NJ: Erlbaum.

NISBETT, R.E., HARVEY, D. and WILSON, J. 1979, *'Epistemological' Coding of the Content of Everyday Social Conversations*. Unpublished manuscript, University of Michigan.

NISBETT, R.E. and ROSS, L. 1980, *Human Inference*. Englewood Cliffs, NJ: Prentice-Hall.

NORMAN, D.A. and SHALLICE, T. 1980, *Attention to Action: Willed and Automatic Control of Behavior* (Tech. Rep. No. 99). San Diego: University of California, Center for Human Information Processing.

NORTH, R.C., HOLSTI, O.R., ZANINOVICH, M.G. and ZINNES, D.A. 1963, *Content Analysis: A Handbook with Applications for the Study of International Crisis*. Evanston, IL: Northwestern University Press.

OGILVIE, D.M. 1987, The undesired self: A neglected variable in personality research. *Journal of Personality and Social Psychology* 52, 379–85.

O'KEEFE, B.J. and BENOIT, P.J. 1982, Children's arguments. In J.R. COX and C.A. WILLARD (eds), *Advances in Argumentation Theory and Research*, pp. 154–83. Carbondale, IL: Southern Illinois University Press.

O'KEEFE, B.J. and McCORNACK, S.A. 1987, Message design logic and message goal structure: Effects on perception of message quality in regulative communication situations. *Human Communication Research* 14, 68–92.

O'KEEFE, B.J. and SHEPARD, G.J. 1987, The pursuit of multiple objectives in face-to-face persuasive interaction: Effects of construct differentiation on message organization. *Communication Monographs* 54, 396–419.

O'KEEFE, D.J. 1977, Two concepts of argument. *Journal of the American Forensic Association* 13, 121–8.

——1980, *Is Argument a Speech Act?* Paper presented at the annual meeting of the Speech Communication Association, New York City, NY.

OMANSON, R.C. 1982, An analysis of narrative: Identifying central, supportive, and distracting content. *Discourse Processes* 5, 195–224.

OSIPOW, S.H. and SPOKANE, A.R. 1984, Measuring occupational stress, strain and coping. In S. OSKAMP (ed.), *Applied Social Psychology Annual*, Vol. 5, pp. 67–86. Beverly Hills, CA: Sage.

PACE, R.C. 1983, *Group Discussion as a Rhetorical Process: The Influence of the Small Group Setting on the Process of Accedence.* Paper presented at the annual meeting of the Speech Communication Association, Washington, DC.

——1985, Patterns of argumentation in high and low consensus discussions. In J.R. COX, M.O. SILLARS and G.B. WALKER (eds), *Argument and Social Practice: Proceedings of the Fourth SCA/AFA Conference on Argumentation*, pp. 770–81. Annandale, VA: Speech Communication Association.

PARKS, M.R. 1985, Interpersonal communication and the quest for personal competence. In M.L. KNAPP and G.R. MILLER (eds), *Handbook of Interpersonal Communication*, p. 171–201. Beverly Hills, CA: Sage.

PASAHOW, R.J. 1980, The relation between an attributional dimension and learned helplessness. *Journal of Abnormal Psychology* 89, 358–67.

PATTERSON, M.L. 1976, An arousal model of interpersonal intimacy. *Psychological Review* 83, 235–45.

PAVITT, C. and HAIGHT, L. 1985, The 'competent' communicator as a cognitive prototype. *Human Communication Research* 12, 225–41.

PELZ, D. 1952, Influence: A key to effective leadership in the first line supervisor. *Personnel* 29, 3–11.

PERELMAN, C.H. and OLBRECHTS-TYTECA, L. 1969, *The New Rhetoric: A Treatise on Argumentation* (J. Wilkinson and P. Weaver, trans). Notre Dame: University of Notre Dame Press.

PERREAULT, W.D., Jr and MILES, R.H. 1978, Influence strategy mixes in complex organizations. *Behavioral Science* 23, 86–99.

PERVIN, L.A. 1978, *Current Controversies and Issues in Personality*. New York: Wiley.

——1986, Personal and social determinants of behavior in situations. In A. FURHAM (ed.), *Social Behavior in Context*, pp. 81–102. Boston: Allyn and Bacon.

PETERSON, C., BETTES, B.A. and SELIGMAN, M.E.P. 1982, *Spontaneous Attributions and Depressive Symptoms.* Unpublished manuscript, Virginia Polytechnic Institute and State University, Blacksburg.

PETERSON, C., LUBORSKY, L. and SELIGMAN, M.E.P. 1983, Attributions and depressive mood shifts: A case study using the symptom–context method. *Journal of Abnormal Psychology* 92, 96–103.

PETERSON, C., NUTTER, J. and SELIGMAN, M.E.P. 1982, Unpublished data, Virginia Polytechnic Institute and State University. Cited in C. PETERSON and M.E.P. SELIGMAN (1984), Casual explanations as a risk factor for depression: Theory and evidence. *Psychological Review* 91, 347–74.

PETERSON, C. and SELIGMAN, M.E.P. 1981, Helplessness and attributional style in depression. *Tiddsskrift for Norsk Psykologforening* 18, 53–9.

PEW, R.W. 1984, A distributed view of human motor control. In W. PRINZ and A.F. SANDERS (eds), *Cognition and Motor Processes*, pp. 19–27. Berlin:

Springer-Verlag.

POOLE, M.S. 1983, Decision development in small groups III: A multiple sequence model of group decision development. *Communication Monographs* 50, 321–41.

POOLE, M.S. and DOELGER, J.A. 1986, Developmental processes in group decision-making. In R.Y. HIROKAWA and M.S. POOLE (eds), *Group Decision-Making and Communication*, pp. 35–62. Beverly Hills, CA: Sage.

POOLE, M.S., SEIBOLD, D.R. and MCPHEE, R.D. 1986, Group decision-making and theory development: A structurational approach. In R.Y. HIROKAWA and M.S. POOLE (eds), *Group Decision-Making and Communication*, pp. 237–64. Beverly Hills, CA: Sage.

POPPER, K.R. 1963, *Conjectures and Reputations: The Growth of Scientific Knowledge*. London: Routledge and Kegan Paul.

PORTER, L., ALLEN, R. and ANGLE, H. 1981, The politics of upward influence in organisations. In LARRY L. CUMMINGS and BARRY M. STAW (eds), *Research in Organizational Behavior*, vol. 3, pp. 109–49. Greenwich, CT: JAI Press.

PORTER, L.W., LAWLER, E.E. and HACKMAN, J.R. 1984, *Behavior in Organizations*. New York: McGraw-Hill.

PRICE, R.H. and BOUFFARD, D.L. 1974, Behavioral appropriateness and situational constraint as dimensions of social behavior. *Journal of Personality and Social Psychology* 30, 579–86.

PRUITT, D.G. 1971a, Choice shifts in group discussion: An introductory review. *Journal of Personality and Social Psychology* 20, 339–60.

——1971b, Conclusions: Toward an understanding of choice shifts in group discussion. *Journal of Personality and Social Psychology* 20, 495–510.

PUTNAM, L.L. and WILSON, C.E. 1982, Communicative strategies in organizational conflicts: Reliability and validity of a measurement scale. In M. BURGOON (ed.), *Communication Yearbook 6*, pp. 629–54. Beverly Hills: Sage.

PYSZCZYNSKI, T. and GREENBERG, J. 1987, Depression, self-focused attention and self-regulatory perseveration. In C.R. SNYDER and C.E. FORD (eds), *Coping with Negative Life Events: Clinical and Social Psychological Perspectives*, pp. 105–29. New York: Plenum.

——in press, Towards an integration of cognitive and motivational perspectives on social inference: A biased hypothesis-testing model. In L. BERKOWITZ (ed.), *Advances in Experimental Social Psychology*, Vol. 20. New York: Academic Press.

QUIRK, R., GREENBAUM, S., LEECH, G. and SVARTVIK, J. 1987, *A Comprehensive Grammar of the English Language*. London: Longman.

RANCER, A.S., BAUKUS, R.A. and INFANTE, D.A. 1985, Relations between argumentativeness and belief structures about arguing. *Communication Education* 34, 37–47.

RANCER, A.S. and INFANTE, D.A. 1983, *The Impact of Physical Attractiveness and Trait Argumentativeness as Predictors of Responses to an Argumentative Situation*. Paper presented at the annual meeting of the Eastern Communication Association, Ocean City, Maryland.

RARICK, D.L., SOLDOW, G.F. and GEIZER, R.S. 1976, Self-monitoring as a mediator of conformity. *Central States Speech Journal* 27, 267–71.

RATLEDGE, N.E.T. 1986, *Theoretical and Methodological Integrity of a Structurational Scheme for Coding Argument in Decision-Making Groups*. Unpublished doctoral dissertation, University of Southern California, Los Angeles.

RAVEN, B.H., CENTERS, R. and RODRIGUES, A. 1975, The bases of conjugal power. In R.E. CROMWELL and D.H. OLSON (eds), *Power in Families*, pp. 217–31. New York: Wiley.

RAVEN, B.H. and KRUGLANSKI, A.W. 1970, Conflict and power. In P. SWINGLE (ed.), *The Structure of Conflict*, pp. 69–109. New York: Academic Press.

READ, S.J. 1987a, Constructing causal scenarios: A knowledge structure approach to causal reasoning. *Journal of Personality and Social Psychology* 52, 288–302.

——1987b, Similarity and causality in the use of social analogies. *Journal of Experimental Social Psychology* 23, 189–207.

REED, E.S. 1982, An outline of a theory of action systems. *Journal of Motor Behavior* 14, 98–134.

REEDER, G.D. and SPORES, J.M. 1983, The attribution of morality. *Journal of Personality and Social Psychology* 44, 736–45.

REIS, H.T., WHEELER, L., SPIEGEL, N., KERNIS, M.H., NEZLEK, J. and PERRI, M. 1982, Physical attractiveness in social interaction: II. Why does appearance affect social experience? *Journal of Personality and Social Psychology* 43, 979–96.

REITHER, F. 1981, Thinking and acting in complex situations—A study of experts' behavior. *Simulation and Games* 12, 125–40.

REST, J.R. 1984, The major components of morality. In W.M. KURTINES and J.L. GEWIRTZ (eds), *Morality, Moral Behavior and Moral Development*, pp. 24–38. New York: Wiley.

RICHARDSON, K.D. and CIALDINI, R.B. 1981, Basking and blasting: Techniques of indirect self-presentation. In J.T. TEDESCHI (ed.), *Impression Management Theory and Social Psychological Research*, pp. 41–56. New York: Academic Press.

RICHMOND, V.P., DAVIS, L.M., SAYLOR, K. and McCROSKEY, J.C. 1984, Power strategies in organizations: Communication techniques and messages. *Human Communication Research* 11, 85–108.

RIORDAN, C. 1981, *The Effectiveness of Post-Transgression Accounts*. Paper presented at the American Psychological Association, Los Angeles, CA.

RIZZO, J.R., HOUSE, R.J. and LIRTZMAN, S.L. 1970, Role conflict and ambiguity in complex organizations. *Administrative Science Quarterly* 15, 155–63.

ROGERS, C.R. 1954, The case of Mrs. Oak: A research analysis. In C.R. ROGERS and R.F. DYMOND (eds), *Psychotherapy and Personality Change*, pp. 359–88. Chicago: University of Chicago Press.

ROGERS, J.W. and BUFFALO, M.D. 1974, Neutralization techniques: Toward a simplified measurement scale. *Pacific Sociological Review* 17, 313–31.

ROKEACH, M. 1973, *The Nature of Human Values*. New York: The Free Press.

ROLOFF, M.E. and BARNICOTT, E.F. 1978, The situational use of pro- and anti-social compliance-gaining strategies by high and low Machiavellians. In B.D. RUBEN (ed.), *Communication Yearbook 2*, pp. 193–205. New Brunswick, NJ: Transaction Books.

ROLOFF, M.E., JANISZEWSKI, C.A., McGRATH, M.A., BURNS, C.S. and MANREI, L.A. 1988, Acquiring resources from intimates: When obligation substitutes for persuasion. *Human Communication Research* 14, 364–98.

ROSCH, E. 1973, On the internal structure of perceptual and semantic categories. In T.E. MOORE (ed.), *Cognitive Development and the Acquisition of Language*, pp. 111–44. New York Academic Press.

———1978, Principles of categorization. In E. ROSCH and B.B. LLOYD (eds), *Cognition and Categorization*, pp. 27–48. Hillsdale, NJ: Erlbaum.

ROSCH, E., MERVIS, C.B., GRAY, W.D., JOHNSON, D.M. and BOYES-BRAEM, P. 1976, Basic objects in natural categories. *Cognitive Psychology* 8, 382–439.

ROSEN, S. and TESSER, A. 1970, On the reluctance to communicate undesirable information: The MUM effect. *Sociometry* 33, 253–63.

ROSENBAUM, D.A. 1984, The planning and control of movements. In J.R. ANDERSON and S.M. KOSSLYN (eds), *Tutorials in Learning and Memory: Essays in Honor of Gordon Bower*, pp. 219–33. San Francisco: Freeman.

ROSENBAUM, D.A., KENNY, S.B. and DERR, M.A. 1983, Hierarchical control of rapid movement sequences. *Journal of Experimental Psychology: Human Perception and Performance* 9, 86–102.

ROSENBERG, M. 1965, *Society and the Adolescent Self-Image*. Princeton, NJ: Princeton University Press.

ROTHWELL, N. and WILLIAMS, J.M.G. 1983, Attributional style and life events. *British Journal of Clinical Psychology* 22, 139–40.

ROTTER, J.B. 1966, Generalized expectancies for internal vs. external locus of control of reinforcement. *Psychological Monographs* 80 (whole No. 609).

RULE, B.G. and BISANZ, G.L. 1987, Goals and strategies of persuasion: A cognitive schema for understanding social events. In M. ZANNA, J. OLSEN and P. HERMAN (eds), *Social Influence: The Fifth Ontario Symposium on Personality and Social Psychology*, pp. 185–206. Hillsdale, NJ: Erlbaum.

RULE, B.G., BISANZ, G.L. and KOHN, M. 1985, Anatomy of a persuasion schema: Targets, goals, and strategies. *Journal of Personality and Social Psychology* 48, 1127–40.

RUNGE, T.E., FREY, D., GOLLWITZER, P.M., HELMREICH, R.L. and SPENCE, J.T. 1981, Cross-cultural stability of masculine (instrumental) and feminine (expressive) traits. *Journal of Cross-Cultural Psychology* 12, 142–62.

SAINE, T.J. and BOCK, D.G. 1973, A comparison of the distributional and sequential structures in high and low consensus groups. *Central States Speech Journal* 24, 125–30.

SALTZMAN, E.L. 1979, Levels of sensorimotor representation. *Journal of Mathematical Psychology* 20, 91–163.

SALTZMAN, E.L. and KELSO, J.A.S. 1983, Toward a dynamical account of motor memory and control. In R.A. MAGILL (ed.), *Memory and Control of Action*, pp. 17–38. Amsterdam: North Holland.

———1987, Skilled actions: A task-dynamic approach. *Psychological Review* 94, 84–106.

SCHANK, R.C. 1975, The structure of episodes in memory. In D.G. BOBROW and A. COLLINS (eds), *Representation and Understanding: Studies in Cognitive Science*, pp. 237–72. New York: Academic Press.

———1982, *Dynamic Memory: A Theory of Reminding and Learning in Computers and People*. Cambridge: Cambridge University Press.

SCHANK, R.C. and ABELSON, R.P. 1977, *Scripts, Plans, Goals and Understanding*. Hillsdale, NJ: Erlbaum.

SCHEFF, T.J. 1968, Negotiating reality: Notes on power in the assessment of responsibility. *Social Problems* 16, 3–17.

SCHENCK-HAMLIN, W.J., WISEMAN, R.L. and GEORGACARAKOS, G.N. 1982, A model of properties of compliance-gaining strategies. *Communication Quarterly* 30, 92–100.

SCHILIT, W.K. 1986, An examination of individual differences as a moderator of upward influence activities in strategic decisions. *Human Relations* 39, 933–53.

SCHILIT, W.K. and LOCKE, E.A. 1982, A study of upward influence in organizations. *Administrative Science Quarterly* 27, 304–16.

SCHLENKER, B.R. 1980, *Impression Management: The Self-Concept, Social Identity, and Interpersonal Relations*. Belmont, CA: Wadsworth.

——1986, Self-identification: Toward an integration of the public and private self. In R. BAUMEISTER (ed.), *Public Self and Private Self*, pp. 21–62. New York: Springer-Verlag.

SCHLENKER, B.R. and LEARY, M.R. 1982, Social anxiety and self-presentation: A conceptualization. *Psychological Bulletin* 92, 641–69.

SCHMIDT, D.F. and SHERMAN, R.C. 1984, Memory for persuasive messages: A test of a schema-copy-plus-tag model. *Journal of Personality and Social Psychology* 47, 17–25.

SCHMIDT, R.A. 1975, A schema theory of discrete motor skill learning. *Psychological Review* 82, 225–60.

——1976, The schema as a solution to some persistent problems in motor learning theory. In G.E. STELMACH (ed.), *Motor Control: Issues and Trends*, pp. 41–65. New York: Academic Press.

SCHMIDT, S. and KIPNIS, D. 1984, Managers' pursuit of individual and organizational goals. *Human Relations* 37, 781–94.

SCHNEIDER, D.J. 1981, Tactical self-presentations: Towards a broader conception. In J.T. TEDESCHI (ed.), *Impression Management Theory and Social Psychological Research*, pp. 23–40. New York: Academic Press.

SCHNEIDER, D.J., HASTORF, A.H. and ELLSWORTH, P.C. 1979, *Person Perception*. Reading, MA: Addison-Wesley.

SCHÖNBACH, P. 1980, A category system for account phases. *European Journal of Social Psychology* 10, 195–200.

——1985, *A Taxonomy for Account Phases: Revised, Explained and Applied.* Unpublished manuscript, Fakultat für Psychologie, Ruhr-Universität, Bochum, West Germany.

——1986, *A Theory of Conflict Escalation in Account Episodes.* Unpublished manuscript, Fakultat für Psychologie, Ruhr-Universität, Bochum, West Germany.

——1987, Accounts of men and women for failure events. In G.R. SEMIN and B. KRAHE (eds), *Issues in Contemporary German Social Psychology: History, Theories and Application*, pp. 97–118. London: Sage.

SCHULTZ, B. 1980, Communicative correlates of perceived leaders. *Small Group Behavior* 11, 175–91.

——1982, Argumentativeness: Its effect in group decision-making and its role in leadership perception. *Communication Quarterly* 30, 368–75.

——1983, Argumentativeness: Its role in leadership perception and group communication. In D. ZAREFSKY, M.O. SILLARS and J. RHODES (eds), *Argument in Transition: Proceedings of the Third Summer Conference on Argumentation*, pp. 638–48. Annandale, VA: Speech Communication Association.

SCHWARTZ, S.H. 1977, Normative influences on altruism. In L. BERKOWITZ (ed.), *Advances in Experimental Social Psychology*, Vol. 10, pp. 221–79. New York: Academic Press.

SCHWEIGER, D.M. and FINGER, P.A. 1984, The comparative effectiveness of dialectical inquiry and devil's advocacy: The impact of task biases on previous research findings. *Strategic Management Journal* 5, 335–50.

SCHWEIGER, D.M., SANDBERG, W.R. and RAGAN, J.W. 1986, Group approaches for improving strategic decision making: A comparative analysis of dialectical inquiry, devil's advocacy, and consensus. *Academy of Management Journal* 29, 51–71.

SCHWENK, C.R. and COSIER, R.A. 1980, Effects of the expert, devil's advocate, and dialectical inquiry methods on prediction performance. *Organizational Behavior and Human Performance* 26, 409–24.

SCOTT, M.B. and LYMAN, S.M. 1968, Accounts. *American Sociological Review* 33, 46–62.

SEARLE, J. 1969, *Speech Acts*. Cambridge: Cambridge University Press.

SEARS, D.O. 1983, The person-positivity bias. *Journal of Personality and Social Psychology* 44, 233–50.

SEIBOLD, D.R., CANARY, D.J. and TANITA-RATLEDGE, N. 1983, *Argument and Group Decision-Making: Interim Report on a Structurational Research Program*. Paper presented at the annual meeting of the Speech Communication Association, Washington, DC.

SEIBOLD, D.R., CANTRILL, J.G. and MEYERS, R.A. 1985, Communication and interpersonal influence. In M.L. KNAPP and G.R. MILLER (eds.), *Handbook of Interpersonal Communication*, pp. 551–611. Beverly Hills, CA: Sage.

SEIBOLD, D.R., McPHEE, R.D., POOLE, M.S., TANITA, N.E. and CANARY, D.J. 1981, Argument, group influence, and decision outcomes. In G. ZIEGELMULLER and J. RHODES (eds), *Dimensions of argument: Proceedings of the Second Summer Conference on Argumentation*, pp. 663–92. Annandale, VA: Speech Communication Association.

SEIBOLD, D.R. and MEYERS, R.A. 1986, Communication and influence in group decision-making. In R.Y. HIROKAWA and M.S. POOLE (eds), *Group Decision-Making and Communication*, pp. 133–56. Beverly Hills, CA: Sage.

SEIBOLD, D.R., POOLE, M.S. and McPHEE, R.D. 1980, *New Prospects for Research in Small Group Communication*. Paper presented at the annual conference of the Central States Speech Association, Chicago, IL.

SELIGMAN, M.E.P. 1986, *Explanatory Style: Depression, Lyndon Baines Johnson, and the Baseball Hall of Fame*. Paper presented at the 94th Annual Convention of the American Psychological Association, Washington, DC.

SEMIN, G.R. and MANSTEAD, A.S.R. 1983, *The Accountability of Conduct: A Social Psychological Analysis*. London: Academic Press.

SHAW, M.E. 1968, Attribution of responsibility by adolescents in two cultures. *Adolescence* 3, 23–32.

SHEA, B.C. and PEARSON, J.C. 1986, The effects of relationship type, partner intent, and gender on the selection of relationship maintenance strategies. *Communication Monographs* 53, 352–64.

SHULTZ, T.R. and WRIGHT, K. 1985, Concepts of negligence and intention in the assignment of moral responsibility. *Canadian Journal of Behavioral Science* 17, 97–108.

SIEGEL, S. 1956, *Nonparametric Statistics for the Behavioral Sciences*. New York: McGraw-Hill.

SILLARS, A.L. 1980a, Attributions and communication in roommate conflicts. *Communication Monographs* 47, 180–200.

——1980b, The sequential and distributional structure of conflict interactions as a function of attributions concerning the locus of responsibility and stability of conflicts. In D. NIMMO (ed.), *Communication Yearbook 4*, pp. 217–35. New Brunswick, NJ: Transaction Books.

——1980c, The stranger and spouse as target person for compliance-gaining strategies: A subjective-expected utility. *Human Communication Research* 6, 265–79.

SKINNER, B.F. 1953, *Science and Human Behavior*. New York: Macmillan.

——1974, *About Behavior*. New York: Knopf.

SMITH, M.J. 1982, Cognitive schemata and persuasive communication: Toward a contingency rules theory. In M. BURGOON (ed.), *Communication Yearbook 6*, pp. 330–62. Beverly Hills, CA: Sage.

——1984, Contingency rules theory, context, and compliance behaviors. *Human Communication Research* 10, 489–512.

SMITH, S.W. and CODY, M.J. 1986, *Communication Apprehension and the Selection of Influence Tactics*. Paper presented at the annual meeting of the International Communication Association, Chicago.

SNODGRASS, S.E. 1985, Women's intuition: The effect of subordinate role on interpersonal sensitivity. *Journal of Personality and Social Psychology* 49, 146–55.

SNYDER, C.R. 1985a, Collaborative companions: The relationship of self-deception and excuse-making. In M.W. MARTIN (ed.), *Self-Deception and Self-Understanding*, pp. 35–51. Lawrence, KS: Regents Press of Kansas.

——1985b, The excuse: An amazing grace? In B.R. SCHLENKER (ed.), *The Self and Social Life*, pp. 235–60. New York: McGraw-Hill.

SNYDER, C.R. and HIGGINS, R.L. 1986, *Excuses: Their Effects and Their Role in the Negotiation of Reality*. Paper presented to the Second Attribution-Personality Theory Conference, Los Angeles.

——in press, Excuses. Their effective role in the negotiation of reality. *Psychological Bulletin*.

SNYDER, C.R., HIGGINS, R.L. and STUCKY, R.J. 1983, *Excuses: Masquerades in Search of Grace*. New York: Wiley/Interscience.

SNYDER, C.R., LASSENGARD, M. and FORD, C.E. 1986, Distancing after group success and failure: Basking in reflected glory and cutting off reflected failure. *Journal of Personality and Social Psychology* 51, 382–8.

SNYDER, C.R., SCHENKEL, R.J. and LOWERY, C.R. 1977, Acceptance of personality interpretations: The 'Barnum' effect and beyond. *Journal of Consulting and Clinical Psychology* 45, 104–14.

SNYDER, C.R., SMITH, T.W., AUGELLI, R.W. and INGRAM, R.E. 1985, On the self-serving function of social anxiety: Shyness as a self-handicapping strategy. *Journal of Personality and Social Psychology* 48, 970–80.

SNYDER, M. 1974, The self-monitoring of expressive behavior. *Journal of Personality and Social Psychology* 30, 526–37.

——1977, Impression management. In L.S. WRIGHTSMAN (ed.), *Social Psychology*, pp. 115–45. Monterey, CA: Brooks-Cole.

——1979, Self-monitoring processes. In L. BERKOWITZ (ed.), *Advances in Experimental Social Psychology*, Vol. 12, pp. 85–128. New York: Academic Press.

——1983, The influence of individuals on situations: Implications for understanding the links between personality and social behaviors. *Journal of Personality*

51, 497–576.

——1987, *Public Appearances, Private Realities: The Psychology of Self-Monitoring*. New York: Freeman.

SNYDER, M., BERSCHEID, E. and GLICK, P. 1985, Focusing on the exterior and the interior: Two investigations of the initiations of personal relationships. *Journal of Personality and Social Psychology* 48, 1427–39.

SNYDER, M. and CANTOR, M. 1980, Thinking about ourselves and others: Self-monitoring and social knowledge. *Journal of Personality and Social Psychology* 39, 222–34.

SNYDER, M. and DeBONO, K. 1985, Appeals to images and claims about quality: Understanding the psychology of advertising. *Journal of Personality and Social Psychology* 49, 586–97.

SNYDER, M. and GANGESTAD, S. 1986, On the nature of self-monitoring: Matters of assessment, matters of validity. *Journal of Personality and Social Psychology* 51, 125–39.

SNYDER, M., GANGESTAD, S. and SIMPSON, J.A. 1983, Choosing friends as activity partners: The role of self-monitoring. *Journal of Personality and Social Psychology* 45, 1061–72.

SNYDER, M. and JONES, E.E. 1974, Attitude attribution when behavior is constrained. *Journal of Experimental Social Psychology* 10, 585–660.

SNYDER, M. and SIMPSON, J.A. 1984, Self-monitoring and dating relationships. *Journal of Personality and Social Psychology* 47, 1281–92.

SNYDER, M. and SWANN, W.B., Jr 1975, When actions reflect attitudes: The politics of impression management. *Journal of Personality and Social Psychology* 34, 1034–42.

SPENCE, J.T. and HELMREICH, R.L. 1978, *Masculinity and Femininity: Their Psychological Dimensions, Correlates, and Antecedents*. Austin: University of Texas Press.

SPIVACK, G. and SHURE, M.B. 1974, *Social Adjustment of Young Children: A Cognitive Approach to Solving Real Life Problems*. San Francisco: Jossey-Bass.

STAATS, A.W. and STAATS, C.K. 1958, Attitudes established by classical conditioning. *Journal of Abnormal and Social Psychology* 57, 37–40.

STEFFEN, V.J. and EAGLY, A.H. 1985, Implicit theories about influence style: The effects of status and sex. *Personality and Social Psychology Bulletin* 11, 191–205.

STEIN, N.L. and NEZWORSKI, T. 1978, The effects of organization and instructional set on story memory. *Discourse Processes* 1, 177–93.

STELMACH, G.E. and DIGGLES, V.A. 1982, Control theories in motor behavior. *Acta Psychologica* 50, 83–105.

STONER, J.A.F. 1961, *A Comparison of Individual and Group Decisions Involving Risk*. Unpublished master's thesis. Massachusetts Institute of Technology, School of Industrial Management.

STOTLAND, E. and DUNN, R. 1963, Empathy, self-esteem, and birth-order. *Journal of Abnormal and Social Psychology* 66, 532–44.

STOTLAND, E., ZANDER, A. and NATSOULAS, T. 1961, Generalization of interpersonal similarity. *Journal of Abnormal and Social Psychology* 62, 265–74.

STUDENT, K.R. 1968, Supervisory influence and work-group performance. *Journal of Applied Psychology* 52, 188–94.

SULLIVAN, H.S. 1953, *The Interpersonal Theory of Psychiatry*. New York: Norton.

SUMMERFIELD, A.Q., CUTTING, J.E., FRISHBERG, N., LANE, H., LINDBLOM, J.S.,

RUNESON, J.S., SHAW, R.E., STUDDERT-KENNEDY, M. and TURVEY, M.T. 1980, The structuring of language by the requirements of motor control and perception: Group report. In U. BELLUGI and M. STUDDERT-KENNEDY (eds), *Signed and Spoken Language: Biological Constraints on Linguistic Form*, pp. 89–114. Weinheim: Verlag Chemie.

SUSSMAN, L. and HERDEN, R. 1982, Dialectical problem solving. *Business Horizons* pp. 66–71.

SVARTVIK, J. and QUIRK, R. 1980, *A Corpus of English Conversation*. Lund, Sweden: Gleerup.

SYKES, G.M. and MATZA, D. 1957, Techniques of neutralization. *American Sociological Review* 22, 667–9.

TAYLOR, S.E. and BROWN, J.D. 1988, Illusion and well-being: Some social psychological contributions to a theory of mental health. *Psychological Bulletin* 103, 193–210.

TAYLOR, S.E. and FISKE, S.T. 1978, Salience, attention and attribution: Top of the head phenomena. In L. BERKOWITZ (ed.), *Advances in Experimental Social Psychology* Vol. 11, pp. 250–88. New York: Academic Press.

——1981, Getting inside the head: Methodologies for process analysis in attribution and social cognition. In J.H. HARVEY, W. ICKES and R.F. KIDD (eds), *New Directions in Attribution Research*, Vol. 3, pp. 459–524. Hillsdale, NJ: Erlbaum.

TEDESCHI, J.T. (ed.), 1981, *Impression Management Theory and Social Psychological Research*. New York: Academic Press.

——1984, A social psychological interpretation of human aggression. In A. MUMMENDEY (ed.), *Social Psychology of Aggression: From Individual Behaviour Towards Social Interaction*. New York: Springer.

——1986, Private and public experiences and the self. In R.F. BAUMEISTER (ed.), *Public Self and Private Self*, pp. 1–20. New York: Springer-Verlag.

TEDESCHI, J.T. and BONOMA, T.V. 1972, Power and influence: An introduction. In J.T. TEDESCHI (ed.), *The Social Influence Processes*, p. 1–49. Chicago: Aldine.

——1977, Measures of last resort: Coercion and aggression in negotiations. In D. DRUCKMAN (ed.), *Negotiations: Social Perspectives*, pp. 213–42. Beverly Hills, CA: Sage.

TEDESCHI, J.T., BONOMA, T.V. and SCHLENKER, B.R. 1972, Influence, decision, and compliance. In J.T. TEDESCHI (ed.), *The Social Influence Processes*, pp. 346–418. Chicago: Aldine.

TEDESCHI, J.T., HORAI, J., LINDSKOLD, S. and FALEY, T.E. 1970, The effects of opportunity costs and target compliance on the behavior of a threatening source. *Journal of Experimental Social Psychology* 6, 205–13.

TEDESCHI, J.T., LINDSKOLD, S. and ROSENFELD, P. 1985, *An Introduction to Social Psychology*. St Paul, MN: West Publishing.

TEDESCHI, J.T. and MELBURG, V. 1984, Impression management and influence in the organization. In S.B. BACHARACH and E.J. LAWLER (eds), *Perspectives in Organizational Psychology: Theory and Research*, pp. 56–98. Greenwich, CT: JAI Press.

TEDESCHI, J.T. and NORMAN, N. 1985, Social power, self-presentation and the self. In B. SCHLENKER (ed.), *The Self and Social Life*, pp. 293–322. New York: McGraw-Hill.

TEDESCHI, J.T. and RIESS, M. 1981, Verbal tactics of impression management. In C. ANTAKI (ed.), *Ordinary Language Explanations of Social Behavior*, pp. 3–22. London: Academic Press.

TEDESCHI, J.T. and ROSENFELD, P. 1981, Impression management and the forced compliance situation. In J.T. TEDESCHI (ed.), *Impression Management Theory and Social Psychological Research*, pp. 147–80. New York: Academic Press.

TEDESCHI, J.T., SCHLENKER, B.R. and BONOMA, T.V. 1971, Cognitive dissonance: Private ratiocination or public spectacle? *American Psychologist* 24, 685–95.

——1973, *Conflict, Power and Games*. Chicago: Aldine.

TENNEN, H., AFFLECK, G., ALLEN, D., McGRADE, B.J. and RATZAN, S. 1983, *Causal Attributions and Coping in Juvenile Diabetes*. Unpublished manuscript, University of Connecticut, Storrs.

TESSER, A. and ROSEN, S. 1975, The reluctance to transmit bad news. In L. BERKOWITZ (ed.), *Advances in Experimental Social Psychology*, Vol. 8, pp. 193–232. New York: Academic Press.

TESSER, A., ROSEN, S. and BATCHELOR, T. 1972, On the reluctance to communicate bad news (the MUM effect): A role play extension. *Journal of Personality* 40, 88–103.

TESSER, A., ROSEN, S. and TESSER, M. 1971, On the reluctance to communicate undesirable messages (the MUM effect): A field study. *Psychological Reports* 29, 651–4.

TETLOCK, P.E. 1981, The influence of self-presentation goals in attributional reports. *Social Psychology Quarterly* 44, 300–11.

THIBAUT, J.W. and RIECKEN, H.W. 1955, Some determinants and consequences of the perception of social causality. *Journal of Personality* 24, 113–33.

TOBEY, E.L. and TUNNELL, G. 1981, Predicting our impressions on others: Effects of public self-consciousness and acting, a self-monitoring subscale. *Personality and Social Psychology Bulletin* 7, 661–9.

TOCH, H. 1969, *Violent Men*. Chicago: Aldine.

TOULMIN, S. 1958a, *The Structure of Argument*. New York: Random House.

——1958b, *The Uses of Argument*. Cambridge: Cambridge University Press.

TRABASSO, T., SECCO, T. and VAN DEN BROEK, P.W. 1984, Causal cohesion and story coherence. In H. MANDL, N.L. STEIN and T. TRABASSO (eds), *Learning and Comprehension of Text*, pp. 83–111. Hillsdale, NJ: Erlbaum.

TRABASSO, T. and SPERRY, L.L. 1985, Causal relatedness and importance of story events. *Journal of Memory and Language* 24, 595–611.

TRABASSO, T., STEIN, N.L. and JOHNSON, L.R. 1981, Children's knowledge of events: A causal analysis of story structure. In G.H. BOWER and A.R. LANG (eds), *The Psychology of Learning and Motivation*, Vol. 15, pp. 237–81. New York: Academic Press.

TRABASSO, T. and VAN DEN BROEK, P.W. 1985, Causal thinking and the representation of narrative events. *Journal of Memory and Language* 24, 612–30.

TRACY, K. 1984, The effect of multiple goals on conversational relevance and topic shift. *Communication Monographs* 51, 274–87.

TRACY, K. and MORAN, J.P. 1983, Conversational relevance in multiple-goal settings. In R.T. CRAIG and K. TRACY (eds), *Conversational Coherence*, pp. 116–35. Beverly Hills, CA: Sage.

TRAPP, R. 1983, Generic characteristics of argumentation in everyday discourse. In D. ZAREFSKY, M.O. SILLARS and J. RHODES (eds), *Argument in Transition: Proceedings of the Third Summer Conference on Argumentation*, pp. 516–30.

Annandale, VA: Speech Communication Association.

——1986, The role of disagreement in interactional argument. *Journal of the American Forensic Association* 23, 23–41.

TRAPP, R. and HOFF, N. 1985, A model of serial argument in interpersonal relationships. *Journal of the American Forensic Association* 22, 1–11.

TUNNELL, G. 1980, Intra-individual consistency in personality assessment: The effects of self-monitoring. *Journal of Personality* 48, 220–32.

TURIEL, E. and SMETANA, J.G. 1984, Social knowledge and action: The coordination of domains. In W.M. KURTINES and J.L. GEWITZ (eds), *Morality, Moral Behavior, and Moral Development*, pp. 261–82. New York: Wiley.

TURNER, R.G. 1977, Self-consciousness and anticipatory belief change. *Personality and Social Psychology Bulletin* 3, 438–41.

TURVEY, M.T. 1977, Preliminaries to a theory of action with reference to vision. In R. SHAW and J. BRANSFORD (eds), *Perceiving, Acting, and Knowing: Toward an Ecological Psychology*, pp. 211–65. Hillsdale, NJ: Erlbaum.

TVERSKY, A. 1977, Features of similarity. *Psychological Review* 84, 327–52.

VALLACHER, R.R. and WEGNER, D.M. 1987, What do people think they're doing? Action identification and human behavior. *Psychological Review* 94, 3–15.

VINOKUR, A. 1971, Review and theoretical analysis of the effects of group processes upon individual group decisions involving risk. *Psychological Bulletin* 76, 231–50.

VINOKUR, A. and BURNSTEIN, E. 1974, Effects of partially shared persuasive arguments on group induced shifts: A group problem-solving approach. *Journal of Personality and Social Psychology* 29, 305–15.

——1978a, Depolarization of attitudes in groups. *Journal of Personality and Social Psychology* 36, 872–85.

——1978b, Novel argumentation and attitude change: The case of polarization following group discussion. *European Journal of Social Psychology* 8, 335–48.

VINOKUR, A., TROPE, Y. and BURNSTEIN, E. 1975, A decision-making analysis of persuasive argumentation and the choice-shift effect. *Journal of Experimental Social Psychology* 11, 127–48.

VON CRANACH, M., KALBERMATTEN, U., INDERMUHLE, K. and GUGLER, B. 1982, *Goal-Directed Action*. London: Academic Press.

WARREN, W.H., NICHOLAS, D.W. and TRABASSO, T. 1979, Event chains and inferences in understanding narratives. In R.O. FREEDLE (ed.), *New Directions in Discourse Processing*, pp. 23–52. Hillsdale, NJ: Erlbaum.

WEARY, G. 1988, *Depressive Self-Presentation: Beyond Self-Handicapping*. Paper presented at the annual meeting of the Midwestern Psychological Association, Chicago, May 1988.

WEARY, G. and ARKIN, R.M. 1981, Attributional self-presentation. In J.H. HARVEY, W. ICKES and R.F. KIDD (eds), *New Directions in Attribution Research*, Vol. 3, pp. 223–46. New York: Erlbaum.

WEINER, B. 1985, 'Spontaneous' causal thinking. *Psychological Bulletin* 97, 74–84.

WEINER, B., AMIRKAN, J., FOLKES, V.S. and VERETTE, J. 1987, An attributional analysis of excuse giving: Studies of a naive theory of emotion. *Journal of Personality and Social Psychology* 52, 316–24.

WEITZ, B.A. 1981, Effectiveness in sales interactions: A Contingency framework. *Journal of Marketing Research* 45, 85–103.

WHEELER, L. and NEZLEK, J. 1977, Sex differences in social participation. *Journal of Personality and Social Psychology* 35, 742–54.

WHEELESS, L.R., BARRACLOUGH, R. and STEWART, R. 1983, Compliance-gaining and power in persuasion. In R.N. BOSTROM (ed.), *Communication Yearbook* 7, pp. 105–45. Beverly Hills, CA: Sage.

WICKER, A.W. 1969, Attitudes vs actions: The relationship of verbal and overt behavioral responses to attitude objects. *Journal of Social Issues* 25, 51–78.

WILENSKY, R. 1978, Why John married Mary: Understanding stories involving recurring goals. *Cognitive Science* 2, 235–66.

WILLARD, C.A. 1976, On the utility of descriptive diagrams for the analysis and criticism of arguments. *Communication Monographs* 43, 308–19.

——1978, *Epistemological Functions of Argument Studies: A Constructivist/ Interactionist View.* Paper presented at the annual meeting of the Speech Communication Association, Minneapolis, MN.

——1979, The epistemic functions of argument: Reasoning and decision-making from a constructivist/interactionist point of view. *Journal of the American Forensic Association* 15, 169–91.

——1981, The status of the non-discursiveness thesis. *Journal of the American Forensic Association* 17, 190–214.

WILLIAMSON, R.N. and FITZPATRICK, M.A. 1985, Two approaches to marital interaction. Relational control patterns in marital types. *Communication Monographs* 52, 236–52.

WILMOT, W.W., CARBAUGH, D.A. and BAXTER, L.A. 1985, Communicative strategies used to terminate romantic relationships. *Western Journal of Speech Communication* 49, 204–16.

WILSON, E.O. 1975, *Sociobiology: The New Synthesis.* Cambridge, MA: Harvard University Press.

WILSON, T.D. and LINVILLE, P.W. 1982, Improving the academic performance of college freshmen: Attribution therapy revisited. *Journal of Personality and Social Psychology* 42, 367–76.

——1985, Improving the performance of college freshmen with attributional techniques. *Journal of Personality and Social Psychology* 49, 287–93.

WINE, J. 1971, Test anxiety and direction of attention. *Psychological Bulletin* 76, 92–104.

WISEMAN, R.L. and SCHENCK-HAMLIN, W. 1981, A multidimensional scaling validation of an inductively derived set of compliance-gaining strategies. *Communication Monographs* 48, 251–70.

WISH, M., DEUTSCH, M. and KAPLAN, S. 1976, Perceived dimensions of interpersonal relations. *Journal of Personality and Social Psychology* 33, 409–20.

WOLFE, R.N., LENNOX, R.D. and CUTLER, B.L. 1986, Getting along and getting ahead: Empirical support for a theory of protective and acquisitive self-presentation. *Journal of Personality and Social Psychology* 50, 356–61.

WORTMAN, C.B., COSTANZO, P.R. and WITT, T.R. 1973, Effects of anticipated performance on the attribution of causality to self and others. *Journal of Personality and Social Psychology* 27, 372–81.

WYLIE, R.C. 1974, *The Self Concept.* Lincoln, NE: University of Nebraska Press.

YINGLING, J.M. and TRAPP, R. 1985, Toward a developmental perspective on argumentative competence. In J.R. COX, M.O. SILLARS and G.B. WALKER (eds), *Argument and Social Practice: Proceedings of the Fourth SCA/AFA Conference on Argumentation*, pp. 619–33. Annandale, VA: Speech

Communication Association.

YOUNG, R.M. 1978, Strategies and the structure of a cognitive skill. In G. UNDERWOOD (ed.), *Strategies of Information Processing*, pp. 357–401. London: Academic Press.

ZIMBARDO, P. 1977, *Shyness*. New York: Harcourt Brace Jovanovich.

——1988, *Psychology and Life*. Glenview, IL: Scott Foresman and Co.

ZOELLER, C.J., MAHONEY, G. and WEINER, B. 1983, Effects of attribution training on the assembly task performance of mentally retarded adults. *American Journal of Mental Deficiency* 88, 109–12.

Index